MIMI SHERATON
NEW YORK'S BEST RESTAURANTS 1989

OTHER BOOKS BY MIMI SHERATON

THE GERMAN COOKBOOK

VISIONS OF SUGARPLUMS:
A Cookbook of Cakes, Cookies, Candies & Confections

FROM MY MOTHER'S KITCHEN:
Recipes & Reminiscences

MIMI SHERATON
NEW YORK'S BEST RESTAURANTS 1989

Weidenfeld & Nicolson
New York

Copyright © 1986, 1988 by Mimi Sheraton

All rights reserved. No reproduction of this book in whole or in part in any form may be made without written authorization of the copyright owner.

Published by Weidenfeld & Nicolson, New York
A Division of Wheatland Corporation
841 Broadway
New York, New York 10003-4793

Published in Canada by General Publishing Company, Ltd.

The following reviews appeared, in a slightly different form, in the restaurant newsletter *Mimi Sheraton's Taste:* Aquavit, Bice, Bouley, Brive, Bukhara, Café de la Gare, Café Luxembourg, Carnegie Delicatessen & Restaurant, Chinatown Seafood, Chin Chin, Le Cirque, Claire, Da Umberto, David K's, Dawat, Flamand, Huberts, Maurice, Memphis, Metro, Moe's Steakhouse, Odeon, Pamir, Periyali, Sam's, Shinwa, Sido Abu Salim, Sushisei, Time & Again, Vico, and Zarela.

Library of Congress Cataloging-in-Publication Data

Sheraton, Mimi.
   [New York's best restaurants]
   Mimi Sheraton New York's best restaurants : 1989 / by Mimi Sheraton. — 1st ed.
       p.   cm.
   Includes index.
   ISBN 1-55584-220-8
   1. Restaurants, lunch rooms, etc.—New York (N.Y.)—Guide-books.
   2. New York (N.Y.)—Description—1981-   —Guide-books.   I. Title.
             TX907.'S457   1988
647'.95747'1—dc19   88-9639
                                                                   CIP

Manufactured in the United States of America

This book is printed on acid-free paper

Designed by Irving Perkins Associates

First Edition

1   3   5   7   9   10   8   6   4   2

ACKNOWLEDGMENTS

To write alone is one thing. To eat alone is quite another. And so my thanks to a dedicated band of loved ones who stick by my side, ever at the ready. First, there is my husband, Richard Falcone, who is the loyalest of eaters, even when he would rather be home with a bowl of pasta in front of the television set. Our son, Marc, is another Green Beret among eaters. But there are also many others, good and true friends who go with me to any restaurants I choose and order the food I want to try, all way above and beyond the call of friendship.

I also owe thanks to Betty Lee, who kept a chaotic manuscript organized and made sense out of my errors and scrawled notes. Dan Green, my editor, has my gratitude for his careful attention to details and for his patience. I hope all feel the effort was worth it, and to all I wish a never-ending bon appétit.

CONTENTS

Introduction to the New Edition   *xi*
A Guide to This Guide   *xix*
RESTAURANT INDEX   *xxiii*
    Ratings   xxv
    Type of Food   xxvii
    Location   xxxi
    Breakfast and Brunch   xxxiv
    Facilities for Private Parties   xxxv
    Open Late (after theater)   xxxvi
    Open Twenty-four Hours   xxxviii
    Open Sunday   xxxix
    Outdoor Dining   xli
    Take-out Food   xlii
RESTAURANT REVIEWS *(arranged alphabetically by type of food)*   1
Alphabetical Index   269
Mimi Sheraton's Taste . . .
    A restaurant newsletter   273

INTRODUCTION TO THE NEW EDITION

No one could have been more surprised than I was to realize how much this revised collection of my favorite New York restaurants differs from the one published two years ago. Only when I finally tallied the results of the final manuscript and compared it to the previous edition did I realize that about one-third of the restaurants included here were not on the earlier list. That great change in so short a period of time is due primarily to several factors that reflect the current state of the New York restaurant scene. First, there is the frenzied proliferation of new restaurants. Even if many of those offer gimmicky menus and indifferent cooking, a large number do serve interesting and well-prepared food. (And we now even have a welcome newcomer serving Scandinavian, an ethnic category not included in the earlier book.)

Second, the competition engendered by those highly publicized newcomers has spurred some savvy owners of older restaurants to perk up their menus and kitchens, and so actually improve, during the past two years. Lastly, and most unhappily, a number of old favorites have not kept up their standards, often because aging owners without heirs to take over from them have lost interest, or perhaps lack ability. Since picking a restaurant is a relative thing, I found myself choosing a number of newcomers over my former standbys.

What I cherish most in this latest collection are the old favorites that have kept up their standards and, like dependable friends, have remained consistent through the years, offering fondly remembered flavors and dishes in familiar but well-kept settings. Unfortunately, that category becomes smaller each year.

"What is your favorite restaurant?" is the much-asked question that I still find difficult to answer. "Favorite restaurant for what?" is all I can counter with. For though I think the food prepared by André Soltner and his staff at Lutèce makes his the best French restaurant in the city, and I feel that French food is the world's best, there are many instances when Lutèce would not be my first choice for dinner.

Being a restaurant buff and living in New York, I favor different eating places for different moods, dishes, styles, and even prices. If I feel like eating linguine with white clam sauce, or a lusty, fragrant pizza, or a red-hot Korean fish soup, or do not want to get dressed up or spend $100 a person for dinner, none of André Soltner's delectables will suffice.

And so this book is a collection of personal favorites in various categories. That the number totals 104 is a tribute to New York's culinary diversity and my own reluctance to exclude any place I really like, if only for a single dish. This book is, in fact, a strategy for eating in New York, knowing where to eat what, in which neighborhood, and at what price. To make comparisons easy for the reader, I have grouped restaurants by the type of food they serve—American, French, Steak, and so on. That way it is easy to tell, for example, the basic differences between Lutèce, La Grenouille, La Tulipe, and Le Cirque. All are top French restaurants, but they provide quite different dining experiences. If I were entertaining someone who loved glamorous, gorgeous settings, I would choose La Grenouille. If it were someone who wanted to dine midst a mad social whirl, it would be Le Cirque. And if it were someone who preferred simple, countrified settings in which to appreciate magnificent food, it would be Lutèce.

Although some might expect that a book of best and favorite restaurants would include only those that are French, Italian, and perhaps Chinese and Japanese, this collection ranges over a much wider variety because I find almost all cuisines enticing, and I would rather have a first-rate Korean meal than a third-rate French alternative. Not every cuisine available in New York is included here because some are so badly represented, German and Czechoslovakian being cases in point. Several years back that would not have been true. And even with the spurt of Mexican restaurants we have had in recent years, the cooking of that country barely squeaks through to be included.

Not all favorites are equally favored, of course; hence the rating system in the book. There are even a few I like to go to for the view, the setting, or the scene, and they are reviewed for that reason, along with suggestions as to the best food to eat in such surroundings, another kind of strategy. I love to sit in the Grill Room of The Four Seasons, for example, and watch the movers and shakers, but there are only a few good dishes there and so I stick to those.

Listing favorites may seem to imply that I go to all of them all the time. Given the choice in New York, that would not be possible, and

Introduction to the New Edition

so even favorites have to be checked to see if they are still performing as I remember them. Therefore, specifically for this edition, I revisited every restaurant at least once—more often two or three times—and in no instance was a free meal accepted. All were paid for. Obviously nothing too new can be a favorite, for consistency has to be part of the evaluation.

I am now recognized in about half the restaurants I visit. To minimize the effect of recognition I almost never make reservations in my own name. The few exceptions occur in four or five restaurants in which I might interview someone, or where my family likes to go for celebrations and we want a special table. At other times reservations are made in the names of friends we dine with, and those friends usually arrive first to see what sort of table and attention they will receive. At times friends even order appetizers before I arrive, so some food will be served before the management sees me.

To anyone who is not a restaurant nut I would suggest limiting one's repertory of restaurants to about six. By becoming a regular at a few places, you will get better food, service, and all-around satisfaction. Although in the best of all worlds restaurateurs would be equally nice to everyone, it is understandable that a frequent customer who spends a great deal of money will be given the preferred table and more special treatment. However, rude service and bad food for anyone are never excusable.

Unfortunately, in many new restaurants, the subject is not food. Rather it is the scene, the living theater that is the restaurant with food merely a prop. What too many critics regard as "interesting" or "brave" is merely the immaturity of chefs who feel that anything they do should be taken seriously. I find it impossible to admire a bad dish simply because it is a brave effort. If a chef served garlic-flavored ice cream topped with ketchup, chocolate, and capers, would that be brave or disgusting? Or, God forbid, "interesting"? Food writers who award premature kudos to chefs-in-training have a lot to answer for in the decline of cooking all over the country. It's too bad they cannot declare a young talent as promising, without having to state that he or she has arrived. Perhaps the hunger for superstars is greater than that for good food.

Despite such depressing recent developments, New York remains the best and most exciting city for food in this country. We still hear much about California cuisine, but that tide seems to be ebbing. True, there is a lot of good food in Los Angeles and San Francisco, but if one goes only to the "in" places, there still is bound to be an overwhelming sense of déjà vu, for all are virtually alike in menu and execution of dishes. What is lacking there that New York has in abundance is a treasury of older chefs experienced in many ethnic cuisines, allowing one to eat the new or old at will and retain gastronomic perspective. I hope this book does the city justice and is a dependable guide through the maze of temptations it offers.

OF FAVORITES, PAST AND PRESENT

Favorite is a relative term, especially in a restaurant scene as fickle and changing as New York's. Following are the changes made between the 1986 edition of this book and the present one. Some restaurants have been dropped because they have fallen in performance, others simply because they have been supplanted in my affections by newcomers. A few have closed, as noted.

Changes in Ratings

PROMOTIONS

Restaurant	New rating	Old rating
Huberts	★★★★	★★★
Memphis	★★	★
Sabor	★★	★
Young Bin Kwan	★★	★

DEMOTIONS

Café Luxembourg	★	★★
The Captain's Table	★★	★★★
Carnegie Delicatessen & Restaurant	★★	★★★
Cent' Anni	★★	★★★
Le Cirque	★★	★★★
The Four Seasons	★	★★
La Gauloise	★★	★★★
Kitcho	★★★	★★★★
Pesca	★★	★★★
Rao's Restaurant	★★	★★★
Saigon Restaurant	★	★★
Shun Lee West	★	★★
Siu Lam Kung	★★	★★★
Tanjore	★★	★★★
Woo Lae Oak of Seoul	★	★★

Restaurants Dropped in This Edition

The Beach House
Le Bistro (new management)
Bombay Palace
Café 58
El Charro
Christ Cella
Csárda
Dardanelles East Ararat
Da Silvano
Ennio and Michael
Georgine Carmella
Grove Street Café
Jane Street Seafood Café
Maxwell's Plum (closed)

La Métairie
Mogul '57 (closed)
Nada Sushi
Peter Luger Steakhouse
La Ripaille
The Ritz Café
Roxanne's (closed)
Table d'Hôte
Tamu
The "21" Club
Xenia (closed)
Y.S. (closed)
Yun Luck Rice Shoppe

New and Welcome Additions to This Issue

Aquavit
Bice
Bouley
Brive
Bukhara
Le Café de la Gare
Chinatown Seafood
Chin Chin
Claire
La Côte Basque
Da Umberto
David K's
Dawat
Erminia

Flamand
John Clancy's
Manhattan Island
Maurice
Metro
Moe's Steakhouse
Periyali
Russian Tea Room
Sam's
Shinwa
Sushisei
Time & Again
Vico
Zarela

RESTAURANTS LEFT OUT AND WHY

After the publication of the previous edition of this book, I received a number of letters asking why certain restaurants were not included. "Are they not favorites, or do you simply not know about them?" The following is an attempt to anticipate such questions on a few high-profile restaurants.

Le Bernardin in the Equitable Center is the French fish restaurant much lauded by critics and patrons. I have been there and revisited it for this book, but still do not think it exceptional. I find the fish preparations overly complex and all much alike, and the tone of service pretentious. One specialty, lobster and mashed potato pie, is a sticky purée that is perhaps the worst travesty ever perpetrated on that elegant crustacean. I have had a few very good things there, but nothing that could not be matched at one of our best French or Italian restaurants.

Gotham Bar & Grill in Greenwich Village is another place I have visited half a dozen forgettable times. Again food is overly contrived, and fish and pasta are undercooked to my taste. I have also found service unprofessional and slow, but the room is handsome.

Lafayette in the Drake Hotel offers spacious, quiet surroundings in a pleasant if undistinguished setting. I have had some dishes that are very good and some zapped with overdoses of herbs and vinegar. But at these high prices I can get food much like this in settings I prefer. Desserts are inexcusably limited and unremarkable. Twice I have asked about a hot dessert, to be told none was available, and on a recent spring evening, a friend asked for fresh fruit and was told there was none. That, even though the Café Suisse in the same hotel had a large display of strawberries as we passed it to enter Lafayette. Service tends to be frantic with long lapses before main courses.

Il Mulino in Greenwich Village is the jam-packed setting for a lot of very good Italian food. I would go gladly if it were not so dark and noisy and if the management honored reservations without necessitating a half-hour (at least) wait. And as much as I like the copious house antipasto giveaway, I find it ruins the appetite for other, more varied appetizers, if not for the whole meal.

The Quilted Giraffe, now in the AT&T building, is a place I have not been to in several years and am unlikely to try again because the owner, Barry Wine, once refused to give me a table. In the past, I rated the original Quilted Giraffe on Second Avenue two stars, finding it very good, if not the hallowed temple of gastronomy many considered it to be. In 1984, I said as much in an article, "The 10 Most Overrated Restaurants in America," that appeared in *Vanity Fair.* After that, Wine would not seat me when I tried to have lunch at what was then the Casual Quilted Giraffe. Therefore, I cannot tell whether I like it more or less than I used to. Hardly a favorite!

The Rainbow Room, atop the RCA building, is a place I would love to have gone to more often, but it has been impossible to get reservations under a name other than my own. I did have one dinner there with friends, and went to one private party. At both, the food was quite good, and certainly a big improvement over what it was. But in the beautifully restored Art Deco set-piece that is The Rainbow Room, the real emphasis is on dancing and so the bands play non-stop. As I do not dance, and find that the music makes conversation impossible, I doubt that it could become a favorite. It might well be for dancers who also want a decent meal, if they can manage to get in.

The River Cafe and *The Water Club*, both operated by Michael "Buzzy" O'Keefe, would probably not serve me if I was recognized. I was refused service at The Water Club, overlooking the East River in Manhattan, when it opened. Nevertheless, I managed to get in unrecognized for lunch in the spring of 1987 and found the food just passable. The River Café, in Brooklyn, offers a more spectacular view of lower New York, but O'Keefe's fear that I will not like his food probably makes it impossible for me to decide for myself.

The "21" Club, alas, can no longer be considered a favorite because of its frequent changes, its rollercoaster ups and downs, and its dwindling coterie of the macho regulars I loved to watch. That was the scene I really cherished, with high-powered denizens at the downstairs bar, and I would stick to uncooked food—smoked salmon, crab meat, etc.—so that I could be there. Then along came the new owner, Marshall Cogan, who put Ken Aretsky and Anne Rosenzweig in charge. They hired Alain Sailhac as chef, and the food gradually improved. When Sailhac left, I revisited to try several things (most especially the chicken hash "21") that had been so good during his reign, and I found that the cooking had quickly become uneven. When "21" settles down to a new identity, I'll try again.

A GUIDE TO THIS GUIDE

Although each review in this book is self-explanatory, some elaboration is necessary on the symbols used for ratings and for the precise meaning of price ranges. Knowing what to expect about a few other details on dining out should also help make those experiences more rewarding.

Ratings

Most restaurants in this book are at the very least good, meaning they have good food. Even so, I have degrees of preferences among them. One important consideration in arriving at these ratings is price; I expect more and give less margin for error in an expensive restaurant than in one that is moderately or low priced. Food counts for about 75 percent of my ratings, with atmosphere and service making up the rest. But at times even the most exquisite food can be overshadowed by downright rude and inept service. And as much as I like a beautiful setting, it matters least to me, as long as the dining room is clean and pleasant. Dirty restaurants are not reviewed *if* I know they are dirty.

What the stars say:
> ★★★★ The Best of the Best
> ★★★ Excellent
> ★★ Very Good
> ★ Good

Money Matters, and How

Because prices change (rise) so rapidly, it seemed best to indicate a relative range with the following meanings. Prices are for food for one person at dinner, before tax, tip, and wine or liquor are added.

> *Expensive*—More than $50
> *Moderately Expensive*—$39 to $49
> *Moderate*—$20 to $38
> *Inexpensive*—Less than $20

Tipping is, of course, optional, and if more people would leave nothing when service is poor, there would be marked improvement rapidly. In general, tips should run between 15 and 20 percent of the check, before the tax. The higher amount is in order when everything has been perfect and you're feeling generous, and in expensive, formal restaurants where there are both a captain and a waiter. The division there is roughly one-third of the check to the captain, two-thirds to the waiter. It is necessary to tip the maître d' only if he has done something extraordinary, or if you are a regular. An easy rule of thumb for most tipping is to double the city sales tax—$8\frac{1}{4}$ percent—meaning that you leave $16\frac{1}{2}$ percent, enough in most cases.

Always scrutinize your check to be sure you are not being overcharged in one way or another—by paying more for something than its menu price, by being charged for something you did not have, or by incorrect addition. To avoid unpleasant surprises, always ask the prices of dishes that are not on the menu but that the captain or waiter describes. Such specials usually cost more than most things on the menu. Restaurants should be required by law to have lists (if only typed or handwritten) of specials with prices. Customers have only themselves to blame for this annoying practice, because most are too embarrassed to ask.

Credit Cards

Do not assume all restaurants take all credit cards. Even the information on those cards that is printed in this book can change. Unless you have all cards or enough cash to pay the check, call and ask what cards are accepted. Restaurants should say which, if any, credit cards they accept when customers call for reservations, but few do.

The key to credit card initials in this book is as follows: AE—American Express; CB—Carte Blanche; DC—Diners Club; MC—MasterCard; V—Visa.

Dress Code

As with credit cards, when in doubt, call and ask about any required dress. A restaurateur has the right to set any policy he or she wants to as long as it is applied to everyone. You have the right to go elsewhere. If a restaurant has a dress code, it is noted in these reviews.

Smoking

With the new smoking regulations now in effect in New York, one should be able to assume that there will be separate sections for smokers and non-smokers. However, remember that the law applies only to those restaurants that have more than fifty seats, and excludes bars and certain other facilities. If it matters a great deal to you, ask about regulations when making reservations and request the part of the room you want.

Favorite Meals and Favorite Dishes

Knowing which dishes a restaurant does well is one thing. Knowing how to combine them into a harmonious meal is quite another, especially when one is in an unfamiliar setting and feels pressured by an impatient captain or waiter. It seemed helpful, therefore, to include my favorite meals in the various restaurants reviewed.

Because menus change, recommended dishes may not always be available. Obviously, I can report only on those I have tried, but even if some are unavailable, the reader will have an idea as to what sort of things the kitchen does best.

Wine and Liquor

Unless otherwise stated, assume that full liquor service is available. Wine and beer only or bring-your-own-bottle policies are indicated in individual reviews. Remember that you usually cannot take your own wine to a place with a liquor license.

Reservations

Except where they are not accepted, reservations should be made. Where it is stated that they are needed well in advance, make them two to four weeks ahead.

Complaints

Food that is not what you want it to be should be quietly, politely, but firmly returned. If service is poor, a manager or owner should be told. And if food or service is not as described in this book, please let me know for future editions. Address such complaints, or any comments, to:

        Mimi Sheraton
        P.O. Box 1396
        Old Chelsea Station
        New York, N.Y. 10011

RESTAURANT INDEX

RATINGS

Four Stars
Arcadia
Huberts
Lutèce

Three Stars
Aquavit
Brive
Carolina
Chanterelle
Chinatown Seafood
Claire
The Coach House
Da Umberto
Dawat
La Grenouille
Hatsuhana
Kitcho
Lusardi's
Maurice
Il Nido
Palm
Pamir
Petrossian
Sistina
Trastevere Ristorante
La Tulipe

Two Stars
The Ballroom
Bice
Bouley
Bukhara
Cabana Carioca
Café de Bruxelles
Le Café de la Gare
Café des Artistes
The Captain's Table
Carnegie Delicatessen & Restaurant
Cent' Anni
Chalet Suisse
Chikubu
Le Cirque
La Côte Basque
Darbar
Ermina
Felidia
Flamand
La Gauloise
Hwa Yuan Szechuan Inn
John Clancy's
Lattanzi
Manhattan Island
Memphis
Moe's
Odeon
Omen
Oyster Bar & Restaurant
Periyali
Pesca
Positano
Quatorze
Raga
Rao's
Sabor

Seryna
Shinwa
Shun Lee Palace
Siam Grill
Siam Inn
Siu Lam Kung
Takesushi
Tanjore
Terrace
Texarkana
Time & Again
Vico
Young Bin Kwan

One Star
America
Beijing Duck House
Le Biarritz
The Blue Nile
Brazilian Pavilion
Café Luxembourg
Charles' Green Tree
   Hungarian Restaurant
Chin Chin

Le Cygne
David K's
Four Seasons
Inagiku
Metro
Mocca Hungarian Restaurant
Nanni
Peking Duck House
El Rincón de España
Russian Tea Room
Saigon Restaurant
Sam's
Say Eng Look
Shun Lee West
Sido Abu Salim
Sushisei
Tavern on the Green
Tibetan Kitchen
Toons
Windows on the World
Woo Lae Oak of Seoul
Yellow Rose Café
Zarela

TYPE OF FOOD

Afghan
Pamir

African, see Ethiopian

American—New, Traditional, and Regional
See also Casual Eating—Cafés, Luncheonettes, and Pâtisseries; see also Chili, Ribs and Barbecue, Hamburgers, and Hot Dogs
America
Arcadia
Café des Artistes
Café Luxembourg
Carolina
Claire
The Coach House
The Four Seasons
Huberts
Manhattan Island
Memphis
Metro
Odeon
The Pink Tea Cup
Sam's
Tavern on the Green
Texarkana
Time & Again

Windows on the World
Yellow Rose Café

Belgian
Café de Bruxelles
Flamand

Brazilian
Brazilian Pavilion
Cabana Carioca

Casual Eating—Cafés, Luncheonettes, and Pâtisseries
Bleecker Luncheonette
Chez Brigitte
Christine's Polish Restaurant
Elephant & Castle
Kiev Luncheonette
Il Nido Café
Pasta & Cheese Café
Patisserie J. Lanciani
The Pink Tea Cup
Sant'Ambroeus
Sarabeth's Kitchen
Serendipity
Terrace-five
Viand Coffee Shop

Caviar
Petrossian

xxvii

Chili, Ribs and Barbecue, Hamburgers, and Hot Dogs

Café de Bruxelles
Carolina
Corner Bistro
Gray's Papaya
Hamburger Harry's
Katz's Delicatessen
Lone Star Café
Manhattan Chili Co.
Memphis
Paley Park
Serendipity
Taste of the Apple
Yellow Rose Café

Chinese

Beijing Duck House Restaurant
Chinatown Seafood
Chin Chin
David K's
David K's Café
H.S.F.
Hsin Yu
Hwa Yuan Szechuan Inn
Lan Hong Kok Seafood House
Oriental Town Seafood Restaurant
Peking Duck West
Say Eng Look
Shun Lee Palace
Shun Lee West
Siu Lam Kung

Cuban, Caribbean, and Tropical

Claire
Sabor

Ethiopian

The Blue Nile

French

Le Biarritz
Bouley
Brive
Le Café de la Gare
Café des Artistes
Café Luxembourg
Chanterelle
Le Cirque
La Côte Basque
Le Cygne
La Gauloise
La Grenouille
Lutèce
Maurice
Metro
Odeon
Petrossian
Quatorze
Terrace
La Tulipe

Greek

Periyali

Hungarian

Charles' Green Tree Hungarian Restaurant
Mocca Hungarian Restaurant

Indian

Bukhara
Darbar
Dawat
Raga
Tanjore

Italian

Arturo's Pizzeria and Restaurant
Bice
Bleecker Luncheonette
Cent'Anni
Da Umberto

Due
Erminia
Felidia
Lattanzi
Lusardi's
Manganaro's Hero Boy
Nanni
Il Nido
Il Nido Café
Orso
Positano
Rao's
Sant'Ambroeus
Sistina
Trastevere Ristorante
Vico

Japanese
Chikubu
Hatsuhana
Inagiku
Kitcho
Omen
Sapporo
Seryna
Shinwa
Sushisei
Takesushi

Jewish and Kosher
Bernstein-on-Essex Street
Carnegie Delicatessen & Restaurant
Katz's Delicatessen
Ratner's Dairy Restaurant
Sammy's Famous Roumanian Restaurant
2nd Avenue Kosher Delicatessen and Restaurant

Korean
Woo Lae Oak of Seoul
Young Bin Kwan

Mexican
Zarela

Middle Eastern and North African
Sido Abu Salim

Pizza, see Italian Tidbits

Polish, see Christine's Polish Restaurant in Casual Eating

Russian, see Russian Tea Room in The View, the Setting, and the Scene

Scandinavian
Aquavit

Seafood
The Captain's Table
Claire
John Clancy's
Oyster Bar & Restaurant
Pesca

Spanish
Ballroom
Harlequin
El Rincón de España

Steak
Moe's
Palm

Swiss
Auberge Suisse
Chalet Suisse

Thai
Siam Grill
Siam Inn
Toons

	Type of Food
Tibetan Tibetan Kitchen	**The View, the Setting, and the Scene** America Café des Artistes The Four Seasons Russian Tea Room Tavern on the Green Windows on the World
Vietnamese Bo Ky Restaurant Saigon Restaurant	

LOCATION

Lower East Side and Chinatown
Bernstein-on-Essex Street
Bo Ky
H.S.F.
Hwa Yuan Szechuan Inn
Katz's Delicatessen
Lan Hong Kok Seafood House
Oriental Town Seafood Restaurant
Ratner's
Saigon Restaurant
Sammy's Famous Roumanian Restaurant
Say Eng Look
Siu Lam Kung

SoHo, TriBeCa, World Trade Center
Bouley
Chanterelle
Elephant & Castle
Hamburger Harry's
Moe's
Odeon
Omen
Windows on the World

Greenwich Village and East Village
Arturo's Pizzeria & Restaurant
Bleecker Luncheonette
Café de Bruxelles
Le Café de la Gare
Cent' Anni
Chez Brigitte
The Coach House
Corner Bistro
Elephant & Castle
La Gauloise
Gray's Papaya
Harlequin
John Clancy's
Kiev Luncheonette
Lone Star Café
Manhattan Chili Co.
Patisserie J. Lanciani
The Pink Tea Cup
El Rincón de España
Sabor
2nd Avenue Kosher Delicatessen and Restaurant
Texarkana
Toons
La Tulipe

14th through 34th Streets, West of Fifth Avenue
The Ballroom
Claire
Da Umberto
Periyali
Quatorze

14th through 34th Streets, East of Fifth Avenue

America
Pesca
Positano
Sido Abu Salim
Tibetan Kitchen

Midtown West, 35th through 57th Streets, West of Fifth Avenue

Aquavit
Le Biarritz
Cabana Carioca
Carnegie Delicatessen & Restaurant
Carolina
Darbar
Kitcho
Lattanzi
Manganaro's Hero Boy
Manhattan Island
Maurice
Orso
Raga
Sam's
Sapporo
Siam Grill
Siam Inn
Sushisei
Russian Tea Room
Woo Lae Oak of Seoul

Midtown East, 35th through 57th Streets, East of Fifth Avenue

Auberge Suisse
Beijing Duck House
Bice
Brazilian Pavilion
Bukhara
The Captain's Table
Chalet Suisse
Chikubu
Chin Chin
Christine's Polish Restaurant
La Côte Basque
Le Cygne
The Four Seasons
La Grenouille
Hatsuhana
Inagiku
Lutèce
Nanni
Il Nido
Il Nido Café
Oyster Bar & Restaurant
Paley Park
Palm
Seryna
Shinwa
Shun Lee Palace
Takesushi
Taste of the Apple
Terrace-five
Time & Again
Young Bin Kwan
Zarela

58th through 72nd Streets, West of Fifth Avenue

Café des Artistes
Café Luxembourg
Gray's Papaya
Pasta & Cheese Café
Peking Duck West
Petrossian
Shun Lee West
Tavern on the Green

58th through 72nd Streets, East of Fifth Avenue

Arcadia
Brive
Le Cirque
David K's
David K's Café

Dawat
Felidia
Huberts
Serendipity
Tanjore
Viand Coffee Shop

73rd Street and Above, West of Fifth Avenue
The Blue Nile
Charles' Green Tree
　Hungarian Restaurant
Chinatown Seafood
Memphis
Sarabeth's Kitchen
Taste of the Apple
The Terrace
Yellow Rose Café

73rd Street and Above, East of Fifth Avenue
Christine's Polish Restaurant
Due
Erminia
Flamand
Lusardi's
Metro
Mocca Hungarian Restaurant
Pamir
Rao's
Sant' Ambroeus
Sistina
Trastevere Ristorante
Vico

BREAKFAST AND BRUNCH

Bo Ky Restaurant
Café de Bruxelles
Café des Artistes
Café Luxembourg
Carnegie Delicatessen &
  Restaurant
Claire
Christine's Polish Restaurant
Dawat
Elephant & Castle
La Gauloise
H.S.F.
Kiev Luncheonette
Lan Hong Kok Seafood House
Manhattan Island

Maurice
Odeon
Omen
Oriental Town Seafood House
Patisserie J. Lanciani
Petrossian
The Pink Tea Cup
Ratner's Dairy Restaurant
Russian Tea Room
Sant' Ambroeus
Sarabeth's Kitchen
Tavern on the Green
Time & Again
Windows on the World
Yellow Rose Café

FACILITIES FOR PRIVATE PARTIES

America
The Ballroom
Beijing Duck House
The Blue Nile
Bouley
Brazilian Pavilion
Brive
Bukhara
Cabana Carioca
Café de Bruxelles
Carolina
Chikubu
Chin Chin
Chinatown Seafood
Le Cirque
The Coach House
La Côte Basque
Le Cygne
Darbar
David K's
David K's Café
Dawat
Erminia
Felidia
The Four Seasons
La Grenouille
Huberts
Hwa Yuan Szechuan Inn
Inagiku
Kitcho

Lusardi's
Lutèce
Manhattan Island
Memphis
Odeon
Periyali
Petrossian
Positano
Raga
Russian Tea Room
Sabor
Sammy's Famous Roumanian
Sam's
Say Eng Look
Seryna
Shinwa
Shun Lee Palace
Shun Lee West
Tanjore
Tavern on the Green
Terrace
Texarkana
Tibetan Kitchen
Time & Again
Toons
Windows on the World
Woo Lae Oak of Seoul
Young Bin Kwan
Zarela

OPEN LATE
(AFTER THEATER)

America
Aquavit
Arturo's Pizzeria
The Ballroom
Beijing Duck House
Brazilian Pavilion
Cabana Carioca
Café de Bruxelles
Café des Artistes
Café Luxembourg
The Captain's Table
Carnegie Delicatessen & Restaurant
Carolina
Chin Chin
Chinatown Seafood
Claire
Corner Bistro
Darbar
Da Umberto
David K's
David K's Café
Due
Elephant & Castle
Felidia
The Four Seasons
Gray's Papaya
Hamburger Harry's
Harlequin
John Clancy's
Katz's Delicatessen
Kiev Luncheonette
Lattanzi
Lone Star Café
Manhattan Chili Co.
Manhattan Island
Memphis
Metro
Odeon
Orso
Palm
Peking Duck West
Pesca
The Pink Tea Cup
Quatorze
Raga
El Rincón de España
Russian Tea Room
Sammy's Famous Roumanian Restaurant
Sam's
2nd Avenue Kosher Delicatessen and Restaurant
Serendipity
Seryna
Shun Lee Palace
Shun Lee West
Siam Grill

Siam Inn
Sido Abu Salim
Sistina
Taste of the Apple
Tavern on the Green

Texarkana
Time & Again
Vico
Yellow Rose Café

OPEN TWENTY-FOUR HOURS

Carnegie Delicatessen & Restaurant (Well, practically. It closes only from 4:00 to 6:30 A.M.)

Gray's Papaya
Kiev Luncheonette

OPEN SUNDAY

America
Arturo's Pizzeria &
  Restaurant
Beijing Duck House
Bernstein-on-Essex Street
  Delicatessen & Restaurant
Bice
The Blue Nile
Bo Ky
Bukhara
Cabana Carioca
Café de Bruxelles
Le Café de la Gare
Café des Artistes
Café Luxembourg
Carnegie Delicatessen &
  Restaurant
Carolina
Cent' Anni
Chin Chin
Chinatown Seafood
Christine's Polish Restaurant
Claire
The Coach House
Corner Bistro
Darbar
David K's
David K's Café
Dawat
Due
Elephant & Castle
Flamand

La Gauloise
Gray's Papaya
Hamburger Harry's
Harlequin
H.S.F.
Hwa Yuan Szechuan Inn
Inagiku
John Clancy's
Katz's Delicatessen &
  Restaurant
Kiev Luncheonette
Kitcho
Lan Hung Kok Seafood House
Lone Star Café
Lusardi's
Manhattan Chili Co.
Manhattan Island
Maurice
Memphis
Metro
Mocca Hungarian Restaurant
Odeon
Omen
Oriental Town Seafood House
Orso
Pamir
Patisserie J. Lanciani
Peking Duck West
Pesca
Petrossian
The Pink Tea Cup
Quatorze

Raga
Ratner's Dairy Restaurant
El Rincón de España
Russian Tea Room
Sabor
Saigon Restaurant
Sammy's Famous Roumanian
  Restaurant
Sant' Ambroeus
Sapporo
Sarabeth's Kitchen
Say Eng Look
2nd Avenue Kosher
  Delicatessen and Restaurant
Serendipity
Shun Lee Palace
Siam Grill
Siam Inn
Sido Abu Salim
Sistina
Siu Lam Kung
Tanjore
Taste of the Apple
Tavern on the Green
Texarkana
Time & Again
Toons
Trastevere Ristorante
La Tulipe
Vico
Windows on the World
Woo Lae Oak of Seoul
Yellow Rose Café
Young Bin Kwan

OUTDOOR DINING

Manhattan Chili Co.
Paley Park

Tavern on the Green
Terrace-five

TAKE-OUT FOOD

Take-out food is available from all Chinese, Indian, Thai, and Korean restaurants in this book, and sushi and sashimi can be ordered from most Japanese restaurants. All coffee shops, luncheonettes, and delicatessens do take-out, as do places specializing in chili, ribs, and hamburgers. In addition, take-out food is available from the restaurants below, generally ordered from the day's menu and picked up by the customer.

America
The Ballroom
Carolina
Charles' Green Tree
   Hungarian Restaurant
Claire
John Clancy's

Manhattan Island
Memphis
Mocca Hungarian Restaurant
The Pink Tea Cup
Sant' Ambroeus
Sido Abu Salim
Tibetan Kitchen

RESTAURANT REVIEWS

AFGHAN

PAMIR

1437 Second Avenue, between 74th and 75th streets
Telephone: 734-3791

Favorite meal:
Shared by two
Scallion dumplings (aushak) and meat-filled crisp pastry (sambosa goushti)
Grilled ground beef on skewers (kofta kebob)
Spiced spinach (chalaw sabsi)
Pumpkin with yogurt (buranee kady)
Baklava (baghlawa)
Afghan tea
Other favorite dishes: All appetizers, all palaws, lamb in spinach sauce (sabsichalaw), chicken, lamb, and ground spiced lamb kebobs (shish kebob), eggplant, spinach, and pumpkin side dishes, gosh-e-feel.
Setting: Intimate, exotic, and informal; seating is cramped in some areas.
Service: Generally considerate and efficient, but can be perfunctory at busiest times.
Dress code: None.
Facilities for private parties: None.
Hours: Dinner, Tuesday through Sunday. Closed Monday.
Reservations: Recommended.
Prices: Moderate.
Credit cards: MC, V.

Exotic and romantic are the words that come to mind in this small jewel of a restaurant. Dimly lit, but sparkling with small pinpoints of light and mirrors, it is a fanciful stage set, with Oriental rugs, intricately woven fabrics, and glints of copper all contrasting with the deep green walls. The handsome, swarthy staff members add to the effect. If the somewhat cramped quarters make a truly confidential tête-à-tête impossible, one can still enjoy the sense of being vaguely conspiratorial.

In the early days of Pamir, the staff was naively gracious and genuinely concerned that customers understand and like their food. Success has brought more self-assurance and professionalism, a trade-off perhaps for the sometimes distracted service when there is a lineup for tables.

Although somewhat lustier and more rustic, the food of Afghanistan resembles that of the Middle East, modified by Indo-Persian spicing. In fact, because Afghanistan was on the path of Mogul warriors who swept down into India, Afghan cooking, it is believed, found its way into the Indian cuisine, most especially with the tandoor-oven method of roasting.

What customers gladly wait for is moderately priced food that is deeply satisfying, with savory meat and yogurt sauces, grilled meats and seductive palaw stews on rice, and palate-tingling combinations of mint and chili peppers, cinnamon and pepper, scallions and coriander. Soup is the only course to skip, not because the two noodle, meat, and vegetable combinations are not well prepared, but because they are served tepid, and so become greasy.

Better to start with an assortment of appetizers, sharing them among two to four diners. Included in such are the sambosa goushti, pastry half circles crisply fried and filled with mashed chick-peas and ground beef; bulanee gandana, scallion-stuffed crisp pancakes with a cloudlet of yogurt on top; bulanee kachalou, turnovers with an aromatic beef and potato filling; and aushak, flat dumplings also with scallions, enriched by a minty meat and yogurt dressing.

All kebobs are properly juicy and tender. This includes the chunks of chicken (kebob-e-murgh), the nuggets of lamb (shish kebob), and the ground, spiced lamb and beef kofta kebobs. It is a good idea to combine these simple unsauced kebobs with one of the palaws, such as the quabilli, with its gilding of saffron and carrot and orange-rind slivers, or the sabsi chalaw, lamb swathed in a garlic- and onion-accented spinach sauce. The vegetable side dishes of spinach, eggplant, and pumpkin can also be ordered in large portions for a completely vegetarian meal.

The tantalizing flat, crisp, yeast bread, Afghan naan, has, unfortunately, deteriorated and now appears limp and almost completely devoid of the fragrant little black onion seeds that distinguished it. Perhaps as compensation, desserts show marked improvement. The baghlawa is a dense, rich confection of walnuts, flaky phyllo, and light golden syrup. A new addition to the menu, gosh-e-feel—huge crisply fried disks of thin golden pastry, lightly sprinkled with sugar and almost as fragile as butterfly wings—is an intriguing alternative. It is a fine accompaniment to soothingly spiced Afghan tea. There is full bar service, but beer best suits the food.

AMERICAN

NEW, TRADITIONAL, AND REGIONAL

Trying to separate the new from the traditional and the regional in American cooking is one of the more difficult and futile tasks facing the writer of a restaurant guidebook. The true name for most of this food should be new Continental anyway, for almost all the menus in these so-called new American restaurants owe much to French or Italian kitchens, and increasingly to those of China, Japan, and Southeast Asia. That kind of mix, leading to a whole new style, is uniquely American, for combining diverse influences has always marked the development of this country's cooking, thus enriching it.

America, see The View, the Setting, and the Scene

ARCADIA

21 East 62nd Street, between Fifth and Madison avenues
Telephone: 223-2900

Favorite meals:
Lunch
Country salad
Chicken hash with lemon and chili
Caramel pears with ginger ice cream and chocolate sauce
or
Dinner
Corn cakes with crème fraîche and caviars
Roast squab with beer batter potatoes and rhubarb
Chocolate bread pudding with brandy custard sauce
or
Smoked trout, pear, and curly endive salad
Chimney smoked lobster with celery root cakes
Pink grapefruit terrine with macadamia nut brittle

American

Other favorite dishes: All pastas; wild mushroom tart; grilled leeks in puff pastry; "mussels like snails"; black bean soup with goat cheese and spinach turnovers; grilled salmon on red orange hollandaise; roast chicken with zucchini and carrot pancakes; duck confit with a turnip, sweet potato, prune gratin; quail, either with beet sauce, kale, and orange or with kasha; grilled veal steak with wild mushrooms; braised short ribs of beef with split peas; roast lamb; warm banana dumpling with sticky caramel sauce; bittersweet chocolate terrine; cinnamon apple turnovers with maple-pecan ice cream; poached prunes in red wine with cinnamon ice cream.
Setting: Sylvan, seasonal mural creates a peaceful and graceful backdrop for this small, posh dining room; peacefulness is badly compromised by tables too closely set and noise.
Service: Attentive, polite, and efficient if a bit self-consciously preppie.
Dress code: Jacket and tie required for men.
Facilities for private parties: None.
Hours: Lunch, Monday through Friday. Dinner, Monday through Saturday. Closed Sunday, major holidays, and last week in August through Labor Day.
Reservations: Necessary well in advance.
Prices: Expensive.
Credit cards: AE, DC, MC, V.

Despite her new role as chief operating officer and almost Lord High Everything Else at The "21" Club, Anne Rosenzweig has managed to keep up the extraordinary level of cooking at Arcadia. Creative yet solidly grounded in traditional cooking techniques, she does the very best kind of innovation at this new-American-style restaurant. She develops dishes that at once surprise yet impart a sense of comfortable recognition. Some chefs apparently think surprise is enough and that "Wow, how did he ever think of this?" is the prize. Rather, the surprise should be expressed more as "Of course! How come no one has ever done this before?" Cooking is, after all, different from painting or composing. A nice try that is an artistic failure is one thing if you are looking at or listening to a brave effort, but food has to be swallowed, and shock beyond a frame of reference had better be extraordinary.

What Arcadia is not a mecca for is peacefulness and comfort, about which more later, and no cooking less exceptional could draw me to such a cramped, noisy scene. Anne Rosenzweig has developed a repertory of brilliant and refined creations using American ingredients and regional expressions in a very European way.

The setting for this gastronomic triumph is as engaging as the food, a small, slim supper club of a room, with mauves and beiges set against an around-the-room mural of the four seasons evolving in a sort of stylized impressionist shimmer painted by Paul Davis. Although closely set, banquette tables are comfortable, much more so than the line of deuces that runs down the center of the room. The noise level is high except for larger corner banquettes, but it is still possible to have a conversation without emerging hoarse.

There is a stylish bar at the entrance, somewhat in the Parisian-bistro mode, but what could be a pleasant place for an aperitif used to be a nightmare from about eight on as the crowd stood three to four deep so that the entrance became impassable, with, at the same time, people eating, or trying to, at the few tables also in that room. Although somewhat better, it is still an uncomfortable area.

The saving grace is that once you have run the gauntlet and are seated, the sylvan aura of the dining room takes over; hence Arcadia deserves top rating for both the friendly, accommodating, and efficient service and the wonderful food. It would be only a slight exaggeration to say that I never met a Rosenzweig dish I didn't like. Her appetizers manage to combine solidity of flavor and intriguing ingredients without being overpowering, and the selection is so well balanced that those who want to eat lightly but enjoy variety can order two or three to make a complete meal. From the verdant simplicity of her impeccable country salad of mixed greens to the lusty pastas (buckwheat with country ham, sweet potato, kale, and onion marmalade or the curliques with salmon and dill cream), and including such subtle delicacies as the wild mushroom tart with endive and greens, Anne Rosenzweig maintains the balance of flavors and textures and manages to juxtapose mutually enhancing ingredients. Perhaps the true appetizer triumph is the combination of small, slim corn pancakes mellowed with crème fraîche and a combination of caviars, one being the so-called golden whitefish, which reads better than it tastes, and the richer, more authoritative osetra. Her now classic poached leeks packeted in high and handsome puff pastry set on a bittersweet onion marmalade and further accented by chive butter is a lesson in the variations on the onion family and how deftly a knowing hand can contrast them. Mussels baked on the half shell are savory with a topping of garlic and parsley snail butter and, among the smoked fish salads Rosenzweig likes to invent, a current winner is trout gentled with pear and sparked by a curly endive. Duck sausage is an old favorite that sometimes reappears here with white beans and pine nuts.

Very few soups have been offered, which I consider a minor shortcoming, but awhile back there was a lovely lobster bisque strewn with wisps of carrot and snappy with the true deep-sea lobster essence. And more recently there has been a darkly thick, smoky rich black bean soup contrasted to crunchy spinach turnovers.

Some of the appetizers occasionally appear as main courses, among them the pastas and the duck sausage. Add to that such elegant treatments as succulent quail improbably but delectably sauced with a cream-enhanced beet dressing, all complemented by lightly cooked kale and fresh orange to clean and separate the otherwise heavy flavors. Miraculously, the delicate quality of the quail comes through the other ingredients. Another masterpiece is the chimney-smoked lobster that gets a sprightly touch of tarragon butter and is well contrasted with fried celery root cakes.

This dedication to humbler ingredients—celery root, parsnip, rutabaga, kale, and the buckwheat kasha that is another foil for quail—typifies Rosenzweig's knowing eclecticism. Roasting salmon is tricky business, that heating method being so potentially drying, but the salmon prepared that way here is miraculously moist and flavorful whether done with onions and Jerusalem artichokes or nestled against good, grainy couscous that absorbs the hollandaise blushed with blood oranges. Duck may be braised with Swiss chard or grilled and served with a warming apple and sweet potato gratin. Rosenzweig has a penchant for pancake creations based on unlikely ingredients, such as the zucchini and carrot combination that adds crunch to roast chicken or the beer batter potato crisps that are a fine foil for squab and the rhubarb sauce that glosses them.

Rarely is veal more tender or pinkly à point than in the grilled steak here that gets earthy richness from wild mushrooms and softness from a potato-tomato tart. Lamb in any version is rendered fragrantly tender, and braised short ribs of beef at lunch have all the down-home heft they need, without being inelegant.

And then of course there are the desserts, the chef-owner's real calling since that is where she began. Chocolate bread pudding is little short of a miracle, the dense, intense chocolate-sauced brioche with a brandy custard sauce. Warm pecan tart with praline-flecked whipped cream and an apple timbale swimming in a lagoon of burnished caramel sauce are close runners-up. Lemon curd mousse is gently soft yet sharply pungent, and the chestnut ice cream with brandy pecan brittle and warm chocolate sauce is the kind of dessert men leave home for. Or should.

To this classic Rosenzweig repertory, add such current winners as warm banana dumpling slices gilded with a blissfully sticky caramel sauce, a densely moist bittersweet chocolate terrine lightened with whipped cream, and the cinnamon-apple turnover mellowed by cinnamon-scented ice cream. Lighter choices include an icy dish of pink grapefruit sherbet that gets crunchy contrast from macadamia nut brittle, and a parfait of cinnamon ice cream topped with wine-drenched prunes.

In fact, I have had only one dish at Arcadia that I think is basically ill conceived, and it is a best-selling luncheon choice, the lobster club sandwich. As appetizing as the combination of lobster, tomato, bacon, and lettuce may sound, layering it all between three pieces of toast makes it, first of all, impossible to pick up and eat as a sandwich. The toast breaks and one struggles through, biting now, cutting with a knife and fork then, and finally winding up with what looks like a messy leftover salad. Anyone who likes that combination would do well to order it as an open sandwich or merely as a salad; the kitchen presents those ingredients in all such variations.

It is hard to tell whether the early bar room crush has subsided a bit because business is slower or because booking is done more carefully. Either way, it's an improvement, as is the more polite telephone voice and the willingness to give reservations at peak hours, instead of shunting unknowns to early or late seatings.

There is a fine, careful selection of California and French wines in a good range of prices, which is perhaps why members of the city's wine trade congregate here.

Café des Artistes, see The View, the Setting, and the Scene

CAFÉ LUXEMBOURG ★

200 West 70th Street, between West End and Amsterdam avenues
Telephone: 873-7411

Favorite meal:
Asparagus soup
Calves' liver with mustard sauce and fried leeks
Lemon tart
Other favorite dishes: Country salad, crabcakes with sweet red pepper rouille, roast baby chicken (poussin), roast duck with brandy sauce, banana roulade.
Setting: White tiled walls and Art Deco theme; convivial if cramped and noisy. Inadequate facilities for coats.
Service: Friendly, helpful, but often very slow. There can be a long wait at the bar.
Dress code: None.
Facilities for private parties: None.
Hours: Dinner, until 12:30 A.M., Sunday through Thursday, and to 1:30 A.M., Friday and Saturday. Sunday brunch. Closed Christmas Day.
Reservations: Necessary, especially before and after Lincoln Center events.
Prices: Moderate.
Credit cards: AE, DC, MC, V.

If not quite what it used to be, this remains a good choice for pre– and post–Lincoln Center meals. With its gleaming tiles, Art Deco overtones, and lively bar, where hard-boiled eggs are set out on old-fashioned wire stands, Café Luxembourg is still one of the best options on the Upper West Side. Noisy and lively, the dining room has a certain Parisian, La Coupole kind of activity. For some reason, however, it has never run quite smoothly and at peak hours there remains a back-up at the door, waiting at the bar, confusion over coats (best but uncomfortably hung near tables), and slow service. It is a credit to the good-natured staff that all of this rarely results in annoyance unless, of course, the kitchen is operating at its slowest.

Along with Odeon, Luxembourg is owned by Keith McNally, and he has replaced the departed executive chef, Patrick Clark, with Tony Shek. He follows the Clark menu style with many of the same dishes that appear on the Odeon menu. However, his efforts are a shade (say, one star) dimmer than those of his downtown counterpart. But keep your ordering simple here and you do well.

That would mean, for example, beginning with hot, rich cream of asparagus soup or the country salad of sprightly greens tossed with Roquefort cheese, garlic croutons, and crisp bacon, all sparked by a mustardy vinaigrette dressing. Crabcakes gentled with a sauce of puréed sweet red pepper spiked with cayenne are delicious as an appetizer, and a double order would make a fine main course.

Fish main courses are less reliable than those of meat, judging by an order of stiff, overcooked mahi-mahi and some rather bland medallions of rock bass. But a juicy, buttery roast baby chicken given a meaty edge with the Italian bacon, pancetta, and a garnish of bright spinach proves altogether satisfying. Calves' liver seems to be a winner at both of McNally's outposts. The version here, done impeccably pink as ordered, has a nicely sharp mustard sauce and an accompanying cloud of crisply fried filaments of leeks. Brandy adds pungency to a sauce underlining crisply roasted duck, and, for the simplest tastes, there is the classic steak frites. Pastas are to be avoided, as they are overly greasy and complex. There is a chicken salad with a warm, freshly grilled, sliced breast nested on Jerusalem artichokes and vegetables that is fine if you ask to have the overpowering, warm chèvre cheese omitted.

Desserts need work. The best so far are the astringent, thick lemon tart and a rich banana roulade with dark chocolate sauce and coconut-flecked whipped cream. The sauce of grapefruit sections and poached rind is the best part of the otherwise junketlike cold grapefruit soufflé. Neither the white nor the dark chocolate mousse has convincing flavors; only the bittersweet chocolate sauce saves them.

Brunch follows the pattern at Odeon (see page 25) with the same prevailing favorites. Breads are a little less interesting here, but the same sort of nicely varied, moderately priced wine list is on hand.

CAROLINA

355 West 46th Street, between Eighth and Ninth avenues
Telephone: 245-0058

Favorite meals:
Corn chowder
Brisket of beef or assorted barbecue platter
Carolina slaw
Pecan fingers dipped in chocolate sauce
or
Dinner
Barbecue on lettuce
Red pepper shrimp or crabcakes
Corn pudding
Carolina mudd cake
Other favorite dishes: Penthouse chili, salmon or swordfish steak, barbecued ribs, smoked breast of chicken, meat loaf with mashed potato topping, barbecued lamb chops, gazpacho salad, ice cream with walnuts in maple syrup or with black currant sauce, strawberry shortcake in season.
Setting: Urbane modern but plush bar area with comfortable seating for meals; back dining room is romantically lit and sparkling mirrors reflect palms; upstairs dining room with brick walls is handsome and stylish; noisy but convivial.
Service: Excellent but tends to slow a bit before main courses and when the check is requested.
Dress code: None.
Facilities for private parties: Upstairs dining room accommodates between 20 and 35; also outside catering.
Hours: Lunch, Monday through Friday. Dinner, seven days. Open late, Monday through Saturday. Closed most major holidays but open on Thanksgiving.
Reservations: Necessary.
Prices: Moderate.
Credit cards: AE, MC, V.

Few restaurants have become classics as soon after opening as did Carolina, the enchanting effort of Martin Yerdon and Eileen Weinberg, she one of the originators of the stylish and successful take-out food shop Word of Mouth. Since it opened in 1983, it has been among the rare restaurants in the Theater District worth a visit for its own sake, whether or not one is attending a performance. Basing their menu on the barbecues and seafood specialties of the South Carolina coast, and going along that coast as far as Boston, the owners blended influences and have evolved a style of cooking that is sui generis and, even more important, delicious. Not even the opening of their Manhattan Island (see page 19) has compromised quality here.

There are three different atmospheres in which to have lunch or dinner, my favorite being the front room, where the handsome bar has a clublike feeling. Although the back room is prettier, with its skylight, twinkling lights, and a single palm that wall mirrors reflect as a veritable tropical forest, it is best for parties larger than four. I prefer round or square tables for four or more and the added elbow room in the bar. The newer upstairs room is also a stylish and different setting, suggesting a Village brownstone floor-through, with natural brick walls, a mellow antique French screen, and a certain air of privacy. It is also available for private parties and is one of the best-looking facilities for that purpose.

And, of course, the food, much of which is based on the no-nonsense smoker and mesquite-fired open hearth grill in the windowed kitchen that one passes going from entrance to back dining room. The most spectacular Carolina offerings are cooked in that smoker, most especially the huge, meaty, and tender ribs and the meltingly fatty, succulent beef brisket and the breast of chicken that magically never dries out. With such dishes the barbecue sauce is the only mild disappointment, it being a bit sweet and tomatoey for my taste, but not too damagingly so. Barbecue in big nicely charred chunks nestles on lettuce for another lusty first course. The city's best crabcakes are made here with hints of mustard and mayonnaise and are as tantalizing a main course as they are an appetizer. Corn chowder with flecks of smoky sweet pink ham is at times pallid, but one of the town's best chili representations is here.

Broiling fish and seafood over the hot grill is a job not easily accomplished with success as those foods dry so quickly. But here the red pepper–zapped shrimp, the swordfish, and the salmon generally emerge juicy, their own natural flavors softly enhanced by smokiness. The shell steak and the barbecued lamb chops are meaty and tender. Baked Cajun meat loaf with a golden mashed potato topping is as heart-warming as it is hefty.

There are also enticing side dishes, some to be ordered à la carte, others served as garnishes. One way or another, get the custardy corn pudding and the Carolina slaw and go easy on the marvelous butter and corn breads and biscuits in the basket, or you'll regret it when it is time for dessert. Imagine not being able to indulge in the earth-rich Carolina mudd cake, the crunchy pecan fingers dipped in bittersweet chocolate sauce, or the ice cream with walnuts in maple syrup or with black currant sauce. For gentler palates there is fruit crisp in the best American tearoom tradition and, in the right season, old-fashioned biscuit strawberry shortcake, which is a meal in itself.

In fact, the single most consistent flaw at Carolina is that every dish is a meal in itself (the combined barbecue platter is an exception; it is three meals in itself). Even the light fish dishes seem heavy because of flavor more than substance. Somehow smoke and a similar spicing format makes for less contrast on the menu than is needed. Also, anyone not used to true barbecue should avoid having more than one dish cooked that way as it can be difficult for a novice stomach to digest, especially if much hard liquor has been consumed at the same time. Beer is a more judicious drink than wine with this food; not that wine is hard liquor, but it seems to have more acidic overtones than beer, and besides, its flavor is knocked out by the smokiness of the food.

The staff at Carolina could not be more sincere, polite, or efficient. Slowdowns before main courses appear to be a kitchen problem, and at times there is also a slowness about bringing checks, which can be unsettling before theater. It is best to ask for those checks when desserts are served.

Claire, see Cuban, Caribbean, and Tropical

THE COACH HOUSE

110 Waverly Place, between Washington Square Park and Sixth Avenue
Telephone: 777-0303

Favorite meals:
  Black bean soup with Madeira
  Roast duck with quince or other fruits on the side
  Grand Marnier bavarois
  or
  Deviled crabcake
  Boneless black pepper steak
  American pecan pie
  or
  Sausage with lentil salad
  Whole red snapper roasted with fresh dill sauce, for two
  Apple tart Tatin
Other favorite dishes: Eggplant Provençale, snails, fried oysters, poached fish in court bouillon, roast prime ribs of beef, rack of lamb, brochette of lamb, chocolate cake, dacquoise, chef's custard.
Setting: Handsome and much like an urbane club in an old coach house with English hunting and food paintings; Hayloft room is uncomfortable and is set aside for non-smokers.
Service: Impeccable but can be overbearing to unknowns.
Dress code: Jacket required for men.
Facilities for private parties: Small upstairs room accommodates up to 37.
Hours: Dinner, Tuesday through Sunday. Closed Monday, major holidays, and for the month of August.
Reservations: Necessary.
Prices: Moderate to moderately expensive.
Credit cards: AE, CB, DC, MC, V.

Celebrating its fortieth birthday in 1989, The Coach House is a restaurant that is part of my own private Greenwich Village history. When I began going to N.Y.U. in the mid-forties, the premises was known as Helen Lane's Tearoom and even then was a sort of homey, American tradition students saved for. Shortly after I moved to the Village, Helen Lane's became The Coach House, and for years I stayed away, hearing it was expensive. Going once, I knew immediately I would try to return often and did, though for the first ten years of my association I was just another customer and not even a food writer. Throughout I had nothing but wonderful food and impeccable service, albeit the tone and style of both changed through the years.

Starting with the history of the building itself—once the coach house of the Wanamaker estates—and the character it took on as Helen Lane's, the new owner, Leon Lianides, created an American menu with wonderful fried chicken and chicken pot pie, pecan pie, cornsticks, and similar fare. Gradually the place developed a combination of urbanity and authenticity. The Greek-born Lianides introduced more Continental sophistications. Brick walls were trimmed in their present deep-but-subtly-bright Victorian red, and he began to collect nineteenth-century English paintings of food and horse scenes. Always impeccably maintained, with simple but graceful flowers and a buffet of desserts at the entrance, The Coach House soon took on the sophistication of the Guinea Grill in London. Steak au poivre as dark and enchanting as midnight, always perfect prime ribs of beef, rack of lamb done rose-red and crusted with parsley, garlic, and bread crumbs, and a fresh bright bouillabaisse took their places on the menu. Eggplant in a garlic and tomato sauce Provençale, garlicky snails, and oysters fried in beer batter join appetizers such as crabcakes based on nuggets of the whitest Florida lump crab meat and coarse, garlicky saucisson nestled alongside a cool lentil salad. Always there was the marvel of black bean soup, a velvety purée with overtones of smoked ham, best accented by a shot of lemon juice or a trickling of wine vinegar and olive oil.

Cornsticks are still passed and are as crunchy as ever, and salads add refreshment by way of their tangy vinaigrette dressing.

Two exceptional fish dishes—the day's catch—are either poached in a court bouillon with slivers of fresh vegetables or roasted and then glossed with dill butter. Duck is parchment crisp yet moistly flavorful, but I much prefer quince to cherries as its garnish. Chicken pie, alas, no longer is the baked-together, richly sauced version it once was and the parchment-crisp fried chicken has disappeared. Fortunately, there is now a buttery roast baby chicken offset by nutty wild rice that almost makes up for the loss.

Desserts are as irresistible as ever. The velvety chocolate cake and the chewy hazelnut-flavored dacquoise, the country's best crunchy pecan pie, and the airy Grand Marnier bavarois are always perfection, as is the chef's custard, really a bread pudding, which I prefer without its raspberry sauce. Apple tart Tatin, though delicious, does not always have the right glassy caramelization, but it is properly thick with tender, buttery apples.

Just as he respects America's ingredients and its culinary heritage, so Lianides was one of the first serious purveyors of American wines, and they are as well chosen as his French bottles. Italian wines are banally represented, but perhaps they are unnecessary in this context.

Failures at The Coach House are the service and treatment of certain unknown guests, whether because of their dress or whatever. I have had reports from people I trust on the cold indifference that can greet them and the short shrift they are given. Also, the balcony Hayloft room is claustrophobic and cramped, and service up there can be perfunctory and slow, all too bad in a New York landmark that still can set an exceptional table.

The Four Seasons, see The View, the Setting, and the Scene

HUBERTS

575 Park Avenue in the Beekman Hotel; entrance on 63rd Street
Telephone: 826-5911

Favorite meals:
Crab meat pierogi on a green sauce
Grilled sirloin with ancho pepper mayonnaise
Blood orange tartlets with ginger-lime ice cream
or
Rabbit sausage with molé
Grilled lobster with leek, tomato, and poblano sauce
Lemon soufflé tart
Other favorite dishes: Salad of grilled venison, Cajun barbecued shrimp, gravlax terrine, oxtail consommé, Roquefort soufflé, warm belon oysters, country captain chicken, roast duck with vegetable strudel, salmon with coriander and cucumber, tuna with endive ragout, rack of lamb with goat cheese lasagne, roast saddle of boar with sage and dried Montmorency cherries, profiteroles with apricot mousse, strawberry roulade with spiced figs and basil or tangerine ice cream, vanilla and orange cheesecake, raspberry rhubarb tart with clove ice cream, chocolate cake with fruit compote, coconut cream puffs with pineapple, plum bisteeya with cinnamon ice cream, all ice creams and sorbets.
Setting: Stunning, elegant, and eclectic modern decor with Japanese overtones. Quiet and spacious. Back dining room is low-ceilinged and stylish and is suited to serious business discussions.
Service: Slightly confused, but polite and friendly.
Dress code: Jackets required for men.
Facilities for private parties: Private dining room accommodates between 35 and 70.

Hours: Lunch, Monday through Friday. Dinner, Monday through Saturday. Closed Sunday, and Christmas and New Year's days.
Reservations: Necessary.
Prices: Expensive.
Credit cards: AE, MC, V.

A brilliant new four star constellation shines on Park Avenue. To find out just how good food can get, and how glowingly classic a modern room can be, waste no time in going to Huberts, opened last spring in the Beekman Hotel, where Le Périgord Park used to be. Fans of Karen Huberts, who oversees the dining room, and her chef-husband, Len Allison, will not be surprised at the delicate, subtle, and esoteric combinations and presentations of ingredients. But they may be dazzled by Adam Tihany's luminous, spacious dining room, with its silk-lined glass wall panels, its stunning and authoritative Japanese structures rendered in intricately grained, golden Australian ash, and the lighting, which is most effective when moderately dim. Dramatic bouquets of fruit blossoms accent the Japanese motifs. Midst all of this are large, widely spaced tables, comfortable chairs, and a benign noise level.

There is also a smartly polished little bar area, an inner lounge for smokers, and a more intimate cafélike back dining room that is conducive to intimate, private conversations and which also will be available for private parties.

A Huberts aficionado since this pair first opened their charming old restaurant in downtown Brooklyn, and remaining one during their Gramercy Park incarnation, I feared for their ability to cope with the grander, larger quarters announced for Park Avenue. Magically, it has brought improvement and, more magically, the new decor reflects the eclecticism of Allison's culinary creations.

To be successful such eclecticism can be practiced only by those experienced in more traditional forms and disciplines. In art, the wave of Abstract Expressionism was a signal to a lot of would-be painters that it was no longer necessary to know how to draw. Similarly, the new all-bets-are-off school of cooking has led to much bad food, based as it is on lack of experience (both in eating and cooking) and no foundation in technique. The wonder of Huberts is how magnificently culinary eclecticism can succeed when practiced by those who have a finely honed sense of aesthetics and craftsmanship. To date no one does it better than Allison, as he guides Japanese, American, and Thai cooks who turn out stylish fare that combines American regional, European, and Oriental influences.

That the kitchen succeeds becomes evident even with the small, beguiling giveaway appetizers that appear each evening. One night it may be a round, molded timbale of eggplant purée or a sweet red pepper mousse tipped with a yellow pepper sabayon, both with distinct Mediterranean overtones. Another night, the Japanese seaweed, nori, may be wrapped sushi style around cool, mildly saline buckwheat noodles lightly touched with soy sauce. Eastern European—inspired crisp pouches of pastry for pierogi are filled with crab meat and sauced with a leaf-green blend of spinach and tarragon; Mexican molé sauce with its counterpoints of chocolate, nuts, and chili powder underlines Allison's now classic, lean and plump rabbit sausage. Grilled venison, rare and slightly warm, is brightened by pungent greens in a salad, and delectable prawns, often with their roe, are fired with a Cajun barbecue sauce heady with thyme and bay. The Japanese horseradish, wasabi, is the surprise sharpening ingredient in crème fraîche layered in with the dill-scented gravlax terrine, and a cushiony cabbage leaf filled with the ricelike pasta orzo and tender flecks of beef is adrift in a clear, bracing oxtail consommé.

Roquefort cheese is so delicately combined with cream that it is not overpowering in a hot appetizer soufflé sauced with apple. Cream is also the protective, gentling topping for barely warm, seabreeze-sharp belon oysters. Of the two dishes I did not like among all of those tried, one is the appetizer of fettuccine with sautéed sweetbreads and oysters; the pasta lacked salt and was oily, and there was not enough textural contrast between the sweetbreads and the oysters.

To get the other negative over with early on, the only failure among main courses is the halibut that is obscured by an overly sweet confit of leeks. This still leaves plenty of other wonders, such as the crisply sautéed salmon cooled with cucumber and piquant with coriander, and the grilled lobster mellowed with leeks, tomato, and a needling of poblano chilies. (The kitchen prefers to cook that lobster rare, but I ask for it medium as I find that less cloying.) The same is true for the grilled, sliced fillet of tuna that gets a sophisticated bittersweet edge from a sheer, golden endive ragout.

Main courses can be as down-homey as traditional country captain chicken, the curry-flavored Southern stew gently sweetened with slivered peppers and contrasted to grainy couscous, or as soigné as organically raised duck basted with soy sauce, then roasted rare and sliced, to be accompanied with seductive vegetable strudel. Goat cheese is of the mildest, creamiest sort and so adds delightful pungency to lasagne noodles that complement rare-roasted rack of lamb.

Fiery red ancho peppers are whipped into a mayonnaise that adds brassiness to grilled sirloin steak. Tender saddle of boar, best blood-rare, is perfumed with sage; a sharp-sweet note comes from the

Montmorency cherries in its sauce. With all of these dishes are inventive vegetable creations, and herbed biscuits or delectable breads that are all too irresistible, considering the hefty portions of main courses.

All of which may make you wish you had more willpower when desserts come around. John Dudek, the pastry chef, is devilishly adept at ruining even the most devout dieter's resolve. The ice creams and sorbets alone are blissfully destructive of waistlines, with their original, supple flavorings such as cinnamon, clove, basil, tangerine, or almond brittle for the creams, and mango-lime, orange-Armagnac, grapefruit-cassis, or lemon-lime for the ices.

That still leaves the heavenly baking—such as the frothy lemon soufflé tart, the plum-filled bisteeya of North African inspiration with its phyllo dough pastry enfolding warm red plums cooled with whipped or liquid sweet cream, and the intensely chocolate cake, served warm with the same two creams. Spicy blood oranges glow ruby red in tiny tartlets sharpened with ginger-lime ice cream, and a silken mousse of dried apricots fills profiteroles of the most interesting, slightly rough-textured pâte à choux (cream puff pastry) that I have ever had. Gentle vanilla plus orange zest is the palate-tingler in a gossamer cheesecake.

Then comes the tiny, enticing cookies, all inspired but paling beside the thin ovals of dark chocolate spiked with cayenne and cinnamon—a crisp, hot, and aromatic finish that surely brings the reserved, well-dressed clientele back for more.

In such a thoughtful environment, it is no surprise to find a carefully devised wine list with excellent choices in all price ranges, and an unusually delicate but well-rounded 1985 Newton, a California merlot, at $28.

What is yet to be accomplished at Huberts is a staff that is more polished and has a quicker awareness of customers' needs. All are polite, jauntily dressed, and willing, but lack the professionalism they had better develop if customers are to hold still for an automatic 18 percent service charge. It would also be an improvement to have salt on the table. Its absence is pretentious. As Fowler pointed out in another context, "The obvious is better than the obvious avoidance of it."

It may be true that nothing is perfect, but surely Huberts is about as close as a restaurant can get to that elusive goal.

MANHATTAN ISLAND

482 West 43rd Street, corner 10th Avenue, in Manhattan
Plaza Health Club
Telephone: 967-0533

Favorite meals:
Lunch, shared by two
Sausage bread
Assorted greens with Island dressing
Key lime pie
or
Dinner
Salad of goat cheese on mixed greens with jalapeño tomato relish
Maryland crabcakes with cole slaw
Orange pound cake with ice cream
Other favorite dishes: Roasted peppers with mozzarella cheese and sun-dried tomato vinaigrette; herb chicken roasted with lemon and garlic; pesto lamb chops; salmon steak with caper crunch; New York shell steak; red pepper shrimp; Oriental chicken salad with noodles, scallions, and toasted pecans; grilled tuna salad Niçoise; sausage pizza; hamburger; peanut butter pie; chocolate mudd cake.
Setting: Palmy, casual tropical duplex overlooking swimming pool, with terraces for outdoor dining.
Service: Polite and helpful, if at times self-conscious and a bit slow before main courses.
Dress code: None.
Facilities for private parties: Two dining rooms and two terraces are available in a variety of combinations.
Hours: Lunch and dinner, Monday through Saturday. Brunch and dinner on Sunday. Open late Tuesday through Saturday.
Reservations: Necessary before theater and for Wednesday lunch. Otherwise, generally recommended.
Prices: Inexpensive to moderately expensive.
Credit cards: AE, MC, V.

Under the careful direction of Eileen Weinberg and Martin Yerdon, the guiding hands behind Carolina, Manhattan Island is the kind of tucked-away, joyous surprise I like to spring on out-of-town visitors. Laid out on two floors, each with a terrace and overlooking the swimming pool and tennis courts of the Manhattan Plaza Health Club, this feels like a stylish suburban country club. Decorated with a sort of Key West motif of palm-patterned wallpaper, fading green shutters, and window frames, it offers surcease from the city's concrete and skyscrapers. An obvious choice in summer when meals are served outdoors as well as in, it is perhaps even more of a delight in winter, having about it a sort of greenhouse glow, enhanced by the view of the turquoise, glassed-in pool with its lavish plantings and lighted trees on the terrace.

Much the same menu prevails here daylong and it is an ingenious mix of the light and the substantial, the casual and the formal. Have a good New York shell steak if you like, or three petite lamb chops grilled rose-red as ordered and spread with a verdant pesto sauce. Start with a salad and end with the cool, yellow-amber Key lime pie, and you have a hearty, delicious, full-fledged meal.

But come in for lunch, or for a light snack before or after theater, and you can choose from salads, sandwiches that include a thick, beefy burger or the thick-crusted, briochelike pizza topped with chunks of spicy fennel-scented sausage, tomato, and melting mozzarella, or the sausage bread, a yeasty loaf centered with garlicky sausage, cheese, peppers, and eggs in the style of pizza rustica. Share either of these along with a freshly green and piquantly dressed salad and you will leave feeling more than satisfied.

Carolina favorites that are on hand here include the firm but nicely moist grilled shrimp fired with red pepper, and the golden cakes of lump crab meat soothed with mayonnaise and accented with mustard. With these comes the coarse, bright cole slaw, now a Carolina classic. The best salads at Manhattan Island are those listed as appetizers—the combination of roasted peppers with creamy mozzarella cheese and a vinaigrette dressing brightened with sun-dried tomatoes, and the goat cheese on mixed greens that are brought to life by a relish of jalapeño peppers and tomato. These, plus the Niçoise based on grilled tuna and garnished with asparagus, olives, and new potatoes, are all better than the half dozen or so cold pasta combinations, something I like only in an Oriental idiom. One such is the Oriental chicken salad tossed with noodles and spiked with scallions and toasted pecans to add crunch. Otherwise, dead, cold pasta always seems to me to be bland and greasy.

Grilled fish choices vary from day to day, but if you are in luck, you will be able to have the thick slab of juicy salmon glazed with a crunchy topping of caper-dotted mayonnaise. Choose it over the somewhat dry and uninspired lime-basted swordfish. Similarly, roasted chicken scented with lemon and garlic is far better than the punishingly dietetic, dry grilled, boneless, skinless paillard of chicken.

Sunday brunch in summer is a jam-packed affair, when a variety of egg dishes and French toast joins many of the house classics, such as the crabcakes, the sausage bread, and more.

The one argument for having the dry chicken paillard or the swordfish is that you would get valuable calorie credits for dessert. In addition to the astringently refreshing lime pie and the golden, citrus-perfumed orange pound cake, there is chocolate mudd cake with a rich, costly chocolate flavor that is neither too sweet nor too cloying, and fluffy peanut butter pie with a veneer of dark chocolate on top.

There is a modest, well-chosen wine list, crusty, chewy sourdough bread, and Riviera toast slices to dip into a creamy garlic spread served along with butter.

MEMPHIS

329 Columbus Avenue, between 75th and 76th streets
Telephone: 496-1840

Favorite meals:
Cajun popcorn with rémoulade sauce
Barbecued ribs
Bread pudding with whisky
or
Shrimp, chicken, and andouille gumbo
Southern fried chicken with mashed potatoes
Creole cream cheese cake
Other favorite dishes: Barataria crabcakes, grilled filet mignon in tortilla shell, snails baked with shiitake mushrooms, split and grilled shrimp with soba noodles, Crescent City crab meat pancakes, jambalaya, pan-roasted filet mignon, pan-barbecued Gulf shrimp, blackened swordfish, pecan pie.
Setting: Huge, noisy café on two levels, with modern, Art Deco accents. Big bar scene.
Service: Polite, quick, and a bit slapdash; slow upstairs.
Dress code: No running suits or tank tops.
Facilities for private parties: Balcony can accommodate 40 to 70, at dinner only.
Hours: Dinner, seven days.
Reservations: Recommended, especially on weekends for peak dinner hours.
Prices: Moderate to moderately expensive.
Credit cards: AE, DC, MC, V.

Believe it or not, some restaurants improve, even if they are on Columbus Avenue. Given the usual dismal quality of eateries on the Upper West Side, the upswing in the kitchen's performance at Memphis is all the more remarkable. If the reason for its name remains a mystery, as does the idea behind having no sign marking the restaurant, we can at least be thankful for the lusty, flavorful Louisiana Creole-Cajun food, now joined by Tex-Mex and Continental dishes.

That savory array is presented both in the noisy clamor of the trim, silver gray downstairs dining room that leads off from the jam-packed singles bar, and on the quieter but boring balcony where service inevitably slows.

A number of dishes on this menu are neoclassics and, among appetizers, such include the snowy, zesty Barataria Bay crabcakes with a spicy mayonnaise, the crisped, breaded crawfish known as Cajun popcorn, here with batons of fried eggplant, and the Crescent

City pancakes—delicately cool crêpes, enfolding luscious mouthfuls of crab meat, avocado and a froth of crème fraiche, counterpointed to a tangy, chili salsa. Almost as good are relative newcomers such as snails baked with shiitake mushrooms in a glossing of garlicky cilantro butter, the succulent, split, grilled shrimp on chewy buckwheat soba noodles and, almost a main course, nuggets of grilled filet mignon doused with a pungent mole sauce, sour cream and guacamole, heaped into a parchmentlike tortilla cup. Gumbo is a good starter, whether based on seafood or the chicken and peppery andouille sausage.

A most welcome improvement is the jambalaya, served more in the style of paella, with mussels and crawfish in shells, and shrimp, smoked chicken, and ripe, saline ham, nested on tomato-moistened rice. If not quite the authentic version, for which shrimp and ham are mixed through rice, this jambalaya is, nonetheless, delicious. Barbecued shrimp in the shell drift in a bowlful of a dense, piquant tomato sauce and, though messy to handle, are worth the effort. The sauce, however, would have more meaning with thick toast croutons than with the boiled potatoes that appear.

Nowhere in town will you find crunchier Southern fried chicken, with a greaseless, flaky breading and, just as impeccable, are the mashed potatoes with cream gravy that profits from a generous shaking of black pepper. Lean, tender barbecued ribs soothed with red country beans and mellow fried bananas are as soul-satisfying as the pan-roasted filet mignon, its bloody juices mingling with the ruby-red cabernet sauce, dusky with wild mushrooms.

Disappointments on the menu include bland pastas, tough yet overcooked green beans, meager pork chops with soggy stuffing, and ginger roast duck, at times dry and stringy. If this is Cajun, the fish must be blackened and so it is. This method of coating fish with spices, then "blackening" (or burning) it on a white hot skillet, seems an insensitive way to cook delicate salmon. Better to leave it for swordfish, the tasteless, boneless darling of yuppies.

Try to resist too many corn-flecked corn muffins or the jalapeño-spiked alternatives, or you'll be sorry at dessert time. Better save room for the thick, cool, whisky-soaked bread pudding, the airy Creole cream cheese cake under a nutty, praline glaze, and the Bourbon-scented pecan pie, or, to cool an overheated palate, vanilla ice cream in a thin cookie "tulip."

METRO

23 East 74th Street, between Fifth and Madison avenues
Telephone: 249-3030

Favorite meals:
Lunch
Mussel and avocado salad
Sautéed calves' liver with sherry vinegar and onions
Fruit sherbet
or
Dinner
Lobster bisque
Clay pot-roasted chicken
Cinnamon ice cream
Other favorite dishes: Cold cream soup of snow peas, buckwheat crêpe with red caviar and poached egg, country salad with goat cheese, sweetbread salad with greens, lobster and squid salad, hot vegetable tart with herb-butter sauce, swordfish with black olive butter, grilled salmon with shrimp sauce, fricassee of Maine lobster, roast squab, roast loin of lamb.
Setting: Clublike blend of traditional and contemporary influences with glowing light and stylish touches; noisy and crowded.
Service: Polite, friendly, and helpful, but agonizingly slow before main courses.
Dress code: None.
Facilities for private parties: None.
Hours: Lunch, Monday through Friday. Dinner, Monday through Saturday. Brunch, Sunday. Closed Sunday night.
Reservations: Generally necessary.
Prices: Expensive.
Credit cards: AE, DC, MC, V.

A glowing, sophisticated setting and food to match make Metro welcome on the Upper East Side. The credentials here are impressive, with Adam Tihany, designer of Bice and Huberts, at it again creating a setting for the food of Patrick Clark, the highly original and deft chef who gave us the original new continental cooking at Odeon and Café Luxembourg. Formerly Adam's Rib in what was the Hotel Volney, the dining room is a clublike setting with wood-paneled walls, the sort of glowing light that is a Tihany specialty, and overtones of old and new, richly combined. Unfortunately noisy, Metro does have comfortable seating and generous tables.

Even after a few months, Clark is again stirring up stylish fare. If he is not quite up to his former high batting average, it is because he has to work out desserts with his pastry chef, and restrain himself a bit in the use of strong seasonings such as ginger. Nevertheless, this mellow new option is understandably attracting a conservative, well-dressed local set, and most especially the art gallery crowd at lunch, an exceptionally pleasant meal here.

It was then that I sampled several of Clark's best new dishes, among them an appetizer salad of cool, unpolluted mussels with a slight bay-pickling spice accent, in a light sauce that seemed like a cross between vinaigrette and mayonnaise, nestling on sliced avocado. Spring vegetable tart with a buttery crust, which included slim French string beans, asparagus, and spinach in a butter sauce flecked with chives, was almost enough to make a main course.

Also midday, I tried a beautiful main-course salad of freshly cooked, satiny lobster meat with tender rings of squid in a basil, lemon, and olive oil dressing and slivers of sweet red peppers and buttery baby lettuce leaves. For heartier appetites there is perfectly sautéed calves' liver, as fresh and rose-pink as one might want, given just the right edge of sweet-sourness from a combination of sherry vinegar and sautéed onions.

Appetizers at dinner are more complex than at lunch with warm nuggets of squab in a tossing of haricots verts, red cabbage, and lettuce, and, similarly, warm sweetbreads with lettuce, endive, and mushrooms in a vinaigrette dressing fragrant with hazelnut oil. Country salad with greens, croutons, bacon, and Roquefort is another Clark standby expertly rendered. Less successful are the wet chicken terrine with a watery, melting aspic and unpleasantly greasy roasted Louisiana shrimp. A better hot first course is the airy buckwheat crêpe rolled around Columbia River sturgeon caviar (good enough for this purpose) that gets luxurious accents from a poached egg, a whipped butter sauce, and chives. Soup is delicious, whether it is the intense, coral-bright lobster bisque or the delicate cool cream of snow pea pod that had a fresh springtime green flavor.

Cream, saffron, and a belt of whisky are combined with enough deftness to prevent them from overpowering lobster (meagerly portioned) in a fricassee, and dark, pungently salty olive butter added zest to otherwise bland grilled swordfish.

As good as several fish dishes are, they are outshone by the poultry, such as the almost falling-apart-tender clay pot-roasted chicken heady with roasted garlic and herbs, and the equally mellow squab banked by a wild mushroom risotto slightly short on salt. Too bad the chicken's potato pancake is such a mass of uncrisp mush. An original use of the curry idiom with spices, fried onions, and almonds setting off roast loin of lamb, is worth trying. Otherwise nice roast breast of duck with figs and red wine is impossible to finish because of its palate-numbing dose of ginger. Overheated butter mars sweetbreads, giving them a waxy aroma.

Don't worry about skipping the crusty country bread or holding back on other courses to save room for dessert. Only the fruit sherbets and the cinnamon ice cream are worth the deprivation. No matter how good they sound, don't be beguiled by the gross crème brûlée, the minted terrine that suggests chocolate toothpaste, the peach charlotte that is all custard and barely any peaches, or the sodden cherry-filled crêpes.

The staff is well-meaning and professional but the kitchen evidently has a hard time getting main courses out. The wait can be agonizing. There is good representation of Italian, French, and California wines, most of them overpriced by about 20 percent.

ODEON

145 West Broadway, corner Thomas Street
Telephone: 233-0507

Favorite meals:
Country salad
Cassoulette of lamb and vegetables
Lemon tart
or
Chilled marinated mussels
Calves' liver with sherry vinegar sauce
Chocolate soufflé
Other favorite dishes: Cream of asparagus soup, seafood chowder, seafood sausage, roast lotte with tomato confit, herb-roasted chicken, paillard of veal, steak frites, pineapple soufflé. For brunch: grilled grapefruit with honey, fresh juices, buttermilk pancakes, roast corned beef hash with poached eggs, smoked salmon and bagel plate, biscuits.
Setting: Handsome Art Deco cafeteria-turned-café that is moderately crowded and noisy.
Service: Polite, informed, but at times disorganized and slow.
Dress code: None.
Facilities for private parties: Will close restaurant for a fee to be negotiated.
Hours: Lunch, Monday through Friday. Dinner, until midnight, seven days. Late supper, midnight to 2 A.M., Monday through Friday, and until 3 A.M., Saturday and Sunday. Brunch, Sunday.
Reservations: Generally necessary.
Prices: Moderate.
Credit cards: AE, DC, MC, V.

How good is the food at Odeon since a new chef took over? Like Café Luxembourg, Odeon is owned by Keith McNally and until recently both shared Patrick Clark as executive chef. The style of Continental–New American food he created had the spirit of a Parisian grand café menu, made contemporary with some Oriental and Latin touches. That format is still being followed by the chefs who succeeded him, with somewhat better results at Odeon than at Luxembourg.

Odeon, an Art Deco cafeteria-turned-restaurant, remains one of the treasures of TriBeCa, even more so for me now that the former crush of high fashion popularity is moderately diminished. It has settled in to become a neo-classic, with its dark wood paneling, mirrors, slow-moving ceiling fans, touches of dark green trim, beautiful flowers, and crisp white paper covering tablecloths. The staff is bright, informed, and only occasionally confused on orders. The slowness between courses seems more the fault of the kitchen than of the waiters, and it is one of the consistent shortcomings here.

That aside, Odeon is the sort of stylishly casual, versatile restaurant every good neighborhood deserves. It offers weekend brunches, weekday lunches, dinners, and late suppers that are accompanied by a jazz trio Monday through Wednesday.

Equally varied is the menu, allowing for light grazing of two appetizers such as, say, the country salad with greens accented by Roquefort cheese, nuggets of bacon, and croutons, and then, perhaps, a plump, subtle, grilled seafood sausage in a light butter sauce. Those of lustier appetites might begin with the creamy, briny seafood chowder and go on to steak frites, the excellent calves' liver brightened by a sheer sherry vinegar and honey sauce, or the cassoulette with meaty chunks of lamb, sausages, and tiny turnips and carrots fleshed out with green fettuccine.

Other Odeon standbys that the new chef, Gonzalo Figueroa, does well include a lusciously rich, verdant cream of asparagus soup and cool, lovely mussels on the half shell topped with a salad of corn kernels and peppers and seasoned with cumin and coriander. Somewhat less successful is the green salad overly sweetened by balsamic vinegar and ravioli with a bland eggplant stuffing. In general, pastas tend to be flavorless and greasy.

Roasted lotte is a better alternative than the same fish sautéed. A whole thick fillet is roasted, then sliced to remain moist but with the nice edge of seared richness, accented by a pleasantly salty tomato and olive confit. Simple dishes such as herb-roasted chicken and paillard of veal with parsley sauce are more dependable than the duck soured by wine vinegar. All dishes have some sort of attractive vegetable garnish, an improvement over the original strictly à la carte pricing.

Brunch dishes range from true breakfast choices such as oatmeal with brown sugar and cinnamon, bagel with smoked salmon, and all sorts of egg dishes to more lunchlike selections, among them soups, pasta, fish, and a steak sandwich. My own favorites for that weekend meal include the warm-cool, sweet-sour, honey-glazed grilled grapefruit, any of the poached egg creations topped with a satiny, lemony hollandaise sauce, and the crusty, properly chewy roast corned beef hash with fried or poached eggs. Lovers of pancakes should appreciate the soufflé lightness of the buttermilk-raised specimens and the maple syrup that is served comfortably warm. Smoky ham or bacon or breakfast sausage rounds out the meal. Well-made waffles and a big crisp potato pancake are other fine choices.

Buns and muffins at breakfast, as well as sourdough bread at other meals, are all distinctive and satisfying, and there is a nicely varied choice of moderately priced wines.

Odeon's piquant, velvety lemon curd tart and the dark, bittersweet chocolate mousse are the best desserts. Soufflés are delicious but why one orders in advance, only to wait 20 minutes for it anyway, is a mystery. Crusts for fruit tarts vary from crisp to soggy and though crème brûlée is based on a soothing custard, its warm (probably grilled to order) sugar topping lacks the glassy crackle it should have.

The Pink Tea Cup, see Cafés, under Casual Eating

SAM'S

152 West 52nd Street, in Equitable Center, between Sixth and Seventh avenues
Telephone: 582-8700

Favorite meal:
Chicken livers with frizzled onions
Grilled salmon with red butter sauce
Yam cinnamon custard
Other favorite dishes: Grilled shiitake mushrooms and roasted red pepper salad, oysters, smoked turkey club sandwich, roast farm chicken with mashed potatoes, sautéed black bass with herbed polenta, duck breast with black beans, sautéed spinach.
Setting: High, spacious, and convivial bar and dining room with Southwest overtones; mezzanine dining room is more private and quieter than downstairs.
Service: Absentminded at the door and on telephone; polite and efficient at tables.
Dress code: None.
Facilities for private parties: Upstairs can accommodate 25 to 55 in one or two rooms. Entire mezzanine can accommodate 100 to 150.
Hours: Lunch and dinner, Monday through Saturday. Closed Sunday.
Reservations: Recommended, especially before theater.
Prices: Moderate to moderately expensive.
Credit cards: AE, DC, MC, V.

Mariel Hemingway is one of the principals here, but don't let that discourage you. We all have a right to be suspicious of celebrity-operated restaurants these days, but one of the nicest things about Sam's is that it is a serious restaurant. Most nights, the only reminder of Ernest's pretty granddaughter is a big, bright James Rosenquist floral painting, through which the famous smile and eyebrows peek. For the rest, this is a surprisingly pleasant, moderately priced place to have a business lunch, or dinner before or after theater. It is, in fact, my favorite in the Equitable Center complex, primarily because it is the least pretentious. With just a little fine tuning that includes serving hot food truly hot, this could easily rate two stars.

The huge, soaring room designed by Philip George is forthright and handsome, with certain Southwestern accents reminiscent of the Santa Fe Bar and Grill in Berkeley. Cactus plants in terra cotta planters, and the same bright red clay color on wall tiles, create this effect. The huge, agate glass chandeliers and comfortable golden oak chairs suggest that the premises might have been a big old bank or a state house. There is a jam-packed bar that turns out stunning bloody Marys, properly cold even when ordered straight up, and a mezzanine dining room that is quiet, private, and intimately decorated with family photographs of Ernest Hemingway, now with a marlin, here with Kilimanjaro, there with Mariel as a child. Seated below, one should avoid the too-low, too-deep banquettes and some of the more closely packed tables.

Food is much in the young-spirited, contemporary vein, and best at its simplest. Pizzas are only fair, primarily because of a soft, almost buttery crust, much like monkey bread. Moreover, they arrive tepid, like the pasta and soups.

Better first courses include the moist, sautéed chicken livers topped with glassy rings of frizzled onions fired with cayenne or Tabasco, the clear, cold oysters and a crinkly green salad soothed with chubby grilled shiitake mushrooms. Crabcakes are a bit thready though nicely seasoned, but the mousse of fresh and smoked salmon is much like a standard mix from a Jewish appetizer store.

There is a lot of two-appetizer ordering here, but for those who want a conventional main course there are two good fish dishes—one a grilled salmon in red wine butter, the other, sautéed black bass with herbed polenta, perhaps a little too creamy but well flavored. Roast farm chicken, meltingly soft and tender, is delicious with creamy mashed potatoes and is better than the dry, bland braised chicken or the paltry lamb chops. Black beans provide a velvety foil for grilled, rare duck breast and though steak and hamburger are passable, both are too lean and, therefore, dry. As for a pork chop with blue cheese sauce, try it and tell me what it's like.

There is an original and lovely smoked turkey club sandwich on the lunch menu, the chunks of meat layered between thin pumpernickel with bacon, tomato, watercress, and a good thousand-island type dressing.

Yam cinnamon custard sounded awful and so took me by surprise, for it is really a wedge of bavarois, coolly taupe and cinnamony and much like pumpkin pie filling. Other desserts are all right for those who must end on something sweet, though all are unremarkable.

The dining room staff is quick, friendly, and professional. Not so the vague, confused voice that takes reservations and some of the help at the desk.

Tavern on the Green, *see* The View, the Setting, and the Scene

TEXARKANA

64 West 10th Street, between Fifth and Sixth avenues
Telephone: 254-5800

Favorite meals:
Southern-style pickled shrimp
Blackened rib steak
Fried okra, shared by two to four
Rum pecan pie
or
Seafood gumbo
Roast suckling pig or breast of duck with jalapeño peppers
Bread pudding with bourbon sauce
Other favorite dishes: Charred raw beef, barbecued pork with lettuce leaves, venison sausage, jicama salad, potato and green chili soup, orange and red onion salad, Southern fried chicken, barbecued chicken, venison chop, calves' liver with bacon and scallions, barbecued lamb chops, barbecued veal chop, fried chicken salad, crabcakes, blackened fish, dirty rice, french fries, lemon cheesecake, plum pie.
Setting: Modern but with romantic French Quarter overtones and colors; crowded and noisy; bar is especially handsome as is the crowd frequenting it.
Service: Staff is professional and accommodating, but the kitchen can be slow.
Dress code: None.
Facilities for private parties: Separate area can be set aside for parties of 15 to 30.
Hours: Dinner, until midnight, Sunday through Thursday, and to 2 A.M., Friday and Saturday. Bar is open until 4 A.M., seven days.
Reservations: Generally necessary.
Prices: Moderate to moderately expensive.
Credit cards: AE, DC, MC, V.

Texarkana is the perfect name for the state of mind that holds sway in the kitchen of this stylishly handsome, convivial restaurant. With Abe De La Houssaye, a native Cajun who is the chef and a partner, that sensibility means combining such Louisiana traditions as gumbo and the suckling pig, cochon du lait, which he does each evening on a spit in the dining-room fireplace with Southwest overtones of green chilies, barbecued and Southern fried chicken, then applying such ingredients and techniques to somewhat Continental dishes. He succeeds here far more than at his other restaurant, Savant, where he proselytizes for food low in fat and sodium, and, as a result, flavor. There are even some Savant specialties along with the bon vivant alternatives at Texarkana, but the smart money is definitely on the latter.

The dishes I love at Texarkana have proved consistently excellent; those that fail also do so consistently. That suckling pig is one favorite, and portions must be ordered when reservations are made. There has been a sliding schedule of hours when that crunchy, mellow-meated piglet is served, so check when making reservations. Usually, the 8:30 time is the safest. Before I get to that or other main courses, I nibble my way through the pickled okra and onions, the good, gritty cornbread, black-eyed peas, and coleslaw. Then there are the fine appetizers, among the best being the charred raw beef in green chili sauce and the chunks of barbecued pork in a smoky sauce nested on lettuce leaves. Crawfish in a cocktail have never had flavor enough, but pickled shrimp in a vinegar, lemon, and oil dressing almost make up for them.

More delicate appetites might prefer an icy jicama salad or the combination of oranges and red onions with vinegar, sesame oil, and black pepper, a welcome palate freshener with the smoky meats. Potato and green chili soup has a Tex-Mex lustiness, and seafood gumbo is delicious.

Two moist, flavorful chicken dishes are the Southern fried and the barbecued, pit grilled and glazed with pungent barbecue sauce. Catfish has lacked flavor, but the blackened fish inspired by Paul Prudhomme, who made the dish famous, is better, more delicately done than the so-called master's version. For the most part, though, I go to Texarkana for a meat fix, and there is that in spades in the thick, bloody, gargantuan, barbecued prime rib steak that two can easily share. (Or leftovers can be taken home to be enjoyed cold the next day.) Barbecuing is also well accomplished on veal or venison chops, neither drying out in the process.

In the mood for lighter fare, I might have the crabcakes or the fried chicken salad with nuggets of fried chicken tossed with greens and mushrooms and moistened with a honey-mustard dressing. Or for more stylish eating, there are the boned, crisp-skinned duck breast zapped with jalapeño peppers and the tender calves' liver with scallions and bacon.

Side dishes I tend to order include dirty rice (dirtied with giblets), the slim, crisp french fries, the jalapeño and cornmeal dressing, and fried okra, depending on what is served with main courses ordered. All, however, are well worth trying.

American   31

Pacing myself to include dessert is a trick I have not yet quite mastered, given other enticements here, but we usually do some sharing on that last course. Rum pecan pie, bread pudding with bourbon sauce, lemon cheesecake, and a surprising (in this format) juicy plum pie are among the temptations I have not always resisted.

Stunningly decorated with Southwest-sunset-pink walls and a balconied dining room that suggests a New Orleans courtyard, Texarkana is an attractive if jam-packed and noisy setting. The magnificent wooden bar was made by George Nakashima, the sculptor, who is the uncle of Mr. De La Houssaye's wife, Alene. The balcony also has tables, but it is airless and remote. Nice preppie waiters hold forth, often apologizing for the occasional slowdowns.

TIME & AGAIN

116 East 39th Street, between Park and Lexington avenues, in Doral Tuscany Hotel
Telephone: 685-8887

Favorite meals:
Phyllo of spinach with feta cheese and red bell pepper sauce
Roast lamb Provençale
Peach charlotte with caramel sauce
or
Cream of asparagus soup
Grilled New York steak with artichokes in a pinot noir sauce
Chocolate terrine with orange segments and vanilla sauce
Other favorite dishes: Marinated shrimp with avocado salsa, spicy crabcakes, grilled swordfish or red snapper, coulibiac of salmon (at lunch), grilled veal chop, roast breast of chicken stuffed with spinach and pine nuts, roast breast of duck with honey thyme sauce, white orange chocolate mousse with chocolate sauce, chocolate mousse with vanilla sauce.
Setting: Formal, spacious, and quiet dining room.
Service: Polite and efficient, if at times unpolished.
Dress code: Jackets required for men.
Facilities for private parties: Private room upstairs in Doral Tuscany with food prepared by Time & Again. Accommodates up to 150.
Hours: Breakfast, seven days. Lunch, Monday through Friday. Dinner, Monday through Saturday. No dinner on Sunday. Open late, Friday and Saturday.
Reservations: Recommended, especially for lunch.
Prices: Moderately expensive.
Credit cards: AE, DC, MC, V.

Can we talk? The answer at this comfortable, attractive newcomer is a blissful yes. Not only talk, but hear, which explains at least in part why this place has become so popular for business breakfasts and lunches and for social dinners at which friends still value conversation. But as desirable as quiet and spaciousness may be, they are not the only reasons for the almost instant success of this

Murray Hill winner. There are the handsome room with its traditional, honey-walnut paneling, its mirrors and crystal and brass chandeliers from the old United States Hotel in Saratoga, and a comfortable bar and cocktail lounge.

And that is exactly what the chef, Derrick Dikkers, usually turns out. Born in Holland and trained in France, Dikkers was responsible for the fine "nouvelle" Russian cuisine he created at Le Bel Age in Beverly Hills. A few of his Bel Age favorites are on the menu at Time & Again, although for the most part the food can best be described as new international. Coulibiac, the Russian triumph of salmon enfolded in pastry, and most traditionally with rice, dill, and the binding substance, vesiga, is here rendered more as white fish mousse with salmon en croûte, and tends to be flakier and lighter at lunch than at dinner. But always, its Chardonnay-accented butter sauce is superb.

Stylized classic dishes (Time & Again?) are the features. A case in point is the glorious appetizer, phyllo of spinach with feta cheese and red bell pepper sauce. Expecting the typical Greek spinach pie, I am surprised by three puffy round packets of the flaky pastry holding luscious mouthfuls of spinach and feta, all enriched with a sweet red pepper purée. Crusty little crabcakes, aromatically spiced and soothed with a sheer tomato sauce, and the large, meaty shrimp in a cool marinade of olive oil and garlic garnished with a rustic version of guacamole are also enticing appetizers. Although fresh and bright, a so-called baby artichoke salad is disappointing, for the name leads one to expect a plateful of artichokes with perhaps a few greens, when in fact the opposite is true. Spinach linguine with wild mushrooms, artichokes, and prosciutto is well flavored but a bit gummy, and a duck terrine is disconcertingly rare.

The chef has a strong predilection for spinach and artichokes, so choose each course carefully or those vegetables will keep reappearing. The excellent, roseate roast lamb, suitably perfumed with Provençale herbs, is rimmed with spinach. That vegetable also garnishes the fine, juicy veal chop and the moist, olive-oil-gilded swordfish, and is the herbaceous filling for the rolled breast of chicken in a green peppercorn sauce. Artichokes trim the beefy, tender New York shell steak and even work with the pinot noir sauce. Grilled snapper is as carefully done as the swordfish, but salmon, though nicely moist, is overpowered by the ginger and garlic topping. Thyme seems to correct the sweetness of honey in a sauce for the rare-roasted, lean duck breast. Custardy timbales of vegetable purées and a variety of fine potato preparations flesh out dishes, but other banal vegetables are unnecessary.

Desserts are hard to resist, whether one considers the creamy domed peach charlotte with caramel sauce or the dark, bitter chocolate terrine set off by orange sections and a blond vanilla sauce. That same sauce modifies the richness of chocolate mousse, and this is one of the few dessert chefs who can make white chocolate mousse taste like anything—a feat accomplished with the addition of orange zest and a velvety bittersweet, dark chocolate sauce. Overly sweet pear tart and a somewhat misbegotten caramelized puff pastry with strawberries, though inoffensive, hardly match the other possibilities.

Breakfast is made much of, with such conveniences as pads and pens at tables, calculators, cassette recorders, and cordless telephones available on request.

The naiveté of the staff is not in keeping with the sophistication of the menu, and a lack of polish is disconcerting in so traditional a setting. But everyone is polite and well meaning, which is a lot these days. And three cheers for whoever decided to list daily specials and prices on a small handwritten card.

There is a well-varied wine list with a careful stepping-up of prices. One fragrant bargain is the 1985 Gigondas Maufaux, a clear-flavored red Côtes du Rhone at only $19.

Windows on the World, see The View, the Setting, and the Scene

YELLOW ROSE CAFÉ

450 Amsterdam Avenue, between 81st and 82nd streets
Telephone: 595-8760

Favorite meal:
  Texas ranch hot sauce with chips, shared by two
  Barbara Ann's Southern fried chicken with mashed potatoes
  Buttermilk biscuits
  Pecan pie
Other favorite dishes: Texas bowl of red chili, Cattle Annie's chicken-fried steak, smothered pork chops, chili and cheese burger, corn bread, french fries.
Setting: Simple, pleasant café with Lone Star flag as decorative focal point.
Service: Pleasant, accommodating, and reasonably efficient except at peak hours, when service slows.
Dress code: None.
Facilities for private parties: None.
Hours: Lunch and dinner, seven days. Open late, Friday and Saturday. Brunch, Saturday and Sunday. Closed major holidays.
Reservations: Not accepted; line begins to form at 6:45 P.M.
Prices: Inexpensive, with a $6 minimum after 6 P.M.
Credit cards: AE, MC, V.

The meal I enjoy most at the Yellow Rose Café is lunch, when this simple café-luncheonette, done in soft Southwest colors and adorned only by the Texas flag, is peaceful and felicitous. That, or early dinner, is best, because no reservations are accepted, and the dinner hour usually brings with it a waiting line. That good the Yellow Rose Café is not.

Sturdy Texas-Southern home-style cooking is the mode, often with a disappointing blandness but always dependable with the dishes recommended here. Far and away the best is Barbara Ann's Southern fried chicken, with a breading as crisp and greaseless as gold leaf and moist, flavorful meat within, and only occasionally undercooked. It would be an improvement if the chicken were cut into smaller pieces before being breaded so there would be a better, crunchier proportion of crust to meat, but it is perhaps ungrateful to carp about a dish so hard to find well prepared in this city. I always have it with some of the inspired, honest-to-God mashed potatoes.

My main reason for ordering the Texas ranch hot sauce is the darling chips it comes with—tostadas stamped out in the shape (more or less) of Texas. Guacamole also arrives with those chips and is fine if doctored with salt, pepper, and hot sauce. Nachos are the sort I dislike, just a big mound of the chips with melted cheese all over them. I much prefer them individually topped and baked. The Texas bowl of red chili, the meat properly cubed instead of ground, also could be spicier, but some Tabasco fixes things just fine. Chicken-fried steak (steak that is floured and pan-fried) is an idiosyncratic preference of mine; I know it's awful yet I love it, but with cream gravy on the side. Barbecued ribs and chicken, as well as the messy and bland cheese enchiladas with green chili casserole, have been disappointing, but the tender, smothered pork chops with potato sauce are satisfying much the way the chicken-fried steak can be. Chili and cheese are enriching toppings on the house hamburger, and the coarse, mildly sweet corn bread and buttered hot biscuits are good enough to be destructive. I always opt for more biscuits and no dessert, taking my calorie credits where they produce the most mileage in taste.

Prices are so low that a $6 minimum is imposed after 6 P.M. Credit cards are now accepted and there is a full liquor license. Try a frosty margarita as an eye-opening starter.

BELGIAN

CAFÉ DE BRUXELLES

118 Greenwich Avenue, corner 13th Street
Telephone: 206-1830

Favorite meals:
Warm salad of string beans with onions, potatoes, and bacon (salade Liégoise)
Waterzooi of chicken or fish
Chocolate cake
or
Flan of chicken liver (gateau Bressan)
Beef in beer stew (carbonnade flamande)
Belgian waffle with ice cream and chocolate sauce
Other favorite dishes: Oysters on the half shell, country pâté, green or endive salad, snails in Roquefort butter and cream, poached sole with shrimp and mussels in white wine, monkfish with leek sauce, grilled white sausage with onions (boudin blanc), filet of beef sautéed in green peppercorn and tarragon sauce, calves' liver with shallots and vinegar, sauerkraut with pork and sausages (choucroute de Breugel), fruit tart. In bar, hamburger Bruxelles (with onions), chicken wings with barbecue sauce (ailerons de poulet frites), grilled ham and cheese sandwich (croque-monsieur), grilled chicken and cheese sandwich (croque-madame).
Setting: Handsome bistro-style café with bearable noise level; sophisticated little bar for eating and drinking.
Service: Polite, friendly, and helpful but often very slow.
Dress code: None.
Facilities for private parties: Large dining room can accommodate up to 48; café section accommodates 24.
Hours: Lunch, Tuesday through Saturday. Dinner, seven days. Sunday brunch. Open late. Closed Christmas and New Year's days. Bar menu, 5 to about 11 P.M., seven days.
Reservations: Recommended for peak dinner hours.
Prices: Moderate to moderately expensive.
Credit cards: AE, DC, MC, V.

Now owned by Thierry Moity, the excellent former chef at La Gauloise, and his wife, Patricia, who is a charming hostess, this stylish bistro offers the lush Belgian dishes it has been known for, plus some engaging, purely French additions.

Located on the triangle where Greenwich Avenue tapers into 13th Street, the restaurant follows that shape. The result is a tiny knife-point of a bar, with a lively crowd and, now, an enticing night menu. There is a long, narrow passageway dining room that some prefer because they can see who is entering and leaving. But because it is a passageway that includes a swinging kitchen door and a heavily trafficked stairway to check- and rest rooms, I find it unsettling. I much prefer the handsome dining room with spacious tables and a view of the street through the windows hung with starchy white lace half curtains. Dark, bottle-green trim, glazed walls that have a peachy antique patina, and decorative modern art make for an urbane room that combines elements of the antique and the contemporary.

Most of the great Belgian specialties are here. The braised beef stew, carbonnade Flamande, is seasoned with onions, nutmeg, and the malty undercurrents of Belgian beer, and the big chunks of beef are lean and juicy. Waterzooi, the Flemish soup-stew of chicken or fish in an egg- and cream-thickened broth, is fragrant with leeks, white wine, and lemon.

Choucroute de Breugel is one of Mr. Moity's additions. The blond, pungent sauerkraut heaped with sausages and cuts of tender pink pork makes this Sunday special a most welcome one. Juicily spurting grilled boudin blanc, the white pork sausage here mellowed by onions, is satisfying without the inappropriate vegetables that surround it. A hint of vinegar gives a pleasantly acidic edge to the onion sauce that underlines perfectly sautéed calves' liver, and it would be hard to find a more carefully prepared pavé de beouf, the rare filet of beef brightened by green peppercorns and tarragon.

Fish dishes show much improvement here. The two best are the moist, snowy poached sole Ostendaise, topped by a light white wine–cream sauce fleshed out with shrimps and mussels, and the firm nuggets of monkfish that get a mild oniony perfuming of leeks or lemon butter. All main courses are accompanied by the famous Belgian frites—slim shoestring fried potatoes now always crisp and hot, that are heaped in a paper cone, to be authentically dipped into mayonnaise.

Appetizers offer a good choice of light to heavy options. Among the former are the refreshing, coolly crisp salads of mixed greens or of silvery endive. Salade Liégoise is a gently warm, delicately vinegared tossing of string beans, onions, and bacon. Country pâté has the right hefty, garlicky overtones, and an inspired creation is gateau Bressan, a soothing warm custard flan made of chicken livers and burnished with a port wine sauce. Clear, properly chilled oysters or tender snails glossed with a mild Roquefort cream sauce are also good starters.

The biggest disappointments here have been two mussel

dishes—an appetizer of those mollusks baked on the half shell with garlic and herbs, and a main course of moules marinière. The mussels used for the appetizer are so tiny that they dry in the baking. Those for the marinière can be rank.

Buttery crisp crusts distinguish the fresh fruit tarts and there is an airy bittersweet chocolate cake that gets a refreshing contrast from lightly whipped cream. The big, thick Belgian waffles with ice cream are better with the chocolate sauce than with the raspberry.

A bar menu is served from 5 to about 11 P.M. Excellent burgers, the spicy grilled chicken wings, and the French grilled cheese sandwiches—croque-monsieur, to which ham is added, and croque-madame, which substitutes chicken, are great late-night sustainers.

In addition to a modest wine list, there is a full range of lusty Belgian beers, from the smoky Duvel to the distractingly sweet, cherry-accented Kriek and the powerful Palm ale.

Service is polite, friendly, and accommodating but the kitchen can be extremely slow between appetizers and main courses.

FLAMAND

349 East 86th Street, between First and Second avenues
Telephone: 722-4610

Favorite meal:
Waterzooi of scallops
Duck confit with cabbage
Croustillant with apples
Other favorite dishes: Dandelion and bacon salad, cheese croquettes, terrine of duck and veal, shrimp with green herbs, chicken liver salad, peasant soup, veal kidneys with juniper, rabbit cooked in beer, veal stew in beer, filet of venison, veal chop, all desserts.
Setting: Informal, homey bistro.
Service: Friendly, but uneven.
Dress code: None.
Facilities for private parties: None.
Hours: Dinner, seven days.
Reservations: Recommended.
Prices: Moderate to moderately expensive.
Credit cards: AE, DC, MC, V.

Do you know a snug, undiscovered bistro with good bourgeois food at moderate prices? That is one of the questions I am most often asked. Having found this relatively new Belgian hideaway on the Upper East Side, I can finally answer yes. This engaging storefront dining room, with its deep rose walls, bright modern art posters, and sweeping white tie-back curtains, is reminiscent of small ethnic restaurants so common in Chicago. A naive charm prevails throughout. Tables are awkwardly placed at strange angles, parallel to nothing, so one feels adrift in space. And the kitchen, at whim, changes garnishes described on the menu.

But stay with it, and enjoy many of the luxurious specialties Belgium is famous for, most prepared with homemade sincerity.

Although you cannot as yet have the Belgian beef-in-beer stew, carbonnade, because the chef says he cannot find the right beef for it, almost all other classics are served. Start with one of two Belgian salads, whether it is the dandelion greens with nuggets of bacon, dressed with hot bacon fat and balsamic vinegar, or the sautéed chicken livers, touched with Rodenbach, the pungent Belgian beer. Tossed with balsamic vinegar, the livers are heaped on vibrant greens. Big, crisp, oval cheese croquettes based on Parmesan-accented Gruyère could not be better, nor could the typical Belgian soup-stew waterzooi, with scallops and wisps of carrots and leeks, in an egg yolk—enriched cream sauce. Waterzooi also appears as a main course, made with fish or chicken.

Homemade terrine of veal and duck gets a nice zapping of green peppercorns, and small fresh shrimp are verdant with tarragon, dill, thyme, chervil, and parsley. Peasant soup is a jade-green blend of cabbage, turnips, lima and white beans, potatoes, and slivers of bacon, and, with the good French bread, is almost a meal in itself.

It would be hard to find kidneys better prepared than they are here, the fresh nuggets sautéed to crisp yet rosy perfection, then seasoned with juniper berries and flambéed with gin. Blanquette de veau, the white veal stew that can be dreary, here is tender and subtly enriched by smoky Duvel beer. Succulent, generously portioned rabbit is braised in the cherry-accented Kriek beer, and the lusciously salty, fat-preserved duck, confit, nests on cabbage mellowed with bacon. Mushrooms in a light wine sauce grace a thick, delectable veal chop and with all main courses comes a rainbow array of al dente vegetables. Game is beautifully handled, judging by a rare roast filet of venison in a poivrade sauce combining red wine and black pepper.

A few menu caveats are in order. At times, there is a bit too much vinegar in the salads and one night the vegetables were cold. That was the same night, I later learned, the chef was off and the difference, though subtle, was observable. Perhaps that is why the cheese sauce topping the baked ham and endive was thick and lumpy, and why the chicken breast filled with ham and goat cheese seemed lackluster. Unfortunately, the chef's night off varies, so it's hard to know which to avoid. It seems a better idea to close one night a week than to serve second-rate fare at full prices.

Desserts are as good as the main courses. That includes the dame blanche, a sundae of vanilla ice cream with hot Belgian chocolate sauce, a miraculous cloud of crisp phyllo pastry enrobing Calvados-spiked apples (croustillant aux pommes), and both the marjolaine with its meringue layers alternating with chocolate and hazelnut, and the intense chocolate cake.

BRAZILIAN

BRAZILIAN PAVILION

316 East 53rd Street, between First and Second avenues
Telephone: 758-8129

Favorite meal:
Brazilian rum (cachaça) and lime juice cocktail (caipirinha)
Codfish patties (bolinhos de bacalhau), when available
or
Brazilian appetizer (sautéed shrimp with hearts of palm)
Chicken fried with garlic (bossa nova)
Custard (flan)
Other favorite dishes: Soup of potatoes and kale or collard greens (caldo verde), broiled shrimp with garlic (camarão Paulista), shrimp Baiana in tomato sauce, hashlike fried chopped meat (picadinho), shellfish in tomato-cream sauce (mariscada), codfish with potatoes and eggs (bacalhau a gomes de sá), roast leg of pork (pernil assado); fish stew (peixe a Brasileira).
Setting: Trim, modern atmospheric dining room with bright colors, plants, and green glass lamp shades; tables are close and both dining rooms are noisy when full.
Service: Polite and helpful.
Dress code: None.
Facilities for private parties: Back dining room accommodates up to 50.
Hours: Lunch, Monday through Friday. Dinner, Monday through Saturday. Closed Sunday and major holidays.
Reservations: Recommended.
Prices: Moderate.
Credit cards: AE, DC.

This is by far the prettiest and most stylish of the city's Brazilian restaurants, and though, despite new ownership, its food is not up to the level of Cabana Carioca's, many diners feel far more comfortable here and so are willing to forgo the more authentic fare. It is a large, bright, and airy restaurant, with plaster white walls, lots of greenery in glass lamp shades, plants, and waiters' jackets, and touches of royal blue-purple here and there. The front dining room, which includes the noisy, nonstop party bar, is the more spacious of the two; the back is more intimate if you define intimacy as being elbow-to-elbow with strangers. That crowding of tables makes it difficult for waiters to take orders and serve.

I also try to get a reservation in the front room so I can sit comfortably as I sip a caipirinha, a refreshing, powerful cocktail based on cachaça (the Brazilian sugarcane rum) with lime juice and sugar, all shaken until frosty. A version prepared with lemon juice (batida de limon) is a little too sharp, but the batida de coco, made of cachaça and coconut milk, is rich and soothing, if slightly filling. With that drink I have some sliced, pan-sautéed Portuguese sausages if they are on hand or, on some days, the tiny fried codfish balls that Brazilians inherited from Portuguese kitchens. More generally, I start with the aperitivos Brasileiros, a salad of shrimp sautéed in their shells with garlic, bedded down on hearts of palm with tomatoes, olives, and crisp but tasteless iceberg lettuce; too bad romaine or escarole is not substituted. Other times I have the soup caldo verde, here somewhat thin, but nevertheless pleasant, with its collard greens, potatoes, and nuggets of the Portuguese sausage linguiça.

Appetizers are not really essential because portions are huge as in all Brazilian restaurants and main courses are fleshed out with rice and lovely stewed black beans. Shrimp are done in many intriguing ways in Brazil, and at this restaurant there is a mildly pleasant shrimp Baiana—simmered in palm oil and coconut milk with green peppers, garlic, and tomatoes, a sauce similar to that used for moqueca de peixes, a soup-stew of fish and shellfish. Camarão Paulista, shrimp sautéed in garlic, is a fine choice if you have not had the similar appetizer. Plain broiled lobster is usually moist and fresh, and peixe a Brasileira—bass and shrimp in a peppery, garlicky tomato sauce—is a delicious stew. More elegant is the mariscada—shellfish in a spicy, pink tomato sauce.

Other fish dishes do not match these, nor does anything even vaguely Continental, such as veal cutlet Milanese or chicken Francesa, with ham and cheese. Churrasco misto, a mixed grill of beef, chicken, and sausages, is dry and flavorless.

Picadinho, a comfortable sort of hash, is fine for tired stomachs. Chicken bossa nova—moist, tender chunks sautéed golden brown with a showering of garlic—is one of the better dishes, as is the dried salt codfish, bacalhau a gomes de sá, when it is offered as a Friday special. The well-soaked snowy codfish is cooked with potatoes and onions, then finished off with black olives and cut-up hard-boiled eggs.

And then, of course, there is feijoada, every Wednesday and Saturday for lunch and every night for dinner. This is Brazil's answer to cassoulet, based on the earthy, meaty black beans cooked with sausages and various cuts of fresh and smoked pork, all served with kale or collard greens, sliced oranges, and the crackling manioc flour, farofa. The version here is lackluster, the meats too darkly overcooked and the beans stodgy. Roast pork, a Wednesday and Saturday special, is generally moist and well flavored.

There are a lot of big fancy cakes on the dessert wagon, all of which are banal and seem impossible to negotiate after the hefty food. Fruit salad or flan is the most I can manage.

Portions are large and sharing is not discouraged; two people could share an appetizer and then a main course and eat inexpensively. There is sometimes terrible confusion at the coat checkroom when the restaurant is crowded, so be braced for it.

CABANA CARIOCA

123 West 45th Street, between Sixth and Seventh avenues
Telephone: 581-8088

Favorite meals:
Shared by two
Brazilian rum (cachaça) and lime juice cocktail (caipirinha)
Clams or mussels in garlic broth
Brazilian black bean and meat cassoulet (feijoada), Wednesday and Saturday
or
Chicken with okra, other days
Flan
or
Soup of potatoes and kale or collard greens (caldo verde)
Grilled shrimp with garlic (camarão Paulista)
Fried potatoes and black beans
Flan
Other favorite dishes: Hearts of palm salad, broiled stuffed lobster, fish stew, oxtail stew with polenta, codfish with egg and potatoes (bacalhau a gomes de sá), roast chicken, codfish croquettes when available, chicken fried with garlic (carioca).
Setting: Upstairs dining room is best and has a trim, clublike look; informal, with a convivial bar.
Service: Seemingly brusque but really good-natured and helpful; nonregulars are discouraged from upstairs dining room.
Dress code: None.
Facilities for private parties: Private dining room accommodates up to 60.
Hours: Lunch and dinner, seven days.
Reservations: Recommended, especially for upstairs.
Prices: Moderate.
Credit cards: AE, CB, DC, MC, V.

This favorite meeting place for New York's Brazilian community is jammed, lively, and much like a private house party. Because it specializes in lusty, delicious, moderately priced food, and because the upstairs dining rooms are so small, in recent years it has sprouted a neighboring annex, a few doors east. I want to make it clear that the only Cabana Carioca this review refers to is the one at the above address.

Cabana Carioca is one of the theater district's enduring delights, but when making a reservation, *always* specify one of the upstairs dining rooms. Then walk up the narrow flight of stairs with its florid folk mural on the walls, and you are in another world. Portuguese is the lingua franca; regulars eat and drink at a small, active bar; and at the closely set tables in the dining room, friends and families share the enormous portions. Wood-paneled walls and spruce-green tablecloths give the room an informal yet serious look, a promise the food fulfills.

A caipirinha, the Brazilian rum and lime juice cocktail, is a fine opener, especially if you nibble some chewy, fried garlic-and paprika-accented linguiça sausage. On days when fried codfish balls are available, they are even better appetizers. Hearts of palm salad with tomatoes and olives is enough for four even if you ignore the insipid iceberg lettuce upon which all of the goodies are bedded down. Soups are excellent whether you have the caldo verde, a kale, sausage, and potato-thickened brew, the aromatic Alentejo garlic soup, or the near-soup that is clams or mussels steamed in a potful of verdant garlic and parsley broth. The last is best shared by two as the dozen or so huge mollusks in it constitute almost a meal in themselves.

Feijoada is the dish to shoot for, served Wednesdays and Saturdays. The black beans with tongue, smoked pork, sausages, oranges, kale, and the nutlike farofa (toasted manioc flour) should satisfy a trencherman of any capacity. It is therefore not the best pretheater choice for it will certainly cause drowsiness even as the curtain rises. If I have dinner at Cabana Carioca before theater, I prefer the shrimp Paulista (sautéed in the shells with a haze of garlic). Shrimp Baiana, in a mellow tomato-coconut milk sauce, can arrive as an unfortunate mix of big, firm fresh shrimp and tiny, pulpy fishy ones, and, therefore, is not a wise choice. But the moderate-sized lobster is tender and sweet, baked under an enormous mantle of a spicy seafood and bread stuffing. The dried salt codfish bacalhau is also a savory choice, either braised with tomatoes or steamed with a sunny garlic egg sauce. Chicken is light but rib-sticking when done Carioca-style, simply roasted, or in a tomato-based stew with fresh okra. Oxtail stew with polenta, available on some weekdays, is a dark, soul-warming, and tender blend of onions, vegetables, and meat in a sauce that gets body from the oxtail bones—a little greasy perhaps but wonderful on a cold, wintry day.

Fish stew with a tomato and onion sauce is fine even if you do have to ignore the sometimes rubbery shrimp. Pot roast (carne assada) and roast suckling pig, when available, offer hearty options. Clams simmered with pork, Alentejo style, a dish traditionally cooked in the hinged round casserole known as a cataplana, can be good if the clams do not toughen.

Steak and pork chops are too tough to be recommendable, and other dishes on the menu have proved to be lackluster.

As always with Brazilian food, main courses are accompanied by rice and black beans and round slices of fried potatoes, which add interest and heft.

Flan is the only dessert to consider, and Brazilian beer is the best accompaniment to the solidly flavored main courses.

CASUAL EATING

CAFÉS, LUNCHEONETTES, AND PÂTISSERIES

Cafés

Elephant & Castle, 68 Greenwich Avenue, just east of Seventh Avenue, 243-1400, and 183 Prince Street, between Thompson and Sullivan streets, 260-3600. At weekend brunches, as well as for lunch, dinner, and late supper seven days a week, both of these pert and stylish café-luncheonettes turn out delicious omelets (I like the Mexican-inspired combination of Cheddar cheese, guacamole, and tomato; the Provençale with zucchini, tomatoes, and onions; and the bacon with scallions), and lusty chowders. Hamburgers are no longer worth ordering. Salads and sandwiches are always heftier than I expect (or want) them to be, and warm dishes tend to be overcontrived, but there are enticing appetizers that can be combined for a meal. The spicy chicken wings with blue cheese dip and the pasta with crushed olives and capers are my preferences. There are many teas to choose from, and in the larger, roomier, and more inviting SoHo branch, there are wine, beer, and full bar service. Speaking of service, it is friendlier and more efficient in the Greenwich Avenue original. Long lines form at both places as no reservations are accepted. Specific hours differ slightly, but both serve all meals described.

Il Nido Café, 875 Third Avenue, corner 53rd Street, 319-6122. An offspring of Il Nido, this shiny, very Milanese café, laid out in the polished lobby of a glassy new building, serves light lunches and early dinners, breakfast, and all-day take-out. Cold food in the form of antipasto items is refreshing, light, and decent, and there are a few hot dishes too, although I can't imagine eating any but the pasta in this setting. The real stars are the homemade Italian gelati, the creamy, custard-thick ice cream marvels of which the tantalizing bittersweet chocolate is the most seductive. Closed Sunday, and Saturday in summer.

Pasta & Cheese Café, in Bergdorf Goodman, 5th floor, Fifth Avenue and 57th Street, 753-7300. This is a spot I cherish when I am alone in midtown and want a light and pleasant lunch. Salads and sandwiches are what I prefer here, especially the Mediterranean salad with tuna, feta cheese, vegetables, and olives; the Café salad with avocado, chicken, raw mushrooms, Gruyère cheese, and baby shrimp; the sandwich of smoked turkey, bacon, and avocado; and the Black Forest sandwich of ham and Gruyère on thinly sliced rye bread. Pastas are a little bland, but soothing on a cold day, and the cheerful room with counter and table service is functional and attractive, though cramped. Service is a bit slow and prices moderately high. Pasta & Cheese is open from 11 A.M. to 5 P.M., Monday through Saturday.

The Pink Tea Cup, 42 Grove Street, just west of Bleecker Street, 807-6755. This is the sort of gentle café tearoom one hopes to find in the Deep South. Soul food is the feature, as is the daylong special breakfast of eggs any style (I like mine fried) with grits, biscuits, and spicy sausages or thick, half-chewy, half-crisp bacon. Breakfast is served from 8 A.M. to midnight, Sunday through Thursday, and from 8 A.M. to 1 A.M., Friday and Saturday.

Sarabeth's Kitchen, 423 Amsterdam Avenue, between 80th and 81st streets, 496-6280. Sarabeth Levine also operates a café on Madison Avenue near 92nd Street, but it has become so shabby, with dirty wallpaper and slovenly housekeeping, that I would not think of eating there. Her Amsterdam Avenue outpost is a place I prefer for weekday lunches or weekend brunches, all light, delicate, and satisfying, in a pretty pastel-colored setting. Juices are fresh and egg dishes delicious, most especially the frittata with red peppers, scallions, Gruyère cheese, mushrooms, and ham. "Goldie Lox," scrambled eggs enfolding smoked salmon and cream cheese, is also diverting, and there is a spicy, creamy tomato soup that makes the morning seem brighter. Buttery cheese blintzes, pancakes, French toast, and waffles are all fine. Salads (especially the smoked chicken) are fresh and substantial. Save room for some of the church-cake-sale muffins and desserts. Prune Danish, rugelach, and poppy seed cake are my favorites. Honey and homemade jams are lovely touches with mild-flavored breads.

Serendipity, 225 East 60th Street, between Second and Third avenues, 838-3531. In addition to the foot-long hot dog (*see* Hot

Dogs), I go to this shop-cum-café for a rich dessert after seeing a movie in one of the nearby theaters. And each dessert is enough for two or three. Choices include drugstore sundaes, the monumental banana split, and a variety of wonderful calorie-packed drinks, hot and cold. Cinnamon toast is soothing with afternoon tea. Monday through Thursday, 11:30 A.M. to 12:30 A.M.; Friday, 11:30 A.M. to 1 A.M.; Saturday, 11:30 A.M. to 2 A.M.; Sunday, noon to midnight.

Terrace-five, fifth level of Trump Tower, 725 Fifth Avenue, between 56th and 57th streets, 371-5030. Though distinctly pricey, this tiny, tucked-away café has the charm of the undiscovered, never mind that reservations are necessary for peak lunch hours. The strengths of this stylish and modern spot, with a small bar and two pocketsize outdoor terraces, where food is also served, are light salads and entertaining appetizers. Dinner is served as is hot food for lunch, but neither appeals to me in this setting. Tea does, however, and it is served 3 to 5 P.M., Monday through Saturday. There is full bar service, and several good wines can be had by the glass. Closed Sunday.

Luncheonettes

A counter is essential to this format, as is take-out. There may also be tables and a menu that features what is most accurately billed as "hot eats," but with a difference.

Bleecker Luncheonette (also known locally as Italian Home Cooking), Bleecker Street, corner Carmine, with no apparent telephone number. From noon to 2 P.M. and from 5 to 7 P.M. on weekdays, this small luncheonette ladles out an extraordinary green minestrone full of vegetables such as potatoes, zucchini, and string beans that seem to be bolstered with split peas. Pastas are overcooked but savory in an old-fashioned, comforting way, and sausage with peppers is first-rate.

Chez Brigitte, 77 Greenwich Avenue, between Bank and 11th streets, 929-6736. With only eleven seats at two counters, Chez Brigitte is uncomfortably elbow-to-elbow at the height of lunch and dinner. I go off-hours for light pea soup, juicy veal fricassee with paprika and softly overcooked vegetables, roast lamb or veal, veal cutlets or meatballs on plates or in sandwiches. Well-made omelets and scrambled eggs, the nice carrot and celery salad, and silky crème caramel are other options. Monday through Saturday, 11 A.M. to 9 P.M. Closed Sunday, holidays, and most of the summer.

Casual Eating

Christine's Polish Restaurant, 332 East 86th Street, 570-4620, and 344 Lexington Avenue, 953-1920. These are the best, most serious, and neatest of the four luncheonettes in this mini-chain, and are eat-in or take-out bargains. Each has counter service and a small, trimmed dining room with glass-covered tablecloths and full liquor service. For best results, stick to egg dishes ($2.65–$5.65), most especially the pancake omelet with kielbasa sausage including potatoes, or the good, grainy buckwheat kasha or the soothing Russian–Eastern European dough turnovers, pierogi ($5.25 for eight). Filled with meat or potatoes, these are better fried than boiled.

Crêpes for blintzes are delicately rolled around a gently sweet cheese filling ($5.25 for three) and the steaming, lusty soups are just what you need to get through the mid-winter frost. Try the creamy mushroom barley ($2.25), the hot Ukrainian cabbage borscht, the split pea, or the golden chicken noodle soup. Sour cream and applesauce abound and both are good with the crisp, oniony potato pancakes ($5.95 for four). Meat, fish, and poultry main courses have been uniformly awful, but the coffeecake, babka, is light and yeasty.

Kiev Luncheonette, 117 Second Avenue, corner 7th Street, 674-4040. Open twenty-four hours a day, seven days a week, this Jewish–Eastern European–very New York eatery serves stupendous breakfast dishes around the clock. The best are the thick French toast made with egg challah and a pancake omelet with garlic- and pepper-sparked kielbasa sausage slices, which will see you through the day.

Viand Coffee Shop, 673 Madison Avenue, between 61st and 62nd streets, 751-6622. There are two lusty, delectable dishes here—the best turkey sandwich in town, freshly sliced from a whole bird roasted on the premises (I like mine without lettuce and with butter), and the best Greek coffee-shop rice pudding around. Served in a tulip glass with plump raisins and smoky dustings of cinnamon, it is enough for three people. I have either the sandwich or the rice pudding for lunch; both would be impossible. Monday through Saturday, 6 A.M. to 10 P.M. Closed Sunday.

Pâtisseries

Patisserie J. Lanciani, 271 West 4th Street, between 11th and Perry streets, 929-0739. Although there are sometimes warm quiche with salad, pizza rustica, and croissant sandwiches here, I really go for coffee and cake—croissant, brioche, or crumb buns with morning cappuccino, or some of the richer pastries midday or late evening. Individual fruit or lemon tarts, the caramel and whipped cream extravagance known as the religieuse, and the chewy, soft-crisp French nut torte are my favorites. Eclairs are also good, and there are real old-fashioned charlotte russes—the little scalloped paper cups holding genoise cake and a swirl of whipped cream. Cookies are also buttery and fragrant with spices. Service is erratic. Obviously everything can be taken out.

Sant' Ambroeus, 1000 Madison Avenue, between 77th and 78th streets, 570-2211. This brass and mirrored local branch of the chic Milan pasticceria dispenses opulent and generally delectable cakes. Those made with chestnut purées and chocolate are especially good, as are coffee and pound cakes and the eggy brioche loaves that approximate challah and so make good French toast. Panini, small rolls with prosciutto, salami, or cheese, are delicious, but other food tends to be tired and limp. The back café is swathed in puffy drapings, making it feel like the inside of a coffin. There is a very Italian stand-up espresso bar, which is popular, and walk-away gelati, of which I prefer the nougatine, coffee, and chocolate. Prices are high and service is slow. Open seven days.

CAVIAR

PETROSSIAN

182 West 58th Street, at Seventh Avenue
Telephone: 245-2214

Favorite meal:
Années Folles (Crazy Years)
Beluga, osetra, and sevruga caviars
Pressed caviar with blinis
Smoked wild salmon
Russian vodka
Apple tart
Other favorite dishes: Salmon roe caviar, duck or goose foie gras, Le Petit Teaser of assorted appetizers, borscht with pirojkis, cream of broccoli soup, turtle soup, quail stuffed with foie gras baked in puff pastry with truffle sauce, noisettes of lamb with thyme, Le Grand Dessert of assorted pastries and mousses.
Setting: Think Belle Epoque opulence, and you'll be on the right track; marble, mink, and mirrors set the stage in remarkably good if theatrical taste; inadequate lighting is the only drawback.
Service: Professional, efficient, and courteous.
Dress code: Jacket required for men.
Facilities for private parties: Will close restaurant for 50 people at lunch any day, and for 70 at dinner, but only on Sunday, Monday, and Tuesday.
Hours: Lunch and dinner, Monday through Saturday. Dinner until midnight. Brunch and supper on Sunday.
Reservations: Necessary, especially after theater.
Prices: Expensive with exceptions of prix-fixe lunch ($27), pre-theater dinner from 5:30 to 7:30 ($35), and Sunday brunch ($23 to $35) including a drink.
Credit cards: AE, DC, MC, V.

If Petrossian is classified here as a Caviar restaurant, instead of one specializing in French food, it is because that is this luxurious haven's true reason for being. Until recently, I could not get past those glorious sturgeon eggs to try the handiwork of the chef, Michel Attali.

Now that I have, the three-star rating applies to the restaurant's entire production. But first things first, which still means caviar.

Petrossian in Paris is a stunning shop purveying the most impeccable caviar, smoked fish, foie gras, and related king's ransom comestibles. That same tradition has crossed the ocean with one exquisite amplification: Now one can consume those solid-gold groceries on the premises. And what premises they are, all roseate marble with a mink-trimmed banquette here and there, sparkling mirrors and brass and an aura of irresistible decadence that suggests the Belle Epoque and the Roaring Twenties combined. Such special fare gets elaborate, intriguing equipment. There is a big ring on a stand to hold three small glass dishes for the caviar sampling, and a silver and vermeil paddle spoon, much like an Egyptian palm, with which to spoon caviar into one's mouth or to spread it on toast. My favorite meal here has a name—Années Folles (Crazy Years)— and at this writing it goes for $110 a throw. It is worth every cent. First comes the big three-ring circus of caviars: thirty grams each of the best silken, diamond gray beluga, which is the largest of the eggs, the slightly smaller, topaz-colored osetra, and the tiny beads of charcoal gray sevruga. With these there are episodes of toast, the cold being replaced by the warm. Butter is also served, but I find it masks the flavor of the caviar, and I allow only an occasional droplet of lemon juice for variety. I also like to eat the caviar straight, nibbling on toast now and then to renew my palate. Alas, the dim lighting here. With eye appeal so much a part of caviar connoisseurship, Petrossian is too dark for the diner to appreciate the color variations.

The next remove, as they used to say, is my personal favorite, fresh pressed caviar or pajasnaya, a thick, licoricelike spread with the most intense, quintessential caviar flavor. Accompanying it are puffy, light yeast blinis, correctly made with wheat instead of buckwheat flour, and a few cloudlets of crème fraîche. If I am with someone else, one of us orders the pajasnaya and the other has the red salmon roe caviar so we can have even more variety.

Smoked wild salmon so thinly sliced that it seems more like the glaze on the plate itself is the final offering, also with toast. Only Danish smoked salmon at its best competes with this rosy, sweet, and gently woodsy fish. There are other lovely smoked fish here— trout, sturgeon, and so on—as well as duck or goose foie gras, whole and unpâtéd, which is the way to eat either.

A variety of champagnes is offered mostly by the bottle but also by the glass. My preference is iced Russian vodka, the best caviar enhancer.

There are other caviar portions that range in price from $29 to $138. Années Folles is a wonderful after-theater or -opera supper, and Petrossian stays open late enough for that indulgence. The best time to stop by, as far as I am concerned, is whenever I decide I can afford the splurge. This is a retail shop too, so all of the goodies, paddle spoon included, can be had at home, a nice touch in this age of carry-out prepared foods.

Caviar aside, there is elegantly prepared French food with Russian touches appropriate to this format. Petrossian is the New York restaurant that has been offering Babette's Feast, the meal prepared by the French-chef-turned-housemaid in the Danish film of the same name. Although I did not have the meal, the captain, after consultation with the chef, allowed us to order two of the Feast choices à la carte. Rarely have I had a more restorative or aromatic turtle soup lightly touched with sherry and dotted with airy gnocchi, and Babette's caille en sarcophage avec sauce Périgourdine (quail stuffed with foie gras and baked in a "sarcophagus" of puff pastry with truffles) blended the sweet tenderness of the quail meat with the supple richness of foie gras, all set off by the flaky crispness of pastry and the velvety richness of the dark sauce.

But other selections are equally good, among them a Petit Teaser of appetizers based for the most part on the superb smoked fish Petrossian features: roulades of smoked sturgeon with wild mushrooms, a bouquet of tiny shrimp with smoked Icelandic cod roe, smoked salmon enveloping avocado touched with salmon roe caviar, and fillets of smoked eel rolled with shiitake mushrooms. A hearty Russian cabbage borscht served with the plump meat-filled pastry turnovers, pirojkis, and a smooth, subtle cream of broccoli were both superb soups.

Alternatives to the famed quail might be the noisettes of rose-pink lamb sautéed with wisps of fresh thyme, a better choice than the characterless veal medallions, unrelieved by their mustard sauce. Nicely done vegetables and potatoes accompany these main courses. Fish is also nicely prepared, if lacking the flavor heft of meats and poultry. Fortunately, portions are not so large that you will want to bypass desserts—one of Petrossian's strong points. The neatly done lemon meringue tart, the fruit tarts, the fluffy Grand Marnier chocolate mousse, and the chocolate cakes are wickedly irresistible, and are included in the "Grand Dessert" extravaganza.

CHILI, RIBS AND BARBECUE, HAMBURGERS, AND HOT DOGS

Chili

Carolina, see American

Corner Bistro, 331 West 4th Street, corner Jane Street, 242-9502. This neighborhood bar, with tables in back, cooks up an above-average, mild beef chili with red beans. Open seven days from about noon to 4 A.M. Closed Thanksgiving Day.

Lone Star Café, 61 Fifth Avenue, corner 13th Street, 242-1664. Although there is a music charge in the evening, at lunch and early dinner anyone can walk in and try the fiery "bowl of red," diced beef chili that can be ordered in first-, second-, and third-degree hotness, that last being my favorite. But I do ask them to hold the cheese, a topping I dislike with chili. Lunch is served Monday through Friday, and dinner from 6 P.M. every night, with a music charge starting about 7:30. Music begins at 9:30 P.M.

Manhattan Chili Co., 302 Bleecker Street, near Seventh Avenue, 206-7163. One of the better things to happen to the Village in a long while, this casual café in Southwest pastels offers a variety of satisfying chili variations to be eaten on the premises or as take-out. My preferences are the Texas Chain Gang version, which is the hottest, with diced beef, jalapeños, tomatoes, and beans, and the Real McCoy, diced chunks of beef zapped with two types of chili powder (hot and hotter) and, as the menu says, no beans, no tomatoes, no bull. Salsa fresca and Calico corn muffins are good go-withs, but the coleslaw and guacamole are innocuous. Brunch is served on weekends, lunch and dinner, seven days. Open noon to midnight. There is a pretty trellised garden where food is served in warm weather.

Yellow Rose Café, see American

Ribs and Barbecue

Carolina, see American

Lone Star Café, see Chili for address and hours. Hickory smoked ribs are fresher, hotter, and better at night than during the day, but sauce is sweet and commercial.

Memphis, see American

Hamburgers

Café de Bruxelles, see Belgian

Carolina, see American

Corner Bistro, see Chili for address and hours. Freshly ground beef in a huge burger is one of the very best, and still only $3.50 plain. Combined with chili, it's a gourmet meal if the gourmet is starving. Lunch, dinner, supper, seven days.

Hamburger Harry's, 157 Chambers Street, between West Broadway and Greenwich Street, 267-4446. Mesquite-broiled plain burgers of moderate size ($3.85) are delicious here but disappointing at the 45th Street Theater District outpost. The only added topping I like is the combination of guacamole with spicy pico de gallo sauce ($5.85), and it's worth the extra 50 cents to get the burger on a toasted English muffin. Seven days, from about noon to midnight.

Taste of the Apple, 1000 Second Avenue, between 52nd and 53rd streets, 751-1445. Huge, seven- to eight-ounce burger, well cooked, juicy, and fresh, is $3.10 at this writing and may be the most economical protein fix in town. Seven days, until midnight. Closed major holidays.

Taste of the Apple has a new outpost at 283 Columbus Avenue at 73rd Street, 873-8892, where the same menu and quality burgers prevail, the latter at the slightly higher price of $3.15. This branch is also open seven days, but stays open until about 1:30 A.M.

Hot Dogs

Gray's Papaya, 2090 Broadway, corner 72nd Street, 799-0243, and on the northwest corner of 8th Street and Sixth Avenue in the

Village, 260-3532. This old-style open luncheonette grills a meaty beef hot dog that is a steal at 50 cents. There's papaya juice if you can stand it, but I prefer the frothy piña colada for old time's sake.

Katz's Delicatessen, 205 East Houston Street, at Ludlow Street, 254-2246. Huge sandwiches are cheap and famous, but the quality of the meat is disappointing. Not so the crisp grilled beef hot dogs (not skinless these, but crackling in natural casings), on rolls with hot sauerkraut and lots of yellow deli mustard. The scene late night is strictly New York, though hours are shorter than they used to be. Sunday through Thursday, 8 A.M. to 11:30 P.M.; Friday and Saturday, 8 A.M. to 1:00 A.M.

Paley Park, 53rd Street between Fifth and Madison avenues. A wall-wide waterfall, ivy, and chairs and tables make William Paley's gift to the city a treasure. The hot dogs are said to be Sabrett made to Paley's taste. What's most special about them is their freshness, the sizzling grilling they get, and the toasted rolls. Then too there's iced tea, coffee, or soft drinks and a sylvan oasis. Closed in January and part of February.

Serendipity, *see* Cafés for address and hours. Skip hamburgers and go for the slender foot-long hot dog. I like mine plain with mustard, but you can have yours also with chili and chopped onions.

CHINESE

Chinese food is so much better, more varied, and less expensive in Chinatown than elsewhere that I rarely venture north of Canal Street to eat it. Uptown Chinese restaurants tend to be overpriced and banal, a condition not mitigated by the recent appearances of highly touted, lackluster, Americanized additions such as Pig Heaven, Fu's, China Grill, Chin Chin, and Auntie Yuan. One notable, new exception is Chinatown Seafood on the Upper West Side.

Other exceptions to the rule appear below, and I go to them when I want to eat in their neighborhoods—midtown, the East Side, and, most of all, Lincoln Center.

One of the most frustrating things about eating Chinese food is having all the dishes ordered arrive at the same time. Not only is the table overcrowded, but some food gets cold and unpleasant. This almost always happens in Chinatown, no matter how one pleads for a few dishes at a time, and it often occurs uptown as well. The reasons for this are custom and the Chinese method of kitchen organization. It is easier for cooks to prepare the complete order for each table than it is to keep track of which table is ready for what. It helps a bit to order only a few dishes at a time, but at the busiest hours, Chinatown restaurants prohibit that. If it makes you feel any better, this is not discrimination against Occidentals; Chinese families get the same treatment and seem undisturbed.

As much as I love the food in Chinatown, I detest the dirtiness of the area and wonder why ours cannot be as clean as San Francisco's. I rarely go to Chinatown on Friday or Saturday nights, and if I go on Sunday, I do so at about 7 P.M. Weeknights and Saturday lunches are my favorite times, as restaurants are less hectic and messy. Weekday lunches are wonderful, but I never get down there unless I am on jury duty.

Most Chinatown restaurants now sell domestic and Chinese beer, and all have soft drinks. A few have full bars (as do all uptown Chinese restaurants), so it is a good idea to ask what is available when you call. It is also a good idea to check on credit cards. The policy in Chinatown changes rapidly and is always somewhat nebulous (a few restaurants restrict the use of cards to a minimum bill, and so on). English is clearly understood and spoken in all of the restaurants mentioned here, but it is also conveniently forgotten when the staff wishes to rush customers.

As a fairly dependable general rule, I find that it is best to skip dishes listed as chef's specials or suggestions on Chinese menus. They usually turn out to be gussied-up tourist creations, rarely as good as standards on other parts of the menu. Clues lie in ingredients; beware of an abundance of red and green peppers and carrots, American broccoli, and dishes that are sweet and sour or made with ketchup. Also any that have "everything" in them, an obvious attempt to appeal to touristic palates.

BEIJING DUCK HOUSE RESTAURANT ★

144 East 52nd Street, between Lexington and Third avenues
Telephone: 759-8260

Favorite meals:
Shared by two
Tientsin bok choy with special hot sauce
Peking duck
Fresh fruit
or
Shared by four to six
All of the above plus
Smoked fish
Fried dried scallops with seaweed
Shrimp in hot and spicy sauce
Eggplant with garlic sauce and pork
Other favorite dishes: Spiced cold beef, duck song, hot and sour soup, diced chicken in hot sauce with peanuts, sliced beef with watercress, pork with garlic sauce, string beans with minced pork, hot bean curd with minced beef, hot fish with crispy skin.
Setting: Informal, disorderly dining room a notch or two above a Chinatown luncheonette setting; housekeeping needs improving.
Service: Adequate, if impersonal; can be impatient when rushed or near closing time.
Dress code: None.
Facilities for private parties: One room that accommodates between 20 and 25.
Hours: Lunch and dinner, seven days.
Reservations: Necessary for lunch.
Prices: Moderate.
Credit cards: AE, CB, DC, MC, V.

This is one of the offsprings of the Chinatown Peking Duck House that specializes in carved-at-the-table Peking duck that need not be ordered in advance. Unfortunately, the Chinatown original has become unrecommendable; crêpes for the Peking duck are dry and leathery, the dining room is a mess, and the help rude. This East Side branch, as well as Peking Duck West (see page 67), has maintained higher standards.

The setting is only slightly more put together than Chinatown restaurants. There is carpeting (often soiled) and some attempt at decor, but in general an informal café atmosphere prevails. The staff is adequate and becomes pushy only at peak hours. The star on the menu is the Peking duck. A whole one must be ordered, and it appears, crisp, golden, and greaseless, to be carved by a chef who wields a cleaver as deftly as a surgeon should. Skin and meat are carved together, for what purists consider an unauthentic version of Peking duck, for which skin and meat should be separated. (It is, however, common practice in China.) But rolled into a rice flour pancake with hoisin sauce and a spray of scallion and cucumber, the flavor is so sensational I have never quibbled. The carcass, still with lots of meat, is carried away unless it is requested by diners, and, when I am a diner, it always is. Or, again on request, it can be cooked with cabbage into a mild, soothing soup served as a last course. If only two people are eating, the duck is about all they will be able to manage, and it is a satisfying meal at that. But there are other good dishes here to be shared before and after the duck.

Tientsin hot and salty pickled Chinese cabbage is a bolting palate awakener, and spiced cold beef, much like corned beef, is another piquant first course. A cool-and-warm tossing of meat and vegetables with gossamer mung bean noodles glossed with a chili soy sauce is delicious, as is the deep-fried seaweed with a sprinkling of crackling fried, crumbled scallops. Chewy, caramelized smoked fish and the hot and sour soup are other first courses I choose here. The Beijing Duck House seems willing to spice food really hot when requested. Previously the kitchen staff had a timid hand, but recent insistence proved more rewarding, even though I was not recognized. What does persist is a tendency toward greasiness.

Spareribs and spring rolls are lackluster, as are soups other than the hot and sour and the duck and cabbage.

If for any reason I do not want Peking duck, or if we are six or eight, other dishes I order include the duck song (lettuce leaves wrapped around moist, meaty strips of duckling moistened by a light sauce); the diced chicken with crunchy peanuts in hot chili sauce; sliced beef pepped up with sautéed watercress; nuggets of tender pork in a light brown garlic sauce; or cushions of bean curd stir-fried with crumbles of beef in hot sauce, which really must be fiery to work. Hot fish with crispy skin, in a meaty garlic, ginger, and chili oil sauce, is also good, as are the eggplant with garlic and the hot and spicy shrimp. Fruit is about all I can manage after the complex aromatic fare.

CHINATOWN SEAFOOD

2544 Broadway, between 95th and 96th streets
Telephone: 316-7033

Favorite meals:
Shared by two
Steamed Cantonese meat dumplings (shiu mai)
Pork chop with chili and salt
Steamed flounder or grass carp with scallions and ginger
"Season" vegetable (hong choy) or watercress with bean curd sauce
White rice
Oranges
or
Shared by six
All of the above, plus bird's nest soup with crab meat, fried bean curd stuffed with shrimp, and Singapore curry noodles.
Other favorite dishes: Subgum winter melon soup; sliced pork soup with season vegetable (hong choy); Cantonese roast duck; conch, scallops, and vegetables in fried taro basket; lobster or crab with ginger and scallions or with black bean sauce; squid with chili and salt or ginger and scallions; baked salted jumbo shrimp; deep-fried soft-shell crabs; braised sea bass; special roast squab; pork chop Peking style; steamed meat cake with salted egg; filet steak with Chinese broccoli; house special steak; Chinese broccoli with oyster sauce; spinach with garlic sauce; Cantonese yi mein noodles; Amoy-style fried rice noodles.
Setting: Pleasant, bright, modern dining room with attractive table linens and decorative touches.
Service: Generally crisp, efficient, and helpful; only perfunctory at peak hours.
Dress code: None.
Facilities for private parties: One claustrophobic glassed-in sort of box wedges in about 12, but there are large tables in back dining room for banquets.
Hours: Lunch and dinner, seven days. Dinner until 12:45 P.M., Friday and Saturday.
Reservations: Recommended for peak hours for more than two.
Prices: Inexpensive to moderately expensive.
Credit cards: AE, MC, V.

Chinatown has definitely come to the Upper West Side, in what is the best Cantonese restaurant I have been to since Lee Man Chiu left his post as chef at Siu Lam Kung (see page 75). Since the end of 1987, he has been up here, stir-frying his pungent green vegetables (watercress or the bitter, springtime hong choy with bean curd sauce, or spinach with garlic sauce), deep-frying crunchy soft-shell crabs, and steaming to custard mellowness fish such as flounder or grass carp, sprinkled with astringent wisps of scallions and coriander.

The word to fix in your mind is Cantonese, for that gentle, subtle regional cooking is what makes the trip worthwhile. "No Hunan! No Szechuan!" the take-out menu heralds, and they're not just whistlin' "Dixie." Stray from the classic Cantonese dishes, or wander over to the list of chef's creations on the inside of the menu cover, and you will be disappointed.

The first pleasant surprise is the place itself, gleaming with mirrors and black tile, a neat little bar, white tablecloths and pink napkins, and a flower, albeit fake, on each table. The managers are young and fluent in English, although they most surely come from China or Hong Kong, and they are bringing a crisp professionalism to the goings-on—directing waiters, wandering around to see that everything is right, checking delayed orders and, occasionally, even arranging to have dishes arrive one or two at a time, instead of all at once. That convenience is possible only at slower times.

This is a huge menu and, though I have made six trips, I have tried only about a third of it, with the following delectable results. Among soups, the snowy, crunch-textured bird's nest sparkling with crab meat and bound with fluffs of egg whites is a soothing starter, expensive though it is at $7.50 a portion. With this and other soups such as the wintermelon with shrimp, pork, mushrooms, and vegetables, and the sliced pork with hong choy or watercress, come freshly fried noodles—warm, greaseless, and pale blond.

Among dumplings, the fluted, pork-filled Cantonese steamed shiu mai are the only good ones; the fried crescents, fun kor, reek of acrid grease and the shrimp-filled har gow have pasty rice flour coverings. Better to save room for such barbecue specials as the soy-mellowed duck nested on tiny white beans or, when available, the cuts of roast suckling pig with cracklings. If not billed as appetizers, several other dishes work well that way. Crisp fried squares of bean curd stuffed with minced shrimp, and thin pork chops either dry with chili and salt or moistened with a thin, saline, soy dressing (Peking style) would be good openers as would the jumbo salt-baked shrimp that you must peel as you go.

In addition to seafood already mentioned you'll find a lightly stir-fried combination of conch and scallops with vegetables in a taro basket; eat everything but the basket, which hints of stale oil. Thick sea bass, braised in a velvety brown sauce enriched with slivers of peppers and bamboo shoots, is crisp, soothing, and pungent all at once, as are mussels steamed in the same sauce and served piping hot in an earthenware casserole. A few flecks of hot green chili peppers get into this, a non-Cantonese touch, but one I enjoy, especially as I eat the sauce on white rice. Both lobster and hard-shell crabs take on brilliance from ginger and scallions, or fermented black beans with a hint of ginger, and are worth the messy fingers they cause. Pan-fried flounder is skippable, again because of stale grease, but also because it is underdone.

Duck with assorted vegetables is another disappointment, not nearly as good as the barbecue, but the golden-skinned, roast Cantonese chicken with its anise-scented salt dip is a miracle of inner moistness and outer crispness. Chinese broccoli, though hard to maneuver with chopsticks, is worth the effort, whether by itself in a dark brown oyster sauce, or sizzling under slices of rare, sliced steak filet. For plainer tastes, there is the lightly breaded house special steak that takes on interest when dipped into brown sauce touched with garlic.

An addictive Cantonese home-style specialty on this menu is steamed meat cake with salted egg, for which ground pork with nutty crunches of water chestnuts and hints of garlic and ginger is steamed right on the serving plate with a topping of salty egg broken over it and setting to a saline glaze—soul food of a high order.

Noodles are more interesting here than fancy rice. Thin rice vermicelli fried and gilded with curry, Singapore style, and the same fine noodles fried with shrimp, pork, and vegetables (Amoy style) round out meals soothingly. So do the Cantonese yi mein, soft fried noodles with straw mushrooms and vegetables.

For dessert, be content with orange wedges and a fortune cookie.

There is full bar service, including a most modest wine list. Beer remains the favored beverage with this food.

A particularly neat and careful job is done here in packing take-out orders. The substantial foil containers with plastic tops are easily reheated and hold food well until the next day. The cold barbecued meats are especially pleasant the following day, eaten as is, reheated, or brought to room temperature and tossed into a salad dressed with rice vinegar and sesame oil.

CHIN CHIN

216 East 49th Street, between Second and Third avenues
Telephone: 888-4555

Favorite meal:
Shared by four
Steamed Shanghai dumplings
Barbecued spareribs
Eggplant with garlic
or
Tea smoked duck
Szechuan prawns
Crisped orange beef
Crispy sea bass
Fresh fruit
Other favorite dishes: Vegetable or shrimp dumplings, cold sliced kidneys Taiwan style, hot and sour soup, lobster Cantonese, clams with black bean sauce, shredded beef with hot peppers and black bean sauce.
Setting: Stunning, modern bar and dining room; uncomfortable chairs.
Service: Ranges from perfect to embarrassingly self-conscious.

Dress code: None, but jackets are preferred.
Facilities for private parties: Back room holds up to 55; smaller café seats up to 20.
Hours: Lunch, Monday through Friday. Dinner, seven days.
Reservations: Recommended at peak hours.
Prices: Moderate to moderately expensive.
Credit cards: AE, DC, MC, V.

Funny, this doesn't look Chinese! But Chin Chin is just that. A newcomer, it is described by its owners, the brothers Jimmy and Wally Chin, as a "Restaurant Chinois." Saying Chinese restaurant in French, in America, and giving it a Western setting are supposed to flash a message, namely that its food, service, and prices are way above Chinatown levels.

A graduate of Auntie Yuan, Jimmy Chin has created a handsome room that suggests a stunning, tailored steak house. This effect is achieved with dark wood trim outlining blush-peach walls rimmed with eggplant-colored banquettes. Sepia-toned Chin family photographs are austerely hung, for a stylish effect. "And where is the family now?" I asked Jimmy Chin. "In Brooklyn," he answered. Then, sensing my disappointment, he added, "But many are in Canton."

A few members of the Canton branch should be imported as tasters, if not as cooks. Two consistent flaws in the beginning were underseasoning and that old Chinese nemesis, the acrid presence of overheated oil. Now, there are improvements.

The diverting specialties are based on traditional Chinese dishes from many regions. Appetizers make up the best course, and a satisfying meal can comprise a varied selection, most suitable at a business lunch. Giveaways may be a bowl of beansprouts, or pickled cabbage, or cold string beans. On most tries, these are crisp and refreshing, but occasionally the bean sprouts and cabbage are over the hill, wilted and off in flavor.

Dumplings are almost always delicious, whether steamed and filled with vegetables, or the traditional shrimp-filled har gow in rice flour dough, or the juicy Shanghai steamed pork specials. Guotie, the half-fried, half-steamed pork-filled crescents, were fine twice, but limp and greasy on a third try. More consistent are the scallion pancakes—always awful—greasy, and with no hint of scallion. Barbecued spareribs and cool, sliced kidneys Taiwan style are excellent and amethyst-bright small eggplants gentled in garlic sauce are among the best dishes. But disappointing choices include soupy chicken soong to be wrapped in lettuce leaves, flavorless vegetable duck pie, and bland shredded roast duck salad.

Seldom have I had a better hot and sour soup, the big bowl here afloat with tree ear and black mushrooms, slivers of pork and bean curd, and a magical counterpointing of vinegar and fiery chili oil.

Prawns and lobster are the bases for some of the best main courses—the lobster Szechuan style or either one in the classic Cantonese sauce, sunny with egg and fleshed out with pork. Crisp fried sea bass in a pungent sweet-hot sauce is admirable, as are the clams in black bean sauce. Not so the dry, overcooked salmon or the greasy seafood in the "love nest."

Orange beef, chewy, aromatic, and tender, and the shredded beef in a hot pepper and black bean sauce outshone the dull veal medallions and even the interesting-looking three-glass-chicken clay casserole with no flavor at all. Among main courses, by far the worst is Peking duck, with cold skin and brittle as glass, followed by meat that hardly seems to be duck at all. Tea-smoked duck, moist and woodsy, is a better choice.

Pretty but impractical dishes are used here—black, glazed pottery already chipped. And, it is hard to eat family style, the tables being too small to hold platters. That is just one Western touch I could skip. Another is the back "White Room," a blazing dining room that suggests a high-toned interrogation center.

DAVID K'S

1115 Third Avenue, between 65th and 66th streets
Telephone: 371-9090

Favorite meal:
  Shared by two
  Sautéed mustard greens with lima beans and pork
  Braised sea bass
  Peking chicken
  Apple tart
Other favorite dishes: Spicy chicken dumplings, home-style bean curd, three seafood soup, hearts of Chinese broccoli, family meat balls with shiny noodles, shrimp steamed in a silver paper, lemon lobster, Danny Kaye's shredded vegetables with Chinese sausage.
Setting: Front room is a pleasant, modern café. Back room is attractive but dim and stuffy.
Service: Excellent, if at times unevenly paced.
Dress code: None.
Facilities for private parties: Back room can be reserved well in advance for 45 to 70.
Hours: Lunch, Monday through Friday. Dinner, seven days. Brunch, Saturday and Sunday.
Reservations: Recommended.
Prices: Moderate to moderately expensive.
Credit cards: AE, DC.

Chinese food has a brand new look. David Keh and his wife, Jean, have returned to their Chinese roots after a brief, unsuccessful journey into the worlds of Mexican food (Café Marimba) and whatever it was that they served at the Safari Grill. Keeping the American obsession with health in mind, Mrs. Keh has adapted traditional Chinese dishes so that they use less oil and fat, less salt (alas), and absolutely no MSG, for which we can all be thankful. Some days, the results are superb, while at other times, flavor is obscure. Often all that is needed is some salt or soy sauce, or perhaps a shot of vinegar, chili, or sesame oil. Yet no condiments appear unless requested. It would seem a gracious accommodation to have them readily at hand. I favor this place, despite these drawbacks, for those things that they do very well are not available elsewhere.

Among them are some delicious little appetizers such as the small, delicate chicken dumplings in spicy oil, "jumping" shrimp, steamed and served heads on and in the shell, and a verdant stir-fry of bitter mustard greens tossed with lima beans and bits of pork, one of the few and flavorful times that naughty meat appears. All outshine the tasteless chicken salad on shredded iceberg lettuce, the tough, unappealing squab that takes forever to get, the gray swordfish muffled with nearly burned scallions, and the cold, greasy noodles with barely visible wisps of lobster at $12.50—much higher than much better choices. The frothy white seafood soup is pleasant enough, if in need of a little more seasoning. One of the most seductive dishes is the cool, custardy, homestyle bean curd, glossed with a pungent green sauce of garlic, ginger, and scallions. Also good are hearts of Chinese broccoli—crunchy, yet tender.

Because healthfulness is the goal, there are some variations in grain products. Wehoni rice, red and cloyingly sweet, and whole wheat flour pancakes in which various foods are wrapped may have more nutrients than their refined cousins, but their flavors are too strong. Neutrality is devoutly to be wished for when such garnishes are foils for other flavors.

But you will have to settle for those pancakes with the Peking chicken, complete with scallions and hoisin sauce, an obvious low-calorie, low-fat takeoff on Peking duck. At one try it is delicious, with moist, crisp-skinned chicken and thin pancakes. On another night, pancakes are heavy and wheaty and the chicken is dry. Big, light, family meat balls and cabbage with slippery bean thread noodles is soul-warming, as is Danny Kaye's shredded vegetables and Chinese sausage in whole wheat pancakes—a tribute to the actor who was a friend of the house.

Ginger, garlic, and scallions accent impeccably braised sea bass. Fresh shrimp steamed in foil with coriander and scallions are delectable. So is the citrusy lemon lobster touched with ginger, and the pork with cashews, leeks, and little firecrackers of hot red peppers. Avoid the greasy lamb with scallions, the nondescript chicken casserole, and the too darkly sautéed sea scallops in Cantonese egg sauce. There are coolly pleasant ice creams and sherbets, but the winning dessert is the house apple tart with a cookie crust much like shortbread and a hint of cinnamon and sugar.

The vaguely Moderne front room is livelier than the back, despite the old-folks-home look of the wicker chairs. The more tailored back room lacks the activity of the bar and open kitchen in front. Service is friendly and professional. Now if only they could find salt and chili oil when they are requested . . .

See also **David K's Café,** under Dim Sum and Other Chinese Tidbits

HWA YUAN SZECHUAN INN

40 East Broadway, between Catherine and Market streets
Telephone: 966-5534

Favorite meals:
Shared by two
Hot spicy Chinese cabbage
Wined chicken
Pork meatball casserole
Oranges
or
Shared by six
All of the above plus
Aromatic sliced beef
Stuffed eggplant
Carp with hot sauce
Noodles with hot brown meat sauce
Dried sautéed string beans with ground pork
Other favorite dishes: Shredded chicken with pepper sauce; sliced kidney with chili and ginger sauce; smoked fish; preserved duck; hot and sour soup; braised fish head casserole; shredded beef or pork with hot green pepper; chunked chicken either with ginger sauce or hot sauce; sautéed kidneys, bean curd, chicken, or pork home-style; eggplant with bean sauce; cold noodles with sesame sauce.
Setting: Modern Chinese with dark wood and brick; has more style than the usual Chinatown setting.
Service: Efficient, patient, and helpful, if rushed.
Dress code: None.
Facilities for private parties: Downstairs dining room accommodates up to 80.
Hours: Lunch and dinner, seven days.
Reservations: Necessary for six or more.
Prices: Inexpensive.
Credit cards: AE, DC, MC, V.

This lively Chinatown outpost really has two menus intertwined—one offering the food Chinese customers eat, the other aimed at tourists. This was not always so and would be a pity except that the kitchen turns out the more authentic dishes with results so enticing they cannot be matched at many places in town.

What I try to avoid are the dishes listed as the "chef's new specialties." Deviating from that resolve, I twice ordered lobster with spicy ginger wine sauce, not remembering it would have the cloying red sweet and sour sauce. The lobster was fresh and tender, but the sauce overpowered it completely. So back to the non-specials, avoiding almost all that are Cantonese, definitely not the kitchen's strong point.

What that leaves is a dazzling array of delicious cold appetizers, an assortment of which would make a wonderful meal. Freshly cooked shredded chicken napped with a tingling sesame and chili oil sauce or the cool wine-marinated breast of chicken are full of flavor and would be perfect for a summer cold buffet. (All of this is sold take-out.) Thinly sliced preserved duck looks as though it were cured with Mercurochrome, but the delicate meat, edged with fat and skin, is succulent and teasingly salty. So is the pickled aromatic spiced beef and the crisp, hot spicy cabbage. Sliced kidney seasoned with ginger and chili and the chewy, slightly sweet smoked fish are also worth trying. Hot and sour soup is consistently rich and properly fiery, especially if you ask to have it that way, but I usually forgo it in favor of one of the bubbling casserole soup-stews served here. Wire-bound stoneware casseroles arrive seething with boiling broth enriched by silken hanks of bean thread noodles, all sorts of vegetables and mushrooms, and five big, puffy pork meatballs. Fish head casserole with similar trimmings is a second choice, and others are based on bean curd or assorted meats and vegetables. Not long ago, my husband and I began with scallion pancakes, the cabbage, and then had this casserole. That copious meal cost exactly $27 for two.

Because they are so substantial, these casseroles must be considered a main course for two, or a soup course for four to six. Ordered that way, they can be preceded by a few of the enticing appetizers.

Among main courses, home-style, meaning a savory brown sauce, is the preparation that produces delectable results with kidneys, bean curd, chicken, or pork. Hot, meaty sauces on fish, like the incomparable fiery carp cooked here, are almost always at Chinese tables, and the carp is an extraordinary dish. Shredded beef or pork with hot green peppers and crisply roasted chicken cut into chunks and bathed with ginger or hot sauce are among the house's best efforts. Good accompaniments include the string beans sautéed with pork and, when available, balls of fried, pork-stuffed eggplant. Scallion pancakes, also an occasional daily special, are thick, crisp, and satisfying. Noodles are specialties here, cold with sesame oil as a refreshing appetizer or hot with brown meat sauce that can be mild or peppery.

I avoid anything with baby shrimp; they are frozen, translucent, and tasteless. Also skip the greasy moo shu pork. But flaws like these leave more than enough pleasurable eating.

Hwa Yuan is acceptably attractive, with brick walls and a sort of postmodern motif, Chinese style, on one end wall and the usual clutter and disorder. There are white tablecloths and a slightly more put-together look than one expects in this location and at these prices. There is a big downstairs dining room, but I do not like it because it seems musty. I therefore wait for a table in the street level dining room and make reservations there when there are six or more people in our party. Such reservations are honored and even held for a while after the appointed hour.

PEKING DUCK WEST ★

199 Amsterdam Avenue, at 69th Street
Telephone: 874-9810 or 799-5457

Favorite meals:
Shared by two
Chinese cabbage with special hot sauce (Tientsin bok choy)
Smoked fish
Peking duck
Pineapple
or
Shared by four to six
All of the above plus
Barbecued beef
Dried scallops with seaweed
Lobster in hot and spicy sauce
Crispy string beans with pork
Other favorite dishes: Meat and vegetables with Tientsin mung bean sheets, cold noodles with sesame sauce, lobster in hot and spicy sauce, steamed sea bass, dried sliced beef with orange flavor, sliced beef with watercress in hot sauce, homemade noodles with bean sauce, hot bean curd with minced beef.
Setting: Once attractive, modern dining room has grown dull and is in need of sprucing up; tables are large and well spaced; noise level is comfortable but lighting is too dim.
Service: Usually polite and helpful but can become perfunctory at busy times.
Dress code: None.
Facilities for private parties: None.
Hours: Lunch and dinner, seven days.
Reservations: Recommended before Lincoln Center performances.
Prices: Inexpensive to moderate.
Credit cards: AE, DC, MC, V.

Just about the same flaws and advantages described for the Beijing Duck House apply to this branch, close to Lincoln Center. It is, in fact, one of my choices for dinner when I am going to a performance, and the Peking duck shared by two makes a wonderful pre-theater meal. It would also be fine as a late supper, but the restaurant is open late enough for that only on Friday and Saturday.

When the Peking Duck West opened, it had a handsome, upholstered modern dining room, but since that time the setting has faded slightly.

Even so, that hot golden duck, carved at the table by a deft, cleaver-wielding chef, is inspired. The crisp skin and moist meat rolled into big, hot rice flour crêpes that have been slathered with hoisin sauce and garnished with wisps of scallions and cucumber makes for sublime eating. Ask to have the chopped carcass to nibble on, or order it cooked with cabbage into a last-course soup. Or take it home and have it cold for breakfast and forget what you read in *Fit for Life*.

As at the Beijing Duck House, there is some greasiness in stir-fried dishes, and here, too, there are some sweet and sour dishes to avoid. That said, I can in good conscience recommend a number of other delectable dishes, all moderately priced. Nice, fresh, big walnut meats caramelized with sugar to crackling succulence have an engaging bite and flavor and are lovely, when available, with drinks. Bok choy, the gentle, flavorful Chinese cabbage, gets fiery pickling with chili oil and salt, and among other fine appetizers are the cold noodles with sesame-chili sauce and the slivered meats and vegetables tossed with slippery Tientsin mung bean noodles. Beef that is marinated and barbecued on a stick is delicious, as are the nutlike fried, dried scallops mingled with crisp-fried seaweed. Fish smoked in a sugar glaze is edible, skin, bones, and all.

Skip rather disappointing soups and save room instead for the tender, fresh lobster developed carefully in the pork and chili sauce that has an astringent belt of ginger, the chewy dried beef with a bitter orange glaze, and the easygoing sliced beef sautéed with wilted watercress, then zapped with a hot garlic sauce. When dieting, I have the delicate steamed sea bass that gets a touch of ginger and scallion. Noodles with crisp bits of cucumber in bean sauce and the bean curd with minced beef are inexpensive, satisfying dishes, as is the crisp string beans tossed with crumbles of lean pork. Forget fried bananas, which almost always taste of overheated oil, and choose instead the fresh pineapple.

SAY ENG LOOK

5 East Broadway, between Oliver and Catherine streets
Telephone: 732-0796

Favorite meals:
Shared by two
Fried fish roll in bean curd sheet
Eggplant with meat in spiced sauce
Lion head pork ball
or
Shared by four to six
All of the above plus
Beef with scallops
Shanghai pork chops
Broccoli with oyster sauce
Other favorite dishes: Fried whole fish with seaweed, prawns in hot spiced sauce, Tai chi chicken in spiced sauce, chicken in brown sauce, dried beef sautéed, shrimp with kidney, hot and spicy carp, dry sautéed string beans, bean curd in spicy meat sauce, ho sai sea or fish head casserole, casserole of chicken and cellophane noodles, pan-fried noodles with mixed topping. Beer and wine are available. Bring your own hard liquor.
Setting: Garish but substantial red lacquer decor; downstairs dining room is more comfortable and in all ways preferable to upstairs.
Service: Generally good, if rushed when busy; impatient upstairs, where food is apt to be cold.
Dress code: None.
Facilities for private parties: Upstairs dining room can be reserved for between 70 and 100 people.
Hours: Lunch and dinner, seven days.
Reservations: Necessary for more than six; rarely honored for fewer than four.
Prices: Inexpensive to moderate.
Credit cards: AE, MC, V.

Shanghai food is the specialty at this very good, very moderately priced Chinatown Mecca. If it is not nearly as wonderful as it used to be (most especially on busy weekend nights when the crush is on), it is still a fine option for some unusual food. The main dining room on the street level is done up to a fare-thee-well in old-style Chinese red lacquer but housekeeping is careless. Though gaudy, it is at least "decorated," which in Chinatown has to be considered a plus. Although the upstairs dining room has been given brief decorative consideration, it is uncomfortable. The service up there ranges from indifferent to rude, and the food is rarely hot. My rule for Say Eng Look, then, is to go Monday through Thursday for dinner, or for an early lunch on other days, and always to sit downstairs.

One of the best dishes in the city, regardless of price, cuisine, or location, is the fried fish fillet rolled in a sheet of bean curd and fried to tissue crispness. Crunchy and peppery, it is a lusty appetizer, but for anyone eating alone it would make a main course, along with one of the fine vegetable dishes such as the eggplant in a spicy meat sauce or the broccoli with brown, pungent oyster sauce. Another amazing seafood creation is the fried whole sea bass, scored for crispness and moistness, and topped with cellophanelike flakes of fried seaweed. Shanghai spareribs, really lean and meaty marinated pork chops, are beautifully cooked. Lion heads, huge but airy ground pork meatballs braised with green vegetables in a gingery brown sauce, is a soothing, subtly satisfying main course, and for contrast, when the group is large enough, I like the hot spicy carp, its sauce fleshed out with ground pork and its chili-based sauce accented by ginger. Oddly, for a Shanghai restaurant, the cold wine chicken lacks wine flavor and is dry.

Two very good chicken dishes are Tai chi chicken in spiced sauce stir-fried with black mushrooms and the chicken in a gentle, meaty brown sauce. Dried beef, chewy and mellow in a light sauce, is enlivened by scallions, ginger, and garlic. If you like spicy sauces really spicy, ask for them that way. The kitchen will comply, thereby doing justice to dishes such as the prawns or shrimp in hot sauce and the bean curd in meat sauce. For palates of milder inclinations, there is a stir-fry of beef with scallops and the improbable but intriguingly textured combination of shrimp and thinly sliced pork kidney.

Unfortunately, two dishes that used to be excellent have become disappointing—the crisp aromatic duck, somewhat like Peking duck but served with steamed buns, and the Peking duck itself. Neither seems freshly roasted, and the crèpes can be stiff and crumbly. Pan-fried noodles tossed with a mix of shrimp, pork, and vegetables are better than fried rice.

Wire-bound stoneware casseroles hold a variety of one dish soup-stews of amazing heartiness and richness. Try the fish head version, with bean thread noodles and Chinese cabbage, or the ho sai sea, a broth plumped up with balls of pork and fish, noodles, vegetables, shrimp, and julienne strips of omelet. Guests may bring their own wine even though there is a limited list offered, along with beer; many carry in hard liquor. Oranges become dessert in the standard Chinatown fashion.

SHUN LEE PALACE

155 East 55th Street, between Third and Lexington avenues
Telephone: 371-8844

Favorite meals:
Shared by two
Tangy spicy shrimp

Fried dumplings
Lobster Szechuan, out of the shell
Smoked duckling with scallion pancake
Fruit
or
Shared by four to six
All of the above plus
Hot and sour cabbage
Broccoli with garlic sauce
Other favorite dishes: Hot and sour soup, cold duck with spicy Hunan sauce, crispy stuffed prawns, soft-shell crabs with black beans, spicy crispy sea bass, shrimp or lobster with black bean sauce, Peking duck, velvety shrimp puffs.
Setting: Neon gives an Art Deco touch to corny, worn, Chinese-screen-type decor for a mismatched blend; most comfortable seating is in back dining room.
Service: Professional and prompt, but pushy toward unknown guests.
Dress code: None.
Facilities for private parties: One private room accommodates between 20 and 30.
Hours: Lunch and dinner, seven days. Closed Thanksgiving Day.
Reservations: Necessary.
Prices: Moderately expensive.
Credit cards: AE, CB, V.

Shun Lee Palace, along with Shun Lee West, Shun Lee Dynasty, and Hunam on Second Avenue and 46th Street, was the creation of T. T. Wang, perhaps the most talented and innovative Chinese chef New York has known so far. Abetted by Michael Tong, who ran all his dining rooms, this wizard of a chef-owner introduced us to a new era in Chinese cooking, one that went well beyond the egg roll, egg drop, wonton, subgum, one-choice-from-A cuisine we were used to. He also introduced staggering prices for Chinese food, all of which we got used to because of the excellence of his cuisine. Since Wang's death, Shun Lee Dynasty and Hunam have closed, and Michael Tong is occupied only with the two remaining Shun Lees. Both have remained among my favorites, although the Palace now has a slight edge. Never mind that the worn mix-match of Art Deco neon and modern ceilings clashes with the old-time flashy opulence of gold and Chinese-screen motifs. The effect is pleasant enough even if the details bring a shudder to anyone with a finely honed sense of design.

This is one restaurant where I am sometimes recognized, sometimes not, and there is a difference, less in food than in service. For reasons that still remain a mystery, unknown guests are offered the least desirable tables even when the place is empty. Only when they ask for a better table do they get one, and even then it can take several requests to get into the quieter, more orderly back dining room. One night we were offered a table in the raised alcove smack up against a noisy party of ten. We asked for a larger table in the half-empty dining room and got it. "Of course," said the host. But if "of course," then why not in the first place?

The other difference is in the pushiness of captains. To unknown guests they quickly suggest assorted appetizers with drinks. That is a quick way of taking care of the first course. What guests then miss is some of the best choices and the fun of putting the hors d'oeuvres assortment together themselves. Similarly, family service is discouraged, as captains dish out food and heap varieties and flavors all over one another. Ask for family service, and the meal will be more enjoyable.

With so many cavils, it might seem surprising that this is a favorite. What makes it so is the very good food and the fact that the staff can be brought to heel in short order. The rewards of the effort are many, beginning with the remarkably bright and cool hot and sour cabbage, which can awaken even the tiredest palate; the cold hacked chicken nestled in a sesame and chili sauce; and the tangy, spiced shrimp, topped with an almost Mexican-type sauce of coriander, scallions, and chili peppers. Crescent dumplings filled with meat are delicious fried (really both steamed and fried). So are the stuffed fried prawns. Velvety shrimp puffs, crunchy with bamboo shoots and water chestnuts, are fine as main course or appetizer. Hot and sour soup is full of delicate goodies—slivers of meat and bean curd, black mushrooms, and peas—but make it clear that you want it very spicy, assuming, of course, that you do. Otherwise it will be thick and rich but bland. That insistence on hotness is essential to be taken at your word here.

Shun Lee was one of the last holdouts for the old-fashioned, authentic method of serving Peking duck—with crisp skin and meat separated to be layered on rice flour crêpes with scallions and hoisin sauce. Now, the method advanced by the Peking Duck establishments prevails here, with the toqued chef carving a whole duck, skin with meat, in the dining room. The result is so juicily, crunchingly tempting, only a churl could quibble with it.

Another marvel of a duck dish is the sweetly woodsy smoked duck, served at room temperature and complemented with a crisp-fried scallion pancake—a really intriguing combination. And as an appetizer, there is yet another cold duck with a spicy Hunan sauce, well worth trying.

Lobster prepared in a spicy Szechuan sauce or in a more mellow fermented black bean purée can be had in or out of the shell; that last, with an extra charge, is a blessing even for the most serious lobster buffs, who have to admit that, with such sauces, extricating meat from shell is not fun.

Dry sautéed shredded beef, once a treat here, is now rendered so stringily dry and sugary that to eat it is to know what candied shoelaces might taste like. Better to choose filet mignon Hunan style, pan-fried with scallions, a haze of garlic, and hot peppers.

Vegetables are nicely done, most especially the broccoli with garlic sauce and the dry sautéed string beans.

Considering how many savory dishes this kitchen turns out, it is hard to understand why so many others—especially the stir-fried meats—are so greasy and tasteless. Hunan lamb, Wang's amazing chicken, family-style eggplant, and Lake Tung-Ting shrimp are enduring examples.

To wind up on a positive note, much as my usual meals there usually do, try crispy whole sea bass. The fresh, plump fish is deep-fried, then blanketed with a gingery, hot Hunan meat sauce.

SHUN LEE WEST

43 West 65th Street, between Columbus Avenue and Central Park West,
at Lincoln Center
Telephone: 595-8895

Favorite meal:
Assortment of appetizers, shared by two
Hacked chicken
Hot and sour cabbage
Shanghai steamed dumplings
Honey baby ribs
Soft-shell crabs with black bean sauce
Szechuan don don noodles
Other favorite dishes: All hot and cold appetizers except giant prawns with black bean sauce, Peking duck, cold sesame noodles.
Setting: Stunning and dramatic interior done in black with stylish touches; long, attractive bar.
Service: Excellent when guests are known; can be perfunctory to unknowns, especially late in the evening.
Dress code: None.
Facilities for private parties: Café accommodates 50 to 100. On Monday and Sunday afternoons, entire restaurant can be booked to accommodate 200.
Hours: Lunch and dinner until midnight, seven days.
Reservations: Generally recommended, especially for 6 P.M. seating before Lincoln Center events.
Prices: Moderately expensive.
Credit cards: AE, CB, DC, MC, V.

Three features of Shun Lee West combine to make this a place I favor on a limited basis: the stunning decor, the excellent hot and cold appetizer array from which a complete meal can be assembled, and the restaurant's close proximity to Lincoln Center, an otherwise hopeless area for good food. Remove any of those considerations, and I would have no reason to go.

Redecorated in 1985, Shun Lee West at first suggested a gaudy

New Jersey nightclub. The main dining room is all tiers of black velour, and around the ceiling cornice winds an almost endless, stiffened-fabric white dragon glowing from within. But by my third visit, I became enchanted. The black shell, with its white accents of tablecloths, is a dramatic backdrop against which women dressed in black, white, or bright red become a wonderful design. Even hands tipped with red lacquer nail polish look deliberately planned. Men look fine, if less dramatic, unless they are in black tie.

Given this stylish backdrop, the generally considerate service that lapses only occasionally when unknowns are pushed to have drinks at the bar as they wait for tables, and the possibility of putting together a savory, satisfying meal of appetizers that is just right before or after a Lincoln Center performance, Shun Lee still has a strong following, albeit one that falls off after 7:30 P.M.

As good as this may sound, it is discouraging to note how inferior almost every main course has become. Having tried at least 15 in the past two years, I can say that too many emerge from the kitchen dark, greasy, and tasteless, and many ingredients, such as sliced pork, duck, and shrimp in various stir-fried combinations, are far from fresh. Sodden with oil and underseasoned, even when asterisks assure hotness and a special plea is made to the captain, they lead to disappointment. The only exception is the Peking duck, no longer served in the traditional Shun Lee way with crisp skin and meat separated. Now the whole duck comes to the dining room with a chef who has a cleaver in hand to do the carving tableside. Then meat and skin together are folded into crêpes with scallions and hoisin sauce, an always fresh and delectable meal.

The key to satisfaction here is in appetizers such as the pungent, cool hot and sour cabbage, the slivers of hacked chicken in their sesame and chili oil sauce, slices of kidney in a coriander-scented, tangy and spicy dressing, and slices of cold duck in a pungent almost fruity Hunan sauce. Equally good hot appetizers include the juicy Szechuan wontons with their chili, scallion, and coriander dip, lean and meaty honey-glazed baby ribs, crisply fried shrimp balls, and delicate steamed Shanghai dumplings or the more bracing, half-crisp, pan-fried Peking variation. Soft-shell crabs, when in season, are delectable in a smoky black bean sauce, but avoid giant prawns because here, as in the main course stir-fry of garlic and scallions, they may taste of iodine, a sign of staleness.

Although soups are no longer as good as they were, and, like other dishes, often include what surely and inexplicably must be canned mushrooms, there is a bracing and delicious alternative in the Szechuan don don noodles. This is basically a soup thick with fine noodles and crunchy, piquant flecks of pickled Szechuan vegetables with a needling of chili oil to add zest. Cold sesame noodles with coriander and chili are also savory fillers and far better endings than the improbable French pastry.

At my most recent Shun Lee meal, a fair dish was the steamed Norwegian salmon, for though underseasoned it had a light freshness. Ordering so-called crisp duck with walnut stuffing, we got soggy, limp duck meat with a pasty filling of rancid nuts. Following the captain's suggestion that we exchange it for duck with ginger, we then were served stale-tasting duck with more ginger than meat, all awash in oil. Smoked duck with scallion pancake, once a house triumph, now also tastes reheated, and the pancakes do not even hint of scallion; and no matter how much I plead for the Szechuan ma-po bean curd to be authentically hotly seasoned, it arrives almost sweet, as do the prawns with garlic, sticky with chili sauce.

You can have really steaming hot tea here, but it may take three firm requests to get it that way.

SIU LAM KUNG

18 Elizabeth Street, between Canal and Bayard streets
Telephone: 732-0974

Favorite meal:
Shared by four to six
Fried bean curd stuffed with shrimp
Pork chops with chili pepper and salt
Bird's nest and crab meat soup
Roasted chicken
Lobster with ginger and scallions
Braised duck with Chinese mushrooms
Oranges

Other favorite dishes: Sliced pork and vegetable soup, sliced abalone with vegetables, braised abalone with oyster sauce, baked chicken with salt, steamed chicken with ham and Chinese broccoli, pork chops Peking style or with pepper and black bean sauce, baked salted shrimp, boiled shrimp, shrimp with scrambled eggs, conch with scallops and vegetables, squid with chilies and salt, mixed seafood in bird's nest, crabs with ginger and scallions, steamed or fried flounder, braised bean curd with black mushrooms and vegetables, broccoli with oyster sauce, fried rice, pan-fried noodles with pork or shrimp.

Setting: Recently redone, pleasantly modern dining room, with usual noisy, disorderly jam-packed scene.

Service: Perfunctory at busiest times, but generally good-natured, helpful, and fast.

Dress code: None.

Facilities for private parties: None.

Hours: Lunch and dinner, seven days.

Reservations: Necessary for more than four, and honored with reasonable promptness.
Prices: Inexpensive to moderate.
Credit cards: None.

Few restaurants in Chinatown have attracted such a steady line of eager eaters as this one. Even when reservations are made, there is usually at least a short wait, and parties of two to four often have to share larger tables. Since it first earned three stars, much has happened to this large, bustling Cantonese restaurant. There have been changes in partner-owners, and clones opened across the street and on Mott Street—and most recently, another on Third Avenue near 34th Street that is a disaster. Perhaps that explains a certain unevenness in the kitchen's performance—often as excellent as ever, but at times lackluster. A few consistent failings persist: black bean sauce on all seafood is too thickly cornstarched, and beef tends to be sinewy and tough.

Despite the Cantonese kitchen, the menu does not offer the usual wonton–spare rib–egg roll trinity or other similar clichés. Instead you can start with puffy, creamy square pillows of bean curd, stuffed with shrimp and lightly, crisply fried, or the pork chops, pounded thin and simmered with pepper and black beans or stir-fried with chilies and salt. Ordered Peking style, they arrive crisply fried, with only a spiced salt dip for seasoning. Shrimp either plain boiled in shells or baked with salt are also good to begin with (not that you can be sure they will arrive before main courses), and there are a couple of delicious soups—one with sliced pork and vegetables, the other a luxurious richness of bird's nest flecked with crab meat. Soup orders are huge and rarely a good idea for two, as much will be wasted. Abalone, which can be as tough as rubber washers, here is pounded and simmered to tenderness and is fine with vegetables or braised with oyster sauce.

Conch, the shellfish the Italians call scungilli, is always tender here, especially as served with scallops and vegetables. Stir-fried seafood of all sorts nests in a crisp fried basket of grated taro root, another understandable favorite at Chinese tables. For an original and altogether pleasing lunch main course, there is sweet pink shrimp folded into softly scrambled eggs, to which I like to add minced scallions.

Other good seafood dishes include the pearly, fresh steamed flounder brightened with ginger and the fried version, so crisply done it can be eaten small bones and all. Scallions added to the clear broth around the fish lend sprightly flavor contrast. Lobster is sea fresh and full of flavor, and the ginger-scallion sauce over it provides the right complement.

Chicken is wonderful in several forms, my favorites being the crisp-skinned, golden, roasted version and the gentler, sunny, salt-baked variation. Delicate too is the chicken steamed with shavings of salty Virginia ham and firm, slightly bitter Chinese broccoli. There is a sensational duck dish that defies the American passion for crispness in that bird. It is braised slowly, tenderly, with spices that include star anise and black Chinese mushrooms to lend an earthy, almost smoky accent. Steak with broccoli is about the only beef dish I order here, and it has never been disappointing.

Very good vegetable combinations round out this menu. Among favorites are the snowy bean curd tossed with black mushrooms and Chinese vegetables, the broccoli with oyster sauce, and, when in season, something called yocca or hong choy, cooked with fermented bean curd. Some waiters know this when asked, others claim never to have heard of it. I always try and hope for the best. It is much like dandelion greens and profits from a dose of garlic. Shrimp or pork fried rice and pan-fried noodles with the same toppings are comforting fillers worth saving room for. Consider them dessert, as oranges are the only alternative.

DIM SUM AND OTHER CHINESE TIDBITS

A specialty of Southern China and Hong Kong, dim sum are the "heart's delights" that you eat while you *yum cha*—drink tea. The array of steamed and fried dumplings made with various types of rice- and wheat-flour doughs, and the small dishes such as stewed spareribs with garlic, peppers stuffed with shrimp, taro pancakes, various innards, and chicken or duck feet, along with big, puffy, filled steamed yeast buns, make up the repertory.

Traditionally these delicacies are served in huge cafeterialike dining rooms, but instead of customers going to the food, it comes to them on little carts rolled by waitresses. You point to what you want, and at the end the empty dishes and steamers are tallied to arrive at the bill.

As this custom has become more popular in Chinatown, the dim sum have become less good, an unfortunate development. Flushed with the easy success of satisfying parvenu dim sum eaters, more and more Chinese cooks turn out carelessly made versions.

The most authentic and best dim summery in Chinatown, **Lan Hong Kok Seafood House**, 31 Division Street (226-9674), is small and decorless, in fact downright raunchy, but it is a great favorite with Chinese for dim sum from 7:30 A.M. to 4 P.M. every day. Because the room is small, waitresses carry trays, and not too many dishes are on each. That assures hotness and freshness. In addition, the dim sum are very well flavored. Meat fillings are copious and coarsely chopped for good texture, the lion head pork balls with ginger are garnished with wilted watercress (or what looks and tastes like that green), and the pinwheels of crisp, shredded taro root packed around flat minced pork are masterpieces. Stuffed crab claw (the stuffing around instead of in the shell) and slivers of roast pork or duck folded into yeast buns are equally good.

There is a full Cantonese menu with a number of inexpensive, sustaining noodle, meat, and vegetable soups.

H.S.F., standing for Hee Sung Feung, at 46 Bowery, just south of Canal Street (374-1319), is my second choice even though it is not as impeccable as formerly. Sometimes overcooked, the dumplings do, however, have more flavor than most others in Chinatown, and they arrive at tables steaming hot, a necessary requirement for most of the offerings. It is also a bit easier for novices to negotiate than Lan Hong Kok.

The only category to avoid at H.S.F. is the crisp-fried specialties such as shrimp toast, fried pork dumplings, sesame chicken, etc. Those always are tepid and ooze grease. Steamed shrimp dumplings either in translucent rice- or opaque wheat-flour dough, shiu mai, which are tulip-shaped pork dumplings, and slippery crêpes filled with chicken, beef, or shrimp are all delicious. So are fried crab claws, fried bean curd sheets filled with vegetables, shrimp-stuffed green pepper sautéed at the table on a grill cart, and the half-steamed, half-fried dumplings finished in the same way. Bowls of hot and sticky fried rice with pork, nuggets of spareribs in garlic and black bean sauce, roast pork, chicken, and duck, and spicy squid are also good.

One of my special favorites is paper shrimp, big butterfly wings of starchy rice paper holding a shrimp filling at the base. It does not come out of the kitchen too often, but ask as soon as you sit down and some will be forthcoming. H.S.F. has a neat and enticingly illustrated leaflet of dim sum at each table, and you can point to what you want and the waiters will generally get it. Sweet pork or red bean paste in steamed buns and a variety of soups are also satisfying. If you are in a large group, finish up as Chinese do, with an order of pan-fried noodles with seafood. That and beer or tea should hold you for the day.

There is also a good selection served fresh and juicily hot at the ***Oriental Town Seafood Restaurant,*** 14 Elizabeth Street, just south of Canal Street (619-0085).

Dim sum are served seven days a week at all of the places

mentioned, starting at 7:30 or 8 A.M. and going through the afternoon until 4 or 5 P.M.

David K's Café, 1115 Third Avenue (935-1161), around the corner from the same restaurant's Third Avenue entrance, specializes in dumplings, noodles, and small dishes based on Chinese street foods. It is a pleasant, bright, and noisy setting, and the menu is intriguing and moderately priced. Dinner until midnight Monday through Friday. Lunch and dinner Saturday and Sunday.

Hsin Yu, 862 Second Avenue, at the corner of 46th Street (752-8943), is an emergency stop I rely on. Primarily a neighborhood take-out place, it also offers a small, attractive café-dining room with big windows overlooking the street. There are delicious fried, pork-filled dumplings here and wonderfully pungent hot and sour soup. Diced chicken with peanuts in hot pepper sauce is another soul-stimulating choice, but the dumplings and soup are usually enough. It is best if two share the eight big dumplings, then each have a bowl of soup. When I am alone, I just leave half of the dumplings, as they do not travel well.

See also **Bo Ky**, under Vietnamese Tidbits

CUBAN, CARIBBEAN, AND TROPICAL

CLAIRE

156 Seventh Avenue, between 19th and 20th streets
Telephone: 255-1955

Favorite meals:
Bahamian conch chowder
Broiled cornish game hen, gai yang
Key lime pie
or
Squid salad
Broiled mahi-mahi from Trinidad with coconut-curry sauce
Chocolate almond angel pie
Other favorite dishes: Smoked trout with horseradish sour cream; gravlax with mustard-dill sauce; seviche of tuna with dill and capers; roasted andouille sausage with Creole mustard; sautéed broccoli with garlic, oil, and pimiento; avocado, tomato, and red onion salad; linguine with white clam sauce; fisherman's harvest (shellfish with marinara sauce on linguine); broiled fish such as tilefish, grouper, monkfish, mahi-mahi, blackened bluefish; broiled filet mignon of beef wrapped in bacon; roasted boned duckling with plum and hot pepper sauce; Carmen's rum pound cake; banana country cake; blueberry crumb pie; rhubarb cobbler à la mode.
Setting: Breezy tropical café that is crowded, convivial, and noisy; lively bar scene.
Service: Polite, efficient, and accommodating, if a bit precious in tone.
Dress code: None.
Facilities for private parties: None, but take-out from regular menu or catering off premises can be arranged.
Hours: Lunch and dinner, seven days, until 12:30 A.M. Brunch, Saturday and Sunday. Closed Christmas Day.
Reservations: Recommended, especially on weekends.
Prices: Moderate.
Credit cards: AE, DC, MC, V.

A palmy, tropical charm plus diverting, original food at moderate prices has made this an enduring favorite with a coterie of neighborhood regulars. An offspring of the restaurant of the same name once operating in Key West, Claire opened in New York in 1982 as a forerunner of the now trendy Caribbean-tropical eateries. Off to a slow if decent start, Marvin Paige, the owner of both the New York and Key West operations, kept at it, and finally has an excellent restaurant that has achieved what is perhaps the ultimate—a style of its own.

This is a casual, cool breezy café on Seventh Avenue in Chelsea just two blocks north of Barney's. In this otherwise restaurantless expanse, it tends to be forgotten, except by its many regulars. Therefore, I am always surprised at how really delectable the food has become, how accommodating the polite staff can be when not being affected in describing daily specials, and how moderate the prices are. Palm green walls, big ceiling fans, natural wood trellis partitions, and tropical plants make this appealing in both hot weather and cold. The bar and closely set tables result in a moderately high level of noise, but the back room (non-smoking) is the more peaceful of the two dining areas.

Smartly serviceable and so almost always open (Christmas Day being the one exception), Claire offers menus based primarily on seafood, a few pastas, salads, a limited group of meats and poultry, all with artfully combined influences of the Caribbean, Thailand, Cajun country, with a few hints of Europe, China, and Japan thrown in for very good measure. That it all works with its hints of hot chili or cool dill here, Provençal herbs and scents of ginger and curry there, and fiery accents of horseradish, both Japanese and European, is a tribute to the chef's refined sensitivity.

I have a hard time resisting the Bahamian chowder full of tender chunks of conch and potatoes in a creamy, cayenne-brightened base. If I do resist, it is for such diverting alternatives as squid in a salad dressing of garlic-scented olive oil and lime juice, the smoked trout with horseradish sour cream, the tuna marinated into a pungent seviche, or, for a heftier start, the roasted Cajun sausage, andouille, dipped into coarse-grained Creole mustard. Broccoli stir-fried with garlic and oil and a colorful salad of avocado slices with tomato and red onion are also delicious.

All go well before any of the grilled fish here, where the more unusual varieties have always been featured. Among such are the snowy, mild-flavored Hawaiian mahi-mahi topped with chopped raw tomato and basil, Orientalized tilefish with black bean sauce, scallions, and a breath of ginger, Key West grouper mellowed with a Provence blend of herbs and tomato, and firm-fleshed monkfish verdant with pesto sauce that gets added interest from capers and pimiento. Parrot fish (no feathers and it doesn't talk) is firm and pearly and needs the liveliness of the coconut-curry sauce with lemony, minty Thai spicing that it gets. Bluefish, something I normally detest, loses its oily heaviness thanks to a Prudhomme-style blackened crust of spices.

Less rewarding among fish are the rather dry Norwegian salmon and the overly salty teriyaki-grilled mako shark. A few other fish dishes suffer from overcomplexities of ingredients. Pastas, however, are just fine, most especially the linguine with white clam sauce, which has a gentle appeal, milder than the Italian original, and the fisherman's harvest of rock shrimp, red snapper, scallops, and mussels in garlicky-herbed red sauce atop linguine.

A Claire classic is the savory broiled Cornish game hen with sprightly hot and aromatic spicing in the Thai gai yang style, served with a sweet and pungent dipping sauce. Boned, crisply roasted duck is lifted by a sauce that counterpoints sweet plums against hot peppers, a palate-entertaining idea. For more conventional tastes, there is a nice, tender and juicy filet mignon that gets smoky accents from the strip of bacon wrapped around its edges. Rice or potatoes and vegetables with main courses are also given careful attention and novel touches.

All that and wonderful desserts too make this an embarrassment of richness. True Key lime pie, piquant and glassily yellow in a flaky crust, is as good as the crumb-topped blueberry cake and the cream-mantled banana country cake. Being a pound cake fan, I especially like Carmen's rum-laced version, enriched with a cloudlet of softly whipped cream. And since I am not a chocolate pie fan, it is worth special note that I find the chocolate almond angel pie a miracle of lightness and airy chocolate flavor. "Angel" refers to its meltingly crisp meringue crust. Mississippi mud cake is the sort of wet, dense chocolate specialty I dislike, and the cream cheese flan is similarly cloying.

Good hamburgers are offered day-long at Claire and the weekend brunch menu has a full array of egg dishes, breakfast meats, and more luncheonlike broiled fish. An appropriate wine list—decent choices at modest prices—is another plus.

SABOR

20 Cornelia Street, between West 4th and Bleecker streets
Telephone: 243-9579

Favorite meals:
Escabeche of fish with vegetables
Pot roast stuffed with chorizo sausage (carne estofada)

Key lime pie
or
Empañadas filled with chorizo sausages
Shrimp in green sauce (camarones en salsa verde)
Baked coconut bread pudding with sherry and cinnamon (coco quemado)
Other favorite dishes: Zarzuela of mussels in tomato sauce; marinated squid (calamares picantes); salt codfish with potatoes and vegetables in tomato sauce (bacalao à la Vizcaina); zarzuela of shellfish; ground sirloin with olives, capers, and raisins (picadillo); chicken in prune sauce (curri de pollo con ciruelas pasas); flan; fresh sliced pineapple; cappuccino ice cream.
Setting: Small, closely packed bohemian bistro that is attractive, if noisy.
Service: Friendly and efficient.
Dress code: None.
Facilities for private parties: Can close restaurant for groups of about 30.
Hours: Dinner, seven days. Closed on major holidays.
Reservations: Recommended.
Prices: Moderate.
Credit cards: AE, MC, V.

There is good news at this small, pretty Village bistro, in that the once contentious service has become relaxed and friendly and the Latin drinks such as lime daiquiris and margaritas are better if still not brilliantly prepared. With its cream-colored brick walls and plum wine trim, Sabor continues to offer the best renditions of Cuban food in town, albeit without a hefty belt of authenticity. Still, considering the subtle flavorings, the freshness, and the moderate prices, it is worth coping with cramped quarters and, at times, intense noise to sample some of the kitchen's better efforts.

To light eaters, that could mean two of the very good appetizers, perhaps the crisp empañada turnovers filled with spicy chorizo sausage and the escabeche, a nice chunk of firm fish pickled with olives and vegetables and served overflowingly on a small lettuce-lined plate. A larger plate would make eating more comfortable. Or the starter might be mussels in a saffron-piqued tomato sauce or the cool, marinated squid, just chewy enough in its pungent peppery dressing.

An excellent main course is the well-soaked salt codfish bacalao, served here à la Vizcaina, a lovely stew of potatoes, vegetables, capers, and olives in tomato sauce, and there is the equally good shellfish stew zarzuela, combining clams, mussels, shrimp, scallops, and squid in a spicy tomato broth. Firm, snowy shrimp in a fluffy parsley and garlic green sauce is one of the better dishes. It is very good with the steamed white rice and stewed black beans that accompany all the main courses. Red snapper, however, in a sourish lime juice and garlic sauce is far less pleasant, especially when the fish is small and little more than skin and bones.

The same escabeche that is offered as an appetizer can be had in a larger main-course portion and is a welcome option on a hot night.

Picadillo is a sort of Spanish hash, ground sirloin tossed with olives, capers, and raisins, and wholly satisfying here. The best meat dish is the carne estofada, a pot-roasted beef stuffed with chopped chorizo sausage, olives, capers, raisins, and prunes. Its sauce is bolstered with puréed vegetables and lightened with dashes of sherry and fresh orange. Lŏmo de puerco, a pork roast, has the impossibly sweet overtones of hot pineapple and sherry in its sauce, so I avoid it.

Prunes also are in the curry sauce on chicken, a surprise and a delight, although mushrooms midst all of this seem strangely out of place. An order of fried plantains was limp and grease soaked and a far cry from the crisp wonders that used to be served at bars in Havana and Veradero Beach.

Individual tarts of Key lime pie and light flan, the custard burnished with caramelized sugar, are easygoing desserts. Lustier and yet soothing is the coco quemado, a sort of coconut bread pudding with sherry and cinnamon, served hot with a soft whipped cream topping. Brazo gitano, an insipid, soft cake roll drenched with custard, Grand Marnier, sherry, and orange sauce, is close to a mini-trifle and cloying.

It is still hard to understand why the two young women who own this place, Gail Stratton and Ronnie Ginnever, do not make a greater effort to get real Cuban bread and serve stain-the-cup Cuban coffee. Both are available in New York, most especially the coffee, and Puerto Rican or even a good, dry and light Sicilian bread would be closer to the mark than the Italian loaves they offer.

Moderately priced California and Spanish wines are offered here, but Dos Equis beer appeals to me more with this fare.

ETHIOPIAN

THE BLUE NILE

103 West 77th Street, just west of Columbus Avenue
Telephone: 580-3232

Favorite meal:
Shared by two
Red lentil salad (azefa)
Kale and potatoes with spices (yegomen wot)
Spicy beef tartare (kitfo)
Lamb in curry-style sauce (yebeg alitcha)
Other favorite dishes: Peas in hot sauce (yekik wot), chick-pea purée (shuro wot), stewed red lentils (yemesir), beef stewed in hot sauce (tibs wot), chicken in hot sauce (doro wot).
Setting: Spacious, attractive dining room with a pretty bar, colorful Ethiopian artifacts, and basket tables and three-legged stools at which food is served native style.
Service: Gracious, helpful, and efficient.
Dress code: None.
Facilities for private parties: Upstairs room that can accommodate up to 75.
Hours: Lunch, Tuesday through Sunday. Dinner, seven days. Closed major holidays.
Reservations: Not accepted.
Prices: Inexpensive to moderate.
Credit cards: AE.

Still the best option for the diverting, heavily spiced curries and stews of Ethiopia, the Blue Nile serves its food native style, at colorful basketry tables with guests sitting on carved wood stools. It's an arrangement not recommended for knees over forty, and one that suggests pants for women, rather than skirts, for complete ease. There is a trim bar, colorful Ethiopian artifacts and Coptic-style religious hangings and decorations, and the service is graceful and helpful.

Although operated by the same management, Abyssinia in SoHo is far less comfortable and appealing, and the food uptown has a fresher savor.

As represented in New York, no one would rank the Ethiopian kitchen as being among the world's finest, but it does offer a number of delicious and diverting dishes, all truly exotic, in the strictest sense of that word. Borrowing from Indian and Arabic cooking, and adding a number of their own creations, the Ethiopian menu will appeal to anyone who likes subtle spicing and soothing textures.

No utensils are used. Instead, food is picked up with pieces of a spongy, crêpe-like bread called injera. The first time I saw it laid out in a wide flat basket, I assumed it was our napkins. Most of the food is stewed or in a curry-like sauce, so that the small pieces and their sauces are easily picked up with torn-off sections of the injera. As in India and other countries where eating is out of hand, it is considered correct to use only the right hand. Among dishes designated as appetizers, my preference is for the azefa, a lentil salad spiked with onions, bitter mustard seeds, green chili peppers, and lemon juice. Kidneys marinated in red wine were overly strong, and a house salad seemed to have been invented to pacify the American passion for such greenery.

If in a party of four or more, start also with the kitfo, beef tartare that profits from a mixing with spiced butter and chili powder and is best when ordered hotly seasoned. For a smaller group, this can be included among main courses.

Kale simmered with potatoes and green peppers and aromatically spiced is a good foil for dishes such as doro wot, stewed chicken and hard-boiled egg in a fiery berberé sauce, the only problem with that dish being the large pieces of chicken with bones that are hard to handle with the bread. Yebeg alitcha (chunks of tender lamb mellowed in an exotically spiced sauce of turmeric, ginger, onions, garlic, and white pepper) and the tibs wot (beef cubes tenderized in a hot sauce that includes fenugreek, garlic, onions, and spices) are easier to handle, as is, of course, the kitfo. Chick-pea purée (shuro wot) with overtones of basil and ginger and the yekik wot (peas in hot sauce) are good company to meat dishes for parties of four or more. Portions are not large, and sharing is convivial since all eat from the same injera-lined tray. Other dishes on the menu are dull by comparison, and occasionally even the best creations seem to have been made too long in advance. On one occasion, the doro wot had obviously been scorched.

Desserts are the Columbus Avenue repertory of heavy, overly rich pies and cakes. Too bad no fresh fruit or sherbet is on hand.

Beer provides a refreshing contrast to this food, and as a less caloric alternative, have a Scotch and soda, as I do.

FRENCH

WITH AN EXPLANATION

Once asked what his religion was, Woody Allen answered, "Jewish, with an explanation." It is a remark that came to mind as I tried to categorize restaurants by the type of food they serve, most especially where nouvelle French and new American come together. Is a French restaurant one in which the kitchen staff is French? Or does it matter if choices are described on the menu in English, French, or Franglaise, or that a certain percentage of dishes are French inspired?

The only solution, when in doubt, was to follow my own perception of a restaurant and let the chips fall where they may. Odeon and Café Luxembourg appeal to me as new American, and so that is where I have put them. In an attempt to make sense out of this stew of confusion, I have indicated the categories of those restaurants that might be looked for under a French heading. That, and the detailed index, should solve the problem.

It is, of course, more important to know if the food is good than to know which category it fits into, but expectations are very much a part of my evaluations. If something is billed as French, I expect something different from food that is called Continental, new American, or abstract expressionist, which is what much of it has become. None of this adds up to the most burning issue of our times, but it is a question raised by the current wave of culinary eclecticism that tends to make all food alike, at least in the "hottest" restaurants. Anyone going only to such places will have a hard time knowing whether the city is Munich, Paris, London, New York, Chicago, San Francisco, or Los Angeles. It's fillet-of-sole-bonne-femme time, all over again.

LE BIARRITZ

325 West 57th Street, between Eighth and Ninth avenues
Telephone: 757-2390

Favorite meal:
Salade Niçoise
Gigot of lamb with beans (flageolets)
Rice pudding
Other favorite dishes: Assorted hors d'oeuvres, artichoke vinaigrette (if it is a fresh, bright green), roast chicken with cèpes or chanterelles, calves' liver à l'anglaise, brains with black butter (cervelles au beurre noir), braised shank of veal (jarret de veau), crème caramel, chocolate mousse, salad of fresh fruits in red wine.
Setting: Beautifully kept, charming red dining room hung with gleaming copper pots; noisy at lunch, but comfortable.
Service: Well meaning but generally distracted.
Dress code: None.
Facilities for private parties: None.
Hours: Lunch, Monday through Friday. Dinner, Monday through Saturday. Closed Sunday and major holidays.
Reservations: Recommended, especially for lunch.
Prices: Moderate.
Credit cards: AE, DC, MC, V.

With restaurants changing so rapidly, it is reassuring to discover that some go on being themselves for better and for worse. Le Biarritz is a perfect case in point, a pleasant, serviceable bistro with moderate prices and dishes you can generally count on to be satisfying. Best of all, perhaps, as settings become wilder and more theatrical, this looks like a restaurant, a feature that offers no small comfort.

It is a maverick of a bistro, beautifully kept, with rows of brightly polished copper pots, and it is one of the last places left at which to find those old bistro flavors. Nevertheless, there are bad days when the service slows to an absentminded smile and when the kitchen has a heavy hand with the Grand Marnier that is poured into the otherwise magnificent rice pudding.

But I risk such hazards to sample what the place does best, and that usually means lunch. Le Biarritz gets a big midday crowd, largely from publishing and broadcasting offices in the vicinity, and the food at that time of day is fresh and sprightly. At night it can be woebegone. Walking in, I always glance at the assorted hors d'oeuvres laid out on a buffet near the entrance. If all looks bright, colorful, and not sodden, I know things will go well. Not many places in town offer this classic array—a substantial salade Niçoise, with the right little Mediterranean black olives, crunches of green pepper, and pink tuna, or the céleri rémoulade, with the good firm bite and mustardy mayonnaise dressing. Even the sardines are moist and plump, and the slices of French garlic salami are always paper thin and pungent. If the artichokes are nice and green, rather than limp and bronzed, I start with one, valuing the leaves as vehicles for a creamy, mustard vinaigrette dressing.

Quiche at lunch has a puffy soufflélike filling, and after that I might have roast chicken with tarragon or cèpes or chanterelles, the wild mushrooms that lend their own earthy color and flavor to the rich brown sauce. Gigot, that marvelous French roast leg of lamb, is always rose pink, and its juices flavor the jade green beans, flageolets, just firm and garlicky enough. Even more classic bistro dishes are the simple fresh calves' liver anglaise sautéed in butter in a light, golden bread crumb dusting, the calves' brains in butter called black but really a deep nut brown, and braised shank of veal with herbs, so tender it melts from the bone. Even broiled lamb chops with watercress and butter are done right here as are traditional desserts such as crème caramel and chocolate mousse. There can be a good apple tart, and there is always cut fresh fruit macerated in red wine. But by far the best dessert is the thick, creamy rice pudding that gets a bittersweet accent from a strip of orange rind and a droplet of Grand Marnier. But, as noted earlier, on days when the hand that pours slips, that liqueur can ruin the dessert.

Dishes to avoid are the greasy, stale duck, the darkly acrid beef bourguignonne, and the salty, alcohol-zapped lobster bisque.

The modest wine list is a good match for the menu, but there can be a bit of favoritism shown to regular customers. Vintages are not listed, and it is not unknown for the management to offer a better year to a regular at the same price a stranger might pay for a lesser year.

BOULEY

165 Duane Street, between Hudson and Greenwich streets
Telephone: 608-3852

Favorite meals:
Fava and green bean salad
Rotisserie duck with nine spices
Orange clafoutis with caramel ice cream
or
Duck liver (foie de canard) with roasted onions and balsamic vinegar
Turbotin or pompano in lobster sauce
Apple conversation with Calvados sorbet
Other favorite dishes: Glazed oysters, fricassee of clams and mussels, lettuce salad with

smoked scallops, eggplant terrine, artichokes "en Barigoule," langoustine with saffron sauce, black sea bass "en Barigoule," rack and loin of lamb, roast and braised pigeon with foie gras and savoy cabbage, venison with red wine and black pepper sauce, cheeses, hazelnut parfait, chocolate terrine.
Setting: Romantic, luminous country chateau atmosphere; seating is cramped and noisy in certain areas.
Service: Polite and friendly, but erratic, slow, and disorganized.
Dress code: Jacket and tie required.
Facilities for private parties: On long notice, might close restaurant for parties of 25 to 85.
Hours: Lunch, Monday through Friday. Dinner, Monday through Saturday. Closed Sunday.
Reservations: Necessary.
Prices: Expensive.
Credit cards: AE, DC, MC, V.

Help wanted: Experienced manager to organize exquisite restaurant with generally superb food. That, in short, is the story so far at Bouley, one of the most romantically beautiful restaurants to open in TriBeCa, if not in the entire city. David Bouley, the chef-owner whose dishes you might have sampled last at Montrachet, has improved markedly since moving to his own establishment, and his delicate, nouvelle-style presentations are backed by lots of old-fashioned flavor. This place is so good, in fact, it ought to be better.

The only thing standing between Bouley and three stars is the poorly organized dining room and, perhaps, the kitchen as well. Courses are unevenly paced, and captains and waiters, though polite, are either out of sight when you need them, or all over you when you don't. There can even be long waits for seating as the hostess goes in search of the maître d' and again at the checkroom while the attendant is being sought out. Such lapses have not discouraged a very stylish, reserved, and attractively dressed uptown clientele from jamming the place.

Considering how much time and effort went into creating this handsome, country chateau setting with its antique wood doors and fanlights, its quarry tile floors, the cream-colored walls with vaulted ceilings, and the graceful bouquets and window boxes of flowering bulbs, it's a shame to compromise the effect with inefficient service. Also with tables under drafts of cold air in the back of the dining room, or by a few too closely set. The room is even more felicitous at lunch, with bright daylight filtering through the sheer white glass curtains to cast an Impressionistic glow on the soft blues, roses, and celadons of the upholstery. There is a tiny, handsome bar area used primarily by those waiting for tables and, downstairs, a dramatic wine cellar that would be an original setting for a small reception or a wine and cheese tasting.

Once you start eating, however, you'll understand why so many people are willing to wait it out and dine here. Right from the first complimentary course of savory tidbits that might include smoked eel or shark, a fluffy miniature goat cheese quiche, a tiny, plump, juice-spurting duck sausage, and bits of dill-cured salmon, you know something wonderful is about to happen. Crunchy toast slices and wheaty rolls add to that feeling and if you order the best appetizers, you'll be convinced. That might mean something as pristine as slips of fresh fava beans with slim haricots verts in a sherry and crème fraîche dressing, or as rich as the duck liver, foie de canard, sharpened with roasted onions and sweet-pungent balsamic vinegar. Other fine choices are the glazed oysters napped with cream, a layered eggplant terrine that exudes the oily, herbaceous essence of Provence, and a sprightly salad of crisp, lacy greens fleshed out with thin slices of smoked sea scallops or a fricassee of Maine clams and mussels given the toothsome contrast of jade-green fava beans. At lunch there is also a refreshing rendition of artichokes "en Barigoule," with crunchy asparagus and diced vegetables in a sauce heady with basil, a preparation that works as well on sea bass.

With such choices, it is best to bypass the overly sweet soup of puréed butternut squash with chestnuts, the uninteresting raw tuna usually substituting for the mahi-mahi on the menu, and the heavy-handed grilled lobster, unrelieved even by its chervil dressing.

There are delectable fish and seafood main courses, none better than the succulent langoustine curled in a blond saffron sauce or the pompano mantled with a rose lobster sauce and a sunny sabayon of sweet yellow peppers. Sea scallops are too darkly sautéed here, and lobster in a sauce of Sancerre rouge is so meagerly portioned, one wonders if the crustaceans were below legal limits when caught.

Game is very well handled, whether it is the rose-rare venison in a red wine and black pepper sauce or the squab, half of which is roasted to roseate perfection and nests on foie gras, the rest enveloped in savoy cabbage. However, if you must have pigeon medium to well done, forget it, because the kitchen will not comply. Lamb arrives as a roasted rack cut into chops and long slim slices of rare loin, richly endowed with a port wine sauce, a buttery purée of potatoes, and ratatouille baked into a sort of clafoutis. Last, but far from least, is the rotisserie duck with its parchment skin and satiny meat counterpointed by a nine-spice mix.

If kidneys with sweetbreads and a misguided pot-au-feu with almost invisible pheasant and melted foie gras miss the mark, at least there is still a lot to choose from. Disappointments on the lunch menu include a greasy gratin of chicken piled onto flattened tubes of rigatoni awash in a soupy brown broth and a better if unremarkable braised veal shank.

In addition to a very good cheese selection, irresistible desserts are the astringent orange clafoutis with caramel ice cream, the crunchy hazelnut parfait with chocolate truffles and coffee sauce, and the apple "conversation," an array of apple desserts, all delicious. Dark, bitter chocolate flavors the ganache terrine.

The wine list includes decent, moderately priced choices. One such was the 1985 Mercurey Clos L'Eveque at $32 and, not on the list but recommended by the wine steward, the 1985 Côtes de Rhone Gigondas at $30.

There is a menu degustation composed of dishes not on the à la carte menu. When unrecognized, I was told I could not order single dishes from the fixed menu. When I *was* recognized and asked, the answer was, "Why not?" Indeed!

BRIVE

405 East 58th Street, between First Avenue and Sutton Place
Telephone: 838-9393

Favorite meal:
  Beef broth, caraway glaze
  Medallions of venison with sauce poivrade and cranberry linzer torte
  Assorted chocolate or nut desserts
Other favorite dishes: As available in season—terrine of leeks and lentils, salmon with gin "snow," poached oysters with finnan haddie, lobster meringue tart, stuffed pigeon breast, sautéed sweetbreads with vegetable glazes, Muscovy duck breast sauté, roast saddle of lamb in cassoulet, calves' liver Dodin-Bouffant, veal shank in bouillabaisse, all desserts.
Setting: Polished, sophisticated jewel that suggests a private club.
Service: Everything it should be.
Dress code: Really none, though jackets and ties seem standard.
Facilities for private parties: Will close for groups up to 50 on two months notice, small alcove-deck accommodates up to 10.
Hours: Dinner, Monday through Saturday. Closed Sunday and major holidays.
Reservations: Generally necessary.
Prices: Expensive.
Credit cards: AE, DC, MC, V.

This petite, polished jewel suggests a private club dedicated to superb eclectic fare. Once known as Dodin-Bouffant, and again guided by chef-owner Robert Pritsker, this boutique restaurant reopened in July 1986 and has improved steadily ever since. Decor was the first step. Gone is the barren, just-moved-into look it used to have. Now all is posh, and vaguely Continental, what with glazed peachy walls, mellow dark burl wood dado paneling, brush-stroked patterned velvet upholstery, and a graceful silvery screen separating front and back sections. Seating is comfortable with the exception of a few deuces up front where they are too closely set to allow for private conversation, and the back can become noisy when a loud group inhabits the alcove-deck.

The staff could not be more polite or professional, though in fairness, it should be said that I was recognized on all visits. Certainly the tone is an improvement over the persnickety pretentiousness that often became embarrassing in the original restaurant.

Because the menu changes with the seasons and because Pritsker is so restlessly inventive, it is difficult to recommend dishes that might not appear on the menu for a long while. In any season there are consistencies to steer by, among them Pritsker's rich and subtle soups, his expertise with pigeon, duck, venison, sweetbreads, and calves' liver, and his delicate touch with desserts. Weaknesses are his occasionally overwrought creations that are at worst harmless. At times they can be so overly complex that they mask flavors, as when monkfish is muffled in a wrapping of eggplant. Usually, however, his innovations are as seductive as they are surprising.

Flavorful fluffs of this and that are giveaway hors d'oeuvres and among the best are shrimp mousse with a drizzle of sauce Nantua and cool, rare lamb slivers sparked with a pungent sauce gribiche and a few furls of the salad green mâche. If you are lucky, one of two magnificently lush soups will be available: the beef broth with dot-size meat balls and a chiffon lacing of savoy cabbage glazed under a caraway-scented cream. Or it might be the cream of chicken wing and giblets, verdant with cloudlets of sorrel dumplings. If not soup, try one of the light terrines, perhaps of lentils and leeks with a fresh tomato purée or of salmon roe with salmon, sparked by a cress aspic and a touch of cream. Poached oysters satiny with puréed finnan haddie and a gratin of potatoes have the right counterpoints of brininess and creaminess, while gin or vodka "snow"—really shaved ices—does wonders for appetizers such as salmon. Lustier appetites should be off to a satisfying start with tender pink rabbit chops Milanese, nicely crisped in their breading and garnished with parsley-flecked fettuccine. A spectacular opener is lobster meringue tart, a name that perfectly describes this melting, savory conceit. Veal tongue ragout with black beans is good, if not quite up to the other appetizer choices.

When pigeon and calves' liver are on the menu, I have a tough time choosing. One time around, it was boneless, roseate, sliced pigeon breast stuffed with bread crumbs, shallots, and thyme, all gentled with herb-green spaetzle dumplings and a satiny purée of celery hearts. Legs and thighs of roasted pigeon round out that main course. Moist, sweet nuggets of sweetbreads, gilded in the sauté pan, take on richness with their three vegetable purées— spinach, celery and leek, and sweet pepper—and calves' liver

Dodin-Bouffant, a Pritsker classic, is burnished with a veneer of grainy mustard.

Typical of Pritsker's overkill are the exquisitely rare and flavorful roast lamb slices, inexplicably layered between brioche slices to form a sandwich—one that could not be picked up in any case, nor would it be in this elegant setting. Another miss was a fist-size lobster chopped "steak," so thick it did not cook at the center. Among great winter treats are the meltingly tender veal shank in a "bouillabaisse" broth of tomato and saffron served with sweet red pepper pinwheeled around Swiss chard, Muscovy duck breast sliced ruby rare alongside hazelnut potatoes, and roast saddle of lamb en cassoulet, nestled among garlic-mellowed white beans.

Wonderful desserts include the assorted chocolate plate, with such components as bavaroise, warm chocolate cake, a tuile with banana ice cream and a Grand Marnier cream sauce, or the equally diverse nut assortment that usually includes the thin meringue cake, dacquoise, a nut mousse, and the like. For a lighter, more refreshing finish there are usually flans, ice cream, or sherbets in tropical fruit flavors. A recent welcome addition is an astringent terrine of lemon-spiked espresso halfway between ice cream and sherbet. Buttery hot apple tart and souffléed rice pudding, aromatic with cinnamon ice cream, are just two more sublime ways of going to hell with yourself. Not to mention petits fours, confections, and candied citrus peel. Pritsker has an especially well-planned wine list, with carefully stepped-up prices and choices. The Château Fourcas-Hosten 1975 ($28), has the classy, rosy overtones that make this red Bordeaux a delicate palate brightener, while Acacia's pinot noir "St. Clair" 1983 ($30), made of the more robust burgundy grape, is a proper foil for the game dishes.

LE CAFÉ DE LA GARE

143 Perry Street, between Hudson and Greenwich streets
Telephone: 242-3553

Favorite meals:
Pâté of rabbit or pork (rillettes de lapin or porc)
Veal stew (blanquette de veau)
Paris Brest
or
Monkfish with beets in honey-mustard vinaigrette (salade de lotte)
White beans with garlic and sausage, duck, and pork (cassoulet)
Lemon tart or fruit-flavored bavarios

Other favorite dishes: Scallop and truffle salad; leek and potato soup; endive salad with Roquefort and walnut dressing; sautéed loin of pork with a sauce of cornichons, capers, tarragon, mustard, and cream (carré de porc charcutière); entrecôte; broth with veal, chicken, and vegetables (pot-au-feu); broth with chicken, sausage, cabbage, and potato (potée); crème caramel.
Setting: Small bistro with intimate casual charm; noisy when full.
Service: Informal, friendly, and efficient.
Dress code: None.
Facilities for private parties: Generally none, but will occasionally close for parties of 20 to 30.
Hours: Dinner, Tuesday through Sunday. Closed Monday.
Reservations: Necessary on weekends; otherwise recommended.
Prices: Inexpensive to moderate.
Credit cards: None.

This sort of snug bistro is hard to find even in Paris, let alone New York. The tiny, convivially crowded Greenwich Village hideaway is a true bistro, which features cuisine de femme, the traditional "woman cooking," that both Balzac and Escoffier considered France's best. Not that Maryann Terillo, the chef-owner, is a strict keeper of the culinary flame, turning out as she does innovative appetizer salads far removed from the everyday home cooking of France. But the mainstays of her menu, and her best efforts, do reflect tradition: the solid cassoulet with its white beans developed in garlicky tomato sauce and fleshed out with salt-cured confit of duck, chunks of pork, and coarsely ground sausage, and her stews such as the soothing, bay-scented, white-sauced blanquettes of veal or lamb, or the brighter, vegetable-dotted navarin of lamb.

Roasted, herbed baby chicken and France's favorite steak, entrecôte, served with gratinéed potatoes dauphinoise, are other winners. These are best preceded by light appetizers such as the spiky endive salad sparked with a Roquefort and walnut dressing, or a black and white harlequin salad of scallops and truffles with vinaigrette dressing. Somewhat more substantial are the snowy chunks of the meaty fish, lotte, contrasted to beets in a mustard dressing that would be even better without the sweetening touch of honey that is added. Rillettes, the threadlike, spreadable pâté of pork or rabbit, is subtly soothing, if perhaps a bit too lean.

Soft-shell crabs Provençale miss when the crabs themselves are too shelly. Though a little tough, the rack of pork is saved by a piquant sauce of cornichons, capers, and a tarragon-scented mustard cream sauce. Fish dishes here are less exciting than meats.

On Thursdays in winter, there is a very rustic pot-au-feu, which generally includes veal shank, chicken, beef brisket, and vegetables in a heady broth. Potée, another classic French boiled dinner, is made here with chicken and pork sausage, bacon, carrots, potatoes, and cabbage. It is a satisfying main course on the prix-fixe menu, now $18.75, although the hot leek and potato soup preceding it is perhaps not the best starter, it being so similar in heft and flavor to the potée. The burnished custard, crème caramel, provides the right, cooling finish, however.

Other good desserts are the cream puff pastry ring, Paris Brest, the pungent lemon tart, or the restorative fruit-flavored bavarois.

With such moderate prices (even more so because you may bring your own wine), the reservation book fills up early, especially for weekends.

Café des Artistes, *see* The View, the Setting, and the Scene

Café Luxembourg, *see* American

CHANTERELLE

89 Grand Street, corner Greene Street, until the end of 1988.
Then at 6 Harrison Street, corner Hudson Street.
Telephone: 966-6960

Favorite meals:
Grilled seafood sausage
Rack of lamb with thyme and mustard
Assorted cheeses
Orange-flavored chocolate torte (reine de saba)
or
Terrine of foie gras and vegetables
Breast of Muscovy duck and chilies
Warm rhubarb tart
Other favorite dishes: Crab or crayfish bisque, sorrel soup, ravioli with seafood, asparagus in puff pastry, white beans with sausage and meats (cassoulet), bass in mustard dill sauce, shad roe with rhubarb and leeks, salmon with tomato and coriander, squab, beef with marrow and red wine, pecan ice cream, fruit tarts, chocolat pavé, poached pears in Sauterne sabayon.
Setting: New decor and location not seen at press time.
Service: Prompt and efficient although precious in tone.
Dress code: Jacket and tie required for men.
Facilities for private parties: None.
Hours: Dinner, Tuesday through Saturday. Closed Sunday, Monday, major holidays, for the first week in January, and all of July.
Reservations: Necessary, well in advance.
Prices: Expensive.
Credit cards: AE, MC, V, DC.

Young American wonder chefs, today's premature superstars, have generally been disappointing, reveling as they do in their own bizarre creations and considering any detractor a Philistine. Amid such disarray of standards, it is reassuring to have David Waltuck, a graduate of the Culinary Institute of America, who opened his original restaurant in 1981 in SoHo. During that time he has care fully invented dishes and honed them to near perfection. At this writing, Waltuck is en route to new digs at the above address. It is to be hoped that once ensconced, he will be able to maintain the same level of quality. Certainly something will be lost in atmosphere, given the delicate peach glow of the simple, original storefront setting, with its magnificent frost-white pressed tin ceiling and glorious bouquets. The new decor remains a mystery as this book goes to press, so we can only hope for the best.

His American-French nouvelle cooking was as beguiling as ever on my last visit to the old quarters, when I checked back for this edition. Unfortunately, a cloying precious tone in service, much improved for a time, had returned, making dinner a little less felicitous than it should have been. But no fault could be found with the food, other than what still seems to me to be unfounded sky-high prices. On a $65 dinner, a $15 supplement for puff pastry filled with wild mushrooms and black truffles seems excessive, delicious though the dish was. And not even the dazzling, perfectly conditioned cheeses seem worth a $12 penalty.

Caveats aside, the food is inspired and beautifully executed.

The menu changes often, so recommendations made here must be taken as indications of what the kitchen does well. A few dishes are almost always available, among the best being the grilled seafood sausage in a pale pink cream sauce, lightly blushed with tomato. Awhile back this specialty emerged from the broiler toughened; more recently it was delicate and gentle. All seafood terrines are delights, whether of fresh or smoked salmon with pike or marblings of caviar, and so are ravioli with a variety of fillings, my favorite being the crab meat version.

Nut-brown cloves of garlic cooked to the gentleness of butter flavor the rare-roasted rack of lamb for one of Chanterelle's more enduring favorites, while thyme and mustard accent it as a variation. Beef with cèpes and venison in a classic, peppery sauce poivrade offer confirmed meat eaters the satisfaction they require. Duck and squab are two birds beautifully prepared. I still remember a crisp-skinned, pink meat squab in a subtle red wine sauce, hoping it will reappear on the menu when I go back. Tart fruits are often sensitively combined with fish and seafood, none more successfully than rhubarb when glossing scallops or shad roe. Similarly, cranberries polish the warm unctuousness of poached salmon. That fish may also be sparked with a tomato sauce, bright with overtones of coriander. A new personal favorite is the rare Muscovy duck accented by chilies and soothed with wilted beet greens.

There are usually half a dozen desserts, which always include a lovely, satiny homemade ice cream (watch out for the overly strong ginger) and the orange chocolate torte, reine de saba; poached pears in Sauterne-brightened sabayon and a buttery apple or warm rhubarb tart may be others.

All sorts of sign-off goodies arrive, compliments of the house, and there are silken dark chocolate truffles, crackling tuiles, and mosaics of petits fours.

LE CIRQUE

58 East 65th Street, between Madison and Park avenues, in the Mayfair-Regent Hotel
Telephone: 794-9292

Favorite meals:
Lunch
Baby artichokes with garlic and basil (petits artichauts à la Barigoule)
Spaghetti primavera
Lemon tart
or
Dinner
Crab meat salad with chervil (crabe frais du Maryland au cerfeuil)
Roast chicken with lemon, garlic, herbs, and oil (poulet croustillant au citron)
Crème brûlée
Other favorite dishes: All pâtés and terrines except those made of all vegetables, aspic of calf's feet and head (tête et pieds de veau), all smoked fish, lobster salad Le Cirque, lobster ravioli, snails in casserole (cassolette d'escargots), gratin of tagliolini with shrimp (gratin de tagliolini aux crevettes), lobster bisque, fried goujonettes of sole, grilled flounder or red snapper with mustard sauce, filet of lamb with foie gras, grilled kidneys with mustard sauce, roast squab, rib-eye steak with marrow (côte de boeuf rôtie à la moelle), beef carpaccio (éffeuillé de boeuf à la Toscane), rack of lamb, almond puff pastry tart (gâteau Pithiviers), all fruit tarts without almond cream (frangipane) filling, fruits with vanilla ice cream and orange sauce, white chocolate mousse with chocolate sherbet, bread and butter pudding.
Setting: Jammed, noisy, and with a corny perception of elegance, now being redesigned; all tables are uncomfortably cramped.
Service: Excellent and attentive, but can be distinctly cool to unknowns.
Dress code: Jacket and tie required for men.
Facilities for private parties: Large attractive room, L'Orangerie, for parties of 30 to 70; smaller room accommodates 20 to 30.
Hours: Lunch and dinner, Monday through Saturday. Closed Sunday and major holidays, and during the first three weeks of July.
Reservations: Necessary well in advance.
Prices: Expensive, with the exception of the prix fixe lunch at $30.75.
Credit cards: AE, CB, DC.

To the casual eye, Le Cirque is exactly what it always has been—a madhouse celebrity zoo, haunt of the rich, famous, and flashily dressed, and the domain of the country's most polished and shrewdest restaurateur, Sirio Maccioni. With a manner that suggests a combination of John Wayne and Marcello Mastroianni, this suave native of Montecatini moves as agilely as a dancer between the tightly packed aisles, placating a blond, lacquered bouffant here and a defunct Baron von This-or-That there, all the while casting an eye about the room to see where wine needs to be poured or an empty plate removed. Air kisses are blown across the room as usual, diamonds bigger than the Ritz sparkle on hands holding glasses of white wine with ice, and a dozen or so faces you almost recognize are seated in the number-one celebrity pit, close to the door along the front right aisle.

But to the most serious eaters, all is not quite as it was a year or two ago, nor, fortunately, as it was in Le Cirque's earliest years. Each time there is a new chef, it is detectable in the food—dreary and mundane under the original, Jean Vergnes, brilliant during the reign of Alain Sailhac, who left for "21," from which he has also departed, engaging if less satisfying under the present chef, Daniel Boulud, late of Le Régence in New York's Hôtel Plaza Athénée.

Somewhat more concerned with arranging separately cooked foods into attractive still-lifes than with actually preparing them together so there is a true exchange of flavors, Boulud is far better with classics than with his please-the-eye inventions. But the still temptingly varied menu allows him to do a full range of the original and the traditional, and so I go, usually for the latter, and to see if the scene is as manic as ever.

The setting in the Mayfair-Regent Hotel remains corny and dated, although its effect is pleasant enough even if the anthropomorphic monkey murals and garish lighting fixtures suggest the Continental dining-salon of a fallen grandeur hotel. The nightmare element at Le Cirque is the jammed-in crowd, the dizzying noise, and the action in the aisles, with trays sailing overhead. Sit on a banquette and you are tightly wedged as in a stock, and if you have an aisle chair, know that it will be kicked all night long, eight to the bar. Sirio Maccioni acknowledges this crush and always says he will remove some tables, but the only furniture moving I ever see is more chairs being added, to cram yet another guest or two around an already tight table arrangement. There is also the nagging knowledge that I would like Le Cirque less if I were not known there. Reliable reports on indifference on the telephone when reservations are called for, and of seating in outer Siberia, persist, although they are much less marked than they were ten years ago. That Siberia is inevitable with so many high-rolling regulars, perhaps, but in a place as pricey as this, there should be no really bad tables, and all guests should be given the same courteous welcome and attention. Recently two friends arrived before me to claim our table for four and were told curtly to wait at the bar until their party was completed, an understandable request in an inexpensive Chinatown restaurant, but hardly acceptable here.

If Boulud lacks Sailhac's sensitivity to flavors, he does an above average job with many of the specialties, all served on a stunning array of china and at tables inventively decked out with flower, fruit, and vegetable centerpieces. Pâtés and terrines have almost always been winners here and still are—my favorites being those based on beef shank with leeks and the silkily gelatinous pork head and feet "fromage" with horseradish cream. Seasonal game pâtés are also meaty and fragrant with brandy, garlic, and peppercorns. Only the vegetable combinations are bland and watery. Two refreshing and beguiling starters are the tiny artichokes gentled in olive oil and flecks of vegetables, then scented with garlic and basil, and a salad of pearly lumps of crab meat verdant with my favorite green herb, chervil, parsley's sophisticated cousin. Firmly al dente, rainbow bright vegetables enhance a lobster salad given an earthy touch of truffles, and moist woodsy smoked fish varieties are of superb quality.

Scallops in hot and cold appetizers are totally lacking in flavor, overpowered as they are by ingredients such as heavy olive oil or truffles, and raw tuna fish suffers much the same fate.

There is absolutely no fault to find with hot appetizers such as the sheer lobster ravioli nested on spinach leaves or snails in a tiny casserole with white wine, basil, and garlic. Shrimp and mushrooms gratinéed on a bed of the thin pasta tagliolini, and the house's signature dish, spaghetti primavera with its flecks of broccoli, mushrooms, peppers, and pine nuts in a gossamer butter sauce, are all unsurpassed. But fettuccine with white truffles or wild mushrooms may be wonderful or milkily oversauced, as both have been several times. Lobster bisque has just the right crackling edge of shellfish zest, but a cold tomato soup with dots of avocado is boringly one-dimensional and suggests a cold tomato sauce mistakenly ladled out as soup.

As attractive as fish dishes are here, Boulud's creations often obscure the delicate essence of the fish themselves. Thus impeccably poached turbot is obscured by a hot citrus sauce, and fillets of Boston sole lose ground to the bitter Italian vegetable broccoli rabe. Better to opt for crisp ribbons of fried goujonettes of sole or grilled flounder or red snapper with a mildly needlelike mustard sauce. Bouillabaisse can be zapped with overdoses of saffron now, but a cold version, really a seafood salad with garlic toast, is pleasant.

Classics rather than inventions is the rule for meat and poultry main courses as well. Roast chicken as golden as toasted butternuts is perfumed with lemon, garlic, herbs, and sunny olive oil, a better choice, say, than the stewy duck confit with its overly reduced wine sauce. Lightly roasted filet of lamb, its pink interior hiding a delectable nugget of foie gras, and the veal kidneys grilled to crackling roseate perfection are both preferable to sweetbreads ruined by a base of stingingly salty spinach. Overcooked carré of beef is not helped by dark greasy potatoes with onions and mushrooms that suggest hash-house cookery, but perfectly grilled rib steak with a mellowing of marrow, and the raw beef carpaccio with a brightly herbaceous olive oil dressing are unbeatable. Try all of the grills of game birds, but bypass duck bludgeoned with blackberries and orange zest. And so it goes, to the worst mess of all, lobster with mashed red beans and hot pineapple.

More beguiling touches here include the trademark Parmesan-encrusted toast slices, the little canapés of garlicky eggplant purée heaped on toast points, magical foie gras in terrines or freshly sautéed, and salads so fresh they still seem to be growing.

The mixed meat and vegetable dinner that the French call pot-au-feu and the Italians bollito misto is less lusty than it used to be, served in an overly stylized, overly petite variation that allows for just a spoonful of this meat or that, diverse though the assortment and garnishes are.

Desserts, by and large, are breathtaking, with full credit going to the Austrian patissier Markus Farbinger, who can even make white chocolate take on brilliance. Tarts of fruit or pungent lemon, the almond paste–filled puff pastry Pithiviers, crème brûlée still rendered in the inspired style of former pastry chef Dieter Schorner, and dozens of other enticements abound. The only downers are tarts filled with overly sweet almond frangipane cream and a cream-stuffed poached pear much too heavy for a finishing touch. The cookies and confections passed with coffee are edible jewels, with which, Maccioni told me, Nancy Reagan's society playmate, Jerry Zipkind, fills his pockets when leaving.

As might be expected, there is an enormous and enormously priced wine list, but if you can get Maccioni's attention, he guides you to the real sleepers, usually Italian, of which he is most proud.

If Boulud and Le Cirque are coasting somewhat on the reputation firmly established by Sailhac, most of the clientele are unaware of it. At Le Cirque, food is not quite what it is all about anyway.

LA CÔTE BASQUE

5 East 55th Street, between Fifth and Madison avenues
Telephone: 688-6525

Favorite meals:
Lunch
Artichoke vinaigrette
White beans baked with lamb, sausage, and duck or goose (cassoulet Toulousain)

Fruit sherbet or berries
or
Dinner
Snails à la Meridionale
Roast duck with two sauces
Chocolate soufflé
Other favorite dishes: All pâtés and terrines, salad of crab and lobster with avocado, asparagus vinaigrette, boned quail stuffed with sweetbreads, "swan" of pastry with foie gras and minced truffles, "couronne" (crown) of shellfish with haricots verts, fish soup with garlic rouille sauce, grilled red snapper or sole with mustard sauce, veal kidneys with green peppercorns, roast rack of lamb with thyme, roast chicken with tarragon, veal chop with champagne sauce and morels, steak au poivre, white and dark marbled chocolate mousse cake, all soufflés.
Setting: Huge, festive, and colorful rooms with famed mural window scenes of Côte Basque harbors and landscapes; crowded, noisy, and hectic.
Service: Polite and professional if at times distracted and disorganized; unknowns can be treated coolly, to say the least.
Dress code: Jacket and tie required for men.
Facilities for private parties: Downstairs room accommodates 10 to 32; semi-private wing of dining room can be reserved for 50 to 60.
Hours: Lunch and dinner, Monday through Saturday. Closed Sunday and major holidays.
Reservations: Generally necessary.
Prices: Expensive.
Credit cards: AE, CB, DC, MC, V.

It would be hard to think of a setting more operatically festive than this one. Ever since it was opened in 1958 by Henri Soulé as a poor man's Pavilion (his famed gastronomic mecca originally on these premises), it has been known for its elegantly casual Mediterranean setting with wood beams against ivory walls and the colorful murals of Basque landscapes and harbor scenes showing through open shutters, a decorative note that suggests a musical comedy stage set. Raspberry-red velvet banquettes, pretty flowers, graceful china, and displays of intricately garnished appetizers add to the effect that has been established by the chef-owner, Jean-Jacques Rachou, since he bought it in 1980.

Enlarged several years ago so that it is now virtually a huge dining hall, La Côte Basque is a fashionably popular madhouse most days, with tables crammed together, lots of noise and table hopping, and general convivial confusion. Though I understand why one would go for a special occasion, I have trouble figuring out how regulars can subject themselves to so much conviviality lunch after lunch, dinner after dinner. Yet that is what the fashion, society, and business sets do, hobnobbing on weekends with a fair representation of celebrants from other boroughs and the suburbs.

The latter will probably be subjected to pretty cool treatment, especially when calling for reservations if they get the pretentious, overbearing maître d' on one of his bad days, although that occurs less frequently now than it did three years ago. Likewise, unknowns are relegated to back tables, no matter how empty the dining room, but though they miss the celebrity action, they do sit in surroundings every bit as attractive as those up front. My own favorite spot here is the area in front of the bar on the left as one enters. It is more privately, smartly pocketed off than the star-studded first aisle that is in a direct path from the door. Only the new wing, far to the left and back, is to be avoided, unless, of course, you are up to no good and do not want to be spotted by anyone who matters.

Rachou's personality is evident in his cuisine, and few chefs wear their hearts on their toques as recognizably as he does. A man of enormous, widely divergent culinary skills with a shy but proud and generous nature, he is never satisfied with a dish until he has gone just a little too far. The result is huge portions of delicious food, elaborately and magnificently garnished, but always, always, too intensely rich. Sauces around food are all mini-paintings, executed in contrasting colors as, for example, with a main course that might have flowers and vines of red tomato-based sauce winding through an ivory beurre blanc, or, for dessert, chocolate sauce trailing its leaves and blossoms across a ground of pale yellow crème anglaise.

It becomes very difficult, therefore, to get anything really light and simple, just as it was at Rachou's first restaurant, La Lavandou on East 61st Street (later to become his Le Festival and now closed). Clearly, excess is his trademark or shortcoming, depending on your point of view. Diligence in the pursuit of lightness can be rewarded with such delicate appetizers as firmly cooked, bright green asparagus in a slightly piquant vinaigrette dressing or an artichoke in the same sauce. And nowhere else will you see an artichoke arranged as this one is, its leaves taken off the base then placed on a sparkling floral and black-rimmed plate in concentric circles centered with the heart, which is crested with minced hard-cooked egg in mayonnaise.

Rachou's kitchens have always been known for their excellent charcuterie, and the pâtés and terrines of duck with green peppercorns, or game centered with a core of foie gras, or an all–foie gras marvel are miracles of subtlety in their contrasting garlic, brandy, herbs, and spices. An apotheosis of pâté has to be the "swan," the wings, neck, and head of which are shaped in the cream puff pastry, pâte à chou, into which goes an oval body of silken foie gras with its ripe, luxurious overtones, and which is pavéd with finely minced black truffles. Eat all of that and you may be able to contemplate nothing else but a green salad, but it's worth the risk.

There are several appetizer salads of glowingly fresh and succulent shellfish, my favorite being the tossing of coral lobster meat and snowy lump crab meat in a slightly mustardy vinaigrette dressing with avocado, and the high-crowned "couronne" of the same seafood plus shrimp and other deep-sea treasures with a ring of France's delicately slim string beans, haricots verts. Terrine of lobster is the one pâtélike creation that does not work for me, because it becomes too moist and also because so much of lobster's appeal is in its meaty texture, which is lost when it is chopped.

Hot appetizers, again, are mini main courses, none more so than the boned quail stuffed with sweetbreads in a light golden brown sauce with overtones of wine and a good veal or game stock. That, following the artichoke or asparagus, would be an intriguing and satisfying lunch. Snails Meridionale, served out of shells in individual ceramic pots, exude essences of garlic, green herbs, and hot butter. A real overkill among appetizers is the goujonettes of sole, the slim crisply fried strips of fish garnished with scallops and overpowered by a saffron sauce—a dish that would be fine as a main course but which is just too complex as a starter. Casserole of fruits de mer, a mix of shellfish in a too-intense sauce Nantua, is another hot appetizer that disappoints.

This same tendency to over-intensity *almost* mars what may well be the world's most glorious soup, the Provençal soupe de poisson, a deep coral seafood essence redolent of saffron and garlic, with hints of wine and brandy, served with the bright pink rouille, a mayonnaise whip enhanced with cayenne pepper and a hefty dose of garlic, all to be spooned on croutons set adrift in the soup.

If there is one dish that is Rachou's signature creation, it has to be his remarkable cassoulet, available at both lunch and dinner but somehow more appropriate midday. Baked in a big earthenware cassoulet, the white beans absorb the juices and aromas of garlic and herbs, sausage, lamb, and duck or goose. Eaten with dabs of hot Dijon mustard and washed down with a red wine from the Rhône or an upstanding Beaujolais such as Moulin à Vent, it is a meal worth seeking out and napping after.

Again for those eating light, fish means only grilled red snapper or sole tipped with mustard sauce. Other choices are so complex the fish flavor hardly comes through. Understandably, lustier meats are more suited to Rachou's style and these include the always fresh, rosily sautéed veal kidneys lifted with the spicing of green peppercorns, the thyme-scented rare-roasted rack of lamb, the butter burnished roast chicken sharpened with tarragon, and the blood-rare, pepper-crunched steak au poivre. The texture and flavor of snowy veal chops come through more clearly when the meat is sauced with cream and morels than when it is stuffed with sweetbreads, and though the meat of boned quail en croûte is tender and sweet, the foie gras filling turns the pastry to a greasy mush.

What has always disturbed me with Rachou's main courses is his practice of giving every dish more or less the same vegetable garnish, perhaps changing only a preparation of potato or rice from one to the next. Otherwise, there are always the little chive-tied bundles of haricots verts and sticks of turnip and carrot, the same purées and flowerets. Perhaps that is his generous way of giving everyone a taste of everything, but it does not make for the most refined and sensitive dining. Better to take a position on which garnishes go best with which dish and make a choice. That is a little harder on the kitchen, for it is then necessary to remember which dish gets what, but whoever said it has to be easy in a restaurant charging $50 and upward for dinner?

Baking has never been a strong point here, but among current choices the best are the marbleized cake of white and dark chocolate mousse and, at times, fruit tarts. "At times," because they can also be sticky-sweet with almond frangipane cream. Berries, fruit sherbets, and the wonderful hot soufflés are really the best desserts, and, with the heaviness of other courses, these are the most welcome, leaving room as they do for the delectable cookies and petits fours that follow.

Rachou is still one of the dated hold-outs who offers only an all-French untranslated menu. Complain, complain, complain.

LE CYGNE

55 East 54th Street, between Madison and Park avenues
Telephone: 759-5941

Favorite meals:
Lunch
Terrine of beef and tongue with horseradish cream
Red snapper with basil and tomatoes
Fruit salad with liqueurs
or
Dinner
Mosaic of salmon and sea bass in aspic
Roast loin and rack of lamb
Lemon soufflé

Other favorite dishes: Snails with wild mushrooms, Norwegian smoked salmon, oysters, soft-shell crabs Provençale in season, veal kidneys sautéed with apple brandy, breast of chicken with leeks and truffles, all soufflés, blueberry tart without mango sauce.

Setting: Beautiful, postmodern, impressionistic dining room with floral murals that create a graceful backdrop; noise level is bearable though some seating is cramped; upstairs dining room is more spacious and best for parties larger than 4.

Service: Excellent.

Dress code: Jacket and tie required for men.

Facilities for private parties: Three rooms including a wine cellar that holds between 12 and 22 and the upstairs dining room, which can accommodate from 55 to 65 or be divided for 25 to 35.
Hours: Lunch, Monday through Friday. Dinner, Monday through Saturday. Closed Sunday and major holidays and for three weeks in August.
Reservations: Necessary, especially for Friday and Saturday nights.
Prices: Expensive.
Credit cards: AE, DC, MC, V.

This remains one of the prettiest restaurants in the city and a favorite choice for lunch if I want to have a nice long talk in a room that instills a sense of privacy, a surprise considering the closeness of the tables and the occasional high noise level. The graceful dining room with its impressionistic floral murals and luminous postmodern decor suggests a dining room aboard a luxurious yacht. There is an even more spacious dining room on the second floor, which I prefer for groups larger than four because the bigger tables are more widely spaced than those downstairs. Service is gracious, correct, and concerned. Such hard-to-find attributes are what continue to draw me back despite the notable decline in the food, due mostly to menu changes that have eliminated just about every dish I loved.

Le Cygne used to turn out a few spectacularly fine soups, along with some of the best chicken and duck preparations in town, and for lunch I almost always had the goujonettes, crisp ribbons of fried sole never more greaselessly, succulently rendered than they were here. Now, alas, I am told they are sometimes featured on Friday, a pale consolation.

Newer, less complex dishes that the management perceives as being more acceptable to a public that demands lightness, are light, all right, most of all on flavor, and resort to some unfortunate combinations, such as an overdose of lemon and thyme that muffle the delicacy of veal medallions or an acidic mango sauce that nullifies the winey depth of blueberries in an otherwise well-baked tart. Saffron in a soupy sauce does nothing for the misbegotten combination of tortellini with chunks of monkfish, a bad idea not only because of lost flavor, but because the textures of the pasta and fish are disturbingly similar. Also too thin is the creamy leek sauce with scallops that again seems more like soup than a main course.

Still, there are enough nicely done dishes to make it possible to enjoy this airy, flattering setting. Norwegian smoked salmon, as moist and dusky-flavored as it should be, is a fine starter, as are the always perfect chilled oysters with a sprightly red-wine and shallot-flecked mignonette sauce. Beef and tongue in a chilled terrine, lightly moistened with aspic and given zest by a horseradish cream sauce, have the right meaty richness, and there is also a checkerboard mosaic of pink salmon and snowy bass in a terrine that looks a bit coarse, but which turns out to be moist, saline, and subtly refined.

Chilled lobster salad with a black truffle dressing is altogether decent, if lacking the brilliance its $15 surcharge on the $56 dinner demands. The wild mushrooms morels add velvety overtones to nuggets of sweetbreads as a hot appetizer, but the portion of sweetbreads is meager. Another good appetizer is the cassolette of juicy snails fleshed out with wild mushrooms.

Among fish main dishes, red snapper lightly cooked and finished with basil-scented sautéed tomatoes is as good as ever, and, when available, so are the tiny soft-shell crabs pan-gilded and perfumed with garlic and aromatic Provençal herbs.

Roast beef, veal, or lamb served from the big silver cart and varying with the day are all beautifully cooked and sauced, the current winner being a piney, rosemary-perfumed loin and rack of lamb served with a gentle corn flan. Leeks and truffles in a sheer cream sauce bring delicacy and interest to moist, tender breast of chicken. Always fresh veal kidneys, sautéed to roseate perfection, take on sophistication with a finishing shot of apple brandy that mellows flavors as it reduces and caramelizes.

In place of the several fine duck dishes formerly available, there is now canard rôti aux baies sauvages, a cloying dessert-sweet substitution with an overly reduced wild berry sauce that obscures the meat's flavor.

Pastry was never a strong point at Le Cygne. Better to choose one of the excellent, light and flavorful soufflés. My own favorites are the sunny, astringent lemon and the darkly intense chocolate, but coffee and Grand Marnier versions are almost as good.

LA GAULOISE

502 Sixth Avenue, between 12th and 13th streets
Telephone: 691-1363

Favorite meals:
Lunch
Salad of slim French green beans with preserved duck (salade de haricots verts et confit)
Skate fish with brown butter
Crème brûlée with ginger
or
Dinner
Snails with garlic

Roast filet of rabbit with mustard sauce
Apple tart Tatin
Other favorite dishes: Rabbit in aspic, country pâté, oysters, rillettes (pâté) of salmon, roast pork with garlic if well-done, "hanger" or skirt steak with shallots, roast saddle of venison, sauerkraut with assorted sausage and pork (choucroute garnie), grilled chicken with herbs, grilled lamb chops with garlic, white veal stew (blanquette de veau), veal kidneys with mustard, crème caramel, chocolate desserts.
Setting: Handsome, faux-antique bistro with dark wood, mirrors, Art Deco lighting fixtures, and pretty flowers; beautifully maintained, but noisy in some areas.
Service: Friendly, polite, and efficient to regulars, but there have been reports of cool indifference toward unknowns.
Dress code: None.
Facilities for private parties: None.
Hours: Lunch, Tuesday through Friday. Dinner, Tuesday through Sunday. Brunch, Saturday and Sunday. Closed Monday, all major holidays except Thanksgiving, and for three weeks in July.
Reservations: Generally recommended.
Prices: Moderate to moderately expensive. Prix-fixe dinner, $19.50 from 5:30 to 6:45 P.M., Tuesday through Friday.
Credit cards: AE, MC, V.

It is hard to believe that this Greenwich Village charmer has been open only about eight years, so classic do its menu and interior seem. With its gleaming mirrors and dark wood paneling, its frosted glass Art Deco light sconces, and bright, single flower arrangements, it suggests a landmark bistro-brasserie such as one would be delighted to find in Paris. Through the years it has been impeccably maintained by the owner, Jacques Alliman, an Alsatian, who is proud enough of his region's dishes to have several appearing on the menu regularly. That means a sparkling choucroute garnie, the wine- and juniper-brightened sauerkraut extravagantly decked out with sausage, fresh pork, ham, and boiled potatoes, for an incomparably bracing winter meal.

If the new chef, Patrick Verré, has not yet achieved the consistent excellence of his predecessor, Thierry Moity, now the owner of Café de Bruxelles, he is certainly doing a far above average job with both inventions and traditional specialties of many French regions.

One of the pleasantest meals here is weekend brunch, when one can choose between true breakfast dishes such as omelets and the various poached egg elaborations sauced with hollandaise and assorted garnishes, or go for heavier lunch items that are among the kitchen's best efforts: snowy, moist, white skate fish burnished with brown butter and sparked with capers, or onglet aux echalottes, the "hanger" or skirt steak, which is puffy and tender when rare, and gets a mellow burnishing of gently sautéed shallots. The subtle French veal stew blanquette de veau receives a lift from white wine, thyme, bay leaves, and pickled pearl onions. Veal kidneys, nicely prepared and freshly pink at brunch with a madeira sauce, are as wonderful at dinner when they take on the sharper flavor of mustard.

Pâtés, whether of game or the simplest country "campagne" with pork, veal, garlic, and brandy, are as good as ever, as are the impeccably cool oysters, the fine smoked salmon, and snails in ceramic pots exuding delectable wafts of garlic. A few new creations are disappointing, among such being the bland, underseasoned bouchée à la reine (creamed chicken in a patty shell), that could be a delight if the chicken were soft and tender and the sauce had any herbaceous overtones, and gâteau bressan, a sort of steamed chicken liver flan which, one night at least, arrived unappetizingly blood rare in the center, a pity because the outer cooked portion was delicious. A soft pâté, rillettes of salmon, served with toast and a flurry of green salad, could not have been better. Nor could the salad of crisp mixed greens and slim haricots verts tossed with morsels of the salt-and-fat preserved duck, confit, all profiting from the delicate touch of wine vinegar and fruity olive oil.

Onion soup is another dependable standby, as are the various grills of herbed chicken, shell steak with a tarragon bright sauce Béarnaise, and rose-pink lamb chops perfumed with slowly cooked and, therefore, sweet garlic. As delicately satisfying as rabbit can be, I hesitate to order it because the tiny bones annoy me. Here, fortunately, it comes as a pink filet, lightly roasted and gilded with mustard sauce. Roast filet of pork with garlic can be equally enticing if it is not served pink, as mine once was, and duck breast is worth trying if sauced with green peppercorns rather than with fruit. Roast saddle of venison, topped with a fine ragout of the same tender meat, is so expertly produced that it needs only a starch such as spaetzle to be perfect.

Cassoulet, coq au vin, and bouillabaise-like fish soups are other satisfying and enduring favorites on this menu. So are such sweet wind-ups as a warm, mildly sweet apple tart Tatin, an Alsatian-style plum tart that would be even better with a dash of cinnamon, and the simple, cool custard crème caramel or its fashionable cousin, crème brûlée, the sugar-glazed variation that here sparkles with ginger. Chocolate cakes and desserts are also moist, dark, and never too sweet.

Seating is rather close, but convivial in a way that suggests Brasserie Lipp in Paris. That means some noise too, objectionable only around the bar on crowded nights. The staff is polite and efficient, but there are intermittent reports of a rather cool hauteur on the part of management toward guests who are unknown or who, for some reason, do not meet with house approval. Let's hope that is a temporary aberration for this is too pleasant a bistro not to be enjoyed.

Another improvement would be English explanations for appetizers and desserts listed in French. They appear for main courses, so why not for the rest of the menu?

The wine list is thoughtful and accommodates even a more modest budget. As an added consideration, very decent reds and whites are available by the glass.

LA GRENOUILLE

3 East 52nd Street, between Fifth and Madison avenues
Telephone: 752-1495

Favorite meals:
Lunch
Assorted hors d'oeuvres
Quenelles of pike in champagne sauce
Raspberries with Grand Marnier sauce, or fruit sherbet
or
Dinner
Cream of pea soup Saint-Germain
Roast chicken with tarragon
Apple soufflé with calvados
or
Lobster ravioli with butter sauce
Rack and saddle of lamb
Brie with truffles and green salad
Hot chocolate torte
Other favorite dishes: Littleneck clams Corsini, all pâtés, hot sausage with potato salad, salad of yellow, green, and red tomatoes with basil vinaigrette, salad with foie gras and truffles, salad of vegetables à la Grecque, lobster bisque, turbot braised with leeks, sautéed frogs' legs with garlic butter and tomatoes, grilled sole with mustard sauce, or tail or daube of beef in red wine, chicken in champagne sauce, veal kidneys flambéed with Cognac, poached chicken with coarse salt and horseradish sauce, calves' liver Lyonnaise, pheasant and venison in season, oeufs à la neige, apple tart Tatin, hot apple tart with ginger and honey ice cream, soufflé harlequin (half coconut, half chocolate), fruit tarts.
Setting: Elegantly posh, high-style setting with flattering lighting and flower arrangements out of Flemish still-lifes; tables are too close together; noisy.
Service: Professional and polite, but perfunctory toward unknowns.
Dress code: Jacket and tie required for men.
Facilities for private parties: Beautiful, chateaulike upstairs room with high ceiling, leaded-glass windows, and baronial fireplace; accommodates 20 to 30.
Hours: Lunch and dinner, Tuesday through Saturday. Dinner until 11:30 P.M. Closed Sunday, Monday, major holidays, and all of August.
Reservations: Necessary, especially for Thursday, Friday, and Saturday.
Prices: Expensive.
Credit cards: AE, MC, V.

Much has been heard of the superstar designers responsible for the interiors of our hot new restaurants, but few achieve the pure, graceful beauty of La Grenouille. Probably it is the loveliest restaurant in New York and, for women at least, the most flattering. The glowing, peach gold light from the ceiling and the silk table lampshades, the springtime lift of the textured, minty green walls, the shimmer of mirrored panels and lipstick red banquettes would be almost enough to create a gorgeous backdrop for elegant dining. The touches that add real splendor, however, are the lavishly exquisite bouquets arranged each day by Charles Masson, who with his mother, Gisèle, owns and manages this jewel of a spot, as did his father, who created it.

The look of the place and the stylishness of the food have kept La Grenouille a favorite with the more refined and immaculately well-dressed members of the haute fashion set, particularly at lunch. At dinner, those designers, editors, and merchandisers are joined by stars of the show business and financial worlds. The bigger the name, the more likely the owner is to be seated in the celebrity alcove, just beyond the bar at the entrance. Although it is amusing to sit there to watch the action, tables in the larger, back portion of the dining room are more comfortable because they are not in a traffic pattern. Unfortunately, comfort anywhere in this restaurant is compromised by the too closely packed tables and, in the rear, by noise. Most uncomfortable of all are unknowns, who are consistently given tables that are much too small (four placed at a table for two; eight crammed at a table that at best can hold five), and rarely are they allowed to make a change or is their request for a round table honored.

The kitchen has had its shaky moments in recent years, as several chefs came and went, but through it all there has been a steady level of quality and delicacy maintained in the house's most famous dishes, which still remain my favorites. For starters, such classics include the wonderfully earthy yet subtly herb-scented pâtés and terrines, whether of duck in a Sauternes-sparkled aspic or of game; the coarse but light, warm, garlic sausage contrasted to potato salad sunny with the golden olive oil of Provence; and the tiny littleneck clams Corsini, tender and salty-sweet in their clear broth of white wine, parsley, and garlic. Grenouille, or the Frog to its most dedicated regulars, displays one of the city's most enticing arrays of cold appetizers, which despite changes in the kitchen staff have remained remarkably consistent since it opened about twenty-two years ago. Never have I detected a change in the cool cucumber salad gentled with cream, the firm shrimp in a tomato-blushed dressing, the snowy bass that never tastes of kerosene, and the thinly sliced sausage and celerí rémoulade.

Also classic is the spring-green creamed pea soup, Saint-Germain, and the lobster bisque with its bright belt of coral butter adding the characteristic shellfish essence. Welcome newcomers among first courses include puffy ravioli filled with lobster in a sheer beurre blanc sauce, tiny crabcakes bedded down on dill-accented slivered vegetables, and the salad of foie gras with greens and slim haricots verts flecked with black truffles. All deserve the rank of instant classics. Even a simple salad of tomatoes—red, green, and yellow—gentled with a basil-scented vinaigrette dressing is impeccable here.

Disappointments are few but marked, among them a rather tasteless cream soup with frogs' legs, overly sweetened by what seemed to be red peppers, and slightly soggy salmon mousse that tends to dissolve in a light purée of tomatoes.

Fish has never been my favorite food here, save only a few simple, well-executed exceptions. Grilled sole gilded with mustard sauce has always been firm, moist, and fresh, and, a new invention, braised turbot with translucent slivers of leeks in a froth of a butter sauce retained the deep-sea flavor of the fish. Sautéed fish always is overdone and at times grilled salmon has a peculiar aroma, either because of overcooking or because it is done over heat that is too high.

Again, classics win; not only the grilled sole, but the huge, airy ovals of quenelles, the heavenly dumplings of pike that are never out of fashion here and at their best with a butter- and cream-rich sauce Lyonnaise. Small but meaty and tender frogs' legs are perfect in the traditional sauté that is finished with garlic butter and lightly cooked fresh tomatoes.

Chicken masterpieces at Grenouille are as good as ever, whether you choose the lunchtime specialty of poached fowl with coarse salt and a pungent horseradish cream sauce, or, at any time, the roast chicken, either with tarragon or a buff-colored champagne cream sauce that has subtle overtones of the broth on which it is based. These poultry dishes are far superior to newer entrées, such as chicken with zappingly sweet-sour sherry vinegar, or the duck that is beautifully roasted but ruined by a cloying honey and lime finish, or by an equally overpowering combination of verjus (clear grape juice) with caramelized apples, cranberries, and quince purée. "Where's the duck?" might be the question to ask. Similarly, the delicate flavor of sweetbreads is muffled by an overly reduced sauce, whether with morels, truffles, or leeks.

Lustier meats are delectable, most especially roseate kidneys, their richness mitigated by the brassiness of caramelized, flambéed Cognac, and the roast-of-the-night, especially if it is rack and saddle of lamb. Game is worth trying if not too many sweet ingredients are included in its preparation. At lunch, there are a number of irresistible bourgeois specialties such as calves' liver sautéed Lyonnaise style with soft, melting onions, and either ox tail or the elegant pot roast, daube of beef, matured in red wine with shallots and herbs to become a soul-satisfying lunch on a crisp autumn or winter day.

As a transition for the palate from main course to dessert at dinner, there is truffled brie cheese, ivory-colored and runnily ripe, sharpened by a petite, lacy green salad. While you eat that, the kitchen can perfect such desserts as the incomparable poufs of soufflés properly runny inside and best when flavored with apple and Calvados or a half-and-half harlequin of coconut and chocolate, or the thin, buttery apple tart that takes on elegance with ginger- and honey-perfumed ice cream. Fruit tarts of berries or plums, the glazed upside-down apple marvel that is tart Tatin, and a miraculously light but rich warm chocolate torte with a cooling, vanilla-scented crème anglaise, are other diet-wrecking delights. As for house classics, none is more consistently ethereal than the oeufs à la neige, the cloudlets of poached egg whites floating in crème anglaise, that inspired, eggy custard sauce.

If there are some faults to find with the Grenouille's performance, they are due mostly to overly sweet main courses, the treatment of unknowns, the inadequate choice of modestly priced wines, and an untranslated French menu. Those flaws are, for me, however, outweighed by the ever-increasing beauty of the place.

An added attraction now is the handsome private dining room with walls of wine racks, baronial high ceilings, and a working fireplace, more graceful bouquets in front of leaded-glass windows, and an overall air of privacy in a chateaulike setting.

LUTÈCE

249 East 50th Street, between Second and Third avenues
Telephone: 752-2225

Favorite meals:
Lunch
Alsatian onion tart
Alsatian sauerkraut with pork and sausages (choucroute garni), when available
Apple charlotte
or
Dinner
Sautéed foie gras with apples
Fish soup with crab meat
Roast chicken with herbs
Rhubarb tart when available, or lemon bavaroise
or
Snails baked in brioche
Cream of frogs' legs soup

Roast pheasant or venison, in season
Lemon succès maison
Other favorite dishes: Foie gras in brioche, home-marinated salmon, mousse of duck with juniper, three fish in brioche, all pâtés and terrines, artichoke stuffed with mushrooms, snails Alsatian style, bay scallops méridionale, salmon or bass in puff pastry, truffles with foie gras in croissant, pumpkin soup, cream of pea soup, roast lobster, casserole of crab meat, scallops Provençale, turbot with lemon butter, chicken or veal with morels in cream, veal kidneys in red wine sauce, filet of lamb with peppercorns, filet mignon or noisettes of veal in puff pastry, all game dishes, chicken sauté au Riesling, sweetbreads with capers, chartreuse of cabbage with duck or pheasant, roast duck with peppercorns (not fruit), sirloin steak in red wine sauce, cold raspberry soufflé, praline ice cream bombe, orange chocolate cake, cassis sherbet, all other desserts except gratinée fruit.
Setting: Four rooms in town house duplex; simple, charming bistro with generally good space between tables and bearable noise level in most rooms.
Service: Generally excellent, but there are intermittent reports of indifference from guests the staff considers unimportant.
Dress code: Jacket and tie required for men.
Facilities for private parties: Limited but possible if planned well in advance.
Hours: Lunch, Tuesday through Friday. Dinner, Monday through Saturday. Closed Sunday and for lunch on Monday; in June and July also closed on Saturday. Closed all major holidays and for the month of August through Labor Day weekend.
Reservations: Necessary three to four weeks in advance, depending on day and time.
Prices: Expensive.
Credit cards: AE, CB, DC, MC, V.

That Lutèce has managed to retain its position as New York's most unassailably superb restaurant, and one of its most consistently popular with both critics and the public, is a tribute to the skill and diligence of its chef-owner André Soltner and his wife, Simone, who keeps the dining room in check. Given the rage for new restaurants these days, no less a talent or dedicated spirit could accomplish such a feat.

Spruced up two years ago, Lutèce's four dining rooms glow with a simple bistro charm, from the inviting little bar with its café tables to its upstairs front room with toile fabric and graceful floral bouquets. My favorite remains the small first room downstairs or either of the two upstairs dining rooms and my least favorite the enclosed garden. There is nothing seriously wrong with that trellised pink room with its Paris café chairs; it's just that I prefer the intimacy of the other settings. Pass the open window of the kitchen, where Soltner and his cooks nod starchy white toques blanches as they finish dishes and greet customers, and you instantly feel relaxed and in good hands.

Soltner himself comes out of the kitchen frequently to tour the dining rooms, make suggestions, take orders, and then to check on the meal's progress. He is as likely to do this with newcomers as with regulars, and Simone tries to seat first-timers near celebrities. Among such, Lutèce can count Woody Allen, Jack Lemmon, Henry Kissinger, and more. The regular clientele ranges from out-of-towners in near frumpy clothes to last-of-the-big-spender Seventh

Avenue types and on to the fashionable wearers of the St. Laurents, Armanis, and Beenes. Here, as in all truly great restaurants, what customers have in common is not social standing or profession but their love of food, and that is what they (and I) come to enjoy.

Proud of his Alsatian culinary heritage, Soltner often features dishes of that region, lightening them and garnishing them with unexpected flourishes. Classic French dishes of other regions as well as daily revisions of nouvelle-style presentations add up to an irresistible and varied repertory. My own dilemma when I plan a meal at Lutèce is whether to opt for the old tastes that I adore or chance a new one. If left to my own whim, it would be the former, but Soltner always seems hurt if I do not try a new dish or two. Rarely am I sorry.

If left absolutely to my own choice, a perfect lunch would be the Alsatian onion tart, always among midday appetizers, followed by his choucroute garni, were it a special. Nowhere else is the blond sauerkraut more subtly scented with juniper and Riesling nor the kraut itself cooked just tender but juicy. Three or four kinds of white and red wursts accompany this as does the most stunning array of pork cuts, including smoked and fresh meat from body and foot to provide the right contrast of soft and firm textures with just enough fat to give it all a luxurious gleam. The star of the assortment for me is the sautéed quenelles of liver Soltner adds along with tiny, perfectly boiled potatoes. A variation on that dish includes roast pheasant when in season, and the bird is so golden and moist, I can forgo some of the other meats to make room for it.

Another wonderful Alsatian specialty sometimes featured for lunch is chicken sauté au Riesling, laced with cream and adorned with tiny dumplings of marrow and semolina.

No one has a better hand with foie gras, and the lush New York State product is here sautéed with sliced apples; at times that combination is scooped into small hollowed brioches. The same eggy, crusty yeast roll is sometimes the vehicle for snails, baked right in the brioche complete with parsley and shallot butter.

Pâtés and terrines of pigeon mousse, foie gras, pork and veal, or game, or a combination of fish and shellfish, are equally extraordinary as is the almost daily special of salmon or bass, perhaps with a mousse, baked en croûte. Crusts are much favored in Alsace, and Soltner is as fine a baker as he is a chef.

Warm salmon smoked at Lutèce and polished with a few drops of oil, bay scallops méridionale sautéed with Provençal herbs, truffles and foie gras rolled into a flaky croissant, and simple classics such as asparagus vinaigrette and artichokes stuffed with mushrooms make the first-course choice a wonderful puzzlement.

And that's without even considering soups, a course I rarely miss here. (Soltner gladly divides a series of his appetizers into tiny portions so a small bowl of soup becomes possible.) Some days it is the cream of frogs' legs with tiny puffs of fish dumplings, and another it may be the incredible soupe de poisson au crabe, a more or less Provençale fish soup given zest with nuggets of sea-fresh crab meat. Pumpkin soup gets just enough cream to give it a peachy glow, and the cream of pea soup Saint-Germain suggests liquid jade.

If not soup, I might have the pungent crab meat in a tiny cassolette or share some sautéed scallops with the Provençal trademarks of garlic and herbs. From the simplest Dover sole meunière through the light mousseline of fish with a Nantua sauce coral pink from its shellfish, to the roast lobster with its beurre blanc sauce, most fish dishes are sublime. The few that disappoint are those based on what are called around town escalopes or paillards of fish—paper-thin slices that invariably stick to the plate and lack the texture to hold their flavor.

Much to Soltner's consternation, I often automatically order my preferred main course at dinner—the roasted baby chicken with herbs. It is immaculately rendered, with the meat juicy and just falling from the bone (there's no nonsense about bloody-at-the-joint fish or chicken here, thank God), and with its skin greaseless and faintly crisp but slightly silken. Or if I am feeling traditional, it might be the filet mignon in puff pastry, which has been on the menu almost since the day Lutèce opened, or sweetbreads in hot brown butter sparked with capers. Roast duck is lovely here too, but I prefer it with peppercorns rather than with fruit or fruity vinegar. Morels give a smoky patina to cream sauce that mellows noisettes of veal, and a classic red wine sauce adds an astringency to sautéed veal kidneys.

There might be a surprise such as a miniature chartreuse with duck or pheasant, the tender bird meltingly delicious in its leafy covering. I wish I could still get rack of lamb persillé at Lutèce as I favor that parsley–garlic–bread-crumb crust to the caramelized honey glaze.

Nowhere in the city can I find more subtly handled game such as boar, venison, pheasant, or rabbit, whether in light mustard sauces, the dark-as-midnight stews that are civets, or roasted and garnished with wild mushrooms.

It can probably go without saying that André Soltner also provides the loveliest vegetable and potato creations to round out main courses, and all of the noodle-spaetzle variations are heaven. One touch I love is the topping of cooked fresh noodles with a few golden crisp strands that have been browned in butter, a custom Soltner learned in his mother's kitchen in Alsace. The crisp noodles add intriguing textural contrast by way of a nutty crunch.

All that and dessert too, and a glance at the array in the garden dining room should hint at the divine perplexity of choosing. One day it may be the apple tart Tatin, perfect if humidity has not melted the caramelized glaze or, even better, an apple charlotte, the barely firm fruit centered in a crisp, toasted bread housing and swathed with vanilla-perfumed crème anglaise. Other fruit tarts, especially those based on Alsatian originals, are wonderful, and I always hope for one with blue plums or rhubarb. Puff pastry layered with berries and cream and the lemony succès maison are usually on hand.

Chocolate mousse is dark, bittersweet, and frothy, and the praline ice cream cake, with its crackling bits of sugared filberts, is cooling and rewarding. So is the frozen raspberry soufflé and the thin, moist chocolate cake brightened by orange. I avoid gratinée fruits if they are on the menu as warm fruits thinly sliced do not appeal to me, but I have no trouble with a hot soufflé, of which the chocolate is an enduring first choice.

What makes eating at Lutèce entertaining is the little extras Soltner sends over—a bit of sautéed foie gras or langoustine when you have ordered none, an extra dessert or a half cup of soup, just to try. He is inclined to do this more with customers whose tastes he knows, but he usually makes some effort along those lines even with newcomers. After dessert that means buttery crisp cookies and bonbons, the best of which are the glazed orange sections that inform the palate in the most benign of ways that a wondrous meal has come to an end.

Soltner has a stupendous wine cellar, with some 40,000 bottles stored in a nearby building, and they reach into the thousands in price with many in the mid-hundreds. He prefers customers to drink more modest bottles to their heart's content and has a suitable list of such choices. His pride is the Alsatian selection of Rieslings and Tokays. He also stocks a fire-and-ice framboise that should, I suppose, be considered the *trou alsacien,* the drink that, like Normandy's Calvados, burns a hole to make more room for food.

And as a bonus midst all that French splendor, Soltner has the good taste to include English translations on his menus.

Expensive though it may be, Lutèce offers greater value than other dining places in its price category, and it is easy to spend more money unsuspectingly at a few other improbable spots. That is especially true at lunch, when Lutèce has a prix fixe that is, by comparison, plainly and simply a steal.

MAURICE

Hotel Parker Meridien, 119 West 56th Street or 118 West 57th Street,
between Sixth and Seventh avenues
Telephone: 245-7788

Favorite meals:
Lunch
Chilled crab consommé with lemon grass
Lobster salad
Hazelnut crème brûlée
or
Dinner
Warm oysters with leeks
Breast of pheasant on cabbage
Chocolate dacquoise with pistachio sauce
Other favorite dishes: Seafood broth with scallops, oysters, and mussels; vegetable soup; salmon and scallops marinated in olive oil with caviar; warm sweetbread salad; red snapper with sweet red peppers; baked salmon with dill; medallions of veal with juniper sauce; calves' liver with wine vinegar; roast chicken with sweet garlic; rack of lamb; fruit sherbets; assorted pineapple dessert; raspberry napoleon.
Setting: Quiet and spacious; attractive if somewhat commercial.
Service: Polite and professional, but sometimes slow.
Dress code: Jacket and tie required.
Facilities for private parties: None in restaurant, but kitchen prepares food for up to 50 in a small banquet room.
Hours: Breakfast and lunch, Monday through Friday. Dinner, seven days.
Reservations: Necessary.
Prices: Expensive.
Credit cards: AE, DC, MC, V.

Superb French food in a spacious, quiet setting may seem like the impossible dream. Amazingly, it all comes true, even in New York. It is not in a celebrated, lavish interior created by a big-name architect, but rather in this relatively anonymous, though comfortably posh restaurant in the Hotel Parker Meridien. When this branch of the French-owned hotel chain opened, its consulting chef was Alain Senderens, the widely acclaimed nouvelle cuisine innovator and, to my palate, one of the most overrated, given the bizarre combinations he served in Paris. But his consultancy ended several years ago, and the longer Christian Delouvrier runs the kitchen, the better the food becomes.

Meals here always begin with some tempting giveaway canapés that lead to equally enticing appetizers. But soups are so marvelously orchestrated, I can rarely pass one up in favor of other choices. That is as true of something as light as the chilled, spicy crab consommé fragrant with Thai lemon grass, as it is of richer soups such as the seafood broth full of succulent nuggets of scallops, mussels, and oysters, or of the delicate vegetable potage, with basil-perfumed pistou.

When I can resist soup, it is for something like the warm oysters bedded down on buttered leeks, or the thinly sliced salmon and scallops marinated in a light olive oil, or a gently warm sweetbread salad with vinaigrette sparkled greens. Simpler starters, such as oysters or Norwegian smoked salmon, are impeccable.

Fish, though never overcooked, is never delivered rare, which is a blessing. When it is red snapper mellowed by a froth of sweet red peppers, or salmon baked with airy dill, it is a fine main course or shared appetizer. Lobster salad with a hint of orange is about the world's best. Game birds are done with special sensitivity that renders them delectable yet rich with complex, traditional flavors. Breast of moist pheasant, roasted then nested on bacon-flavored cabbage, is a prime example and roast squab, whether with endives or cabbage and carrots, is another. One of Senderens' creations that is much improved by Delouvrier is the famed duck "Apicius," with an aromatic spice blend of coriander, saffron, cumin, and caraway, said to date back to that ancient Roman epicure.

Veal, so often tough, dry, or flavorless, is never less than perfect here. It may be enhanced with juniper or dressed with a ginger-lime glaze and nestled against translucent homemade noodles or puffy stuffed zucchini blossoms. A sizzling of wine vinegar deglazing the pan in which calves' liver was sautéed lends an astringent elegance, as does orange zest grated into the accompanying spinach. Rack of lamb with the woodsy herbs of Provence and roast chicken heady with sweet garlic are other fine choices.

As I find it hard to resist soup in favor of an appetizer, so I cannot forgo desserts for soufflés. The fruit sherbets here sparkle like jewels on plate and palate, and an inspired crème brûlée is crunchy with hazelnut praline. Dark, moist chocolate ganache dacquoise in pistachio sauce is extraordinary as is the baked-to-order, thin caramelized apple tart and the raspberry and whipped cream napoleon.

There are a few flaws. At times, combinations are overwrought and meaningless, as with the appetizer of snails, frogs' legs, eggplant, and tomato or in the seafood ravioli, often with undercooked pasta. But the real reason the Maurice gets three stars instead of four is the absence of food excitement—nothing on display, no one comes out of the kitchen to make suggestions, none of that temptation an owner-chef would almost surely generate. Otherwise, the management has thought of everything else—cushy banquettes that afford a sense of privacy, and even an elaborate breakfast, but that's another story.

Wine prices are definitely in the upper stratosphere, but there are a few modest choices such as a 1982 Château Monbousquet at $27, and a 1983 Château Rouget or a sprightly Pomerol for $28. There is also a lusty red Beaune, Clos des Mouches 1982, that is a little young and pricey at $45 but very good with game.

Metro, see American

Odeon, see American

Petrossian, see Caviar

QUATORZE

240 West 14th Street, between Seventh and Eighth avenues
Telephone: 206-7006

Favorite meal:
Salad of chicory with bacon and hot vinaigrette
Sautéed calves' liver with shallot sauce
Crème caramel
Other favorite dishes: Oysters, leek and bacon tart, Alsatian onion tart, smoked chicken breast with horseradish cream, Alsatian sauerkraut with pork and sausages (choucroute garnie), grilled herbed chicken, grilled salmon with sauce Choron, halibut with tomato beurre blanc, omelets, beans with duck, lamb and sausage (cassoulet), apple tart.
Setting: Handsome Parisian brasserie-bistro decor with Art Deco touches; very noisy and crowded, with an active bar.
Service: Professional and efficient, if sometimes perfunctory.
Dress code: None.
Facilities for private parties: None.
Hours: Lunch, Monday through Friday. Dinner, seven days. Closed Christmas Day.
Reservations: Necessary.
Prices: Moderate.
Credit cards: AE.

If ever a restaurant exceeded my expectations, it is this one. Trying to create a new dining room that looks mellow and old and as though it had always been in place without becoming corny or overly theatrical was the first unlikely effort. The dark maroon wood trim, creamy walls, mirrors, French posters, and Art Deco wall sconces establish a brasserie-bistro setting, somewhere between the Parisian classic Lipp and La Goulue on the Upper East Side. The noise and brasserie-packed tables, and the hectic scene at the bar, are less intense than they used to be, for though still popular, Quatorze is no longer at the trendy cutting edge.

That is a blessing because the chef is capable and understands the simple, bistro-brasserie classics, making this a diverting spot for lunch or dinner. Reservations are still needed anywhere from a few hours to a week in advance, but less so than formerly. A few times when I have wanted to eat early, say before the theater, I have walked in at 6 or 6:30 and was told I could have a table if I left by 8—a fair bargain under the circumstances. It is an easy trip up Eighth Avenue to the theater district from this location and so it usually works well. Service is generally crisp and efficient but can be distracted, with waiters looking off in the distance as they take orders. There is also the annoying attempt to give away poor tables first even if the room is empty, something that happened on a few occasions when I was not recognized.

But the food has been consistently good whether I was known or not. The appetizer salad of ice-crisp chicory, its bitter bite gentled by nuggets of meaty bacon and a hot, sharp vinaigrette dressing, is a refreshing starter, and large enough to be shared by two. Though not particularly French, the smoked chicken breast with horseradish cream is delicious, and the Alsatian onion tart is soft, fragrant, and satisfying, as is the similar leek and bacon tart. Unfortunately, the house terrine often has the wet softness of pet food. A lively mignonette sauce is fine with clear, cold oysters, but seafood chowder with overly large pieces of fish and vegetables is bland and stewy.

Thin slices of calves' liver, sautéed to rosy perfection and glossed with a bittersweet mantle of shallots, is a main course I find hard to resist. But other temptations do win out, from time to time, among them the nicely done choucroute garnie, the Alsatian classic of juniper-scented sauerkraut piled with various cuts of pork, sausages, and boiled potato. As presented at Quatorze, the dish is a little heavy on sausage and short on meat, but all is fine otherwise. The better-than-average cassoulet has plenty of pork, duck confit, and coarse cotechino sausage midst the white beans that need just a little more garlic to achieve perfection. Fettuccine with artichokes and fennel or with tomato and basil has been too oily and salty with too much sauce in proportion to pasta.

Grilled chicken, which is properly moist within and herbed outside, is a menu regular. Duck, unfortunately, has tasted either reheated or overcooked. Grilled salmon with sauce Choron is as delicious as the gently poached halibut with its tomato-blushed beurre blanc sauce. As simple as crème caramel is, it is not easy to find an excellent interpretation—properly set yet soft and slightly floppy, its essential egginess modified by vanilla and caramelized sugar sauce. That is how it appears here, and it rivals the wafer-thin baked-to-order apple tart as the best dessert. Chocolate regal, declared a specialty on the menu, is a dark wet cake of the sort I detest. The gooey texture suggests it was not baked at all but is rather like raw dough, a state immature palates favor.

There is a modest wine list befitting the cuisine, but there should be more choices by the glass, carafe, and half bottle.

TERRACE

400 West 119th Street, at Morningside Drive, in Butler Hall
Telephone: 666-9490

Favorite meals:
Eggplant terrine
Steamed and baked lobster, Georges Garin
Crème brûlée
or
Smoked salmon with mousse of smoked trout
Rack of lamb
Chocolate-orange mousse
Other favorite dishes: Oysters in champagne, asparagus vinaigrette, snails with walnuts and Pernod, prawns with pasta, lobster bisque, onion soup, veal chop with morels, quail or partridge with red cabbage, poached salmon, sweetbreads with truffles, endive and arugula salad, chocolate mousse, chocolate cream torte, lemon meringue tart.
Setting: Elegant and romantic candlelit dining room with beautiful view over the city; tables for two are less comfortable than those for four; noise level is bearable even with harp or piano music at dinner.
Service: Polite, helpful, and efficient, but often slow.
Dress code: Jacket and tie required for men at dinner.
Facilities for private parties: Separate room accommodates between 20 and 70; for larger parties it is possible to reserve the entire restaurant on Sunday and Monday.
Hours: Lunch, Tuesday through Friday. Dinner, Tuesday through Saturday. Closed one month in summer and Sunday and Monday, but open most major holidays.
Reservations: Suggested for lunch; necessary for dinner.
Prices: Moderately expensive.
Credit cards: AE, CB, DC, MC, V.

The Terrace is a restaurant I love to take first-timers to for a surprise. Most people cannot believe it even when they are there. Located atop the Columbia University residence Butler Hall, it has a sparkling, three-sided view that takes in Upper Manhattan, the Hudson River, and the George Washington Bridge. The large, beautiful dining room shimmers with candlelight, mirrors, and glass, and this is one place where background music (classical harp or piano) is more welcome than intrusive. Also open for lunch, it offers a different but no less felicitous view by day. Pretty floral bouquets and comfortable seating (except for parties of two, who get short shrift) add to the inviting effect. Belying the adage that rooms with a view have poor food, this one has many excellent dishes produced by a kitchen that seems to have settled in solidly since the death of its founder and chef, Dusan Berniç. Now operated by his widow, Nada, with the kitchen run by Dominique Payradeau, the former sous-chef under Berniç, the restaurant is on an even keel with food much in the style of its originator.

The only problem with the menu is reading it in the too dim

candlelight; a second or larger candle at each table would enable one more easily to find the way to the lovely appetizers of smoked salmon with smoked trout mousse, or the baked oysters lightly puffed under a mantle of champagne sauce. Grilled prawns on herbed fettuccine and brightly firm asparagus are other fine first-course options. Asparagus are better in a vinaigrette dressing than with hollandaise, primarily because the hollandaise is so meagerly applied. Lobster salad is worth the thirty-minute wait required for it if you are not too hungry and want to relax with a drink anyway, but the menu should indicate the wait. Plump snails divided between two ramekins get a herbaceous lift from a sauce combining crackles of walnuts with the anise-scented Pernod and a silken eggplant terrine with sweet peppers has overtones of Provence.

Lobster bisque, though slightly overthickened, has exactly the right crackling shellfish flavor and was served blessedly hot; too often that soup arrives tepid in most restaurants. Onion soup is another steamy winner and almost a meal in itself.

Apparently Berniç had a way with lobster that he imparted to his assistant, for another first-class experience is lobster Georges Garin. This steamed and baked main course, glossed with Pernod butter, is named for the owner of the erstwhile, extraordinary Parisian restaurant Chez Garin. Equally dependable is the rack of lamb lightly touched with garlic and always roasted medium rare as ordered. Sweetbreads are crisply sautéed and nestled against minced truffles. Game birds are deliciously moist, and both the boned morsels of quail and the roast partridge are often served with wonderful red cabbage—at once winy, sweet, and sour and just firm enough. Little flans and timbales of vegetables garnish some dishes. Noisettes of veal, once dry, now emerge from the sauté pan petal pink inside under a beige cream sauce of morels, but wild rice still presents a problem; as usual, it is woody and cold.

Duck and rabbit are not quite up to other dishes, and a couple of my favorite desserts seem to have disappeared, most sadly the ethereal banana mousse cake and the nut-crunched Linzer torte. But that still leaves lofty, aromatic soufflés, a perfect crème brûlée, its custard like satin under a glassy burnt-sugar veneer, and the bittersweet chocolate mousse, which I much prefer to the albinoid interloper. There is also a thin-layered chocolate torte with a light cream filling that might make me forget the much missed banana masterpiece, but not quite, and an orangy, chiffonlike chocolate mousse.

The wine list has very good choices in a wide price range. There is valet parking, and the valet will also call a cab.

LA TULIPE

104 West 13th Street, between Sixth and Seventh avenues
Telephone: 691-8860

Favorite meals:
Mousse of smoked trout
Squab with couscous or cabbage
Cheese
Warm apple tart
or
Croustade Provençale
Soft shell crabs meunière, when in season
Vanilla ice cream with hot chocolate and toasted almonds in a pastry shell (La Tulipe Marie-Louise)

Other favorite dishes: Oysters, sorrel soup, wild mushrooms on toast, game terrines, eggplant Provençale, sautéed sweetbreads, lamb chops or noisettes with herb or mustard butter, roast chicken with garlic, breast of chicken with morels, navarin of lobster, venison medallions, confit of duck with lentils, apricot soufflé, chocolate cake with crème anglaise.

Setting: Urbane and stunning brownstone dining room with plum-colored walls and chic bar; extremely noisy; tables are much too closely set.

Service: Generally efficient and helpful but still pretentious; can be slow between appetizer and main course.

Dress code: Jacket and tie preferred for men but not required.

Facilities for private parties: None.

Hours: Dinner, Tuesday through Sunday. Closed Monday, major holidays, and for the last three weeks in August and the first week of September.

Reservations: Necessary well in advance.

Prices: Expensive.

Credit cards: AE, CB, DC, MC, V.

Charm is the word that comes instantly to mind when I think of La Tulipe, the small, sophisticated French restaurant on a tree-lined street in Greenwich Village where the Darrs—Sally (in the kitchen) and John (in the dining room)—have nurtured this establishment into being one of the city's better options. The only detractors from that charm are a pretentiousness that still seems to pervade the staff, noise, and, generally, slow service, especially before main courses.

If the original brilliance of the cooking has dimmed slightly, Sally Darr maintains a high batting average when it comes to delicacy of seasonings and care in preparations. That, even though the frying can be a bit too dark and the once engaging red snapper baked in "papillote" now seems overcooked and blandly uninteresting. This still leaves much delectable food to be enjoyed in the restaurant's urbane setting, with its plum-colored walls, exquisite country floral bouquets, and soft, flattering lighting. The small front café, with its zinc-topped bar, is a felicitous, very Parisian spot in which to have an aperitif. A small banquette has been added to that room for those who like to eat in the bar.

The menu is not large, and, though it changes seasonally, it always includes house specialties served almost since the place opened in 1979. That is a good idea, because frequent guests require new choices while those coming back only occasionally usually do so for remembered tastes.

Among my favorite remembered tastes are appetizers of zucchini fritters, long slender fingers of that vegetable fried in a crisp veneer of breading and grouped perhaps a bit too cutely in a basket, a picturesque holdover, no doubt, from Mrs. Darr's stint in the test kitchen of *Gourmet* magazine. Delicious when properly, lightly fried, these can at times taste of overheated grease, the same flaw that marred a recent order of sautéed gray sole. Still consistently excellent, however, is the appetizer of fish mousse, whether of smoked trout, scallops, or a roll of smoked eel. Terrines of game, such as venison, or of pork and tongue, have the right al dente bite and the aromatic herbal overtones. Eggplant Provençale, baked with tomato, cheese, oregano, and thyme, blends the enticing combination of Italianate Niçoise seasonings.

That same flavor palette colors the savory croustade Provençale, a variation on the Nice specialty, pissaladière, done here with the onion, olive, anchovy, and tomato mixture heaped into a flaky puff pastry shell.

My single favorite dish at La Tulipe, season permitting, is the soft-shell crabs meunière, which may just be the world's best. Tiny crabs, each about the size of an infant's hand, are lightly floured and gilded in hot butter. But the real miracle of timing is the nut-brown butter poured over them. Mrs. Darr begins by placing butter in a small copper saucepan and melting it to a halfway point in the kitchen. The crabs are brought to the table along with the saucepan, its buttery contents still cooking, to be poured over the crabs in a haze of nut-sweet perfume. Never once has the butter been less than perfect, and because heavy copper retains heat, it could easily burn were the timing even two seconds off. There is a short season for the kind of crabs Mrs. Darr insists on—usually from April to mid-July, at the latest.

Less of a high-wire act and more frequently on the menu are tender, succulent morsels of roast squab ringing steamed couscous with raisins and pine nuts. A variation is grilled squab nested in braised cabbage and "batons" (sticklike slices) of vegetables.

Grilled rack of lamb with mustard butter, accompanied by buttergilded slices of potatoes, is as solidly satisfying. So is any dish made with the rich preserved duck confit Mrs. Darr prepares, smoky lentils being the best accompaniment.

Breast of chicken stuffed with morels, navarin of lobster with tomato and tarragon, and puffy pink venison medallions nicely bittersweet with orange rind and gentled with celery root purée are among other personal favorites, as is the buttery roast chicken sacheted with nuggets of golden roast garlic.

A salad of lacy mixed greens gets just the right sort of winy vinaigrette dressing, and there is generally an earthy, ripe goat cheese to go with it, an un-French combination of courses perhaps, but delicious nonetheless.

Desserts have always been irresistible and lately I have come to like the apricot soufflé, a hot, exotically rich creation that I used to find cloyingly sweet. Whether it is the recipe that has changed, or my own preferences, I cannot say, and it hardly matters. It's just nice to have yet another choice. Other Darr dessert classics endure, foremost among them being the hot, baked-to-order wafer of an apple tart, the true floating island (a huge fez of meringue adrift in a crème anglaise sea), and La Tulipe Marie-Louise, a "tulipe" of a thin, butter-crisp cookie filled with homemade vanilla ice cream, hot bitter chocolate sauce, and toasted almonds. There is also a velvety dark chocolate mousse with contrasting overtones of Grand Marnier, to which a textural counterpoint is added by way of whipped cream and shaved chocolate.

To end on a more delicate note, try sparklingly cool orange sherbet spiked with pear brandy or bombe Javanaise, a dazzlement of coffee ice cream, frozen chocolate mousse with whipped cream, pecans, caramel sauce, and shavings of dark chocolate.

When La Tulipe opened, the prices seemed outrageous, but as they have not increased in proportion to the rest of the New York scene, they now are merely high. Considering the consistent high quality of the food, a $59 prix fixe that includes appetizer or soup, main course, salad, cheese, dessert, coffee, and petits four can no longer be declared exorbitant by players in the New York restaurant game. Also, no choice on the menu carries a supplemental charge. The only problem will be for those who do not want a full meal. Exceptions are made for someone who might want one or two courses, but only if he or she is with others who have the full table d'hôte.

Wines are still expensive here, but there are a few more moderately priced choices than formerly.

GREEK

PERIYALI

35 West 20th Street, between Fifth and Sixth avenues
Telephone: 463-7890

Favorite meals:
Lunch, shared by two
Assorted cooked vegetable salads (paradosiaka orektika)
Fried squid on green salad (calamarakia, tiganita)
Grilled shrimp with herbs and lemon (garides Periyali)
Greek pastry
or
Dinner
Assorted salad purées (pikantikes salates)
Shish kebob or grilled lamb chops
Rice pudding
Other favorite dishes: Grilled cheese slices with salad (saganaki), charcoal grilled octopus in red wine marinade (oktapodi Scharas), cheese in phyllo pastry (tiropita), spinach in phyllo (spanakopita), grilled chicken, rabbit stew (kouneli stifado), custard cake (galaktoboúriko).
Setting: Stylish rustic Greek-island atmosphere. Crowded and somewhat noisy, especially in back rooms, which are also hot.
Service: Good-natured, polite, but a little hectic.
Dress code: None.
Facilities for private parties: Two back rooms accommodate 15 to 25.
Hours: Lunch, Monday through Friday. Dinner, Monday through Saturday. Open late, Saturday. Closed Sunday and major holidays.
Reservations: Necessary.
Prices: Moderate.
Credit cards: AE, MC, V.

If we experience a gastronomic Greek Revival, Periyali will be the reason. This stylishly rustic taverna is the best and most beautiful Greek restaurant New York has ever known, at least in my memory, which goes further back than I care to admit. Opened in 1988 in Chelsea, just around the corner from Limelight, Periyali (pronounced perry-YAHLEY and meaning coast) is laid out in a low-ceilinged floor-through, just a few steps below street level. It is a snug space that lends itself to the Greek-island atmosphere with dark wood, colorful tiles, country floral bouquets, and white stucco walls hung with antique kitchen utensils, the most striking of which are wood bread-baking boards. The canniest decorating ploy is the ceiling, which is festooned with a white muslinlike fabric pulled through dark wood beams and covering unattractive acoustical tiles while serving as an added muffler for noise. Not that the dining rooms here are quiet, what with their closely set tables, but at least the decibel level is bearable. In fact, only the two tiny back rooms are uncomfortable because they are hot and stuffy.

Credit for this charmer must be shared by two sets of partners—Irene and Victor Gouras, who operated a restaurant on the island of Patmos and who directed the preparation of food, and Steve Tzolis and Nicola Kotsoni, who also own the trendy Italian restaurant Il Cantinori. It was Ms. Kotsoni who did the decor. Most surprising, perhaps, is that the very good food is prepared by a young American chef, Charles Bowman, a graduate of the Culinary Institute of America. He gives the traditional Greek food pleasingly contemporary presentations.

Strong points are appetizers (some of which are displayed alluringly in the front dining room) and desserts, with the simple grills the best choices for the main course. Crunchy bread and oily, supple olives are set out for all, and, if you resist overindulging, you can go on to some extraordinarily light and delicate first courses. Among the best is the assortment of marinated vegetables that might typically include rice-stuffed grape leaves, herbed mushrooms, whole fingers of okra mellow in a tomato sauce, spicy giant white beans with flecks of tomato, garlicky cauliflower, and more.

If not that gentle, seductively olive-oiled array, then another wise choice might prevail—perhaps the trio of silken salad purées, including the cool, crunchy diced cucumber in yogurt (tzatziki), the smoky eggplant mousse (melintznosalata), and the salty, pink fluff of whipped cod roe (taramosalata). Fresh field greens are sprightly flourishes with these appetizers, as they are with the impeccably crisp fried squid and the unusual version of the Greek grilled cheese specialty saganaki, here served in charred slices of pungent sheeps' milk cheese. Giant white beans nest on the thick garlic sauce (skordalia) and tiny packets of flaky phyllo dough enfold spinach (spanakopita) or zesty feta cheese (tiropita). Most dramatic are the wild-looking, slender tentacles of octopus, charcoal grilled then marinated in red wine and served at room temperature, perfectly al dente.

After such richness, it's just as well that the more complex cooked main courses are not nearly as well executed as the simple grills of lamb shish kebob, lamb chops, butterflied baby chicken, and shrimp bathed in herb-scented oil and lemon. Choose one of those along with a soothingly moist rice pilaf and you'll be far happier than if you opt for stale tasting, fishy stuffed squid, the dry crumbly moussaka, and overcooked baby lamb, all of which tasted reheated. The one fine exception is the kouneli stifado, a peasant rabbit stew for which the lean, toothsome meat is graced with a thick tomato and onion sauce fragrant with bahari (allspice) that lends cinnamon-clove-nutmeg overtones.

Desserts are as compelling as the appetizers and, though authentically Greek, they are less cloyingly sweet than most. Crisp phyllo pastry is the basis of the nut- and syrup-layered baklávas, the cigar-shaped rolls, plakoúndes, and the crunchy shredded wheat rolls, katáifi. Sugar white almond shortbreads, kourambiéthes, the cinnamon-nut cookies and pound cake, and the custardy sponge cake, galaktoboúriko, are other enticements, as are the coils of deep fried honeyed pastry, diples. Rice pudding done in individual casseroles is plump with rice and redolent of cinnamon. Greek (never say Turkish) coffee should be thicker and better.

The wine list has several interesting Greek selections, among them the white, resin-scented retsina, awful in most situations but neatly astringent with the oily food, and some dry, aromatic red wines from the northern region of Naoussa.

Service is informal, enthusiastic, and generally efficient, but unevenly paced and hectic at peak hours. Though not as low as they were at the start, prices are still fairly moderate, so much so that at the crowded lunch hour a $15 per person minimum is in effect.

HUNGARIAN

CHARLES' GREEN TREE HUNGARIAN RESTAURANT ★

1034 Amsterdam Avenue, corner 111th Street
Telephone: 864-9106

Favorite meal:
Borscht
Chicken paprikash
Napoleon
Other favorite dishes: Fried potato pirogen, Hungarian and szeged goulash, stuffed cabbage, stuffed peppers, chicken fricassee, stuffed roast chicken, apple strudel, crêpes (palachinta). Wine and beer only.
Setting: Bohemian atmosphere in what is a cross between a luncheonette and a café, with a convivial young crowd.
Service: Good-natured and concerned, but sometimes slow when crowded.
Dress code: None.
Facilities for private parties: None.
Hours: Lunch and dinner, Monday through Saturday. Closed Sunday and Christmas.
Reservations: Not accepted.
Prices: Inexpensive.
Credit cards: None.

Despite an $8 to $10 cab ride there and back, I find the Green Tree an exceptional buy, and it is a restaurant I like to go to once in a while just to enjoy the bohemian student café atmosphere, the bright and cheerful room, and the cozy staff. Of course there is some good food too, and, at the prices charged, it is a near miracle. Because the place caters to students of nearby Columbia and Barnard, as well as to the staffs of St. Luke's Hospital and the Church of St. John the Divine, there are all sorts of specials available at very low prices, especially at lunch and in early evening. Cagily enough, the management also refrains from bringing out the two or three super homemade desserts until later at dinner, saving the wonderful cream-filled napoleon and the apple strudel for the more profitable guests. Or so it seems. But the young people and the relaxed neighborhood regulars create an amiable café de quartier that makes me wish I lived in the quartier.

My toughest choice used to be between the chewy, mellow potato pirogen, available boiled or, as I prefer, fried, capped with sour cream or what was unquestionably the city's best chicken soup with matzo ball. Now, the soup is gray and greasy, and only the cold, winy beet borscht is competition. If I am with three or four people, we might share some pirogen and have soup anyway, but that blissful state does not often occur, as my husband and I tend to go up to the Green Tree for Saturday lunch or a weekday dinner on impulse. Cherry soup, unfortunately, is sweet and has less character.

A good general rule in a restaurant as inexpensive as this one is to steer clear of meat cuts that are unlikely to be both good and cheap. That means no steak or roasts, but rather poultry, stews, and braised dishes—preparations that were, in a sense, created to accommodate toughness with long simmering. Among such at the Green Tree are the chicken paprikash, with its fluffy sour cream and paprika sauce, and a version known in kosher homes as chicken fricassee— the same preparation essentially, minus sour cream. But that makes a big difference in creating a thinner, more peppery sauce. That, as well as the fine, juicy beef goulash, comes with light little nockerl dumplings. Spicier szeged goulash is nestled against sauerkraut. Roast chicken with a fragrant herb bread stuffing is delicious, as are the seductive combination of scrambled eggs with brains and onions, and the hefty, sauerkraut-topped stuffed cabbage. Breaded veal cutlet is one exception to the no-costly-meat rule. It is crisp and full of meaty flavor. Dishes that seem to be at equal risk in all Hungarian restaurants in town are the roast duck, pork, and veal shank. All tend to be held over from one day to another if they are not sold, with unappetizing results.

Vegetables, salads, and breads are eminently skippable as are heavy potato pancakes. But with sauerkraut, nockerl, and mashed potatoes, as well as with the other good food at low prices, Green Tree remains a fine value. How many places offer so much satisfaction at $7.95 to about $12 for a three-course meal and coffee? Save room for one of the desserts mentioned above, and, to be sure they are not sold out, reserve what you want when you order the meal. The cinnamon- and sugar-sprinkled crêpes, Hungarian palachinta, are also seductive wind-ups. Beer is favored by many regulars, but the Hungarian red wine Egri Bikavér (Bull's Blood) is less filling and a better complement to the food.

Purchased from its original owners two years ago by Charles Schmidt, their waiter of thirty years, the restaurant altered its name to include his first name. Now that he has that out of the way, he should pay attention to the untidy ladies' room and see that the kitchen turns out hotter food.

MOCCA HUNGARIAN RESTAURANT ★

1588 Second Avenue, between 82nd and 83rd streets
Telephone: 734-6470

Favorite meal:
Breaded mushrooms with tartar sauce
Stuffed cabbage
Rum cake with chocolate sauce and nuts (somloi galuska), shared by two or even four
Other favorite dishes: Sausage with green peppers and onions (lecsós kolbász), fried cauliflower à la Mocca, chopped liver, marinated herring, chicken noodle soup, stuffed roast chicken, beef or veal goulash, stuffed pepper, Wiener schnitzel, warm cheese or apple strudel.
Setting: Simple, crowded informal dining room, one step above a luncheonette, with glass tops over tablecloths.
Service: Good-natured if sometimes distracted and slow.
Dress code: None.
Facilities for private parties: None.
Hours: Lunch and dinner, seven days, including all major holidays.
Reservations: Recommended, especially for dinner on weekends.
Prices: Inexpensive, especially at lunch, when a three-course special is $5.45.
Credit cards: None.

What I enjoy at Mocca, in addition to the soul-warming food at almost impossibly low prices, is the relaxed conviviality of the clientele and the simple approach of the management. This is really a cross between a luncheonette and a café, with glass tops covering tablecloths, paper napkins, and a seating arrangement that is elbow-to-elbow. But with candlelight on tables at night, a shot of slivovitz, or a bottle of Egri Bikavér, the Hungarian red wine, the atmosphere is that of a big friendly family gathering.

The most stunning bargain is the friendly lunch for $5.45. It may begin with golden, fragrant chicken noodle soup, then go on to a mellow, meat-stuffed green pepper or stuffed cabbage on paprika-spiced sauerkraut or the juicy, spicy goulash with flecks of nockerl dumplings. Even at that price, the dessert is palacsinta, the crêpes filled with apricot preserves and topped with ground walnuts. Not a lunch for every day, perhaps, but something I like to do once in a while if I am going to the theater or a concert in the evening and do not want to eat beforehand. That lunch is enough to carry anyone through to a post-theater hamburger or pizza. The scene is friendly at noon too, with neighborhood people dropping in, and service is even warmer and friendlier than at peak dinner hours.

But even in the evening Mocca is a wonderful buy, especially since all portions are generous enough to be shared, something my husband and I do with appetizers and desserts. Fried, breaded foods are much better as appetizers here than as main courses, for reasons I cannot fathom. The breaded mushrooms or flowerets of cauliflower, both with tartar sauce, are never greasy or too dark, failings that often spoil main courses such as liver or breaded veal knuckle. Lecsós kolbász, the rich sauté of garlic sausage, green peppers, and onions with paprika, is a delicious starter as is the marinated herring and the stuffed cabbage. In addition to the noodle soup, there may be a heady brew of giblets, vegetables, and paprika, or a lusty goulash soup that is almost a meal in itself. There is always a nice, cool cucumber and onion salad giveaway, and, unlike many others in town, it is not too sweet.

As in other inexpensive Hungarian restaurants, the braised dishes are the most dependable, which here mean veal or beef goulash, my preference being the former, the stuffed cabbage or pepper, and the roast chicken with a peppery, herb-scented stuffing layered between skin and breast meat. Lecsós roast pork with a paprika sauce and, when available, smoked pork tenderloin with beans have also been satisfying, as has the Wiener schnitzel, an exception to the no-fried-main-course rule. I avoid anything that has a cream-style sauce here, finding the results too starchy. That includes all paprikash preparations, unfortunately, and the veal medallion with garlic. On busy days—Saturday and Sunday—roast duck or veal shank can be delicious—huge, moist, tender, and flavorful. But on off days, both seem stale.

Hot cheese or apple strudel, both exuding the enticing scent of vanilla, are fine desserts, as is the somloi galuska, an almost insanely irresistible indulgence of sponge cake oozing rum, chopped walnuts, a dark chocolate sauce, and whipped cream. *That* can be shared by four.

It's a good idea to check on accompaniments to food, or you can wind up with quite a lot of cabbage in one form or another. One night my husband began with an appetizer of stuffed cabbage, after which he had duck. How could he have known that sauerkraut accompanied the duck and the vegetable served on the side was, you guessed it, cabbage? On the other hand, cabbage is really the only vegetable the kitchen does well, so perhaps this is a good place to fill up on it. Still, turning out a very good three-course meal for as little as $15 is no small accomplishment, and so Mocca can be forgiven stylistic lapses.

INDIAN

BUKHARA

148 East 48th Street, between Lexington and Third avenues
Telephone: 838-1811

Favorite meal:
Shared by two
Cheese kebob
Duck Bukhara
Khyber chicken
Dal and spiced yogurt
Bread (naan)
Frozen orange cream
Other favorite dishes: Stuffed roasted potatoes, vegetable biryani, royal veal, quail, barra kebobs, lamb-e-chasma, mellow cream chicken, bolan rolled beef, firni (rosewater custard), all breads except Khurmi naan.
Setting: Romantically decorated cavelike setting with Oriental rugs and copper. Glassed-in "open" kitchen.
Service: Friendly and well-meaning, if slow and a bit forgetful.
Dress code: None.
Facilities for private parties: Will close on advance request for parties of 40 to 50.
Hours: Lunch and dinner, seven days.
Reservations: Recommended, especially on weekends.
Prices: Moderate to moderately expensive.
Credit cards: AE.

Along with the fabled cities of Samarkand and Tashkent, Bukhara, to me, has always promised the ultimate in exotic travel. Geographically within the borders of the Soviet Union, but akin to India in our frame of gastronomic reference, Bukhara, the capital of Uzbekistan, is the home of spicy, seductive, tandoori oven-grilled meats, crisp, fragrant plain and filled breads, pungent garnishes of stewed lentils (dal), dill- and cucumber-accented yogurt (raita), and piquant sauces that may include ginger, basil, lime juice, mint, onion, and coriander.

It is this counterpoint of hot, sweet, and sour that lights up the palate as one enjoys meltingly tender nuggets of duck Bukhara, roasted after marinating in garlic and spice-flavored yogurt, or in mellow cream chicken, sprightly with overtones of lime, cream, and peppers. Dark rum spikes yogurt fragrant with cumin and adds elegance to "royal" veal chops, and a dry spice mixture distinguishes sausage-like bolan rolled beef, baked on skewers. Ginger, contrasted to garlic and heightened with vinegar, lends fire to the lamb-e-chasma, and at times, there are succulently spiced roast quail and the chunky, mellow barra kebobs of lamb shank.

This lusty cuisine from the northwest frontier of the Indian subcontinent is presented in a most dramatic setting—a sort of luxurious, white-walled cave, improbably installed on 48th Street, just east of Lexington Avenue. Richly colored Bukhara carpets with the characteristic medallion patterns hang on the walls, and around the cushy banquettes are gleaming brass and hammered copper vessels. Those banquettes, by the way, afford quiet, private conversation, a most welcome find for a business lunch, midtown. Carved wood tables and chairs fill the center of the room and, if less snug than the wall banquettes, offer a better view of the glassed-in kitchen, where cooks run quail, chicken, duck, squares of cheese, and meats onto the long-handled skewers that will be lowered into the hive-shaped tandoor. Wonderful breads also come out of those ovens, and many are akin to pizza. My favorites are the plain, crisp, and yeasty naan, the bharvan kulcha that is filled with meat, the flaky whole wheat roti or its variations, the fragile roomali roti, and the crisper khasta roti. A dusting of dry mint perfumes the whole wheat paratha, and a huge oval of crisply baked bread, communal naan, has the patina of ancient history. Only khurmi naan (described by waiters as Indian pizza) disappoints, overpowered as it is by the taste of ketchup that seems to be the main ingredient in its sauce.

Interesting side dishes include baked, breaded cauliflower and delicate stuffed roasted potatoes, filled with peas and green peppers, in a lime, coriander, and green pepper sauce. Not all offerings live up to those described so far. Rice in pulao and biryani can be dry and cold, and all fish dishes, prawns included, are hopelessly overcooked. Skewered salad is a mismatch of pineapple, green peppers, onions, and tomatoes baked on skewers, and frontier roasted lamb emerges stringy, stewy, and short on flavor.

There is also a certain slow, unprofessional tone to service, polite and friendly though it may be; it can be hard to get dishes on time, to order, or to get a check.

Those who want to sample life at its most authentic can don the big colorful bib-napkins handed out here, and then eat with hands, shunning utensils, a neat (or not so neat) trick when it comes to handling the hot, creamy dal (one of the best I have ever had), the yogurt sauce, raita, or the warm, soft duck.

There is full liquor service, with beer or the spiced iced yogurt drink, lassi, being the most appropriate. Desserts, like those of India, are cloyingly sweet; the best is the kulfi orange—citrus ice cream frozen in an orange shell. It is fun to go to Bukhara with a group of six or eight so that many dishes can be shared. That way, the fantastic platter of assorted breads can be appreciated. However, it is better to order individual servings of tandoori meats, rather than the combination, as more care seems to be taken in the cooking that way.

DARBAR

44 West 56th Street, between Fifth and Sixth avenues
Telephone: 432-7227

Favorite meal:
Shared by four
Chick-pea, potato, and onion salad (channe ki chaat)
Onion fritters (onion bhajia)
Chicken in a coconut curry sauce (mughlai korma)
Lamb with spinach and coriander (saag gosht)
Crab Malabar
Rice with vegetables, saffron, raisins, and nuts (shahi sabz biryani)
Yogurt and cucumber sauce (raita)
Deep-fried bread puffs (poori)
Pistachio and rosewater ice cream (kulfi)

Other favorite dishes: All appetizers; Hyderbad chicken and potato soup; tandoori lamb (boti kebob); boneless tandoori-grilled chicken in tomato, onion, and butter sauce (murgh tikka masala); chicken with lemon and cinnamon (murgh Madras); chicken with green peppers, tomatoes, and onions (murgh Jalfrazie); sliced lamb in yogurt, onion, and tomato sauce (khara pasande); lamb with yogurt, cream, and almonds (rogan josh); cheese cooked with spices (paneer Jalfrazie); cauliflower and potatoes in curry spices (aloo gobi masala); grilled eggplant in sauce (bayngan bhurta); rice with lamb, raisins, and nuts (Shahjehani biryani); vegetable bread (vegetarian paratha); onion-stuffed bread (onion kulcha); cardamom-flavored rice; creamy rice pudding (kheer).

Setting: Downstairs is romantic, pukka-sahib Indian with beautiful fabrics, pierced wood screens, gleaming brass and copper; noisy and stuffy but alcoves are comfortable; upstairs dining room is attractive but uncomfortable.

Service: Excellent downstairs; careless for dinner upstairs.

Dress code: None.

Facilities for private parties: Upstairs room seats up to 40. Will close entire restaurant for parties up to 200.

Hours: Lunch and dinner, seven days; Friday and Saturday open to 11:30.

Reservations: Recommended, especially for lunch and before and after theater.

Prices: Moderately expensive for dinner; moderate for lunch.

Credit cards: AE, CB, DC, MC, V.

Darbar, a relatively recent addition to the New York scene, is also one of the more welcome. It is a stylish little supper club of a restaurant with romantic decorative accessories, seductive if eventually wearing background music, and a gracious staff—downstairs. Because it is on a sort of landing, the upstairs makes one feel left out, and at night waiters do nothing to alleviate that feeling, bringing food slowly and usually cold.

But downstairs all is luxury and charm. True, there could be better ventilation in some corners, and the best tables are for four or more, in private alcoves, but the colorful, rich, and fresh food makes up for minor discomforts.

Unlike those in many Indian restaurants, the fried vegetable fritters (pakoras) and turnovers (samosas) are clear and distinguishable here, as are the chicken pakoras, marinated in yogurt, then fried in batter. Onion bhajia is a masterpiece, a forerunner, perhaps, of Tony Roma's onion loaf but an ethereal version, lightly floured and as crackling as gold leaf. Puckery tamarind sauce sharpens yogurt that is folded into chick-peas, potatoes, and onions for the appetizer salad (channe ki chaat), and crab Bombay is a cool, curried salad, lightly spiced. With the exception of the zesty chicken and potato soup, creamy with coconut and piquant with lemon (Hyderbad murgh shorba), soups are not quite worth the better food they displace. I prefer to save room for the nuggets of tandoori grilled lamb (boti kebob), which is the moistest and most flavorful of the grilled specialties, and for the murgh tikka masala, tandoori chicken pieces in a pink and spicy tomato and onion sauce.

Lemon and cinnamon are the complementary seasonings for chicken in the South Indian murgh Madras, and a light green pepper, tomato, and onion saucing enriches the chicken in murgh Jalfrazie. Yogurt tenderizes lamb in two fine dishes—the khara pasande, which also contains onions and tomatoes, and the rogan josh, sweetly accented with almonds. Most unusual and intriguing is crab Malabar, perfumed with fennel and green coriander, mixed with tomato.

Indian vegetarian dishes are so satisfying one has no sense of deprivation when eating them, the spices filling the mouth to lend a sense of completeness. The best examples here are the cheese cooked with spices (paneer Jalfrazie), the curried cauliflower and potatoes (aloo gobi masala), and the grilled eggplant (bayngan bhurta). Rice biryanis are rich as Croesus, whether you choose the simple vegetable version, the lamb with raisins and nuts, or the herbed Punjabi special. All are made with basmati rice, which adds its characteristic sweet-nut flavor. Not all breads are equally good. I concentrate on the vegetarian paratha and the onion-filled kulcha. Cucumber, mint, and yogurt are combined in the cooling raita sauce, and there are lively chutneys, my favorite being the onion and the mint.

As always, I steer away from sugary Indian desserts and opt for the rice pudding, kheer, and the rosewater and pistachio sherbet-ice cream, kulfi.

If Darbar rates two stars instead of three, it is because of the difference between food and service upstairs and down, the stuffiness of the downstairs dining room, and an occasional lapse in the kitchen that renders all sauces virtually identical. Then, too, they fail to make food truly spicy when requested, even for the vindaloo curries.

DAWAT

210 East 58th Street, between Second and Third avenues
Telephone: 355-7555

Favorite meal:
Shared by two to four
Spiced shrimp in curry leaves (Madhur Jaffrey's baghari jhinga)
Pastry turnover (vegetable samosa)
Tandoori grilled chicken
Hotly spiced lamb curry (lamb vindaloo)
String beans with freshly grated coconut (Maharashtrian-style farasvi bhaji)
Flat bread (nan)
Steamed basmati rice
Mango or coconut ice cream
Other favorite dishes: Ground lamb patties (shami kebob); fritters of spinach leaves and potato skins (Madhur Jaffrey's bhaja); chick-peas, crisp wafers, and potatoes in a spicy yogurt and tamarind sauce (dahi aloo poori); all soups; minced lamb (tandoori grilled seekh kebob); shrimp in a spicy sauce of herbs, garlic and ginger (shrimp bhuna); chicken or lamb in spinach sauce (sag); chicken in a mild tomato cream sauce (chicken tikka masala); lamb slices in a creamy, spiced sauce (lamb pasanada); okra with onions and dried mango (bhindi masala); baked eggplant; flat bread stuffed with onion and coriander (onion kulcha); bread with dried fruits or nuts (nan-e-Dawat); whole wheat griddle bread with mint (pudinay ka paratha); rice with vegetables (vegetable biryani); spiced wafers (pappadum); yogurt sauce with tomato and mint (timarar raita); yogurt sauce with cucumber (kheer raita); rice pudding with cardamom and pistachios (special kheer).
Setting: Modern, atmospheric dining room with folk art touches; front section is more comfortable than back because it is quieter and brighter, but it is the smoking section.
Service: Well-meaning and polite if obsequious, but distracted and often slow.
Dress code: None.
Facilities for private parties: Downstairs banquet room accommodates 75 to 100. Food on the menu is available for take-out at menu prices and can be delivered free within 10 blocks. Otherwise cab fare is added. Will cater off premises for a minimum of 40 to 50 people.
Hours: Lunch and dinner, Monday through Saturday. Dinner only, Sunday.
Reservations: Generally necessary.
Prices: Inexpensive to moderately expensive.
Credit cards: AE, CB, DC, MC, V.

Intriguing innovations in food and decor make this Indian restaurant most welcome. The first thing you've probably heard about

Dawat is that its dishes were created by Madhur Jaffrey, the elegant Indian actress and cooking-school teacher whose books are perhaps the best ever done on that country's diversely spiced cuisine. You are not likely to forget that here, as her book is on display, and her name all over the menu, identifying dishes she developed.

Those specialties, plus the modern setting subtly tinted in glowing peach and watery blue and the brightly painted folk head carvings, suggest India without resorting to the usual brass and pierced wooden screen clichés. The dining room is comfortably spacious and divided into front and back sections—the first being quieter with better lighting, but the noisy back offering roomier tables and a view of the glassed-in kitchen. There, wonders are performed in the tandoor, a clay oven from which rosily spiced chicken, chunks of lamb, and the ground lamb seekh kebobs emerge pungent, savory, and miraculously moist, clearly the best tandoori grilling in the city.

Served atop sizzling onion slivers and doused with fresh lemon juice, those tandoori specialties are enriched by the textural contrasts of mellow rice dishes such as the fragrant steamed basmati long-grained rice, or the biryani, studded with vegetables. For a perfect meal, add the yogurt sauce, raita, whether with cucumber or tomato and mint, and the seductive vegetables, as exemplified by the grilled eggplant slices, the firm okra with onions and dried mango, or the bits of string beans mingling with snowy, fresh gratings of coconut.

Considering how much better the tandoori grilling is here than elsewhere, it's no wonder I am a bit ahead of the game, for surely everyone will want to begin with a few of the engaging appetizers or soups. Madhur Jaffrey's baghari jhinga, a saucy, spicy blend of shrimp heightened by mustard seeds and garlic, and scented with dry, baylike curry leaves, is one of the best starters, closely followed by the mixed-to-order salad, dahi aloo poori, a tossing of crisp bits of wafers, potatoes, and chick-peas in a tamarind-sparked yogurt sauce. It is better than the other version, bhel poori, so overladen with cardamom it is reminiscent of Vicks VapoRub. The tiny patties of ground lamb, shami kebob, are peppery and good, as are the crunchy pastry domes, vegetable samosas. The most unusual appetizers are the bhaja, leaves of spinach and potato skins battered and deep-fried.

Soups are also far above average. The standard mulligatawny arrives with a very unstandard freshness, a heady blend of chicken stock, fresh lemon juice, puréed yellow peas, and soft spices. Dal soup is a pale golden cream of lentils with toasted croutons, and the best, the green pea soup, is a soft celadon broth lifted with fresh ginger and cumin. All are served tepid, unless requested hot. Make that request and nibble some of the peppery, tissue-thin pappadum wafers, and you'll be off to a savory start.

It is always a good idea to complement the simple grilled meat with one or two curry sauced selections. At Dawat, the best of those is the blastingly hot lamb vindaloo. The sparkling zapping of chili peppers, black pepper, turmeric, garlic, ginger, and more gives this vindaloo the authentic belt it needs. More subtle but stingingly spiced are the roseate shrimp bhuna, the chicken sag, and the lamb sag gosht, the latter two in a frothy spinach purée. More mildly seasoned but palate-diverting is chicken tikka masala, the tandoori grilled boneless chicken pieces nurtured by a sauce of tomato and cream. Creamy, with a golden hue, lamb pasanda has a nice brassy edge to it.

All of these foods can be portioned out for you by the waiters, but I prefer them family style to avoid having everything mixed on the plate at once. Food is kept hot in small, attractive covered copper casseroles.

Although most of Dawat's food is excellent, not all offerings are recommendable. Kerala-style shrimp one night were stale and tasted mildly of iodine. Home-style rogan josh, a goat curry, disappointed because the meat was sinewy and full of cartilage. A slightly too delicate flavor flaws chicken jal frazie with sautéed vegetables; and, among all the breads tried, only a few held real interest—the crisp, thin onion-filled kulcha and the mint-brightened, whole wheat pancake bread, pudinay ka paratha. Poori arrives dry and crumbling, and the tandoori baked nan is greasy, but there is a diverting texture of dried fruits or nuts in the nan-e-Dawat.

Indian desserts are not among my favorites, but the coconut and mango ice creams here are refreshing, as is the strangely starchy but appealing kheer, a rice pudding scented with cardamom and flecked with pistachios. Spiced tea is a fine finish, and beer is my beverage of choice with the food.

My service of choice would be less obsequious and more efficient. Waiters gaze off into the distance and forget what is being ordered, the kitchen slows at peak times, and if a spoon is requested, it might be one that was used for serving, brushed off on a napkin by the waiter.

Despite its flaws, Dawat is by all odds the city's most ambitious and satisfying Indian restaurant, with a high average of culinary performance for so large a menu.

RAGA

57 West 48th Street, between Fifth and Sixth avenues
Telephone: 757-3450

Favorite meal:
Shared by four
Assorted hot appetizers
Lobster Malabar
Tandoori-grilled chicken
Lamb vindaloo
Roasted and mashed spiced eggplant (baingan bhurta)
Rice with fruits and nuts (Kashmiri pullao)
Puffed whole-wheat bread (puri)
Assorted chutneys
Yogurt and cucumber sauce (raita)
Mango ice cream

Other favorite dishes: Lentil crisps with potatoes in pungent yogurt sauce (dhal papri); shrimp in a spicy Creole-type sauce (shrimp Goa); salmon steak in ginger- and garlic-flavored tomato sauce (machali masala); tandoori chicken pieces in tomato-butter sauce (murg tikke makhani); chicken with green peppers, onions, and tomatoes (murg Jalfrazie); tandoori-grilled minced lamb (reshmi kebob); all lamb dishes; all rice specialties; all vegetarian specialties; flatbread baked in tandoor (nan); flat bread stuffed with onions (onion kulcha); cardamom and saffron ice cream (kulfi); rice pudding (kheer); chocolate-cinnamon ice cream.

Setting: Handsomest Indian restaurant in the city; formal, elegant, spacious; dramatically decorated with carvings, musical instruments, colorful fabrics; alcoves are good for private conversations but are usually reserved for parties of five or more; try to avoid smaller tables for four in back of dining room; bar area is especially comfortable.

Service: Poor at lunch; at dinner it ranges from decent to indifferent.

Dress code: None.

Facilities for private parties: Downstairs room accommodates from 20 to 50.

Hours: Lunch, Monday through Friday. Dinner, seven days.

Reservations: Recommended, especially for lunch.

Prices: Moderate to moderately expensive.

Credit cards: AE, CB, DC, MC, V.

When Raga is good, it is very, very good and when it is bad, it is probably lunchtime. This is a restaurant I love for dinner but dislike for lunch. It is hard to understand why this is so, considering the solid citizens it attracts midday. Perhaps regulars get preferential treatment. But back to that later.

Dinner at Raga is a joy. The dining room is palatial with carved wood doorways, columns, and partitions, beautifully striped silks, and an array of lavishly crafted and painted Indian musical instruments such as sitars, flutes, veenas, and rubabs. The name Raga denotes a particular style of Indian music, and the musical theme is reiterated on most evenings, when live musicians play traditional pieces on these instruments.

The best tables set in romantic alcoves are for five or more, five being the most comfortable number. Otherwise there are cushiony banquettes. Only a few square tables in the back are too small for four, primarily because of all the breads, relishes, and rice dishes set down to make Indian food the delight it is.

Few cuisines light up the palate the way this one does. Spices such as chili, cardamom, turmeric, black and brown mustard seeds, various peppers, cinnamon, cloves, and ginger are contrasted with onions, garlic, mint, and tart tamarind. Soothing notes are to come by way of cool yogurt and the lentil sauce dhal to be spooned over the rich rice pullaos and biryanis. Basmati rice, with its sweet-nut flavor, is the basis for these dishes, and bits of lamb, vegetables, peas, or dried fruits and nuts add crunch and substance.

Most of this is handled expertly at Raga, with only the few lapses noted below. It is one place that does a fine job on assorted appetizers, the fritters known as pakoras and the vegetable turnovers that are samosas. Pieces of chicken marinated in yogurt and fried in batter are delicious (murg ke pakore), and the best of all is dhal papri, nutlike crunches of lentil-flour crisps tossed with potatoes and a tamarind-zapped yogurt sauce. Only two appetizers are disappointing—crab Goa, which is well spiced but based on fishy threads of crab meat, and the hideous oysters Bombay. It is hard to believe the kitchen starts with freshly shucked oysters, so curled, gray, and metallic-tasting are these specimens; at a recent lunch the oil in their sauce was rancid.

On to more pleasant thoughts. Tandoori chicken, with its red coloring and brassy spicing, and the tandoori-broiled ground lamb kebobs (reshmi kebob) arrive moist and succulent. An unusual and delectable dish is the machali masala, two thick, very fresh salmon steaks gentled in a golden sauce of ginger, garlic, tomato, and onion, all applied with enough finesse to allow the salmon's own richness to come through. Another fine seafood choice is lobster Malabar, with a sauce much like that of the salmon but a bit creamier. One daily special, shrimp Goa, in a sort of Creole sauce, was good too, flawed only by a slight oversalting. But the shrimp were firm and fresh.

Vindaloo, the hottest of all curries, can be truly blistering if you insist on it that way when ordering, but be sure you mean it. I prefer that sauce on lamb, a version nicely executed here.

There are several good chicken dishes, among them the tandoori-broiled pieces that are simmered in a creamy, spiced tomato sauce (murg tikke makhani) and another with green peppers, tomatoes, and onions (murg Jalfrazie). Lean and fresh chunks of lamb in a verdant spinach sauce (gosht palak) or in herbed yogurt (gosht dahiwalla) combine heft with subtlety and are especially good with the rice dishes and the plain, pizzalike tandoori bread, nan, or the balloon puffs, puris. Other breads tend to be greasy.

Vegetarian specialties are excellent here, my favorites being the roasted eggplant (baingan bhurta), the cauliflower with potatoes (aloo bhaji), and the mixed vegetables with herbs and spices (subzi Jalfrazie). Add to all of this a red-hot onion chutney, the sharp mango chutney, and the comforting cucumber and yogurt sauce, raita, and you have the makings of a sublime meal. Even desserts are fine—"even" because they are usually cloying in Indian restaurants. But the almond and saffron ice cream, kulfi, the creamy rice pudding, kheer, and both the mango and chocolate-cinnamon ice creams are coolly refreshing. Indian beer is best with this food, and spiced tea is the right finish.

Given the general excellence of Raga in so many directions, it could well deserve three stars. What intervenes, however, is the service, which at best is adequate. At night there can be a certain impatience on the part of the staff, especially if they are in a hurry to wrap things up and go home. At my lunch experiences, service has bordered on the horrendous. Guests (especially women sans men) are directed to poor tables even when the better ones are empty. Orders are confused or forgotten, main courses may be brought before appetizers, and there is a long lapse between first and second courses. The food is less good midday and hints at too much precooking.

Having been in business since 1977, the management should have had time to straighten this out so that the beautiful food in the beautiful room will be just as beautifully served.

TANJORE

1229 First Avenue, between 66th and 67th streets
Telephone: 517-7578

Favorite meals:
Shared by two
Lentil-flour crisps, potatoes, and sweet chutney in yogurt (Tanjore chat)
Tandoori-grilled chicken
Spicy lamb curry (lamb vindaloo)
Vegetable and rice biryani
Cucumber and yogurt sauce (raita)
Pistachio ice cream (kulfi)
or

Shared by four to six
Assorted appetizers
Spiced cold chicken (chicken chat)
Tandoori-grilled cubes of lamb (boti kebob)
Tandoori chicken pieces simmered in butter-tomato sauce (chicken tikka masala)
Lamb with spinach sauce (lamb sagwala)
Rice and vegetable biryani
Mango ice cream
Other favorite dishes: Fried chicken wings (pakora); grilled pieces of lamb with onion on thin bread (kati kebob); spiced vegetable soup (shorba); all breads; all rice dishes; all vegetable dishes; tandoori-grilled ground lamb (seekh kebob); chicken with spinach, garlic, and ginger (tikka sagwala); hot curried chicken (chicken vindaloo); chicken in butter-tomato sauce (makhni chicken); cubes of lamb in spiced onion and tomato sauce (Tanjore rogan josh); onion chutney; mango chutney; creamy rice pudding with nuts and raisins (kheer); spiced yogurt drink (salted lassi).
Setting: Simple, attractive storefront café-restaurant with greenery and mirrors; ventilation could be improved.
Service: Polite, helpful, prompt, and concerned.
Dress code: None.
Facilities for private parties: Can accommodate up to 30.
Hours: Lunch and dinner, seven days.
Reservations: Necessary for dinner on Fridays and Saturdays and for more than four any night.
Prices: Inexpensive to moderate.
Credit cards: AE, MC, V.

Right from the first nibble of the spicy, crisp lentil-flour wafers, pappadum, you know something marvelous is about to happen. If it is all just a little less so than formerly, because of a decline in freshness of fish and seafood dishes and a tendency to overcook vegetables, it is still one of the more delightful if simply decorated Indian restaurants.

Ever since the dashingly handsome Ashok Seth opened this cheerful little storefront café-restaurant, it has turned out engaging food. And when the request for "double dynamite" is made, the curries can blister your gullet. Anyone less insistent than double dynamite will get those sauces mildly needling but not really hot; the kitchen applies a cautious hand because so often Americans ask for really hot spicing and then cannot eat it. "Dynamite" or "double dynamite" indicates that you're not just whistlin' "Dixie."

A really dazzling appetizer is the Tanjore chat, round, crisp puffs of lentil flour, tossed with diced potatoes, onion, sweet chutney, herbs, and a sourish tamarind sauce that contrasts with the yogurt. Chicken chat, marinated breast meat sunny with lemon and coriander, is a close second. All the fried vegetable pakoras and pastry turnovers (samosas) are impeccably done, and chicken wings pakora, marinated, battered, and fried, put their Buffalo cousins to shame. Tender nuggets of tandoori-grilled lamb and onions served in thin bread (boti kebob) is another substantial and tantalizing first course.

I remember the spiced, slightly tart vegetable soup, shorba, as being one of the best versions in the city. Incredible Indian breads—the pizzalike nan that bakes crusty in the tandoor oven, the version filled with lamb (keema nan) or an even heftier specialty fleshed out with chicken—are among the winners. Puffed-up puris, cheese-flavored batura, and aloo paratha layered with potatoes are just a few personal favorites. All rice biryanis and the peas pullao are moist, aromatic, and tantamount to main courses, especially the Shajahani biryani, with tandoori-grilled chicken filets, nuts, herbs, and bits of scrambled eggs. Basmati rice is used throughout, imparting its unique sweet-spice overtones to any combination.

Large quarters of marinated, spiced chicken grilled in the tandoor are moister and have more flavor than the boneless bits (tikka). Cubes of lamb (boti kebob) and ground lamb (seekh kebob) are other good tandoori grills. I prefer them to shrimp, which dry out, or to the assorted mixed grill.

Bits of tandoori-grilled chicken mellow in tomato-cream sauce (chicken tikka masala) or a gingery spinach cream sauce (tikka sagwala) are sprightly, as is the buttery chicken labeled makhni.

Double dynamite is the correct way to order vindaloo, and it's a curry equally enticing with chicken and lamb. Milder palates will appreciate fragrantly spiced lamb rogan josh or the lamb sagwala, in a froth of spinach. Korma is the mildest, creamiest of curries, and though the sauce is nicely turned out at the Tanjore, on one occasion the lamb itself seemed to have been cooked too long in advance.

Lively dips and chutneys are house triumphs. There is a green blend served with the giveaway pappadums that is much like Mexican tomatillo sauce, another that has a brassy tamarind belt, and a bright-red onion chutney that looks like chopped rubies and tastes like flame itself. After that the freshest, richest kulfi, the ice cream flavored with pistachio and rosewater, and the even creamier rice pudding, kheer, studded with nuts and raisins, are welcome, as is the peach-colored mango ice cream.

Lassi, a thin yogurt drink, is lovely with this food. I favor the spiced or plain variations to the sweet. Otherwise, I like Indian beer, the only alcoholic beverage served.

Mirrors and greenery add style to this café-restaurant. I just wish it would move to my neighborhood so I could dine there once a week.

ITALIAN

BICE

7 East 54th Street, between Fifth and Madison avenues
Telephone: 688-1999

Favorite meals:
Lunch
Lobster or seafood salad
Risotto with asparagus, chicken, or gorgonzola
Peach with peach sherbet
or
Dinner
Half order pappardelle with tomato and basil
Roast rack of veal
Mixed berries with ice cream
Other favorite dishes: Assorted hot appetizers, gnocchi with tomato and basil, all pastas, minestrone Milanese, grilled baby chicken, sautéed veal kidneys, calves' liver Veneziana, roast rabbit, chocolate-hazelnut ice cream (gelato giandvia).
Setting: Casual, stylish dining room with chic café-bar; comfortable seating but very noisy.
Service: Friendly and polite, if unevenly paced.
Dress code: None.
Facilities for private parties: Semi-private parties for 20 to 45 can be held on raised back alcove of dining room.
Hours: Lunch and dinner, seven days.
Reservations: Strongly recommended.
Prices: Moderately expensive.
Credit cards: AE.

Opened in the summer of 1987, Bice immediately divided local restaurant buffs into two camps: those who would never enter again because of the somewhat insane service that prevailed at first, and those who would suffer almost anything for the light, stylish, and flavorful interpretations of more or less Milanese food. Never badly treated even when I was unrecognized, I became a follower of the latter camp and remain one.

The New York offspring of da Bice, a 63-year-old Milan institution much favored by the high fashion set, Bice immediately attracted the same very "W" crowd, mid-summer, when many other fashionable dining places were closed for vacation. Given their following and the limited choice, Bice (pronounced BEECH-eh) became mobbed. "What can I do? Everyone wants a table and everyone who calls seems to be a president of something!" says Roberto Ruggeri, whose mother, Bice (for Beatrice), is the founder of the original. Povero! Meanwhile, he has piled up ill will and so resolved to say no and to seat promptly—a blessing because waiting when the smart little bar was jammed with unkempt Eurotrash was a less than felicitous beginning and now occurs only occasionally.

Once inside, however, the glowing beauty of this elegantly tailored room takes over. Designed by Adam Tihany, with candlelight walls, silver-gold glints, and smart little Art Deco flower prints, it has all the cool, sexy appeal of a silk shirt by Armani. Banquettes and chairs are equally comfortable as is the lighting. Not so the acoustics, as the charm of the handsome room is marred by the head-splitting din.

If uneven pacing of service sometimes leaves much to be desired, the staff never has exhibited a trace of snobbishness or pretentiousness even on the two visits when I was not recognized. On all counts, Bice is far better at lunch than at dinner, but food has always ranged from acceptable to sensational, and rarely poor.

At both meals there are sprightly and refreshing appetizer salads, all with a supple, fruity Lucca olive oil which Ruggeri claims to have exclusive dibs on. Cool, plump, and succulent lobster salad nests on snappy arugula, mixed seafood takes on a mellow richness with its oil and lemon dousing, and creamy mozzarella with ripe tomatoes and basil is classically impeccable.

For heartier appetizers there is a hot assortment combining a roulade of eggplant filled with ricotta and gentled with tomato, baked spiedini of tomato and mozzarella, and a few pieces of the warm toast slices crostini, with toppings such as chicken livers or mushrooms. Half orders of pasta are served, though they cost two thirds of the full price and are meagerly portioned. But all have been sublime—light, savory, perfectly cooked. That goes for baked cannelloni with sausage and cheese filling and a gossamer tomato glaze, the Apuglia pasta, orecchiette (little ears) tossed with flowerets of broccoli in a garlic-oil dressing, linguine with clams or mussels, and delicate, puffy tortelloni—round ravioli with spinach and cheese filling nestled in a creamy cheese sauce. Quill-shaped penne in a zesty tomato sauce and the wide ribbons of pappardelle mingling with basil-scented tomato and melting mozzarella vie with the fettuccine that gets a crunchy edge of bitterness from radicchio and a belt of lustiness from the Italian bacon, pancetta. Minestrone takes on new meaning, that classic vegetable soup here rendered with a verdant belt of pesto sauce and a lacing of olive oil. Risotto, whether the saffron-gilded Milanese style, or flecked with asparagus or spiked with gorgonzola, has almost always been juicily, soothingly impeccable—"almost," because one night the risotto Milanese served with osso buco lacked salt, character, and just about everything else.

That osso buco, in fact, represents the most serious failure I sampled—thin cuts of meat that were dry and tasteless instead of the thick, melting slabs of braised shank they should be. Nor was it helped by a puerile tomato sauce. On a happier note there is the rosemary and oregano-perfumed grilled baby chicken—moist within, with a nicely burnished skin—and the pale pink roast veal set off by rosemary-flavored roast potatoes.

Also delicious are tender chunks of rabbit in herb sauce, medallions of roast veal blanketed with olive and caper-dotted tomato sauce, and perfect sliced kidneys sautéed with garlic and butter so skillfully done that they were rosy at the center with just the right outer crackle. Similarly well-executed is fresh, bright calves' liver Veneziana with satiny sautéed onions and an accent of white wine. I've had crisper and more flavorful veal cutlet Milanese, and though the carpaccio is based on plenty of thinly sliced, rose-red beef, it is obliterated by a topping of arugula and shaved Parmesan. Grilled swordfish is thoroughly cooked but still moist—no easy task, but it is accomplished here and the olive, caper, and tomato sauce adds zestiness.

Baked desserts need work. So far, the cheesecake is closer to Sara Lee than to the true Italian pizza de ricotta—thin, overly sweet, and mushy, flaws exacerbated by an intense raspberry sauce. Two-crust apple pie with a sort of thick applesauce filling was sublime on two tries, but limp, sodden, and insipid on three others. Better choices are the frothy, custard-like gelati—the Italian ice cream here available in wonderful vanilla that mixes well with berries or, best of all, the chocolate and hazelnut gianduia that even the most die-hard dieter will not be able to resist.

The wine list has an excellent range at prices that seem fair by restaurant standards. That means a two- to three-time mark-up over retail store prices. There are several decent buys at $15, most notably the rugged ruby-red house Chianti Riserva. More elegantly robust yet subtle selections are the velvety 1980 Poggione Brunello di Montalcino and the Rubesco Riserva each at $35.

Right now Ruggeri is busy with yet another Bice in Beverly Hills. Let's hope he is not dividing his attention so much that the New York branch will suffer.

CENT' ANNI

50 Carmine Street, between Bleecker and Bedford streets,
just west of Sixth Avenue
Telephone: 989-9494

Favorite meals:
Baked soup of beans, cabbage, leek, toast, and cheese (zuppa ortolana)
Broiled squab diavolo
Salad Cent' Anni, shared by two
Chocolate cake with chocolate curls, shared by two
or
Seafood salad (insalata di pesce), shared by two
Wide pasta with rabbit, onions, and tomatoes (pappardelle al coniglio), shared by two
Veal chop with sage
Tirami sù
Other favorite dishes: Sautéed wild mushrooms; beans stewed with tomatoes and garlic; buffalo mozzarella with herbs; roast pepper with anchovies (peperoni arrostiti); fettuccine with smoked salmon in cream; capellini with lobster and clams; wide pasta with porcini mushrooms; pasta shells with bacon, tomato, and onion (amatriciana); red snapper Livornese with clams and mussels; grilled marinated pheasant or chicken; grilled rack of lamb (costolette di agnello); mixed grill with rabbit, lamb, quail, and sausage (grigliata mista); cold zabaglione.
Setting: Pleasant, modern storefront dining room with small, closely set tables; moderately noisy.
Service: Often cool and unsmiling, but efficient.
Dress code: None.
Facilities for private parties: None.
Hours: Lunch, Monday through Friday. Dinner, seven days. Closed Christmas, New Year's, and Thanksgiving and for two weeks toward the end of July when there is a street festival in the area.
Reservations: Necessary.
Prices: Moderate to moderately expensive.
Credit cards: AE.

Raffish food, Tuscan and otherwise, in a relaxed storefront café setting is the combination that continues to draw me back to Cent' Anni. This simple, bright, modern trattoria, with its very close-set, small tables, generally reasonable noise level, and stylish casualness, is the setting for consistently excellent culinary wonders both lean and lavish. Service, unfortunately, is less friendly and hospitable than formerly, and so offhand that two stars seem more appropriate than the former three.

From the small stand at the doorway, where desserts and seasonal provender are displayed, a waiter will bring the latest porcini or oyster mushrooms to tempt a diner, and either is earthy and succulent, sautéed alone or wound into some buttery pasta. Bay scallops, lobster, shrimp, and squid get an efficacious bathing of olive oil, lemon, parsley, and crunches of celery for the seafood salad. An assorted cold antipasto can include chewy, peppery prosciutto that exudes the ripeness of age and tiny rounds of buffalo mozzarella, as good with roasted peppers as they are with fresh or sun-dried tomatoes. Beans are among the glories of the Tuscan kitchen, and two preparations at Cent' Anni show them off at their best. Simmered all'uccelletto with tomato and garlic, they are served ever-so-slightly warm as an appetizer. Or they can be baked into the irresistibly lusty meal-in-itself soup zuppa ortolana, along with cabbage, leeks, toast, and a dusting of grated Parmesan.

Not usually a fan of fettuccine with salmon, I find that dish exquisite as prepared in this kitchen. Thick chunks of the smoked salmon, mildly woodsy and moist, are tossed with the green and white pasta along with a sheer cream and butter sauce. Big, chewy rigatoni or hollow shells can be had at times all'amatriciana with prosciutto, tomatoes, and onions or with a simpler filetto di pomodoro sauce or earthy porcini. Forced to pick my favorite pasta at Cent' Anni, I would deliberate between the wide, flat noodles called pappardelle with a rich topping of rabbit, onions, carrots, and tomatoes or the fine capellini with tomato, lobster, and clams.

Rabbit alla Fiorentina is again simmered with onions, carrots, and tomatoes enlivened by white wine for a main course, and there are particularly good grilled birds—all butterflied, marinated, and charred so that the skin takes on a herbaceous burnishing while the meat remains elegantly dewy. Pheasant, Cornish hen, and, best of all, squab are prepared this way and served with sautéed potatoes, heady with rosemary, and a simple vegetable such as string beans, spinach, or escarole—the sort of accompaniment that goes to virtually every table. The lustiest appetites will be not only satisfied but enchanted, as I have been, with the mixed grill—rabbit, lamb, sausage, and quail—for a meaty binge that might thrombose Jane Brody but never fails to delight me.

A thick, near animal that is the gigantic veal chop is sautéed and sauced with fresh sage and white wine for a main course of stunning proportions, in both size and flavor. For lighter eaters there is red snapper, either grilled and brushed with oil and lemon or simmered with clams, mussels, and tomato and capers, Livornese style.

Less beguiling are such complications as veal with oil, mushrooms, artichokes, and tomatoes, a case of overkill, and a highly touted osso buco, which though acceptable was cooked short of the fall-off-the-bone tenderness that makes the dish the dream it is. Its sauce, however, was velvety and balanced, but I have a hard time contemplating that dish without a slab of grilled polenta or some risotto to absorb the meat juices and gravy. Lobster fra diavolo is also disappointing—lacking in the hot pepper needed to "devil" it, and submerged under a mound of calamari. Fruit tarts have been dull, but tirami sù, the layering of soft sponge cake, custard, and coffee cream dusted with cocoa, is cool and gentle. There is a lovely chocolate layer cake topped with thick curls of milk chocolate that I believe to be Hershey's. If not, it's a dead ringer and as utilized here raises usually insipid milk chocolate to new heights.

DA UMBERTO

107 West 17th Street, between Sixth and Seventh avenues
Telephone: 989-0303

Favorite meals:
Assortment of vegetable antipasto, shared by two or more
Pasta with white beans in tomato sauce (rigatoni fagiolata), half order
Grilled herbed chicken
Napoleon
or
Air-dried beef (bresaola) with raw artichokes, shared by two
Gnocchi all'arrabbiata (a pungent tomato sauce)
Veal chop with cognac
Cheesecake
Other favorite dishes: Prosciutto; fish salad (insalata di pesce); crostini of polenta with gorgonzola; bean, cabbage, and bread soup (ribollita); minestrone; capellini with lobster sauce; pasta primavera (with vegetables); risotto verde (with spinach); fish and shellfish in tomato broth (zuppa di pesce); lobster cooked with shellfish; roasted rabbit (coniglio al forno); sweetbreads with lemon and capers; veal cutlet Milanese with arugula and tomato salad; roast pork with rosemary; tirami sù; chocolate cake.
Setting: Simple, stylishly tailored trattoria with café atmosphere and glassed-in kitchen. Very noisy, especially in front room.
Service: Quick, friendly, casual, and occasionally unprofessional.
Dress code: None.
Facilities for private parties: None.
Hours: Lunch, Monday through Friday. Dinner, Monday through Saturday. Open late, Friday and Saturday. Closed Sunday.
Reservations: Necessary.
Prices: Moderately expensive.
Credit cards: AE.

How good can vegetables be? Go to this stunning trattoria in Chelsea and find out. Formerly a partner in the excellent Cent' Anni, Umberto Assante is working that same Tuscan magic on this menu, albeit with a skillful chef from Genoa. They have created a dazzling assortment of vegetables and salads, meant as antipasto, that is lined up on two groaning boards. Had della Robbia chosen to sculpt cooked vegetables instead of fruit, these oil-slicked, jewel-toned zucchini and eggplants, artichokes, tomatoes, peppers, and olives would have served as perfect models. Some are stuffed, none more deliciously than the meat-filled eggplant slices, the packets of escarole baked with ricotta filling, or the Swiss chard with cheese, sausage, and a whiff of nutmeg.

One or an assortment of these can be had as a starter. There are other appetizers too, but none that quite matches this staggering array. Polenta, baked as a crostini with a slathering of melted gorgonzola, is a hefty choice, and the chewy, air-dried beef, bresaola, is lovely under a mantle of slivered, marinated baby artichokes. But that, like the fine prosciutto, is too lavishly portioned for one as a starter, so plan to share.

Otherwise you will not have room for one of the rich soups or pastas. There is a fragrant green minestrone rarely equaled around town, and ribollita, the Florentine specialty of cabbage, beans, and bread sprinkled with cheese. If not soup then pasta, avoiding only the disappointing linguine with clam sauce that was undersalted and tainted with an iodine aroma, and the somewhat watery pappardelle with porcini. Among the best choices are the light airy dumplings, gnocchi, in a spicy arrabbiata tomato sauce and the rigatoni fagiolata, the tubular pasta given substance with white beans in a lightly garlicked tomato froth. Quill-shaped penne with a thick, rich meat and tomato sauce (strascinate), risotto with a verdant mix of green herbs, and fine angels' hair pasta with lobster are other delectable choices. Panzotti, the Ligurian version of ravioli filled with green herbs and sauced with walnuts, would be sublime if served truly hot, as they were not, nor was an otherwise fine lasagne.

Service can, in fact, be slow, accounting for the cold food now and then. But when the food does come, it is generally worth the wait.

You will not mind having waited after pasta if the main course is the generous zuppa de pesce complete with fish and shellfish (even better in a deep bowl than on the flat plate used here) or the even more grandiose lobster marechiare, which by a variety of names is a collection of shellfish clustered around that great crustacean, all bathed in a hotly peppered tomato sauce. Flattened, grilled chicken, crusty on the outside and mellow within, is among lighter main courses.

Lustier eaters might opt for the thick, pink veal chop laced with cognac or the rosemary-scented roast rabbit or pork. Lemon and capers give a nice, sharp edge to pan-sautéed sweetbreads, and the crisply breaded veal cutlet Milanese profits from a flourish of arugula and cut tomatoes. Calves' liver sautéed with sage can be just about the world's best, but other times it emerges soupy and dark. And quails taste twice-heated, delicate though they are with a herb stuffing. Over-saucing has become a consistent flaw, delicious as the sauces are.

Cavils aside, there are tempting desserts, none better than the true, high, moist Italian cheesecake scented with orange and lemon and crackling with citron, the domed chocolate mousse cake, the pears baked in white wine with sticks of cinnamon, or the crisp napoleon, its flakes of puff pastry intersticed with velvety thick, eggy pastry cream, like cream puffs at Italian weddings. Tirami sù, the now-cliché layering of coffee- or rum-soaked cake with cream, chocolate, and powdered coffee or cinnamon, is almost as good as it gets.

The wine list is not quite stabilized and some of the better buys are not always available. Rose-gold glazed walls, bare floors, and exposed air ducts give this restaurant an informal, authoritative look. Unfortunately, it is head-splittingly noisy, though somewhat less so in the back room, which affords a view of the glassed-in kitchen.

ERMINIA

250 East 83rd Street, between Second and Third avenues
Telephone: 879-4284

Favorite meal:
Pasta with sausage and broccoli (orecchiette Erminia), half portion
Lobster fra diavolo with shrimp, clams, and mussels
Chocolate mousse or tartufo
Other favorite dishes: Homemade mozzarella with roasted peppers and tomatoes; artichokes sautéed in olive oil (carciofi alla Giudia); steamed clams and mussels in tomato sauce; pasta with tomato, olives, garlic, and veal (vermicelli pizzaiola); angels' hair pasta with vegetables (capellini primavera); pasta with white clam sauce (linguine alle vongole); fettuccine with porcini; fish and shellfish soup-stew (zuppa di pesce); squid with tomato-basil sauce baked in a bag (calamari in cartoccio); veal sautéed with peppers and capers in tomato sauce (scaloppina di vitello pizzaiola); chicken and sausages sautéed with herbs (pollo e salsiccia); beef, lamb, chicken, and sausage grilled on a skewer (spiedino di carne); chicken grilled over wood (pollo alla legna).
Setting: Small, rustic Tuscan-farmhouse decor; crowded and moderately noisy.
Service: Efficient but a little offhand and pushy.
Dress code: None is enforced, though ties are preferred for men.
Facilities for private parties: Will close for parties of 30 to 35.
Hours: Dinner, Monday through Saturday. Closed Sunday and major holidays.
Reservations: Necessary.
Prices: Moderately expensive.
Credit cards: AE.

Named for Erminia, the mother of the Lattanzi restaurant family, this tiny, rough, wood-paneled trattoria, with its farm tools, flowers, and candlelight, has grown on me gradually. Opened in 1983, it features the lush appetizers and pastas the Lattanzis are known for but adds simple grills of meat and poultry done over a wood fire. Oddly enough, those grills are less engaging than some of the other cooked dishes turned out here, which are the real attractions that draw me back.

The rustic setting has a special charm in New York, affording one a chance to feel as if in a country inn. Though crowded, the space seems to work; the noise level is high but less clatteringly intrusive than it might be because of the wood surfaces. The only pretentious touch is the dress of the staff; dinner jackets do not seem as appropriate as shirtsleeves and aprons.

Among Lattanzi signature dishes are the mellow artichokes sautéed with garlic in olive oil, delicious even though they are not the true, crisply fried carciofi Giudia promised in the billing. Coolly creamy homemade mozzarella gets a combined sweet-acidic edge from the garnish of roasted peppers and tomatoes, and a lightly garlicked tomato broth adds luster to steamed mussels and clams.

Linguine with white clam sauce has the right touch of garlic that is lightly golden brown, and the thin spaghetti, capellini, is tossed with flecks of vegetables, primavera style. Pastas at Erminia that lend themselves especially well to the simple grilled meats include the Apuglia specialty orecchiette (little ears), a shell-like form that adds a tender bite to bits of broccoli and sweet sausage. The standard pizzaiola sauce gets a sustaining addition of julienne strips of veal to mingle with olives, tomatoes, and salty Gaeta black olives, and woodsy porcini add earthiness to fettuccine touched with cream. The only pasta that doesn't quite work is the sticky combination of wide pappardelle with ricotta, the result being too bland and milky.

The lusty Neapolitan seafood extravaganza, lobster fra diavolo, is garnished with fresh, sweet clams, mussels, and shrimp all swathed in a pungent garlic and spicy tomato sauce. Similarly rich and with irresistible counterpoints of seafood, garlic, herbs, and tomato flavors are the Italian fish soup-stew, zuppa di pesce, and the rings and tentacles of squid baked in cartoccio—a big envelope or bag of foil. Once opened, the steamy ingredients send forth enticing aromas of flavors yet to come. Such dishes, as well as the sautéed nuggets of boneless chicken and sweet sausage with the sweet-sour accents of balsamic vinegar and the thin veal scaloppina with a pizzaiola sauce, are the surprise best choices at Erminia's.

Among grilled meats the best are the baby chicken, the veal chop if ordered without leaves of mushy basil on top, and the skewer of beef, lamb, chicken, and sausage. Other options, including the skewer of mixed seafood, tend to be dry. The wine list is limited but serviceable, with no surprises.

Because the Lattanzis vary the styles of their special dishes from one restaurant to another, the napoleon that is brilliant at Trastevere is here rendered thinner, less opulent, and, therefore, less interesting. Instead, finish with the velvety bittersweet chocolate mousse or the tartufo.

Too bad the family manager here joins friends, sitting with his back to the room and not bothering to say good-night or thank-you to departing guests.

FELIDIA

243 East 58th Street, between Second and Third avenues
Telephone: 758-1479

Favorite meals:
Lunch
Pasta with game sauce (fuzi all'fortuna del cacciatore), half portion
Grilled Italian red snapper with garlic, parsley, and olive oil
Mixed green salad
Fresh fruit or berries
or
Dinner
Assorted cold fish appetizers
Gnocchi al pesto, shared by two
or
Risotto with white truffles or seafood, shared by two
Roast baby lamb or braised squab (piccione al tegame)
Fresh fruit or berries
Other favorite dishes: Crostini of polenta with porcini mushrooms in season; sautéed wild mushrooms (porcini saltati); green and white pasta with mushrooms (paglia e fieno al funghi); cornmeal polenta with game; pasta with mushrooms, sausage, tomato, and ricotta (occhio di lupo alla boscaiola); wild mushroom risotto; pasta al pesto; fried calamari; red snapper with polenta; calves' liver Veneziana; sweetbreads with lemon sauce (animelle di vitello); veal cutlet Milanese, Valdostana, or pizzaiola; chicken with peppery wine sauce (arrabbiata); venison; roast veal; pheasant; beef paillard; cheesecake.
Setting: Tiles and natural wood create a stylish, casual modern dining room with urbane overtones; tables are uncomfortably cramped, noise is deafening, and lighting is inadequate in some areas. Non-smoking area is upstairs.
Service: Good but awkward because of tight space, so that there is much reaching across diners; sometimes slow before main course.
Dress code: Jackets required for men.
Facilities for private parties: One private room seats up to 50.
Hours: Lunch, Monday through Friday. Dinner, Monday through Saturday, until midnight. Closed Sunday and all major holidays and first three weeks in July.
Reservations: Necessary.
Prices: Expensive.
Credit cards: AE, CB, DC, MC, V.

Felidia is a restaurant I enjoy going to now and then despite itself, because its kitchen, overseen by Lidia Bastianich, does some unusual dishes of her native Friuli that are delicious and not available in abundance elsewhere. Versions of the cornmeal porridge polenta served with truffles, wild mushrooms, game, or red snapper, as well as various risotto dishes, are the attractions here, as are a variety of game dishes (venison, pheasant, squab) and innards.

For such dishes that are best eaten in fall and winter, I will withstand considerable discomfort from the jam-packed dining room, with its deafening din and generally inadequate lighting. When my husband could not read the wine list at one dinner, Mrs. Bastianich produced a flashlight she had at the ready, a necessity that should have told her brighter lighting is in order. (You also need a flashlight to read the check, perhaps even more to the point.) The setting, with pink terra-cotta tiles, white walls, and polished natural wood, is pretty enough, suggesting a Mexican-Greek island with Italian provincial overtones, but pretty is as pretty does, and this does not quite work.

A purer strain of inspiration is reflected in the menu, and a fine starting point for a meal is the focaccia, a chewy, yeasty pizzalike flat bread, fine with aperitifs. Bruschetta, toasted bread brushed with oil, is offered most times and is a good foil for the best appetizer, an assortment of beautifully fresh and sparkling seafood salads that unexpectedly includes tripe vinaigrette; it is one of the few interpretations of the spongy innard that I can get down. (Even then, I put a piece in my mouth and wash it down with wine, as though I were taking an aspirin.) That, of course, is a personal dislike, but even I know this tripe is very well prepared. Good prosciutto is sometimes made of boar, and wild mushrooms in season are sautéed in oil and butter with a touch of lemon. They are even better topping a toasted slice of polenta. Wild mushrooms gentled with cream also have a nice bite with the green-and-white noodle combination paglia e fieno (straw and hay), and, again, polenta appears as a stick-to-the ribs course with game such as venison, pheasant, quail, or a mix of several.

The big round pasta known as wolf's eyes—occhio di lupo— holds a rich sauce of ricotta and sausage within the tubes to release a marvelous mouthful when chewed, and fuzi, a homemade, short bow-tie-pasta twist, also gets a smoky, earthy elegance from game sauce. Homemade pasta with a toothsome bite is wonderfully complemented by a pesto blend that also distinguishes airy green gnocchi. When white truffles or porcini are in season, I like them here in risotto, but seafood is a fine alternative.

There is a thickly cut, beautifully roasted veal or baby lamb rustico at Felidia that is much in the Abruzzese style of roasting and cutting. Veal also is dependable in breaded cutlets fried Milanese style or sandwiched with prosciutto and Fontina cheese, then fried Valdostana style. Pizzaiola, the pizzaman's blend of tomato, garlic, and oregano, is a surprise in this context and is lightly, delicately accomplished as a sauce for veal. Greaselessness and freshness distinguish the fried calamari rings and tentacles, and a peppery wine sauce is what angry chicken—pollo arrabbiata—is fired up about. On a more delicate note, there are white, moistly sautéed sweetbreads bright with a lemony dressing and grilled red snapper dressed with fresh lemon and oil. Calves' liver Veneziana and osso buco are far above average, as is grilled paillard of beef.

As good as the dishes mentioned are, a few preparations are blandly executed, tasting of overheated grease or lacking salt.

Baked desserts have seemed overly rich after previous courses, so fresh fruit is a more appropriate choice. An exception is the lofty, creamy cheesecake.

Late lunch—say about 1:45—is the optimum time at Felidia, when it is bright enough so one can see and only half-crowded so one can move and hear.

The upstairs balcony dining room is still a kind of Upper Siberia and is now set aside for non-smokers, but there is a stunning new room for private parties.

Wines are costly and "bargains" can be out of stock.

LATTANZI

361 West 46th Street, between Eighth and Ninth avenues
Telephone: 315-0980

Favorite meals:
Lunch
Mixed antipasto
Grilled scampi
Fresh fruit
or
Dinner
Artichokes cooked in olive oil with garlic (carciofi alla Giudea)
Homemade wide noodles with fresh tomato sauce (tortelloni al pomodoro), shared by two
Broiled chicken with rosemary
Cold zabaglione
or
Dinner
Fine pasta with shellfish (cappelletti con frutti de mare), shared by two
Grilled veal chop
Napoleon, shared by two

Other favorite dishes: Mixed green salad (insalata mista), smoked thin beef with arugula and Parmesan cheese (carpaccio affumicato), homemade mozzarella with tomatoes and basil, mussels in tomato broth (muscoli in brodetto), all pastas, chicken with peppers and onions in tomato sauce (pollo capriccioso), squid with tomato and peas (calamari Lattanzi), veal parmigiana, all desserts.
From Roman Jewish menu served after 8 P.M.: Dried beef with marinated zucchini (carne secca), combination appetizer, fettuccine with braised beef (stracotto), green lasagne, red snapper with raisins and vinegar (orata con uvetta), grilled lamb chops with rosemary and garlic (agnello al rosmarino), ricotta cheesecake (cassola).
Setting: Bright, attractive, brick-walled dining room with brassy, bright accessories and a big open grill.
Service: Polite, professional, and helpful.
Dress code: None.
Facilities for private parties: None.
Hours: Lunch, Monday through Friday. Dinner, Monday through Saturday. Open late, Friday and Saturday. Closed Sunday and all major holidays.
Reservations: Recommended, especially for lunch and before theater.
Prices: Moderate to moderately expensive.
Credit cards: AE.

The second-best thing gastronomically to happen in the Theater District in years (the first is Carolina just next door), Lattanzi is a bright, stylishly rustic, brick-walled restaurant that puts on one of the most entertaining shows in town, local playwrights, actors, and directors notwithstanding. The kitchen is good enough to attract an audience for its own sake, although its major appeal is to the lunch and pretheater crowd who want to be in the area. But from 8 o'clock on, it becomes a peaceful yet lively option for some delicious and innovative food, of the manner this same family has created in its other restaurants. (For the genealogy of Lattanzi, see Trastevere.) After 8 is also the time for the special menu of Roman Jewish classics, an intriguing cuisine from what is said to be history's oldest continuous Jewish community.

But even without those esoteric specials, the menu is full of enticements, only a bit less opulent and a bit less magical than those at the original Trastevere. Many of the same pastas appear here, just as succulently executed, but main courses are lighter and are generally grilled, a good idea considering the work or pretheater schedules of most of the clientele.

One Roman Jewish special that is on all menus is carciofi ala Giudea, artichokes here sautéed in olive oil with garlic. Although delicious, this preparation is not authentic, the real version being whole artichokes pressed open and deep-fried to golden crispness. Nevertheless, the good oil and fresh artichoke hearts make for an enticing first course. Carpaccio of smoked beef that is still rare—a nice change from the standard raw meat—has arugula and Parmesan accompaniments. Homemade mozzarella with tomatoes is as tempting as the shiny mussels in a heady tomato broth. Sautéed porcini mushrooms have had the unpleasant aftertaste of overheated oil, and the assorted antipasto is heavy going before most other courses.

It would be sad to miss one of the pastas, and orders can be split for a $1 charge. Though half orders are possible without sharing, they cost $8, more than half of the $14 full price. Cavil aside, we can go on to the fresh fettuccine Lattanzi tossed with peas, mushrooms, and cream; the thick strands of bucatini amatriciana, meaning there is a satisfying sauce of tomato, onion, and Italian bacon; and my beloved linguine with white clam sauce, steamy hot, aromatic with garlic, and full of the seaside freshness only clams can impart. Fine spaghettini is easily twirled around flecks of vegetables bound by a gossamer cream sauce (capellini primavera), and the floppy tortelloni are simple, classic, and lovely in a marinara sauce. Porcini served with fettuccine is worth having in season.

The same sublime fish soup-stew, zuppa di pesce, with its mussels, clams, fish, and squid, is made here as at Trastevere, and squid alone gets a slightly different treatment, being more lightly presented with tomato, garlic, peas, and basil. Grilled herbed chicken and chops are particular specials, always moist within and gently charred without. Scampi-style shrimp, whether grilled or sautéed with oil and garlic, are among the lightest of main courses. The menu, by the way, offers to prepare dietetic or vegetarian dishes on request, but don't let that worry you. The chef's heart and soul are firmly committed to lusty dishes.

The Roman Jewish menu has its own diverting repertory, including a crostini of chicken livers on toast with artichokes and a combination appetizer that includes marinated eggplant, fresh mozzarella, and the fried rice balls, suppli al telefono. Literally, that means telephone wires, referring to the stringiness of the melted cheese in the rice croquettes.

Zucchini wilted in olive oil is tossed with the short quill-shaped penne, and little ears, orecchiette, is the pasta best suited to the topping of tuna fish, tomato, olive oil, and garlic on the same menu. Pasta keeps me away from the soups on this menu—but maybe one day I'll be strong and deviate. Stracotto is a gentle, crumbling, long-cooked pot roast, and it is an enrichment on fettuccine, while green lasagne layers with artichokes, onions, and tomatoes is a Roman Jewish vegetarian delectable that grinds about as many axes as one dish can be expected to.

As improbable as red snapper with raisins and vinegar may sound, the result is surprisingly good, with a delicate sweet-sour balance well known in all Jewish cooking. Veal scaloppine with artichokes, roast chicken, and lamb with rosemary and garlic are other temptations on this special menu.

The regular Lattanzi menu includes the same napoleon and cream puff miracles as at Trastevere, and the Jewish menu adds yet another—cassola, a sort of ricotta cheese and egg combination, between a cake and thin soufflé. Incidentally, Jewish does not mean kosher here, as anyone familiar with that dietary requirement can tell by the presence of cheese and meat on the same menu.

The help at Lattanzi tends to be better to unknowns than at Trastevere, and prices are slightly lower. Both pluses.

LUSARDI'S

1494 Second Avenue, between 77th and 78th streets
Telephone: 249-2020

Favorite meals:
Bruschetta (tomato and basil on croutons)
Penne with porcini (wild mushrooms)
Veal chop with sage
Berries with balsamic vinegar
or
Fusilli with salmon
Chicken with tomatoes and mushrooms (chicken Abruzzese)
Tirami sù

Other favorite dishes: Buffalo mozzarella and ricotta with artichokes or roasted peppers; crostini of polenta with beans and porcini; carpaccio with green sauce (salsa verde); venison carpaccio; mushroom salad; fish croquettes; veal with tuna sauce (vitello tonnato); corkscrew pasta with basil, tomato, and cream (fusilli ai tre sapori); bucatini with tomato, onions, and prosciutto (bucatini amatriciana); linguine with white clam sauce; penne with basil, tomato, and mozzarella (penne tricolori); risotto with walnuts or porcini; tagliatelle with porcini; rigatoni with sausages; tortellini alla panna; tortelloni with spinach and four cheeses (tortelloni de spinacci ai quattro formaggi); tortelloni with pumpkin and sage (tortelloni de zucca alla salvia); ravioli with walnut sauce; mixed seafood fry (fritto misto di mare); chicken sautéed with garlic (scarpariello); veal piccatina; veal paillard alla Dino; veal chop Valdostana or Milanese; roast pheasant; all vegetables and salads; crème brûlée; caramel custard; berries with cold zabaglione.

Setting: Handsome, tailored, and urbane dining room that suggests a stylish Florentine osteria; tables are not too cramped and noise level is moderate; lighting is exceptionally pleasant, but chairs can be uncomfortable if you stay through four courses.

Service: Professional without being pretentious and with an attractive, casual, but efficient tone.

Dress code: Men are preferred in jackets, but no code is enforced.

Facilities for private parties: Lunchtime only when entire restaurant can be closed to accommodate between 25 and 70.

Hours: Lunch, Monday through Friday. Dinner, seven days.

Reservations: Recommended for lunch, necessary for dinner.

Prices: Moderate to moderately expensive.

Credit cards: AE, CB, DC, MC, V.

Few of the recent Italian newcomers to the local restaurant scene can match Lusardi's for style or consistency. It is developing a classic quality, with a casual but handsome dining room and bar that suggest an upscale wine tavern—trattoria as it might be in Rome, Florence, Milan, or, of course, New York. Cream-colored walls with dark, stained wood trim, the racks of wine, and waiters wearing ties, shirts, and aprons make for a modern, practical, but businesslike tone, much in the tradition of an Italian steak house.

The food matches the spirit of the room, an elusive subtlety that I prize, with choices that range from the most traditional dishes, such as linguine with white clam sauce, through Tuscan-style dishes of the moment (tortelloni with pumpkin and sage) and all sorts of nut and porcini risottos and pastas, to house inventions such as the grilled veal paillard alla Dino, which gets an anointing of balsamic vinegar a second or two before it is taken from the fire, thus taking on a mild sweet-sharp patina.

There are no regional culinary snobbisms reflected in this menu, as the food of all Italy appears at some time or another on the menu, with the kitchens of Naples, the Abruzzi, Rome, Tuscany, Emilia, and Liguria as the standards. All are styled and presented in a manner essentially Lusardian, which is perhaps the most a restaurateur can wish for. This has been true since the restaurant opened in March 1982 and continues even though the original chef is now at Sistina and the Lusardi brothers have opened the more casual Due. Since his successor, Lamberto Terrosi of Pisa, has his sea legs, the food is better than ever. Only one dish that was a personal favorite is not quite up to its former savory self, and that is the flattened, fried small chicken that is cooked under a brick weight (mattone) and is called, therefore, chicken mattone. More salt and black pepper and a touch of olive oil to forestall dryness would do the trick. That is a small cavil midst so many other fine choices.

There are a few seasonal appetizer specials not listed on the menu, a selection that would be even more enticing if waiters quoted prices. One night it might be sautéed porcini or grilled radicchio alongside tiny, fresh buffalo mozzarella and a cloudlet of tangy ricotta, or in winter it could be a toasted crostini of polenta topped with braised white beans and mushrooms. Carpaccio appears in two variations, one with paper-thin slices of raw beef dressed only with oil and vinegar and arranged on arugula salad, while the other, which I prefer, has a grass-green oil-based sauce sprightly with capers, parsley, basil, and garlic.

Mussels steamed in white wine, clams raw or baked oreganata, and high-quality prosciutto and the air-cured beef bresaola can be had singly or in combination. Seafood salad has not always been fresh, so I now avoid it. But I have never been disappointed by the vitello tonnato with thin slices of pale veal mounded on arugula in an enticing pyramid, napped with a sheer tuna sauce—alone, a lovely summer lunch dish.

That veal is too rich a forerunner to pasta, so it is a good idea to refrain when you want to try some of the gorgeous possibilities. Among the best are the short pasta penne mixed with an oil and butter sauce and smoky porcini mushrooms. Say no to cheese if it is offered as it will ruin the flavor of the earthy mushrooms. The three colors in the tricolori sauce on penne are the red of tomatoes, the green of basil, and the white dicings of buffalo mozzarella, and the three flavors—tre sapori—folded into the corkscrew pasta fusilli are basil, tomatoes, and a binding of sweet cream. The large, chewy bucatini have the proper heft to carry the amatriciana sauce of tomato, prosciutto, and onion, while tagliatelle, fresh and medium in width, are the more delicate accompaniment to porcini. Tortellini in cream and linguine with white clam sauce are none the less enticing for being omnipresent around town, and the more unusual large tortelloni are as good with spinach and four cheeses as with pumpkin in a cream and sage dressing. Walnuts are pounded into the cream sauce for ravioli, somewhat in the manner of Ligurian pansotti. Walnuts too add a meaty fresh-air flavor to risotto. Occasionally pasta dishes are lacking in salt. Since all are cooked to order, it is wise to state whether you want yours with or without salt. Without is unthinkable as far as I am concerned, but those whose doctors have warned them off can have it their way.

Frying is immaculate here—light, golden, greaseless—as is true for the slivered zucchini, the rings and tentacles of squid, and the mixed seafood fry, which did indeed need a sprinkling of salt when last tried.

Oddly enough, the meat main courses include two or three clichés, the dated chicken Castelli Romani (breast of chicken with artichokes, mushrooms, cream, and white wine, and a hodgepodge) and veal sette colli (the same as Castelli Romani minus cream). I prefer dishes with fewer complexities and more character than what might well be dubbed "rich American eaters' preferences." Take, for example, the nuggets of chicken, bone and all, as sautéed in oil with garlic to make the scarpariello specialty, or the same chunks browned in olive oil and finished with tomato and mushrooms in the manner of the Abruzzi. Veal scaloppine appears in an Emiliana portfolio, stuffed with prosciutto and cheese and then fried, for a dish timid palates will probably enjoy, as do I when tired and in need of something gentle. That mood might also suggest the perfectly executed veal piccatina, and if you think it's easy to get the scaloppine golden brown at the edges while remaining moist within, try to find it that way in this city. Lemon and capers sharpen the butter-and-oil glossing. A thick veal chop with a pocket holding ham and Fontina cheese, topped with a light brown sauce, is the lusty and delicious veal chop Valdostana, and the crisp-crusted veal Milanese is as simple but as remarkable a triumph here as the piccatina. Sage lends a dry, herbaceous flavor to the well-trimmed, succulently moist sautéed veal chop.

Simple, well-cooked vegetables such as whole string beans or sautéed escarole are served family style with all main courses.

Considering how far the kitchen goes to be sure everything is just right, it's a pity it doesn't go a step further and make all of the desserts in-house. As decent as the store-bought cakes may be, they are now tired and overpowering finishes, but the homemade tirami sù has become one of the city's best—fluffs of golden lady fingers moistened with espresso, rum, and kahlua and layered with whipped cream and dustings of grated chocolate, all heaped into a wine goblet. Cold zabaglione with or without berries is a better choice as are crème brûlée, crème caramel, or berries doused lightly with sugar and either lemon juice or balsamic vinegar. As for that commercial ice cream tartufo, it sells the rest of the menu short.

There is an usually careful wine list at Lusardi's, and one gets the feeling that the owners worked hard to get the best possible representations in all price categories, from $15 to $88. Only a few more half bottles would be welcome, but with so many good choices at $20 or less, it is not a serious omission. The absence of vintage years on the less expensive choices is.

NANNI

146 East 46th Street, between Lexington and Third avenues
Telephone: 697-4161

Favorite meals:
Lunch
Seafood salad
Baked ziti with eggplant (ziti al forno alla Siciliana)
Fresh fruit
or
Dinner
Fettuccine with prosciutto, peas, tomato, and cream (alla Nanni), half portion
Chicken sautéed with garlic and white wine (pollo scarpariello)
Zabaglione
Other favorite dishes: Baked clams oreganata; linguine with white clam sauce (linguine alle vongole); fusilli or spaghetti with tomato, onion, and prosciutto (all'amatriciana); trenette

al pesto; manicotti with cheese; clams or mussels in tomato broth; veal cutlet Milanese; broiled veal chop; sautéed escarole.
Setting: Intimate, trattoria-tavern feeling that is casual but urbane. Tables are closely set, but noise level remains magically moderate except at peak lunch hours.
Service: Friendly, accommodating, professional, and civilized.
Dress code: None.
Facilities for private parties: None.
Hours: Lunch, Monday through Friday. Dinner, Monday through Saturday. Closed Sunday and major holidays.
Reservations: Necessary.
Prices: Moderate to moderately high.
Credit cards: AE, CB, DC, MC, V.

Despite the excellence of many of the new-style Italian restaurants that have opened in New York during the past seven or eight years, every once in a while it is reassuring to go back to the old flavors. That means Neapolitan dishes which were once standard on local menus, but which finally became carelessly prepared and so fell out of favor. Nanni's, though, has maintained its menu through the years, combining the most soul-soothing of the southern Italian cooking with some northern dishes as well. It is those southern specialties that draw me back, especially for a weekday lunch when I want to be in that neighborhood. It is a homey, yet urbane and professional, old-timey Italian restaurant. Newly remodeled with its white walls, travel posters, and white tablecloths, this low-ceilinged, masculine eating place suggests a stylish trattoria. There is a clublike feeling to the intimate surroundings, enhanced by the crowd of obvious regulars who gather at lunch and dinner, and if the tone is essentially masculine, it is for that reason appealing to women—or at least to this woman.

Owned by the renowned Abruzzese chef Luigi Nanni, this restaurant offers all the dishes that were standards about twenty years ago when it opened. In an interview for *Vanity Fair*, Federico Fellini told me that he misses "the soft and gentle flavors of the past." In a sense, that is what Nanni dishes up, with pastas and soups overcooked by today's standards, yet mellow with the soft blending of flavors.

A case in point is the thick, restorative minestrone and all the pastas that are a shade more mellow than al dente and so wrap themselves around their satiny sauces with ease. Among those pastas, my favorite for lunch is the baked ziti with eggplant, Sicilian style—a main course that is just right after the house seafood salad, never on the menu but always on hand. That too is a little soupier than would be considered stylish today, but it is also so damned good I never let a drop of its oil and lemon dressing go back unsopped by the chewy Italian bread.

Perfect linguine with white clam sauce, a dish on which I qualify as the world's leading expert, is dished up with well-salted pasta, plenty of chopped clams and golden garlic, and, for garnish, two clams in their shells. Just a dash of hot red pepper flakes is needed to attain gastronomic Nirvana. Various pastas, such as the filled rings cappelletti, fettuccine, or the fine capellini, may be had alla Nanni, with a nicely sticky cream-tomato sauce flecked with peas and prosciutto. The cappelletti version, with a green salad, makes a satisfying main course, as would the fine noodles trenette in a creamy basil pesto sauce. Clams and mussels as fresh as sea breezes are heaped in bowls and are wonderful dipped into their garlicky tomato broth for another house triumph.

Meats can be disappointing, generally because they are tough. That was true recently of very dry pork chops that were not helped by their spicy pizzaiola sauce and of osso buco that needed a sharp knife for cutting, an unthinkable requirement with meat that should almost fall from the bone. In the past, grilled chops have been far better choices, as has been the veal cutlet Milanese with its golden breading. Nuggets of chicken sautéed with garlic and white wine (scarpariello) are better with bone-in pieces, and it is offered both ways. Sautéed escarole with garlic is a bright contrast with meat dishes.

Cheesecake here is awful—gummy and insipid. Better to have fresh berries, with or without the winey warm egg froth that is zabaglione.

Nanni is the kind of raffishly serviceable trattoria every neighborhood needs, but satisfaction will depend on the amount you spend. Order a lavish meal with an expensive wine, and you'll suddenly feel as though you should have gone someplace else. Order modestly, and you'll feel you had a bargain. It is still that kind of place.

IL NIDO

251 East 53rd Street, between Second and Third avenues
Telephone: 753-8450

Favorite meals:
Lunch
Risotto with asparagus
Red snapper with clams
Homemade ice cream
or
Dinner
Mushroom salad
Spinach and cheese dumplings with tomato sauce (ravioli malfatti), half portion

Mixed fry of sweetbreads, brains, veal, calves' liver, and lamb or goat chop (fritto misto all' Italiana), shared by two
Mocha meringue cake
Other favorite dishes: Prosciutto, the cured beef bresaola, baked clams (vongole oreganate), broiled scampi, mussels marinara, clams in tomato broth (vongole alla Capri), carpaccio, crostini of polenta with mushrooms, all soups, all pastas, fried squid (calamaretti fritti), shellfish marinara, mixed seafood in broth (zuppa di pesce), chicken cacciatore, brains (cervella) or sweetbreads (animella), veal kidneys (rognone trifolato), grilled veal chop, veal cutlet Milanese, paillard of beef, all vegetables, arugula and endive salad, homemade ice creams, zabaglione, cheesecake (torta di formaggio), tirami sù.
Setting: Beautifully elegant country restaurant with mirrors and etched-glass panels; most tables are comfortably spaced, but noise level is high and there is an occasional ventilation problem in corners.
Service: Always wonderful for well-known customers, but there are reports of rudeness to unknowns.
Dress code: Jackets required for men.
Facilities for private parties: None.
Hours: Lunch, Monday through Saturday. Dinner, Monday through Saturday. Closed Sunday and major holidays.
Reservations: Necessary.
Prices: Expensive.
Credit cards: AE, CB, DC, MC, V.

Il Nido still is as close as New York gets to having a four-star Italian restaurant. All it would take is the replacing of a few overly complicated, dated chicken and veal main courses with lighter, cleaner, and more subtly herbed specialties that might be Tuscan, Venetian, Ligurian, or Abruzzese in style. This beautiful, polished little restaurant, with its paneled mirrors, etched glass, and generally professional and accommodating staff, raises an aesthetic question I have long pondered: the difference between the classic and the dated where food is concerned. The best comparison can be made with clothing fashions, in which, for example, an A-line dress is considered dated but a silk shirt and a turtleneck cashmere sweater are classics.

On the Il Nido menu the classics are all of the appetizers, fish and pasta offerings, and the meats such as golden fried veal cutlet Milanese, the chicken cacciatore, or the sautéed sweetbreads and brains. But things such as chicken or veal "sette colli," wet sautés of meat with artichokes, mushrooms, and white wines, are the culinary A lines. The difference, I suppose, is that the dated dishes are those once considered at the cutting edge of a trend. In the case of Italian food in the United States, the sette collis represent a special era that peaked about five years ago. In the beginning we had only what has come to be called "red" Italian cooking, based on the tomato-sauced dishes of Naples. Then about thirty-five years ago, Northern Italian food was introduced, and the color was white and creamy. Examples of such are fettuccine Alfredo, risotto Piemontese, and meats such as vitello tonnato and calves' liver Veneziana.

Then came the Il Nido era and the masses of mushrooms and white wine and, for good measure, some even glued together with melted mozzarella, although the latter have been dropped from the latest menu. Given the current rage of nuova cucina, the clichés-to-be are the fruited risottos, the nearly raw grilled birds, the overabundance of sage and rosemary, and pasta or rice only half-cooked and therefore unpleasant and flavorless. Fortunately, Adi Giovannetti, the proprietor, stands fast against such travesties.

But because the menu is so large, it is full of wonderful choices, despite its shortcomings. Appetizers I especially like include the grilled crostini of cornmeal polenta that is topped with sautéed wild mushrooms, the carpaccio with a green sauce far more suitable to it than the creamy bland mayonnaise-type dressing of the original dish, and all sorts of sprightly hot shellfish appetizers such as baked clams, mussels and clams in tomato broth. I also recommend the impeccable prosciutto and the air-cured beef bresaola as well as the sautéed wild mushrooms or raw mushrooms in a lemony olive oil dressing. In season the fragrant white truffles of Alba are as heavenly in a raw salad as they are shaved over fettuccine or risotto, although they carry outrageous prices compared with those at several other places in town. There is only one appetizer I dislike at Il Nido and that is the house version of spiedino alla Romana, because the bread is always wet at the center and the anchovy sauce is so heavy it wipes out the flavors of toasted bread and melting mozzarella.

Pasta e fagioli, that lusty soup of short ditali and beans in a tomato-pink herbed base, here takes on elegance without losing character. Clear, heady broths are the vehicles for spinach and egg or the meat-filled cappelletti, and minestrone is so full of vegetables and flavor one might almost be tempted to have it instead of pasta.

Almost, but not quite. How to resist the airy dumplings of spinach, egg, and cheese that are ravioli malfatti—"badly made" because they have no pasta covering—trimmed with a light sauce of fresh, barely cooked tomatoes, or the good, chewy tortellini in a glossing of cream or the lacy capelli d'angelo—angels' hair—that is easily twirled around bits of shellfish or vegetables and cream? Lasagne with green pasta and a bolognese filling, linguine tossed with the matriciana sauce of tomato, prosciutto, and onions, and the white and green straw and hay that is paglia e fieno with cream and ham provide further embarrassments of choice. Gently soft polenta can be had bolognese-style, and risotto here has always been perfectly cooked, firm but never with a crackle at the center of the rice kernels, meaning that each grain has been fully developed in broth, wine, and whatever flavors it should absorb. "Whatever flavors" could be seafood, tomato, asparagus, saffron, or wild mushrooms, the determining factor usually being the season.

Anyone who feels it is necessary to go to a fish restaurant to get great seafood should know about Il Nido. The assortment and freshness are incomparable and so is the preparation, whether as simple as fried squid or as subtle as the imported Italian striped bass, branzino, that may be roasted and dressed with lemon and oil, or simmered in a translucent tomato brodetto. Red snapper in brodetto with clams is a lunchtime favorite of mine, and once when I was there with a dieting friend, the kitchen produced a sublime, oil-free variation, relying on tomato and a dash of white wine to keep fish and mollusks succulent as they bake in cartoccio—a big envelope of foil. When the little pink Mediterranean triglie are available, they are worth trying grilled, and the house also does a properly hefty fra diavolo sauce for lobster or shrimp.

Many Americans who go to Italy come back disappointed with meat dishes, finding them lacking in interest. But most Italian meat is simply cooked—grilled, fried, or roasted and not too often sauced because it follows rich antipasti and pastas. That is why at Il Nido I generally have some of the sautéed innards or, if my husband is in the mood to share it with me, the mixed fry of sweetbreads, brains, liver, veal, and a lamb or goat chop, with which we usually have some fried zucchini. That or grilled veal chop or a paillard of beef (veal being too dry for this sort of cooking) is my choice.

Desserts have improved markedly in recent years, but in fall, when pears are ripe and juicy, none surpasses that fruit peeled, sliced, and arranged with chips of aged Parmesan cheese and shelled walnut meats. It is really my idea of an elegant finish, especially when followed by a glass of Giovannetti's pride, the golden dessert wine Vin Santo, served with crunchy almond biscotti.

Those with sweeter longings will be happy with the warm, airy whipped egg and Marsala zabaglione, the ice cream homemade around the corner at Il Nido's new café (*see* Cafés, under Casual Eating), of which the vanilla, nougat, and dark chocolate are destructively alluring. There is also a marvelous, nearly indescribable dream of a mocha, almond, and crushed meringue cake that must be eaten to be believed.

Prices are supremely high here, and that includes the array of excellent wines.

I much prefer the front dining room at Il Nido to the even more crowded, even noisier back area, and at certain tables in need of ventilation there can be eye-stinging fumes from the source of heat on the tableside cooker. That does not happen often, which is lucky, because it would ruin what is perhaps the single most felicitous Italian dining experience in New York.

POSITANO

250 Park Avenue South, corner 20th Street
Telephone: 777-6211

Favorite meal:
Steamed mussels with crushed black pepper
Braised rabbit Saracena, with onions, celery, garlic, and tomato
Berries, in season
Other favorite dishes: Garlic focaccia (bread); fried squid with marinara sauce; scallops Partenopea with prosciutto, mozzarella, and tomato; bowtie pasta with broccoli, sun-dried tomatoes, black olives, and garlic; pasta with homemade sausage and cream sauce; pasta shells with periwinkles, tomato, garlic, and herbs; risotto with quail, tomato, peas, herbs, and cheese; warm salad of mozzarella, tomato, olive oil, garlic, and basil; "vigorosa" salad of tomato, tuna, olives, scallions, and capers; chicken Dragona, with sausage, mushrooms and tomato sauce; veal scaloppine Partenopea with proscuitto, mozzarella, and tomato sauce; medallions of beef sautéed with peppers, mushrooms, tomato, garlic, and oregano; chocolate-almond torte.
Setting: Airy modern café in limpid pastels with tiered seating; noisy and hectic especially around and overlooking bar; quieter and more relaxed in side booths.
Service: Friendly and good-natured but often very slow.
Dress code: None.
Facilities for private parties: Can be arranged only for large groups on Sunday, when restaurant is closed.
Hours: Lunch, Monday through Friday. Dinner, until 11:30 P.M., Monday through Thursday, and until 12:30 A.M., Friday and Saturday. Closed Sunday and major holidays.
Reservations: Recommended.
Prices: Moderately expensive.
Credit cards: AE, CB, DC, MC, V.

Just as the town of Positano on Italy's Amalfi coast is built up on a mountainside in ledges, so this namesake restaurant was designed with tiered seating. Even the butter emphasizes that point, stamped out as it is in a mini-three-stepped design. Limpid Mediterranean pastels such as seafoam blue and pink, and clear, comfortable lighting add to the graceful effect, but are not quite enough to dispel the hectic and noisy activity that prevails on weekends. Owned by TV commercial director Bob Giraldi and his production partner, Phil Suarez, this café-restaurant has become a hangout for denizens of the advertising world, most of whom are casually and attractively gotten up. The only oasis of quiet is a downstairs row of booths, which is where I like to sit unless I am with someone who wants to catch the scene. In that case, the upstairs balcony tables are the ones to reserve.

Usually the kitchen of a restaurant as "in" as this one doesn't exert itself unduly, but at Positano the chef, said to be from that Campagna town, offers unusual and enticing dishes, many of which are beautifully prepared. Recent changes in the original menu are even more reflective of Neapolitan cooking at its best, stressing the light and fresh tomato sauces, the olive oil glossed pastas and salads that make southern Italian cooking so right for current dietary preferences. Weaknesses remain appetizers and desserts, but that leaves a lot of very good and savory eating in between. Former favorites such as braised quail, shrimp sautéed in shells with hot peppers, and chicken livers grilled with parsley, garlic, and lemon appear now only as occasional specials. But a flavorful array of regulars has replaced them.

Pastas remain delectable and are now available as half-order appetizers for a little more than half of the full-portion price. But that is better than having to share, and allows for more variety around the table. Among the best is the bowtie pasta, farfalle, tossed with flowerets of broccoli, bits of tart-sweet sun-dried tomatoes, salty black olives, garlic, and a light bath of clear green olive oil. The wide, short tubular pasta, rigatoni, has the heft to carry the tomato-mushroom sauced sausage combination, and marruzelle, a form of shells, is filled lusciously with the tiny sea-snails periwinkles, enriched with a garlic and herb-scented tomato sauce. Spicy sausages assuaged with cream are folded into radiatori (little channeled radiator-like pasta) and provide the right chewy foil to the meat- and cheese-accented cream. Risotto lacks some of the juicy but firm texture the rice should have, but is satisfying when combined with the gentle meat of quail, tomato, peas, herbs, and a sprinkling of Parmesan cheese.

Whether as a light main course or as a shared appetizer, try the salad of tomato, tuna, olives, scallions, and capers (vigorosa) or the Caprese calda, with slightly warm mozzarella and tomato nestling into a basil-scented olive oil dressing. They are better choices than the dry roasted chicken with walnuts and peppers, or the sweetish carrot-dressed Vesuviana with mozzarella, tomato, zucchini, beans, and croutons.

Most fish dishes have become overly complicated on the new menu, the exceptions being the wonderfully fried calamari that can be dipped into a frothy marinara sauce spiked with hot pepper and which, if you have a double order, make a fine main course, and the scallops Partenopea, with slivers of prosciutto and a sheer topping of melted mozzarella and fresh tomato. Otherwise, there are overly sweet-sour touches to things such as salmon and snapper.

Braised rabbit Saracena, on the menu since Positano opened, is fortunately still there and as good as ever, with its savory hints of onion, celery, garlic, and rosemary and its sauce enriched with sundried tomatoes. Being boneless, the rabbit meat arrives as succulent morsels. Sausages, tomato, and mushrooms lend richness to braised thighs of chicken Dragona, and veal scaloppine Partenopea is our old friend veal parmigiana redesigned to appeal to more delicate palates. Typically Neapolitan and well rendered is the beef pizzaiola cut in cushiony medallions and sauced with mushrooms, peppers, tomato, garlic, and oregano. Less satisfying are the bland veal chop with washed-out porcini mushrooms and the stingingly acidic grilled breast of marinated chicken.

Desserts never have tasted as good as they sound here, and the mushily soaked tirami sù, the banal ice cream tartufo, and the textureless chocolate mousse cake do not improve the situation. Better to have refreshing fresh fruit or berries, or the light, gently moist Capri classic chocolate almond sponge torte.

You begin here with fragrant focaccia (garlic- and herb-perfumed flat breads) and small, luxuriously oily herb-flecked olives, all wonderful with red wine. And there are homey, warming vegetables such as roasted new potatoes with rosemary or escarole sautéed with garlic and oil that go with most main courses. The staff is friendly, genuinely helpful, and accommodating, although the kitchen can be slow at peak times. Wines are moderately priced and a personal favorite is the dry, woodsy, red 1983 Carmignano Riserva Cappezzana, at $28.

RAO'S

455 East 114th Street, corner Pleasant Avenue
Telephone: 534-9625

Favorite meals:
Pasta with marinara sauce and ricotta, shared by two
Chicken with lemon sauce
Fresh fruit
or
Fresh broccoli salad
Liguine with white clam sauce, shared by two
Pork chops with vinegar peppers
Fresh fruit
Other favorite dishes: Roast pepper salad; clams in tomato broth; all soups combining pasta with various beans; all pasta; escarole or broccoli with garlic and oil (aglio olio); chicken fried with garlic, onions, and vinegar peppers; veal, beef, or pork chop pizzaiola; broiled veal chop; sausages broiled or with peppers and onions; shrimp fra diavolo or arreganate; squid (calamari) in red or white sauce.

Setting: Small, bohemian bar and grill with only eight tables and year-round Christmas decorations adding a festive touch.
Service: Highly personal and superb, once they let you in.
Dress code: None really, but most regulars wear jackets.
Facilities for private parties: None.
Hours: Dinner, Monday through Friday. Closed Saturday, Sunday, and major holidays.
Reservations: Necessary for first-timers about three months in advance.
Prices: Inexpensive to moderate.
Credit cards: None.

Rao's is undoubtedly the most special Italian restaurant in New York. It's virtually a private club because of its large, loyal following, its limited capacity of eight tables, and its short workweek. Determined always to reserve a few tables that can be booked on short notice by regulars, the management doles out reservations to newcomers so stringently that a call two to four months in advance is not excessive. Whether you think it is worth all that depends upon how you feel about finding a unique classic, totally without pretense or obeisance to fashion, and how much you like no-frills southern Italian food, fresh and lustily prepared.

Even when cook-owner Vincent Rao (now in his 80s) and his wife, Anna, take a night off, there is well-trained help to continue the tradition. Their nephew, Frank Pellegrino, who has become a skillful restaurateur and host, is canny enough to maintain the style and standards. However, cooking is less consistent than it used to be, and you can get a lackluster seafood salad or soggy baked clams.

Rao's is much favored by Woody Allen, among other serious eaters, and he cast Frank Pellegrino in a role in his delicious film *Broadway Danny Rose*. Still, Frank remains levelheaded enough to run the dining room single-handed, sitting at each table to write the order, making suggestions and warning against over-ordering, taking reservations, and generally being a sort of one-man-band restaurateur, all with charm and aplomb.

Usually in the kitchen is tall, ramrod-straight Vincent Rao, cowboy hat in place, grilling his incomparable chicken to charred perfection, then sprinkling it with lemon. He sautés the veal chop and fires up sausages with pungent vinegar cherry peppers while the equally imperturbable Anna, never a pale blond hair out of place, pitches in with pastas, salads, and desserts. Anyone who thinks fast, good cooking can be done only in a torrent of confusion should glance in here. I have a feeling that Mr. and Mrs. Rao are the only people who indeed can make omelets without breaking eggs.

That is not all that is unusual about this New York landmark. Its location gives lie to the oft-heard excuse of failed restaurant owners, namely that they were ruined by being in a bad neighborhood. Looking at Rao's, as well as at Sammy's, one has to believe that going to improbably disastrous sections is in itself a kind of reverse chic, witness the big fancy cars parked out in front of each. At Rao's you will want a car of some sort, for this deserted slum neighborhood, formerly a thriving Italian community, is hardly the place to take a stroll looking for a taxi. But any car you bring will be safe, as Rao's seems to have reached a détente with local troublemakers. A glance at the outside of this tiny corner bar and grill, which usually has letters missing from its shabby sign, and the sheets of metal covering windows in the rest of the building, and it would not be hard to feel that you have come to the wrong address and that the street name, Pleasant Avenue, is someone's grim idea of a joke.

At Rao's it is always Christmas, thanks to the colored lights and tinsel the management keeps the year round. There is a long bar, where customers wait for tables or friends of the management drop by for drinks, and then the eight small, immaculately set tables stand against the dark walls that suggest years of varnishing and revarnishing.

The menu has much the same sure, simple, and satisfying quality as the room, and it is the sort that is a forerunner of such great Italian steak houses as the Palm. It is essentially a grill and hot-stove kitchen, where everything is cooked to order and nothing prepared in advance. That means no lasagne or ravioli or tortellini, no stews or roasts.

The rich and soul-nourishing choices are appetizers such as the satiny, sweet, and pungent salad of slivered roast peppers just oily enough to smooth the bite of the anchovies that accompany them or clams simmered in a light tomato "zuppa." By far the most brilliant first course used to be fish salad, a tossing of sea-fresh lobster and crab meat with tender rings of squid and magenta-tinged octopus bits, and the chewy, smooth conch meat, scungilli. Celery, lemon juice, mild olive oil, and parsley do the rest, which is plenty. When it is up to snuff, I cannot let a drop of that dressing go back to the kitchen, sopping it up with the good, crusty Italian bread provided.

Which leaves me already half sated by the time I choose soup or pasta. But I manage, as the house is good about half portions, sharing, and other civilized practices. Clear, fragrant broths may be adrift with escarole and white beans, and the thicker soup-stews combine short tubular pastas (I prefer ditali) with peas (piselli), or white beans (fagioli), smoking brown lentils or chick-peas (ceci). A light glossing of tomatoes, garlic, and mellow onions flavors these restorative soups, best eaten in fall and winter.

But it's a tough choice between those and the pastas when I consider the perfection of the linguine with white clam sauce, which almost always has the right amount of nut-brown chips of garlic and plenty of salt, or the similar sauce minus clams and known as aglio olio—garlic and oil—a favorite of mine when it is sprinkled with hot red pepper flakes. Or short pasta tossed with broccoli, oil, and garlic or spaghetti or linguine marinara, which I like very much with a little ricotta stirred in for a creamy thickening touch.

Aglio olio works magically on firmly cooked broccoli or blanched and sautéed escarole, vegetables that take on new meaning with that dressing. There are five ways to have chicken at Rao's, but the two I always choose are the grilled with the sunny, sharp lemon sauce or the fried that is zapped with garlic, onions, and hot and pungent vinegar cherry peppers. Those same peppers lend their fresh sting to pork chops and to sausages, with or without chicken.

The more delicate veal scaloppine dishes are disappointing here, the marsala, piccata, and Francese versions among them. That sort of delicacy is just not what the kitchen does best, and so that same pink and tender meat is better ordered with pizzaiola sauce (tomatoes, garlic, oregano), or breaded and fried Milanese style.

There is good, beefy steak and again the pizzaiola sauce can be had as an enhancement. Grilled veal and pork chops are flavorful and rarely dry out, and fried sweet peppers and onions give lean, plump, fennel-seasoned sausages the classic treatment. Again, lighter shrimp dishes impress me less than those baked with garlic, bread crumbs, and oregano (arreganate) or in a hot and spicy fra diavolo tomato sauce. Fresh tender rings of squid in white (garlic and oil) or tomato sauce are delicious plain or sheer heaven atop some steaming al dente linguine.

Frank wisely suggests a fresh fruit platter after such filling fare, and with a commercial tartufo as the only alternative, who could argue? Modest Italian wines are all the house offers, with a Chianti Riserva being as classy as it gets. But those strong, fresh wines go well with this food. Menu prices seem so low you'll hardly believe it, but everything is à la carte, so it adds up faster than you might suspect.

SISTINA

1555 Second Avenue, between 80th and 81st streets
Telephone: 861-7660

Favorite meals:
Fried zucchini (zucchine fritte), shared by two or more
Gnocchi with white beans
Seafood stew in tomato sauce (caciucco)

Tirami sù
or
Risotto with four cheeses (ai quattro formaggi), shared by two
Grilled, herbed chicken (Sisto IV)
Sautéed spinach (spinaci saltati)
Pear in red wine
Other favorite dishes: Sautéed scampi when available; sautéed porcini or other wild mushrooms when available; veal with tuna sauce (vitello tonnato); crostini with mozzarella, tomato, and anchovy; crostini of cornmeal polenta with porcini; vegetable soup (zuppa di verdure); all pastas; fried calamari; veal cutlet Val d'Aosta or Milanese; veal nodini with herbs.
Setting: Small, polished café; cramped and at times noisy; lighting is flattering and felicitous.
Service: Polite, informed, and professional.
Dress code: Jacket preferred for men.
Facilities for private parties: None.
Hours: Lunch, Monday through Saturday. Dinner, Monday through Sunday. Sunday, open until midnight.
Reservations: Necessary, especially for dinner.
Prices: Moderately expensive.
Credit cards: AE.

Sistina is doing exactly what it always did, but much better. It is as though lighting in a room has been turned up several levels, to reveal nuances and richness heretofore missing. A surer hand in the kitchen may be the reason. In addition, there are some delicious new touches such as the fresh garlic-and tomato-topped bruschetta given away as an appetizer with crisply fried zucchini or squid, the marvelous soft-yet-crisp, delicately sweet macaroons passed with coffee, and the expanded choice of exotic mushrooms and shellfish.

In keeping with the vogue to make "in" restaurants hard to find, Sistina's sign remains practically invisible, being only a tiny engraved brass plaque unlighted on the front of the building. But that sign is worth seeking out more than most, for unlike so many of the new and the "in," Sistina also has delicious, rich, North Italian food and a lively, friendly dining room. The setting suggests a small, posh café, with a pleasant roseate glow and a convivial tone that manages to dispel the drawbacks of a slightly cramped and noisy room. The only pretentious touch is what looks like a photostat of Michelangelo's "hand of God" detail from the famed fresco on the ceiling of the Sistine Chapel. It is an obvious reference to the origin of the restaurant's name, but a reproduction so tacky that were Buonarroti to see it, he might well regret those years on the scaffolding.

However art critics feel about this, there should be little to displease food buffs, for the food prepared by chef-partner Antonio Bruno (formerly of Lusardi's) is by and large delicious and diverting. His brother Giuseppe, also a Lusardi graduate, oversees the dining room, and two other brothers trained in top New York restaurants divide assorted chores. The result of all this experience is a consummate professionalism that keeps things running smoothly.

After the generous giveaway appetizers, one needs a hearty appetite to order yet another first course. When I skip pasta, it is to indulge in the pink and tender vitello tonnato—the cool meat mantled with a creamy tuna sauce—or perhaps the golden cornmeal polenta earthy with wild porcini mushrooms. Other times it might be baby eggplants baked with a ricotta filling to be topped with a sheer tomato sauce, or an array of wild mushrooms, each grilled, sautéed, or sauced to its best advantage.

Pastas are brilliantly executed, cooked perfectly al dente, and only occasionally need an extra dash of salt. Now even spaghetti alla carbonara, so difficult to find in an authentic version in New York, is near perfect, its tossing of egg and pancetta bacon with plenty of black pepper added being a far zestier sauce than those overly rich with cream. Green gnocchi contrasted to gentle white beans is an inspired combination. Satisfaction comes by way of the meat-filled circlets tortellini in cream, the large rigatoni with vegetables, or linguine in a light, saline tomato-seafood sauce. Risotto is beautiful whether made with asparagus or four cheeses. The grains of rice are firm and juicy, but not crackling at the center as when underdone. Spinach-filled ravioli, also with four cheeses, is another fine alternative, as is the light vegetable soup that gets added zest from grated cheese.

Fish is especially well handled, whether as simple as sautéed sole with lemon juice and olive oil, or as complex as caciucco alla Mediterranea—the soup stew that here combines shrimp, scallops with their roe, sweet, sandless mussels, squid, clams, crayfish, and, in season, the tiniest soft-shell crabs, all bathed by a garlicky, herbed tomato sauce best sopped up with toasted croutons.

Simple and superb are the flattened, pepper-grilled chicken Sisto IV, piney with rosemary, and the lemon-glossed shrimp, grilled scampi style. On a more lavish scale there is the veal cutlet Val d'Aosta, the veal sandwiching Fontina cheese and prosciutto before being lightly fried with what seemed like a hint of shallots. Veal pounded to tenderness for the cutlet Milanese has a greaseless veneer of breading, while woodsy herbs spark sautéed nodini (thick slices from the filet) of veal. Garnishes are deliciously prepared vegetables and potatoes, another big improvement.

There is a tendency for daily specials to be overly complex. A case in point one night was a veal chop filled with foie gras and prosciutto, dipped in an eggy coating and then fried for a mushy, cloying effect.

Desserts tend to be extremely sweet but the ricotta ice cream and lemon sherbet are light and restorative. And then there are the heavenly macaroons, tirami sù, and pear in white wine with cold zabaglione.

Most wines are moderately priced, considering and in keeping with the menu range.

The menu suggests, "Please ask for prices of Daily Specials . . ." Why not just type them on a menu?

TRASTEVERE RISTORANTE ★★★

309 East 83rd Street, between First and Second avenues
Telephone: 734-6343

Favorite meals:
Linguine with white clam sauce (linguine con vongole), shared by two
Veal cutlet with tomato salad (vitello Trastevere)
Napoleon, shared by two
or
Vegetable antipasto, shared by two
Combination seafood stew (zuppa di pesce)
Chocolate tartufo
Other favorite dishes: Mussels in tomato and garlic broth (cozze in brodetto); vegetable soup (especially broccoli with tomato); brochette of mozzarella and prosciutto (spiedini alla Romana); all pastas; chicken with garlic, white wine, and mushrooms (pollo alla Gaetano); chicken with peppers, onion, and rosemary (pollo alla Romana); squid in spicy tomato broth (calamari Trastevere).
Setting: Tiny, cramped, but atmospheric trattoria.
Service: Generally excellent but can be brusque toward those wanting half orders of pasta; at times check is presented before it is requested.
Dress code: None.
Facilities for private parties: None.
Hours: Dinner, seven days. Closed major holidays.
Reservations: Necessary.
Prices: Moderate to moderately expensive.
Credit cards: AE.

Of the five Manhattan restaurants now owned by the Lattanzi family, this is the first, the best, and in every way my favorite. (Of those five, Erminia and Lattanzi are included in this book, but the second Trastevere, on 84th Street, is not, nor is the overly elaborate Albero D'Oro.) This despite a recent redecorating during which the simple brick walls were paneled in dark wood and the casual, bohemian memorabilia gave way to slicker accessories. That, like the dinner jackets on waiters, is a pretentious addition in a restaurant that gained its first success as a simple trattoria. But though something is lost in atmosphere, the kitchen has not suffered at all.

In this narrow, dark, and convivial setting, one can still marvel at the dishes created by Paul Lattanzi and his mother, Erminia (brothers Maurizio and Vittorio manage other outposts). Their specialties are best described as larger than life and might be considered nuova cucina were they not so copious and lavish. I suppose casalinga, home-style, is the safest description, but you have to be lucky to have it come from a home like this. Consider the antipasti di vegetali, to be shared by two—assorted vegetables, each cooked in a different way and gently slippery with good olive oil. Zucchini or eggplant might be grilled or stewed with tomatoes; broccoli might be steamed and dressed with olive oil and garlic; peppers might be fried and sparked with capers, and more. Some are cool, others warm or hot. If not those, have the sandless, briny mussels heaped in a bowl and underlined with an authoritative, garlic-scented tomato broth or the perfect spiedino alla Romana, the chunks of mozzarella melting between crisp-toasted bread slices with slivers of prosciutto and a golden anchovy sauce. Crisp salad of greens and radicchio, an inspired vegetable soup that is especially good when it is broccoli cooked with tomato, and a very fine pasta are other irresistible first courses.

As for pasta, the four at Trastevere create only one problem, and that is choosing. Feeling delicate, I might have the fine capellini primavera tossed with cream and vegetables. Other times it might be fettuccine Trastevere with peas, mushrooms, prosciutto, and cream, or the thick, hard-to-wind, marvelous-to-eat bucatini with an amatriciana sauce of tomato, onion, and pancetta bacon. My single favorite pasta dish, linguine with white clam sauce (con vongole), is nowhere better, with clams always as fresh as a sea breeze and plenty of garlic bravely cooked to a golden brown patina. At times there are gnocchi that get a frothy marinara sauce, further complicating the delicious dilemma.

The management is not always willing to do different half orders of pasta for members of the same party, a complaint I have had from unknown guests. They will, of course, permit sharing, but with so many enticements, a party of four understandably might want to have different pastas before moving on to the main course, and at $17 per portion, an accommodation seems in order.

Among main courses I have always been happy with are pollo alla Romana, the sautéed chicken fleshed out with green peppers and onion and seasoned with white wine, garlic, and rosemary, or the chunky, tender bits of chicken browned with garlic, wine, and mushrooms—pollo alla Gaetano. Skipping the overly sweet pollo alla Elvira, made with Marsala wine, which I dislike, there is veal to be considered, and here we come to a house classic now being copied (badly) all over town. It is the huge, flat, crisp, and golden breaded veal Trastevere, a cutlet topped with a room-temperature, basil-scented tomato salad. The tomato's juices lend a sense of sauce to the veal without making it soggy, and the contrasting temperatures of meat and salad have a tactile appeal that is almost Oriental in its sensibility. However, that is the only veal dish I really like here, the piccante and Anna being perfectly decent but short on character.

Two seafood dishes are spectacular, both based on similar garlic and herb tomato-broth sauces: calamari Trastevere, the rings and tentacles of squid tender but full of flavor, and the fish and shellfish soup-stew zuppa di pesce. Both are brightened with hot pepper and are served with thick croutons, much in order for blotting up the sauce. Scampi sautéed with garlic and white wine is fine, as is the sole with mushrooms, but with so many other more breathtaking choices, I usually pass them by.

Wonderful desserts are the homemade napoleon, a miracle of flaky puff pastry with a custardy whipped cream filling, or the equally ethereal cream puffs, or tartufo, that chocolate-glazed ice cream puff that is better here than in most places because it is homemade.

Trastevere is crowded and the staff is at times pushy about hustling diners out; stand your ground and they will subside.

VICO

1603 Second Avenue, between 83rd and 84th streets
Telephone: 772-7441

Favorite meals:
Fried zucchini, shared by two
Tortelloni San Remo, shared by two
Lamb chop with rosemary
Capri chocolate-almond torte
or
Rigatoni Siciliana, shared by two
Grilled Cornish hen with herbs
Arugula, radicchio, and endive salad
Tirami sù
Other favorite dishes: Raw beef with mustard sauce (carpaccio Veneziana) or with truffle oil (al funghetto), roast peppers with anchovies, all pastas, mussels in tomato broth, grilled red snapper, chicken with sausages and mushrooms, sausages with broccoli di rape, veal chop with green peppercorns, raspberry tart.
Setting: Small, bright trattoria.
Service: Friendly and crisply professional.
Dress code: None.
Facilities for private parties: None.
Hours: Dinner, seven days.
Reservations: Necessary after 7:15.
Prices: Moderately expensive.
Credit cards: None. Checks are accepted.

Like a $1,000 Missoni sweater, new-wave Italian restaurants have a casual elegance. Among such, Vico, on the Upper East Side, is an engaging prime example. In this trattoria, informally dressed waiters are crisply professional and friendly. They exhibit what should become a modern service politesse. Bright white walls in this long, narrow "vico," or alley, are relieved by handsome black-and-white photographs of nineteenth-century Naples. One senses that the owners, Nino Esposito and Gennaro Vertucci, are not hiding their southern Italian backgrounds, neither in manners nor in food.

Northern and southern specialties are rendered with equal respect. Among appetizers, that may mean Sicilian caponata with eggplant, tuna, tomato, olives, and capers graced with a fruity olive oil, or carpaccio Veneziana, the raw beef sparkling in a light mustard sauce. Even better is the carpaccio al funghetto with truffle-scented oil drizzled over the bright beef. Crisply fried, golden zucchini is an all-Italian favorite, as are succulent roasted peppers accented with plump anchovy fillets. Overheated oil mars both the Tuscan toast, bruschetta, topped with tomatoes, and the Mediterranean antipasto of grilled mixed vegetables.

When available, an excellent first course is New Zealand mussels developed to saline perfection in a sheer tomato broth—Naples at its most delicate. Pastas have been exceptional, whether the northern trenette (a narrow fettuccine) primavera with firm vegetables, or the tortelloni San Remo with tomatoes and peas in a tomato-cream sauce, or the juicy, ravioli-like panzotti with a creamy sauce of four counterpointed mild and pungent cheeses.

From the south comes the incomparable linguine with white clam sauce that has just the right belt of light golden garlic, the corkscrew fusilli gentled with crumbles of sausage, earthy porcini mushrooms, and a lacing of cream, as well as the notorious whore's pasta, penne puttanesca, with sharply salty capers and olives lending an edge to mild eggplant and peppers. Lasagne, though decent, can be a bit watery and thin, but risotto, when fleshed out with smoky wild mushrooms, is hard to beat.

Main courses do not quite live up to appetizers and pastas. Among the most successful choices are the flattened Cornish hen grilled with a piney rosemary and the pollo zingara, pan-browned chicken tossed with garlic, sausage, and mushrooms. Pollo campano, on the other hand, is a misguided overkill of chicken, eggplant, tomato, and peppers. Green peppercorns brighten a thick grilled veal chop done medium-rare as requested, a better choice than the cutlet Milanese or the paillard that is overly sweetened by balsamic vinegar.

No fault can be found with the hefty coarse-ground sausages

nesting on the bitter broccoli di rape, or the lamb chop in a rosemary sauce. Moist and snowy grilled red snapper takes on elegance when gilded with the minty, basil-scented oil.

Good chewy, crusty bread and a few impeccable desserts do more damage to the waistline. But it's worth it to sample the light, sweet-scented chocolate and almond torta Caprese, the crisp-crusted raspberry tart, or the lush tirami sù which indeed "draws you close" with its blandishments of liqueur-soaked cake, cool custard, powdered coffee, and chocolate shavings.

Only the chokingly sweet chocolate salami is a dessert to be missed. There is a good selection of moderately priced wines, but an inexcusable lack of prices given for off-menu specials.

TIDBITS

Heroes

Hero sandwiches filled with eggs and peppers, eggplant parmigiana, meatballs and peppers, and potato omelet are still what one wants them to be at *Manganaro's Hero Boy*, 492 Ninth Avenue, between 37th and 38th streets (947-7325). I skip veal, doubting its quality at these modest prices.

Pizza

Despite a few above-average versions of thin-crusted "new" pizza, I prefer the chewier old pizza, and currently my favorite spot for that is *Arturo's Pizzeria and Restaurant*, 106 West Houston Street, corner of Thompson Street (475-9828). Now that John's on Bleecker Street has gone commercial, Arturo's coal oven heats up the most delectable char-blistered crust, thick with creamy mozzarella and spicy tomato sauce. It's usually jammed with young people digging into the inexpensive, luscious pies (I'm a margherita fan myself and rarely have pizza with other toppings, but the full range is offered) and the live music—guitar, jazz, or whatever—that goes on most nights.

For thin new pizza with stylish, free-association toppings, I prefer *Orso*, 322 West 46th Street (489-7212), where the tomato, mozzarella, and sausage combination, and the tomato with cheese, red peppers, and onion are good before-or after-theater bracers, as is the tomato-cheese-basil classic. Pastas are also satisfying, but cooked foods pale by comparison.

Focaccia, rounds of spongy yeast bread, make savory sandwiches at ***Due***, 1396 Third Avenue (772-3331), run by the Lusardi brothers, in a polished, sophisticated setting designed by Charles Gwathmey. Focaccia with artichoke, mozzarella, and capers is my preference, followed by those with prosciutto, mozzarella, and tomato. Other fillings work less well for me.

*See also **Bleecker Luncheonette**, under Luncheonettes, **Il Nido Café**, under Cafés, and **Sant' Ambroeus**, under Pâtisseries*

JAPANESE

SUSHI AND SASHIMI

Because all Japanese restaurants serving these raw fish specialties do most of the same classic combinations, it seemed a better idea to describe the basics without repeating them for each of the favorites below. Both raw fish forms are best when eaten at the counters behind which they are prepared. Master sushi chefs are few and far between in this country, where novices who are often completely untrained perform for unknowing audiences. Japanese sushi connoisseurs look for important telltale signs of quality even before they bite into a single slice of raw fish (sashimi) or one of the rice and seafood packets (sushi). Very short hair, clipped fingernails, and clean shaves are considered essential for sushi makers, and the real purists do not even condone eyeglasses. The sushi master's work surface should be scrubbable wood. The flat sheets of seaweed (nori) used to enfold maki or rolled sushi should be crisp, golden-green, and lightly heated for a second so their flavor freshens and becomes toasty. That slight warming also provides temperature contrast to the room-temperature rice that has been flavored with rice vinegar and the slightly cooler-than-skin-temperature fish.

Nigiri or squeezed sushi are simply pressed into packets—fish on top, rice on bottom. They are sometimes bound with a strip of seaweed to keep fish in place. Gunkan-maki are wrapped with sidebands of seaweed for loose toppings such as salmon caviar (ikura) or the beautiful orange sea urchins (uni) that taste like very intense lobster coral.

Temakisushi or hand-rolls are often called Japanese ice cream cones, and they mark the finish to the sushi meal for many aficionados. They are cone shapes of folded seaweed filled with rice and such ingredients as tuna, cucumber, grilled salmon skin, or warm, glazed grilled eel. The customer or the sushi master makes the choice. As with all sushi, there is a touch of pungent green horseradish (wasabi) added, and soy sauce is used as a dip. Sushi may be handled with chopsticks, but fingers are preferable, and it is best to invert the sushi so that the fish, rather than the rice, is dipped into the soy sauce. It is also considered preferable to have the fish touch the tongue before the rice. Chirashi or scattered sushi combines the elements of sushi in loose fashion—slices of typical sushi fish, sweet omelet, and pickles over vinegar rice in square lacquer boxes or bowls.

Fish for the plain sashimi slices or the sushi are generally raw. A few types are served cooked or marinated, among them squid, mackerel, most shrimp, octopus, and salmon, which is smoked. Saltwater fish are the only kind served raw, although in Japan some buffs risk the parasites common to freshwater fish and eat those raw. When fresh river shrimp are available, they are served raw. One sushi-sashimi ingredient that has become common despite its inferiority is known as either surimi or kameboko—fish formed and colored to imitate a fish cake or Alaskan king crab, which itself seems an imitation of something anyway. There is also a tendency to use a very salty and unpleasant red fish roe for assorted sushi, rather than the fine salmon roe caviar used for à la carte orders. That rule prevails, by the way. It is always better to sit at the counter and order à la carte. Why that is so is a mystery, as the same chefs make sushi for counters and tables.

Besides, sitting at the counter one sees a floor show as the sushi masters work their magic with knives, hands, and rice. Ask what is especially fresh and good for the day, then order gradually. My own favorites among nigiri-sushi are fluke, snapper, yellowtail, the meaty clam muscle called geoduck, mackerel, shrimp, and grilled eel. I like all the rolled sushi except futo-maki—a big, rather gross checkerboard mix of fish, plums, and pickles. So-called California roll, an inside-out sushi with rice on the outside and with a filling of Alaskan king crab and avocado, is to me skippable. I always finish with a hand-roll and begin with a few slices of tuna sashimi, preferably the fatty pink toro. Miso soup and pickles (tsukemono) and spinach salad with sesame seeds (oshitashi) are also good accompaniments. Scotch is the drink I favor, with sake as a second choice.

Small dishes that we would consider appetizers are often served in sushi parlors, but the best do not have large main courses such as tempura, sukiyaki, and so on. Full-fledged Japanese restaurants rarely produce great sushi. I know of none that does in New York. One sure sign of a good sushi restaurant is the crowd that gathers. If it is not absolutely full, with a waiting line by 12:15 at lunchtime or by 5:45 in the evening, mediocre sushi are the best you can expect.

If there are vacant seats at 12:30 or 6:30, forget it. An early crowd is the best assurance of top quality.

The sushi restaurants included here—Hatsuhana, Sushisei, and Takesushi—do the above dishes, with a few variations as noted.

CHIKUBU

12 East 44th Street, between Fifth and Madison avenues
Telephone: 818-0715

Favorite meals:
Lunch
Lacquer box with assorted foods (makunouchi bento)
Tea
or
Lunch or dinner, shared by two
Cold noodles in soy sauce (soba)
Grilled fatty tuna or salmon
Breaded, fried pork cutlet (tonkatsu)
Shrimp with rice (kamemeshi)
Fruit
Other favorite dishes: Raw fish slices (sashimi); hot buckwheat noodles (kake soba); spinach salad (oshitashi); marinated seafood (nuta); red caviar with grated radish (ikura-oroshi); chicken teriyaki; sea urchin with yam base (konowata); broiled clams (yaki-hamaguri); steamed clams in sake (hamaguri-sakamushi); broiled crab meat with shell (kami-korayaki); fried fish tail cooked in soup with grated radish (amadai-oroshini); miso-covered eggplant (beinasu-shigiyaki); steamed egg custard with chicken, shrimp, and ginkgo nuts (chawan-mushi); day's special casserole (nabe) selection.
Setting: Subtle Japanese modern dining rooms, with counter and upstairs tatami rooms. Gray tile and blond wood create a clean, soothing, and casual setting; noisy when crowded.
Service: Quick, polite, and helpful at tables, but indifferent at counter.
Dress code: None.
Facilities for private parties: Four tatami rooms that accommodate 4 to 8.
Hours: Lunch, Monday through Friday. Dinner, Monday through Saturday. Closed Sunday and New Year's Day, but open other major holidays.
Reservations: Necessary, especially for lunch and weekday nights.
Prices: Moderate to expensive.
Credit cards: AE, DC.

This tiny, barely visible Japanese restaurant is one I have favored since it was in its original, even more obscure Upper East Side setting. Oddly enough, I value it now for reasons exactly opposite to those that formerly existed. Under its original owner, Hironobu Kishimoto, Chikubu's real action was at the long back counter, where the master dished up endless progressions of delectables, determined by him when one ordered "omakase," meaning it was up to him. In those days, food at tables was comparatively lackluster. Now the opposite is true. The counter is there and, under the new owner, omakase can be ordered, but it is a dull and stodgy array compared to former choices, and only a few are prepared in view, the rest coming cooked from the kitchen. Those cooked dishes are delicious, but as they are available at more comfortable tables, it is pointless to sit at the counter.

Food, though, at tables has become very good indeed, and so this sparklingly clean, crowded eatery, with its subtly contrasting gray stoneware tile and blond wood, its handsome dishes, and polite, quick staff, remains a favorite, especially at lunch when I am eating alone. The diverting and varied combination I like to order is the makunouchi bento, a trim lacquered box with divided compartments that hold a kaleidoscopic array of Japanese specialties such as sashimi, tiny skewers of the grilled, marinated chicken (yakitori), bits of kushikatsu (fried pork), pickles that gave a fine, salty crunch, warm rice, flecks of seaweed, and other delectables that change daily. Served with soup and tea, it is a pleasant lunch, as are the various "teishoku" or specials. Nabe (or casseroles), filled with rice that may be topped with slivers of chicken and a sort of steamed omelet with bits of vegetables, are inexpensive, stomach-warming fillers. The soy-and-rice-wine glazed grilled eel, kabayaki, is mellow and rich in its lacquer serving dish and kamemeshi, the Japanese version of risotto, is delicious whether the rice is cooked with chicken, shrimp, or oysters. Slim, firm tan buckwheat noodles are delicious cold, topped with scallions and dipped into soy sauce, or hot with broth.

Enticing small dishes, best enjoyed in a progression, include oshitashi, the wilted spinach salad flecked with silvery bits of dried bonito; nuta, a raw marinade of squid, tuna, or fluke that has a seductively satiny texture; a mound of pale red-gold salmon caviar nested beside grated white radish; and uni, or sea urchin, a coral glob with a characteristic shellfish flavor that contrasts to a base of softly cooked yam. Clams, whether steamed in sake or grilled, are tender and redolent of their salt-sea home, and crab is subtly rendered whether as sautéed soft shells or blue crabs grilled in the shell. Salmon broiled in salt with a crackling edge of its own skin and the fried tail of flounder that is adrift in broth with shavings of radish are more sophisticated. Dishes not done well here include limp and greasy tempura and lackluster sushi.

If one does sit at the counter and has the chef do the planning, a few dishes at least are bound to be above average. Among such have been tiny octopus marinated in plum juice and served with a tart, green miniature plum, slivers of jellyfish marinated in orange juice, and a bracing clear fish broth peppery with green radish sprouts.

Fresh fruit about does it for dessert, a better alternative than green-tea or red-bean ice cream. In the usual fashion, Westerners seem to drink sake while the Japanese stick to Scotch and beer.

HATSUHANA

17 East 48th Street, between Fifth and Madison avenues
Telephone: 355-3345

Favorite meal:
Miso soup
Sashimi of toro
Squid with sea urchin
Assorted sushi
Pickles
Other favorite dishes: Nuta, natto, oshitashi spinach salad, broiled scallops, fried soft-shell crabs, mackerel in white radish wrap, salt-broiled squid, chawan-mushi, pickles, and all sushi except futomaki, kameboko, and California roll.
Setting: Simple, brightly attractive modern dining rooms; table space is more comfortable upstairs; counter is livelier downstairs; crowded and noisy.
Service: Generally good, but when rushed staff seems to fall back on a language barrier that at other times does not exist.
Dress code: None.
Facilities for private parties: One room, seats four to six.
Hours: Lunch, Monday through Friday. Dinner, Monday through Saturday. Closed Sunday.
Reservations: Necessary for both counter and tables.
Prices: Moderately expensive to expensive.
Credit cards: AE, DC, MC, V.

To be very clear, the Hatsuhana I like is the original on East 48th Street. The later clone on East 45th Street is neither as comfortable nor as dependable. At this original, quality and workmanship are still exceptional, and a seat at the street-level counter provides one of the best floor shows. Sashimi slices are presented on glossy ti leaves, sushi are pressed perfectly so the textures feel right against the teeth, and rice is firm but tender. Miso soup has an almost lemony edge to it and is the best in the city.

This is one place where sushi at the table match those at the counter, and if four people order a deluxe array, they can be prepared for a huge round black lacquer box filled with a bright mosaic of delectables.

Though at times fish can be a bit too cold here, and the ginger cut in overly large slices, Hatsuhana offers the best sushi in the city. It also has the widest and most exotic array of ingredients, including fresh sweet water shrimp, served raw over lemon slices, flakes of scallops heaped in nori-wrapped, rice-based ovals, and a tantalizing hand-roll of grilled salmon skin.

Small dishes are also nicely turned out in the upstairs dining room, where we sometimes plan a menu that includes squid or scallops broiled in salt or butter, the custard chawan-mushi, squid enveloped in coral sea urchin roe, and the fermented soybean salad, natto, broiled clams and squid that have a rich burnish about them, and pickles. It is a costly but delightful way to eat unless, of course, there is a rush of business and waiters feign a language barrier.

INAGIKU

111 East 49th Street, between Park and Lexington avenues,
in the Waldorf-Astoria Hotel
Telephone: 355-0440

Favorite meal and favorite dishes:
At the tempura bar only!!
Tempura assortment ending with mixed fritter of fish, shrimp, and vegetables (kakiage), shared by two.
Setting: Tempura bar is simple, modern, somewhat crowded, and in disarray.
Service: Chefs are especially obliging and informative at night. Service is slow and careless at lunch.
Dress code: Jacket required for men.
Facilities for private parties: Two tatami rooms that take five to eight; one Western-style dining room that takes 15 to 20. Outside catering is done.
Hours: Lunch, Monday through Friday. Dinner, seven days. Closed major holidays and January 1–5.
Reservations: Recommended for tempura bar.
Prices: Moderately expensive.
Credit cards: AE, CB, DC, MC, V.

Although this sprawling, confused, modern restaurant in the Waldorf has a full menu of Japanese dishes, the only thing that lures me is the tempura bar. At dinner this is the best tempura in the city, done piece-by-piece by chefs in high black-mesh hats who are masters of this frying technique. Using what is described as a blend of olive, sesame, and camellia oils and constantly skimming off fried bits of batter so they do not burn, the chefs fry, and present at intervals, shrimp, fillets, whole tiny fish, squid wrapped with seaweed, zucchini, asparagus, green peppers, onion slices, lotus root, sweet potatoes, and eggplant. The assortment is slightly less varied and interesting at lunch. Preceded by the lovely miso bean soup, the tempura meal is a delight. The batter is always lacy and crunchy, and with dips of radish-flavored soy sauce or lemon juice with salt, it achieves a magical brightness. Kakiage, the traditional tempura windup in Japan, must be ordered à la carte. It is a solid, sustaining fritter formed of minced squid, shrimp, fish, and vegetables, fried as a sort of croquette, which is meant to use up the bits and pieces left from making the main tempura items. One kakiage is enough for two, and it can be ordered as a main course in itself instead of other fish choices.

Better ventilation, more orderly housekeeping, and more careful service at the tempura bar would be welcome, but the slight discomfort is worth experiencing for the extraordinary food. Not so the disorganized staff, the high prices, and the uneven preparations of other Japanese specialties in the rest of the dining rooms.

KITCHO

22 West 46th Street, between Fifth and Sixth avenues
Telephone: 575-8880

Favorite meals:
Shared by two
Salmon caviar with grated radish (suzuko)
Miso bean soup
Fried pork cutlet (tonkatsu)
Pickles
Seafood and rice (seafood Kamemeshi)
Green tea ice cream
or
Shared by two
Fatty tuna (toro)
Crab meat and cucumber salad (sunomono)
Steak grilled on a stone (ishiyaki)
Spinach salad (oshitashi)
Steamed custard with shrimp and vegetables (chawan-mushi)
Fruit
Other favorite dishes: Grilled clams (yaki-hama), all sliced raw fish (sashimi), all soups, breaded fried pork (kushikatsu), teriyaki grilled beef or chicken, chef's special dinners. Scotch and sake are the best drinks with this food; beer is also good.
Setting: Simple, pleasant, modern dining room downstairs that is informal and usually crowded; private tatami rooms upstairs must be reserved; no sushi bar.
Service: Friendly, helpful, and professional.
Dress code: None.
Facilities for private parties: Eight tatami dining rooms that accommodate between 3 and 25.
Hours: Lunch, Monday through Friday. Dinner, Monday through Friday and Sunday. Closed Saturday and major holidays.
Reservations: Necessary.
Prices: Moderately expensive.
Credit cards: AE, DC.

Although Kitcho now rates three stars instead of the four it earned in the previous edition of this book, it remains New York's very best option for a full Japanese menu with serious cooking and an enormous menu. If the previous glow is somewhat dimmed by slightly less exciting presentations, the kitchen's performance is still remarkably high. The biggest change now is in comfort, an unfortunate result of the new smoking laws that require restaurants to have separate sections for smokers and non-smokers. At Kitcho, smokers get the more attractive back dining room, while the overly bright, workaday front section is for non-smokers. Furthermore, because that back room is small and close, the smoking fumes build up mightily at peak hours.

Kitcho is a surprisingly casual restaurant. Although pleasant and brightly modern, the downstairs dining room has a café informality, with closely set tables that make for a fairly high noise level at peak hours. There are more atmospheric tatami rooms that can be reserved upstairs, but groups of dark-suited Japanese businessmen seem equally fond of both settings. As in so many Asian restaurants, some of the more esoteric dishes do not appear in English on the menu, so it is a good idea to ask for what you want, whether from the descriptions here or by spotting enticing-looking choices at other tables. That way I found that the kitchen turned out a fine, creamy nuta (the small salad of tuna, squid, or fluke), that in autumn there were the golden matsutake mushrooms to be had grilled or steeped in a fragrant broth, and that at all times ishiyaki (tender filet of beef sliced and grilled on a hot stone at the table) was on hand. Do not be embarrassed to ask about dishes you see, even if that means pointing—never mind what Miss Manners thinks.

Through the years only sushi (not served at a counter) and tempura (deep-fried seafood and vegetable assortments) have been disappointing compared with other examples around town. But that leaves dozens of exceptional alternatives, all nicely presented by an interestingly diverse staff—male waiters in trim, conventional white jackets, women gracefully dressed in kimonos, and a waitress or two in a starchy white uniform suggesting a very efficient nurse. All seem intent upon being of service; if there is a hierarchy, it is not imposed on customers, or at least not on non-Japanese.

The current American dining phenomenon, grazing or eating small amounts of several appetizer-size dishes, comes naturally to the Japanese, who have been doing exactly that for centuries. Not only is it a diverting way to eat, but it makes it possible to maintain a nutritionally varied diet, as one eats through a tempting progression of fish, vegetables, bean curd, rice or noodles, small amounts of meat, and finally fruit. The raw, transparently thin slices of saltwater fish that make up the sashimi selections are glowingly fresh at Kitcho, whether you choose the delicate fluke, the zesty yellowtail, the marinated mackerel, or the favorite tuna, sliced in thicker strips as the lean, beefy makura or the prized fatty belly portion, toro. Dipped into soy sauce spiked with the fiery green horseradish, wasabi, sashimi can be an appetizer or a complete meal. Yaki-hama (broiled clams that are reminiscent of the Italian clams casino) are savory and satisfying, and other tiny enticements include the refreshing salad of crab meat and wilted cucumbers (sunomono); warm grilled seaweed with wasabi (yakinori); and cool wilted spinach accented by sesame seeds (shitashi).

Cold buckwheat noodles (soba), sprightly with minced scallions and mellowed by soy sauce, are as delicious as they are restorative, and for an elegant touch, there is pale golden salmon roe caviar nestled against pungent grated Japanese radish. Clear or miso soups, salty crisp pickles, and tiny nuggets of marinated chicken grilled on skewers (yakitori) are other delectable choices. More substantial dishes that would be considered main courses to Westerners are the breaded chicken or pork, crisp and greaselessly deep-fried in vegetable oil, and all of the teriyaki meats, poultry, and fish. Salt-broiled salmon with a crackling edge of silvery skin and a sort of Japanese risotto—clam kamemeshi—served in a handsome, rustic wooden steamer are favorites. I can almost never leave without having chawan-mushi, a winy custard flecked with ginkgo nuts, bright greens, bits of shrimp and fish, and grated lemon rind, steamed in a pretty porcelain cup. It ranks among the world's great soul foods.

Ripe melon or spiral-sliced orange, a nashi (Oriental pear-apple), and green tea ice cream are the best desserts. I prefer Scotch with this food as do most of the Japanese, judging by the bottles of "Pinch" and Black Label that stand on their tables. Sapporo beer is a second choice, and warm sake seems to be an obligatory, ritualistic starter before Scotch. Wonderful banquets of chef's specialties can be ordered here for either the tatami rooms or the tables. They are best for groups of six to eight.

OMEN

113 Thompson Street, between Prince and Spring streets
Telephone: 925-8923

Favorite meal:
Shared by two
Spinach, scallops, and peanuts (peanut-ae)
Nuta with clams or shrimp
Marinated chicken (sansho)
Broth with noodles and vegetables (omen)
Ice cream

Japanese

Other favorite dishes: Spinach and mushrooms with sesame (goma-ae); spinach salad (oshitashi); tofu tempura; clams steamed with sake; miso bean soup; chicken with radish (mizor); broiled salmon (yaki-jake); mixed sashimis; shrimp, octopus, or clams with fermented soybean sauce and scallions (nuta); pickles (tsukemono).
Setting: Trim, rustic Japanese country café; informal and a bit noisy when full.
Service: Generally good but slow.
Dress code: None.
Facilities for private parties: None.
Hours: Dinner, Tuesday through Sunday. Brunch, Saturday and Sunday. Closed Monday.
Reservations: Recommended.
Prices: Moderate.
Credit cards: AE, DC.

Men is one Japanese word for noodles, a derivation of the Chinese *mein*. (Larmen Dosanko, which we think of as a chain featuring Japanese-style noodle soups, is to the Japanese a Chinese-inspired noodle dish—lo mein.) Starting then with *men* for noodles and affixing the Japanese honorific *o* we get *Omen*, a three-hundred-year-old traditional soup enriched with burdock root, spinach, scallions, noodles, and sometimes bean curd. Ribbons of the seaweed kelp add a salty tang as well as minerals, as do the dried flakes of bonito fish. Ginger, hot pepper powder, and roasted sesame seeds make Omen as sustaining to the palate as it is to the body.

Although that is the specialty of this casual, rustic SoHo eating place, it is not the only unusual and pleasant offering. Small dishes to be had before or, in a progression, instead of Omen include coolly marinated sansho chicken or another cold chicken and radish salad, tori-mizore. Tuna sashimi is generally as fresh as it should be; for some strange reason the fluke (hirame) is even more dependable. Maybe that is what they mean by a fluke. Spinach with scallops and peanut sauce (peanut-ae), and nuta of clams or octopus are other tantalizing appetizers. Clams are sometimes on hand, steamed in sake, a subtle blend of the winey and the briny, but too substantial if Omen is to be had. Another sustaining main course alternative is yaki-jake, carefully broiled salmon that remains moist and tender. Skip tempura, chawan-mushi, and the soybean salad natto, which are not as well prepared as the other choices. Good brown rice provides a solid underpinning for most of these dishes, and fresh fruit or ice cream is a refreshing finish. There is a smart little bar where singles can eat or meet; beer and wine are available.

The young staff members at Omen are good-natured and more efficient than formerly. Small, closely set tables make for a convivial din that no one seems to mind. Those who want quiet can ask for the back alcove-balcony, which has a curious out-of-it feeling. But take your choice between quiet and being part of the entertaining scene.

SERYNA

11 East 53rd Street, between Fifth and Madison avenues
Telephone: 980-9393, 980-9394

Favorite meals:
Lunch
Japanese fish soup
Stuffed Dover sole
Green tea ice cream
or
Dinner
Stuffed fried crab (kohra age)
Sirloin steak, grilled on a stone (ishiyaki)
Pickles
Fruit
Other favorite dishes: Salt-broiled scallops, steamed red snapper with vegetables, beef cooked in broth at table (shabu-shabu), grilled salmon, crab meat dumplings (shumai).
Setting: Inviting, stylish dining room that somewhat suggests a tropical cocktail lounge in an international hotel; large tables are generally widely spaced; seating and noise level are comfortable.
Service: Polite, professional, and efficient.
Dress code: Jackets required for men.
Facilities for private parties: Four rooms, each accommodating up to 20.
Hours: Lunch, Monday through Friday. Dinner, Monday through Saturday. Closed Sunday and major holidays.
Reservations: Necessary.
Prices: Moderately expensive.
Credit cards: AE, CB, DC, MC, V.

Every restaurant critic is asked if there is a restaurant he or she does not write about so that it will remain an undiscovered private retreat. I have rarely been tempted to do that, always wanting credit for a good find. Seryna is one of the few exceptions, not because the food is extraordinary (just very good) or because it is a bargain (it is fairly expensive), but because it is a perfect place in which to talk. Being relatively invisible, it offers large tables, widely set apart from one another, comfortable upholstered lounge chair seats, a noise level that is usually benign, a charming and efficient staff, and diverting food that is not too heavy. Also, although Japanese, it is not unremittingly so; that means even the least adventurous palate can be satisfied.

Apparently, there is no cause for worry. For though it does a nice brisk business, Seryna remains more or less undiscovered, apparently not dramatic enough to be the focus of the restaurant-madness set. In addition, it is very hard to find, laid out as it is in a set-back building with no name at the street line and only the most discreet lettering at the entrance. If the management wanted to keep it a secret, they could not do it better. Seryna is a chain in Tokyo and Yokohama (there is also a branch in Los Angeles) and exemplifies the Japanese idea of a Western restaurant. Here they take one more turn and make it the Japanese idea of a Western notion of a Japanese restaurant. Hence the conventional seating, the forks and knives offered right along with chopsticks, the tropical-cocktail-lounge look, and the simple Japanese grill menu.

There are entertaining Western accents on that menu. The Japanese ishiyaki, steak sliced and grilled on a hot stone at the table, is accompanied here by french fries that have a fine potato flavor. Both filet and sirloin are available; the filet is easier to bite when held with chopsticks, but the sirloin has a better flavor, as usual. With the steak (best blood-rare) there are two dipping sauces—one aromatic with chili, the other gentled with garlic. Very Japanese and very good is the shabu-shabu, the boil-at-the-table combination of paper-thin sliced beef, noodles, and vegetables, all to be dipped into ponzu—a soy and lime sauce.

Stuffed Dover sole with crab meat in a spicy dark sauce is now almost as good as the steamed whole red snapper, seasoned with exotic herbs and garnished with steamed vegetables. Sushi leave much to be desired, but the sliced raw fish sashimi is fresh and flavorful, although at times too cold. Salt(shio)-broiled scallops and the stuffed, greaseless fried crab in a shell are good starters, as are the petite crab meat dumplings, shumai. Not so the soups, the salads, and the too-liquid version of the steamed custard, chawan-mushi. Teriyaki broiled scallops are decent, and the salt pickles make a refreshing contrast to the steak. Tempura could be crisper, and the oil used for frying it should be fresher.

The green tea ice cream has been unusually good, and fruit is always ripe.

SHINWA

645 Fifth Avenue, corner 51st Street, in Olympic Tower
Telephone: 644-7400

Favorite meals:
Lunch
Hot noodles with duck in soup, served with baby clams in rice (kamo nanban, asari gohan)
Pineapple
or
Dinner, shared by two
Sushi filled with pickles (oshinko maki)
Custard with shrimp, vegetables, and noodles (odawara mushi)

Grilled marinated salmon (salmon teriyaki)
Cold noodles with soy dipping sauce (zaru)
Melon
Other favorite dishes: Wooden box with assorted fish, vegetables, and buckwheat noodles (kyo shiki bento); lacquer box filled with rice topped with grilled pheasant (kiji bento); marinated octopus (sunomono); salmon roe caviar with grated Japanese radish and lemon (ikura oroshi); assorted raw fish sashimi (tsukuri moriawase); meat, vegetables, and noodles in curry soup (curry nanban).
Setting: Simple, attractive Japanese-style café, bar, and downstairs dining room, adjacent to indoor waterfall; fairly crowded and moderately noisy.
Service: Alternates between polite efficiency and blank confusion; hectic during lunch hour.
Dress code: None.
Facilities for private parties: One waterfall-side room accommodates 10 to 30.
Hours: Lunch and dinner, Monday through Saturday. Closed Sunday.
Reservations: Generally necessary, especially for lunch, *if* they answer the phone.
Prices: Inexpensive to moderate.
Credit cards: AE, CB, DC, MC, V.

"By Japanese for Japanese" should be the motto here. Step through the revolving door into the lobby of Olympic Tower, and see if you think you're in New York or Tokyo. The sea of faces of earnest, fast-talking, fast-eating, young Japanese office workers and junior executives could be just a few steps off the Ginza. Once a French café, this two-level restaurant is now the place for relatively quick, intriguing, and serviceable Japanese lunches and dinners, most typically built around the noodles said to be made on the premises—the long, thick, chewy, white udon of wheat flour and the slender, sophisticated, tan buckwheat soba, my preference.

Main courses with side bowls of pickles, vegetables, rice, or salad and tea are served on trays, so that service moves quickly. Ask for à la carte sushi at lunch and you will be discouraged with the warning of a 30-minute wait, one not worthwhile, considering the sorry specimens that appear. In fact, most elegant Japanese delicacies are second-rate here. The winners are the deeply satisfying, soul-soothing tray meals.

One of the best centers around moist, boneless slices of grilled pheasant brushed with a salt-sweet teriyaki sauce and nested on rice in a lacquer box (kiji bento), complete with a winy miso bean soup and pickles that are wise substitutes for the iceberg lettuce salad. As an alternative, there are tender flecks of lean duck meat floating in hot broth with noodles (your choice of soba or udon), alongside a dish of clam kamameshi, a sort of Japanese risotto. Pickles, again, give a cutting edge to the flavor. Smaller variations on the above include hot noodles with beef and broth (niku-nanban) and a ribsticking, scalding hot, spicy curry broth (curry nanban) in a huge bowl with flakes of beef, shreds of scallions and greens, and, in this case, the more appropriate udon.

Things to avoid include all foods that are fried because they are pallid and taste of overheated oil. That means no tempura or the skewered appetizers, kushi-age. Crab meat dumplings (shumai) are doughy and dull, but any raw fish (sashimi) and the steamy custard "soup" (odawara mushi), set with udon, shrimp, ginkgo nuts, fish, and vegetables, are fine. Sharply pickled Japanese vegetables rolled with rice in seaweed (oshinko maki) are enlivening sushi to have with a drink and there are some unusual salad bowls of Japanese vegetables such as the colorful wafu salad. Tender marinated octopus and fresh salmon caviar are also dependable.

The teriyaki grilled wafu steak, though decent, is skippable, though the boiled potatoes with it are unusually flavorful. Better to have them with the thick cuts of teriyaki broiled salmon that remains moist and coral-bright.

I found dishes such as the grilled eel (kabayaki) and beef with scallions (negimaki) to be lackluster. Not so the cool, blessedly fresh and ripe fruit, whether you choose melon, oranges, or pineapple. Tea is properly scalding, and there is, of course, full bar service, including sake and Japanese beer.

The entire Shinwa menu is also available at the long, pleasant bar-counter on the lobby level, for those eating alone or in a great rush.

Fortunately, the drowning gush and flickering brightness of the waterfall have been muted. It would be a bit too much to bear along with the hectic staff that is disorganized at lunch, although more relaxed at dinner. At times there is a language barrier. Ask one of the Occidental waiters to describe a dish or explain what the restaurant's name means, and he looks blank, unable to grasp your English. He summons a Japanese waitress who answers perfectly, saying that Shinwa means "new communications." It's hard to tell what that means when you call for reservations and no one answers the phone. Once they do, be sure you know what you want, or they hang up. New communications?

SUSHISEI

123 West 49th Street, between Sixth and Seventh avenues,
in the Exxon Building.
Telephone: 265-1277

Favorite meals:
Sushi and sashimi, at counter
Other favorite dishes: Spinach salad (oshitashi); radish sprouts (kaiware salad); hand-rolls; assorted raw fish, pickles, and rice (Sushisei chirashi); box of assorted foods (Sushisei bento); tuna or yellowtail with scallions.

Setting: Tiny, trim dining room with sushi counter. Tables are cramped; inadequate ventilation.
Service: Efficient and courteous, if sometimes slow.
Dress code: None.
Facilities for private parties: None.
Hours: Lunch, Monday through Friday. Dinner, Saturday. Closed Sunday and major holidays.
Reservations: Recommended at peak hours.
Prices: Inexpensive to moderate.
Credit cards: AE, MC, V.

Sushi that is pleasantly fresh and moderately priced is hard to find, most especially close to the Theater District. Also hard to find is this semi-secret source—Sushisei, a trim, tiny Japanese luncheonette that is pocketed away in the lobby of the Exxon Building. Enter through that lobby, or through the unrelated but adjacent Larmen Dosanko on 49th Street.

Under the same management as the Sushisei that has been a fixture in Tsukiji (Tokyo's wholesale fish market) since 1888, the New York offshoot provides satisfying food and service to match. By far the best choices are sushi and sashimi, with a full selection of such favorites as tuna (both lean and fatty), yellowtail, fluke, clam muscle, octopus, cooked shrimp, salmon, mackerel, and the more luxurious salmon caviar and sea urchin roe with the salt-sea tang that is balanced by soothing vinegar rice and smoky seaweed. Unlike really impeccable and elegant sushi establishments, Sushisei does not toast the seaweed before it is used, and so it is sometimes limp though well flavored, and the crafting of the sushi is a bit casual.

Nevertheless, the raw fish slices (sashimi) are fresh and bright. For a good, moderately priced lunch, try a selection of them in the Sushisei chirashi, the various fish layered over vinegar rice along with pickled vegetables prettily arranged in a lacquer bowl. For larger appetites, more of the same are fitted into the bento meals, typically set out in a bright mosaic of colors, flavors, and textures in a lacquer box.

As in most such places, sushi are best enjoyed at the counter, where one orders a progression as desired, and where I always end up with a hand-roll—a cone of seaweed holding vinegar rice and fish such as salmon, yellowtail, or, my favorite, anago—eel grilled with a sweet and pungent soy glaze. Silken minced tuna or yellowtail flecked with wisps of scallions is another satisfying last course.

To be avoided here are "small dishes" served at dinner—not because they are bad, but because the sushi and sashimi are so much better. Also ask to have kameboko (fake crab meat formed of pressed fish) eliminated from your selections.

Soups are weak here, but I like to round out a raw fish meal with either the wilted spinach salad (oshitashi) or the refreshing, slightly stinging kaiware, a mound of crisp, bitter radish sprouts tossed with slivered scallions and dried bonito fish flakes.

It is possible to have a satisfying light meal for as little as $12 to $15 not including tip or alcoholic beverages such as sake or beer. Given those prices and the quickness of meals, the cramped quarters are bearable, but better ventilation would be welcome, especially in corners that become stuffy.

Sushisei can be crowded at peak lunch and dinner hours, so make reservations, especially before the theater. This place also prepares attractive take-out arrangements of the bento and chirashi specialties, as well as of sushi, sashimi, and salads.

TAKESUSHI

71 Vanderbilt Avenue (230 Park Avenue), at 45th Street
Telephone: 867-5120

Favorite meals and favorite dishes:
Shared by two at a table
Spinach salad (oshitashi)
Deluxe "omakase" sushi or sashimi combination
or
Clam soup
Grated radish with salmon caviar
Nuta with tuna fish
Chicken grilled on skewers (yakitori)
Grilled squid
Sunomono salad of tuna
Custard steamed with shrimp and vegetables (chawan-mushi)
Pineapple
or
At the sushi bar
Any sushi or sashimi

Setting: Attractive modern dining room with blond wood and grass-green carpet; sushi bar and booths are the most comfortable locations; ventilation could be improved.
Service: Polite and well-meaning but very slow at peak hours.
Dress code: None.
Facilities for private parties: One tatami room accommodates four or five; another tatami room accommodates four to eight. Outside catering is available.
Hours: Lunch, Monday through Friday. Dinner, Monday through Saturday. Closed Sunday and major holidays.
Reservations: Necessary for tables and sushi bar.
Prices: Moderately expensive.
Credit cards: AE, DC, CB, MC, V.

Beautifully cool, fresh, well-crafted sushi and delicate, flavorful slices of sashimi are the main attractions of Takesushi, tucked away on Vanderbilt Avenue and humming with activity day and night. It is also the most attractive of the sushi restaurants, with its blond wood trim, grass-green carpet, and partitioned alcoves, which allow for more privacy and protection from noise than do the open tables. Otherwise, this is a hectic place with unfortunately slow if courteous service. When the management is aware that things have bogged down, complimentary dishes are sent to the table—a nice touch if it doesn't go on too long. On one such evening, we had oshitashi, the refreshing wilted spinach salad, set off with flakes of dried bonito fish, and baked scallops in a shell—good but uncharacteristically greasy.

The real action is at the sushi bar, where efficient, helpful sushi masters deftly turn out trim versions of all the standard specialties. They also do artful platters of sushi and/or sashimi assortments to be shared by two or more at the bar or at tables. Order the "omakase" version of either, meaning that the choice is left up to the sushi master. I like to finish up with a satisfying hand-roll, the best being yellowtail with scallions.

Both the golden miso bean soup and the invigorating clam broth with clams are good before sushi or a progression of small dishes.

Among such, my favorites are the snowy mound of grated white radish crested with red salmon caviar (sushi restaurants traditionally buy the best available specimens of that caviar); the grilled squid (tender, but with a nutty bite); nuta, which is raw fish stirred through a velvety golden sauce; sunomono (any salad that has a clear vinegar dressing) made with octopus, tuna, squid, or yellowtail, accented by cucumbers and marinated seaweed; and yakitori, the nuggets of boneless chicken glazed with teriyaki sauce and grilled on skewers. Tempura is hopelessly awash in grease, and it's pretty stale grease at that. I therefore avoid anything fried here. Salt-grilled salmon is fresh and cooked to moist perfection.

Chawan-mushi, the steamed custard with bits of fish, shrimp, vegetables, and ginkgo nuts, is a lovely finish. Fresh pineapple has always proved a better dessert than the underripe melon.

At lunchtime only sushi, sashimi, and soups are served downstairs, with all other dishes offered upstairs. At dinner the upstairs is closed, and the full assortment is served downstairs. Reservations are essential at both meals.

TIDBITS

Sapporo, 152 West 49th Street, just east of Seventh Avenue (869-8972), is the place to sample the ramen that was so memorably introduced to Americans in the film *Tampopo*. The thick, chewy noodles served in broth along with a choice of vegetables, fish, meat, or chicken are derived both gastronomically and linguistically from the Chinese lo mein. In this always-crowded, tiny luncheonette, at either the steamy counter behind which cooking is done or at small tables, devotees eat their fill for $5 or $6, and sometimes less, depending on the garnishes chosen. Only the shoyu soups are not recommended because they are stingingly salty. This is a fine, quick, and inexpensive option for a pre-theater meal. Open for lunch and dinner, seven days.

JEWISH AND KOSHER

Considering the size of New York's Jewish population, it is hard to understand why there is no really fine and attractive kosher restaurant and why so few serve excellent Jewish food even if it is not kosher. Thirty or forty years ago, there were a number of savory options in this category, including full-fledged white-tablecloth restaurants, dairy restaurants, and far more great delicatessens than we have now.
The best of the sparse possibilities follow.

CARNEGIE DELICATESSEN & RESTAURANT

854 Seventh Avenue, between 54th and 55th streets
Telephone: 757-2245

Favorite meals:
Breakfast
Fresh orange juice
Cheese blintzes with sour cream
Coffee
or
Dinner
Chicken or boiled beef in the pot
Cheesecake
Coffee
Other favorite dishes: All smoked fish with or without bagels and especially smoked whitefish plate, oatmeal, French toast, chicken soup with matzo balls, cabbage soup, tongue and eggs, jumbo all-beef frankfurters with sauerkraut, Nova Scotia salmon and onions with scrambled eggs, tongue or salami and eggs.
Setting: Typical, huge, sprawling, and crowded New York deli decor.
Service: Generally good, but can be rude and pushy late-night.
Dress code: None.
Facilities for private parties: None, but they do catering and take-out.
Hours: Seven days, from 6:30 A.M. to 4 A.M. Closed the first day of Rosh Hashanah and Yom Kippur Eve and Day, opening after 6 P.M. on Yom Kippur night.
Reservations: Not accepted.
Prices: Inexpensive to moderate.
Credit cards: None.

When Leo Steiner died at the end of 1987, we lost not only the greatest deli man this city, or any other, has ever known, but a brilliant, quintessential New Yorker. Not only was the generous, convivial, and beautifully, brassily loud Leo the spirit of the Carnegie, but its brain as well, what with his instinct for quality and his knowledge of his trade. He was also a natural genius in the way he handled people—employees and customers alike, working with a mix of languages and backgrounds that would have driven less gifted restaurateurs to throw in their toques. His kitchen was a Babel of tongues, but Leo respected each man for what he could do and knew how to get the best out of each, always taking care of his help, as he did his customers.

Because of his knowledge and dedication, without Leo Steiner anyone who loved the Carnegie and its pastrami, corned beef, and other cholesterol-defying delectables feared for the future of the deli. Having been back several times, I can report that almost all is as it was before, but almost is what accounts for a two-star rating instead of the previous three. Not nearly as good as before are the pastrami and the corned beef. Both now lack their former supple softness and the edge of spicy flavor. The pastrami needs more pepper and smoke, the corned beef a more generous marbling of fat, so that it will not become dark and dense as it cools. Most noticeable of all, the pastrami seems to be made of a different, narrower, and more sinewy cut of beef.

Nevertheless, the meats are layered up in the characteristically mountainous stacks to be eaten along with wonderfully firm and succulently sour garlic-deli pickles and cool, saline, pickled green tomatoes. Coleslaw is coarser and perhaps better than it used to be, and, just so the crowd doesn't go away hungry, knishes are now available, the best being those filled with mashed potatoes. Skip the mealy kasha and stale-tasting meat fillings in favor of the potatoes.

Milton Parker, one of Leo Steiner's partners, oversees kitchen and dining room, and the staff exudes a special pride in knowing that their customers are still going away happily satisfied. The scene remains an only-in-New York classic, despite the addition of an awful revolving pastry display case that has more to do with Greek coffee shops than with an authentic deli. Only late-night does the staff lack the friendliness expected here.

In rating the Carnegie two stars, I must point out that there is a whole category of dishes I ignore. They are far less than wonderful and to me are out of keeping with the spirit of the place. They include cooked food such as goulash, short ribs, etc., not specifically recommended here, and salad platters of tuna, egg, or chicken, piled high with iceberg lettuce.

Other dishes I continue to avoid at the Carnegie are chopped liver (not chicken liver and too pasty), leaden potato pancakes, and gefilte fish, which is commercial.

My favorite times at the Carnegie are between meals, when the peak crushes are not in force. That means mid-morning breakfast, at which I might have freshly squeezed orange juice, expertly cooked eggs (three is the standard portion), or smoked salmon with cream cheese on a bagel, or a slab of nice, woodsy smoked whitefish with a toasted bialy, or homemade cheese blintzes with sour cream.

For early or late lunch or dinner, I might start with the matzo ball soup that is the city's best, or the cabbage soup. Usually, I have a half portion of soup, something the house willingly serves, and follow it with a pancake omelet of tongue and eggs, always asking that the tongue be center slices—for which there is an added charge, but worth it. Or one of the spectacular sandwiches such as rare roast beef, pot-roasted beef brisket, or salami that has been allowed to dry and age. Meats can be combined in sandwiches, although I do not like them that way. Rather, my husband and I order two different sandwiches and switch halves, for variety. I also like to order those meats on a plate if I am not in the mood for a super-sandwich; their flavor and texture are even better appreciated that way. Chicken in the pot and boiled beef, both with noodles, matzo balls, and vegetables, are juicy and flavorful and are improved with fresh carrots and celery instead of canned string beans and soggy peas.

Salami and eggs is another of my preferred dishes, as is the combination of scrambled eggs with smoked salmon and onions. Although I do not often have one here, the Carnegie broils a terrific hamburger. Big thick jumbo beef frankfurters are served either boiled or, as I like them, split and grilled, and I choose sauerkraut rather than canned baked beans as an accompaniment. Cold sauerkraut, by the way, is the side dish I prefer to coleslaw with deli meats.

"Beer is the wine of the great deli," the menu advises, to which I must add, so is hot tea. That, along with the firm but slightly custardy cheesecake, is all the finish a meal requires.

Carnegie does a huge take-out business and caters parties and business meetings, all with the same flourish. As the Carnegie is opening outposts in other parts of the country and around the New York area, I want to make it clear that anything I write refers only to the original; I have not been to the others.

SAMMY'S FAMOUS ROUMANIAN RESTAURANT ★★★

157 Chrystie Street, near Delancey Street
Telephone: 673-5526, 673-0330, 475-9131

Favorite meals:
Shared by two
Stuffed derma (kishka)
Eggplant salad, Sammy's style
One order of Rumanian tenderloin steak, large size
Silver-dollar potatoes
or
Shared by six
Sliced brains
Broiled chicken livers and unborn eggs
Grated radish with onions and chicken fat
Rumanian beef sausages (karnatzlach)
Grilled rib steak
Stuffed cabbage
Breaded veal cutlet
Mashed potatoes with chicken fat
Other favorite dishes: Calf's foot jelly (patcha), chopped eggs and onions, fried kreplach, chicken soup with noodles, mushroom-barley soup, eye of the rib steak (mush steak), broiled veal chops, broiled chicken, boiled beef flanken with mushroom-barley gravy, kasha varnishkes with onions and dried mushrooms, seltzer, lots of hot tea, Alka-Seltzer.
Setting: No-frills dining room bursting with conviviality; jam-packed, noisy, and with live music every night.
Service: Cheerful, patient, and efficient.
Dress code: The management says, "Comfortable," which means no tight belts.
Facilities for private parties: Separate dining room accommodates 40 to 100.
Hours: Dinner, seven days. Closed Yom Kippur eve, day, and night. There are special Seder dinners with songs and services on the first two nights of Passover with one seating only, beginning at 6:30.
Reservations: Necessary.
Prices: Moderate.
Credit cards: AE, CB, DC.

About twice a year—perhaps when the first cold snap of autumn arrives and when there has been a damp, wet snow in late February or early March—I get a yen for Sammy's. That longing builds slowly, but I know what's coming when I begin to dream about the garlic-zapped roasted green peppers always on the table and find that in the midst of serious business conversations my thoughts are on a big bowl of creamy gray mushroom soup fluffy with barley, and my teeth almost ache for a bite of that rare and bloody, sublimely tender and beefy Rumanian tenderloin, the skirt steak so impeccably grilled in the best Rumanian-Jewish tradition. Then my husband and I round up about four friends (six is my favorite number for this knockdown-drag-out evening of food and song) and go. The rest becomes history, written in yet another inch on my waistline.

Everything about Sammy's needs an explanation, beginning with its name. Stated fully, it is "Sammy's Famous Roumanian Jewish Steak House Restaurant." Variations on that abound, including whether "Famous" goes before or after "Sammy's" and the correct spelling of Roumanian-Rumanian-Romanian—take your pick. What also needs explaining is how a restaurant in this disaster of a Lower East Side neighborhood can pack people in, night after night, year after year, as big fancy cars pull up to the curb and the waiting line spills out of the three-steps-down doorway on weekends.

And how does this kitchen manage to maintain such high levels of excellence, turning out voluminous portions of hot, steaming, and savory food at a rapid pace while the dining-room staff moving through the jam-packed room full of demanding, food-crazed customers maintains an air of cheerful goodwill and efficiency throughout? It should also be explained that though the food is Rumanian-Jewish, it is not kosher, witness the containers of milk on every table to be mixed with Fox's U-Bet chocolate syrup and seltzer to make egg creams. That milk with a menu featuring meat is all the tip-off one needs to the non-kosherness of Sammy's.

The clientele includes yuppies in jeans or *Miami Vice* regalia and loyal middle-class devotees from Manhattan and the suburbs, and the local pols, theater folk, judges, writers, and painters. It is that kind of place. The only people who do not go, because they have been and have not liked it, are those who are tone-deaf to New York. This is, in fact, the restaurant that separates true New Yorkers from lily-livered poseurs, those who are reluctant to mix it up with an essential element in the city's makeup.

Even to use the word decor in relation to Sammy's is stretching a point. It has none. It is just a room full of tables and chairs and people, clanging with voices of staff and customers against a backdrop of live singing and piano playing of a Jewish, Israeli, and Eastern European repertory that sometimes includes a wild-card number from a Broadway show, or even a French-inspired ballad. When the professionals take five, it is not unusual for a customer to get up and perform, often to be shouted down by fellow diners. There are a lot of memorabilia on the walls—photographs, newspaper clippings, and signatures of happy eaters—but in general, this nonstop Jewish wedding takes place in a no-frills room. Through all the din and dining, the guiding light behind this establishment, owner Stan Zimmerman, circulates, schmoozing here, taking a sip from someone's drink there, being a little too insulting once or twice during the evening, but always keeping things moving.

It is, of course, unnecessary to eat oneself into stupefaction to appreciate the spirit of the place. I suspect that almost all Sammy-goers stuff themselves because they go infrequently, so each time they order everything. But there is no house rule requiring such gorging, and my husband and I have enjoyed a number of dinners when we have shared an order of the frothy light eggplant salad that gets textural contrast from chunks of tomato, green pepper, and onion, then shared a grilled Rumanian tenderloin steak, some crisply fried silver-dollar potatoes, and hot tea. That is in no way an outrageous meal, even if we indulge in the garlicky peppers and pickles before other food arrives.

If desserts are short on appeal, the wonderful appetizers more than make up for that shortcoming. There is the city's best stuffed derma, the natural casing filled with a spicy meal of flour, chicken fat, onions, and paprika, sliced and grilled. That final grilling makes the difference at Sammy's, giving a lean crispness to what can otherwise be soft and fatty. Unborn eggs, really yolks of unformed eggs taken from butchered chickens, are lightly browned and served with sautéed chicken livers, or by themselves, or in the rich chicken soup that is also garnished with noodles. The chopped onions with hard-boiled eggs is light and refreshing. Black radish, grated and tossed with onions and chicken fat (a supply is on every table in syrup pitchers), stuffed cabbage in a gentle sweet and sour tomato sauce, and fresh, cool poached brains dressed with lemon and a little oil and minced onion are all among my favored openers. Hefty but delectable grilled beef sausage that are the garlic- and pepper-accented karnatzlach are wonderful as first or main course. Although I am not usually fond of calf's foot jelly (patcha), Sammy's is a meaty, flavorful exception. Only the very wet chopped liver and the greasy chicken fricassee have been disappointing. Soups never are, whether the rich mushroom-barley brew or the chicken soup with garnishes, which can also include meat-filled kreplach.

Rumanian broiling is a tradition as it is in all Balkan countries and is the forerunner of the Jewish steak house that existed in New York years ago. At Sammy's those expertly broiled cuts include the tender eye of the rib steak known as "mush," the whole rib steaks (or what the French call entrecôte) here served with the bone for maximum flavor, veal chops that do not dry out, Rumanian tenderloin, and moist, well-charred chicken. Sweetbreads and calves' liver fare less well, and can be very dry and dense, so I avoid them. All of the broiled meats are served in portions huge enough to share.

"Jewish veal cutlet breaded" is another larger-than-plate-size wonder, which is based on a big floppy veal rib chop, thickly breaded and crisply fried. Perhaps it is necessary to have grown up with that powerful dish to appreciate it, but as I did, I do. I especially like to chew the bone, which has bits of the breading clinging to it, but my Italian husband, used to thinner cuts of breaded veal, cannot even contemplate it with equanimity.

Boiled beef flanken is meltingly tender and succulent at Sammy's, and I like it with a thick mushroom-barley gravy spooned over it.

A choice of vegetables at Sammy's means the following: boiled potatoes that can be topped with chicken fat and sautéed onions, the sliced rounds that are fried to become silver dollars, mashed potatoes with chicken fat and cracklings (greeven, on this menu), overly thick potato pancakes, fried onions, kreplach, the stuffed derma, or kasha (buckwheat groats) varnishkes (pasta bow ties) tossed with sautéed onion and dried Eastern European mushrooms. Not exactly what vegetarians might have in mind, but then Sammy's is not really their glass of tea anyway.

There is a full bar here and that includes wine, but beer and the seltzer on every table are more suitable. The egg creams that are stirred up and enjoyed all over the room leave me cold. As much as I like that drink, I cannot understand downing it with this food, and it is the one custom that I regard as a bizarre aberration.

After all that food it is probably just as well that Stan Zimmerman has not come up with good desserts. The strudel is more like candy, with its heavy clogging of candied fruits, the chocolate pudding is the most banal packaged product, and rugelach are dry and tasteless. That still leaves applesauce and stewed prunes, but leave them is what I do.

To give you an idea of how low prices are, there has to be a five dollar minimum charge per person, and there is a one dollar ninety-five cent cover charge on weekend and holiday nights after 5. Monday and Tuesday the entertainment is a violinist and a joke teller; piano and singing take over from Wednesday through Sunday.

TIDBITS

Delicatessens

Though not in the same league as the Carnegie, a few kosher delis do have several very good choices on their menus.

At *Bernstein-on-Essex Street,* 135 Essex Street, between Delancey and East Houston streets (473-3900), they have Rumanian pastrami—a leaner, narrower cut of meat that has a strong smoke-pepper flavor, making it much like Jewish barbecue. That and the bay-leaf-flavored corned beef are excellent and now surpass even Carnegie's. Other food leaves much to be desired. I have not tried the kosher-Chinese menu in years, so you're on your own. Bernstein is glatt kosher and so is closed from 3 P.M. Friday until Saturday after sundown. Open Sunday.

2nd Avenue Kosher Delicatessen and Restaurant, 156 Second Avenue, corner 10th Street (677-0606), is kosher but not glatt. Corned beef is delicious, but pastrami is sinewy and waxen. Soups, however, are wonderful, including the city's second best matzo ball chicken soup and a smoky, earthy mushroom-barley masterpiece. Open seven days, and until 2 A.M. on Friday and Saturday.

See also **Katz's Delicatessen,** under Hot Dogs in Chili, Ribs and Barbecue, Hamburgers, and Hot Dogs

Dairy

Meat is out at kosher dairy restaurants for obvious reasons, and what that leaves is a whole array of salads such as tuna, egg with peppers, egg with mushrooms, egg with onions, vegetarian liver (mushrooms, beans, onions, etc.), a variety of hot and cold fish and herrings, soups, blintzes, French toast, pirogen dumplings filled with cheese or potatoes that can be had boiled or fried with sour cream, and coffeecakes. Here too, present options are pale shadows of former marvels such as Hammer's, Rappaport's, and the Garden in its heyday. Most now are sloppy in both housekeeping and cooking. Unfortunately, R. Gross, the best dairy restaurant, has closed, and Ratner's is the only decent option.

Ratner's Dairy Restaurant, 138 Delancey Street, between Norfolk and Suffolk streets (677-5588), is fine for soups, egg dishes, fried potato pirogen, and cheese blintzes. There are some cakes satisfying in this genre—the marble cake, the Russian coffeecake, poppy seed cake, rugelach, and the crisp, bubbly sugared egg boards chremslach. Open seven days, from breakfast through dinner.

KOREAN

WOO LAE OAK OF SEOUL

77 West 46th Street, between Fifth and Sixth avenues
Telephone: 869-9958

Favorite meals:
Shared by two
Grilled beef (sogum gui)
Pickled cabbage (kimchee)
Pickled radish (kaktoogi)
Stir-fried vermicelli, beef, and vegetables (chap chae)
Fresh fruit
or
Shared by four
All of the above plus fish casserole (me-oon tang)
Other favorite dishes: Grilled chicken leg (dak gui); grilled beef tongue (hemmit gui); grilled beef heart (yumtong gui); grilled marinated pork (daeji gui); meatball, fish, and vegetable casserole (shin sul lo); raw beef in sesame oil (yook hwe bibim bap); mixed plate dinner (jung sik); mixed cold noodles (bibim naeng myun); dumpling soup (mandu kuk); deep-fried fish and vegetables (twikim). Beer and whiskey are best with this food.
Setting: Big modern dining room with large, well-spaced tables that allow for private conversations; housekeeping and ventilation could be better; pleasant bar and cocktail area.
Service: A language barrier stands in the way of totally helpful service; staff is otherwise polite and prompt, if sometimes sloppy.
Dress code: None.
Facilities for private parties: Three private dining rooms accommodate between 12 and 50.
Hours: Lunch and dinner, seven days. Closed New Year's Day.
Reservations: Necessary for four or more.
Prices: Inexpensive to moderate.
Credit cards: AE, DC, MC, V.

Large and spacious, informal and friendly, Woo Lae Oak is a branch of a Korean chain that is also represented in Seoul, Los Angeles, and Jakarta. Charming and polite waitresses in colorful costumes are as helpful as they can be given the language barrier, but any customer who is really stymied can ask for a hostess or a manager. Menu items are explained in English that is often confusing, and I always point at anything that looks interesting at a neighboring table. Never mind Emily Post on pointing; when gourmandise is the goal, manners bend. Things are a little less gracious here than formerly, and service can be messy and careless though never rude.

Because Mongolian-style meats grilled at the table are featured, each table is set under a ventilating hood, which rarely seems to work. Nevertheless, it does provide a sort of divider that suggests privacy. Such grilled meats can be ordered as first or main courses. The best at Woo Lae Oak include strips of unmarinated beef served with scallions (sogum gui), nuggets of chicken leg (dak gui), soft, gentle beef tongue (hemmit gui), meaty beef heart (yumtong gui), and pork (daeji gui), all sparked with a vinegar and soy sauce that is best when fired with a dab of hot chili paste. Diners cook these meats themselves, using chopsticks for turning and cooking to the desired degree of doneness. (Except for the chicken and pork, I prefer these meats rare.) All are fine if the grill has been properly heated. Sesame-flavored raw beef (yook hwe bibim bap) is an intriguing variation on steak tartare.

Once delicious morsels such as fish fillet or tiny meatballs dipped in a frothy egg batter and lightly fried are now stodgy and greasy. For parties of four or more, a special appetizer assortment (koo jul pan) can be pre-ordered, and it is an enticing array of abalone, octopus, squid, fried or salt-cured fish, cold egg preparations, and crisp vegetables.

Pickled in salt with fiercely hot chili peppers, kimchee (made of cabbage) is standard with any Korean course, and variations on it include radish, cucumber, turnip, spinach, and bean sprouts. Here, as in most Korean restaurants, if you order kimchee, the whole assortment arrives.

Whether they are so-called or not, many dishes turn out by our standards to be soup. At Woo Lae Oak one extraordinary example is the fish casserole (me-oon tang) that appears seethingly hot, both in temperature and flavor. Fish, slippery bean thread noodles, vegetables, and bean curd make this a fine one-dish meal, but order some rice on the side as beer or tea will not assuage the effect of the chili oil. Another soupy casserole (koong joong jungol) combines tripe, intestines, meat, noodles, vegetables, and hard-boiled eggs in an aromatic broth. Shin sul lo, cooked on a brazier at the table, has many of the same ingredients, usually minus the intestines. In midsummer the hefty noodles and greens in cold broth (bibim naeng myun) is sustaining and restorative. More conventionally, there is a broth with large meat-filled dumplings (mandu kuk). To all of these add hot sauce, coriander, or soy sauce to taste, as recipe writers say.

For beginners, there is an assorted plate dinner (jung sik), a good idea that includes dishes described above, a winy bean soup, and the soothing traditional filler, chap chae, a stir-fried blend of noodles, meat, and vegetables.

Japanese specialties such as sushi and sashimi are available, but I always skip them, having found them far from fresh and ineptly crafted. Twikim, the Korean version of tempura, is preferable, if not the most diverting dish here.

Other dishes I avoid on this menu are the jungol, a sort of sukiyaki based on ropy beef, and any grilled meats other than those mentioned, as they tend to be greasy and stringy.

After so many complex flavors, fresh fruit and ice cream are the most welcome desserts. Ginseng tea is available, but its publicized palliative effects are lost on me. Scotch and beer have more to offer.

Because of all the table cookery and the less-than-perfect ventilation, I avoid wearing clothes that have just come from the cleaners as I find they always have to go right back. Washables are preferable.

YOUNG BIN KWAN ★★

10 East 38th Street, between Fifth and Madison avenues
Telephone: 683-9031

Favorite meals:
Shared by two
Egg-rolled fish fillet (saeng sun jun)
Assorted pickled vegetables (kimchee)
Grilled skirt steak (bank ja)
Stir-fried vermicelli, beef, and vegetables (chap chae)
Fresh fruit
or
Shared by four
All of the above plus yellowtail fish casserole (jogi mea-wuntang) and fried dumplings (mandoo tui gim).
Other favorite dishes: Assorted appetizers of pickled vegetables; grilled marinated pork (je yook gui); grilled marinated chicken (dak gui); brazier with tripe, beef, chicken, mushrooms, and vegetables (shin sul lo); egg-rolled stuffed green pepper (go chu pa jun); roast whole red snapper (domi gui); whole snapper with sweet and pungent sauce (hong cho); dumpling soup (mandu kug); raw marinated beef (yook hwe bibim bab); plain buckwheat noodles (naeng myun sari). Beer or Scotch goes best with this food.
Setting: Attractive, two-story dining room with buffet upstairs; large and lively bar scene; ventilation is poor in back portion of downstairs dining room.
Service: Polite, efficient, but limited because of language barrier.
Dress code: None.
Facilities for private parties: Two rooms that hold between 20 and 50.
Hours: Lunch and dinner, seven days.
Reservations: Recommended.
Prices: Inexpensive to moderate.
Credit cards: AE, CB, DC, MC, V.

Newer than Woo Lae Oak, Young Bin Kwan is far cleaner and more modern and attractive, with a polished bar and cocktail lounge and a big upstairs for private parties. Nevertheless, the low ceiling in the back portion of the main dining room can be intolerably smoky as meats are grilled on table braziers, so when making reservations, I always ask for the front of that room. Although I do not think I have ever been recognized there, I have always been given the requested part of the room.

Waitresses now have a fine understanding of English and provide more careful service than those at Woo Lae Oak. Among the best dishes are skirt steak, a juicy, meaty cut that is marinated and grilled (bang ja), the flavorful grilled pork (je yook gui), and the moist leg of chicken dipped in the pungent soy-chili sauce (dak gui). Guests do the cooking on grills set in tabletops, and long chopsticks facilitate turning. Rare is the way to cook beef, with well done being more suited to chicken and pork. I like to nibble on the sharp Korean vegetable pickles stung with chili oil, most especially the cabbage (kimchee) and the cucumber (oi kimchee).

Other wilted, salt-cured vegetables such as spinach and bean sprouts, gentled with sesame oil, are refreshing foils for egg-dipped fish fillet (saeng sun jun) and the similarly prepared stuffed green pepper (go chu pa jun). That same fragrant oil adds subtlety to raw beef tartare (yook hwe bibim bap). Shin sul lo, the casserole of tripe, beef, eggs, noodles, and vegetables, is good and sprightly with chili oil.

Chap chae, the lovely sauté of delicate, silky noodles, slivered beef, and vegetables, is to the Korean meal what fried rice is to the Chinese. I like to have it after something like the roast snapper, the more sophisticated whole snapper in sweet and pungent sauce, or the casserole of yellowtail in a paprika-bright sauce. Another soother for this aromatic food is naeng myun sari, cold buckwheat noodles with a belt of soy sauce.

Broiled meats other than those mentioned are disappointing, but the meat-filled dumplings are satisfying fried (mandoo tui gim) or in soup (mandu kug). Fresh fruit is the best choice for dessert.

At dinner there is a generous eat-all-you-want steam table buffet of Korean dishes in the balcony dining room. At $11.50 it is a bargain, especially early in the meal hour, when the food is firm and fresh. Later on, vegetables grow limp, and anything fried in batter is to be avoided.

Raw fish for Japanese sushi and sashimi looks awful here, especially on Sunday, when specimens at the sushi bar seem well past their prime.

MEXICAN

ZARELA

953 Second Avenue, between 50th and 51st streets
Telephone: 644-6740

Favorite meal:
Fried squid in spicy tomato sauce, shared by two
Eggplant salad shared by two
Chicken Yucatan
Walnut pie
Other favorite dishes: Flautas, chilaquiles, shrimp in olive oil with garlic and chili, grill-smoked salmon, pan-fried liver marinated in pickled jalapeño juice, rice baked in sour cream, stewed pinto beans, chocolate pecan and mocha layer cake, white almond cajeta torte.
Setting: Festive, lively, cramped, and noisy bar and upstairs dining room.
Service: Polite, but uneven and talky.
Dress code: None.
Facilities for private parties: Downstairs can accommodate 25 to 30.
Hours: Lunch, Monday through Friday. Dinner, Monday through Saturday. Closed Sunday.
Reservations: Recommended for lunch; necessary for dinner.
Prices: Moderate.
Credit cards: AE, CB, DC, MC, V.

Most of what passes for Mexican food in New York ought to be illegal. The usual mess of assorted, tortilla-wrapped mush glued together with melted cheese gives a bad name to what on home ground is a subtly complex and enticing cuisine. If Zarela Martinez, the highly touted cook at the erstwhile Café Marimba, does not yet redeem the reputation of her native fare at her new restaurant, she at least offers some enticing appetizers and a menu that indicates there's more to Mexican cooking than meets the palate in New York. Here, as at Marimba, Zarela seems to prefer the party atmosphere of the dining room to the rigors of the kitchen, so it is difficult to know just who is responsible for the sometimes lackluster food.

Laid out in the two-story premises formerly occupied by Tastings on Two, this noisy, cramped, and festive restaurant is gradually being Mexicanized, with the more or less provincial trappings of its former tenant giving way to white brick walls, Mexican textiles, and bouquets of bright paper flowers. The tiled bar turns out very good margaritas, frozen or cold and straight up as I prefer them, and equally limey, heady daiquiris. Sipping those drinks, one can almost fail to notice that the tortilla chips are tasteless and that the sometimes piquant salsa of tomato, onion, peppers, and cilantro can be stale and wilted. Similarly, guacamole can be brilliantly seasoned with just the right overtones of jalapeño, or oily and pallid.

Crammed in at tables in the convivial downstairs bar, or in the slightly roomier upstairs dining room, diners shout over the noise of voices, compounded by live music on the stairway landing. If waiters finally come and hear you, you can get some delectable appetizers. Try the lightly fried squid in a chili-sparked tomato sauce, the cool, pale eggplant silky in an onion-jalapeño-oregano dressing, the crackling, tightly rolled flautas filled with somewhat dry chicken improved by guacamole and the sensuously rich chilaquiles—a simmering gratin of melted white Cheddar blanketing bits of chicken and tortilla, set off by a spicy ranchero sauce. Less successful are the red snapper hash (a house specialty, but musty and stale the night I tried it), the heavy enchiladas, and chili relleno filled with a cloyingly sweet mix of dried fruit and chicken.

Skip the starchy, leaden soup of corn and crab and move on to a refreshing jicama and watercress salad or shrimp sautéed with garlic, olive oil, and piquant Anaheim chilies. Shrimp with coconut in a chili and cilantro sauce was once fiery and lovely, but at lunch arrived stingingly salty. A heavy mole (pronounced mole-ay) sauce totally obscures any flavor of the tuna it covers, but nuggets of smoke-cooked salmon contrasted to crackling cool vegetable salads are pleasant. Except for the spit-roasted chicken Yucatan and the pungent, nicely pan-fried liver with onions, bacon, and a needling of pickled jalapeño juice, all meat courses are drab and disappointing, as are most side dishes. Exceptions are the pink country pinto beans with tomato, onion, chilies, and beer, and rice baked with sour cream, Cheddar chilies, and corn. The tortillas are awful— cold, dry, and floury, as is the starchy rice torta and grease-soaked fried plantains.

The best dessert by far is the chewy, rich upside-down walnut pie, followed by a chocolate-pecan-mocha layer cake and a light, white almond-scented torte.

Service ranges from polite to pretentious and erratically paced, and, like the setting, is more pleasant at lunch.

MIDDLE EASTERN AND NORTH AFRICAN

These sensuous, unctuous cuisines are badly represented in New York, a pity because they are so good on their home ground, most especially as they are in Turkey and used to be in Lebanon. We did have a much better representation, and perhaps with luck we will again. Meanwhile, whenever I am in the mood for the shish kebob, vine leaves, couscous, and moussaka repertory, I go to the restaurant below and pick my way carefully through the menu, much as though I were picking daisies in a briar patch. Or I go to the Greek Periyali. Too bad that the relatively new Turkish restaurant, Anatolia, is as dreadful as it is. Not that all those national cuisines are the same, but they do satisfy the same longing in me, given the limitation of choice.

SIDO ABU SALIM

81 Lexington Avenue, corner 26th Street
Telephone: 686-2031

Favorite meal:
Sido mezze for two, as follows:
Chick-pea and sesame purée (hommus)
Eggplant purée (baba ghannouj)
Sesame purée (tahini)
Bean and vegetable croquettes (felafel)
Homemade yogurt cheese (labanee) with yogurt and cucumbers
Rice-stuffed grape leaves
Fried ground lamb croquettes with bulgur (kibbee)
Stewed fava beans (foul moudammas)
Mint tea
Other favorite dishes: Broiled kafta kebob, raw lamb tartare (kibbee naya), meat-stuffed grape leaves.

Setting: Bright new modern decor with café overtones is inviting.
Service: Good-natured, helpful, and prompt.
Dress code: None.
Facilities for private parties: None, but it does outside catering and take-out.
Hours: Lunch and dinner, Monday through Friday, noon to 11 P.M.; Saturday and Sunday, 1 P.M. to 11:30 P.M.
Reservations: Accepted for dinner.
Prices: Inexpensive to moderate.
Credit cards: AE, MC, V.

Run by Palestinians formerly of Haifa, this trim, brightly clean restaurant is newly installed a few blocks south of its original location. With its dark-stained wood-paneled walls, glass-topped white tablecloths, and flower prints, it is now an inviting setting, halfway between a tavern and a café. Regulars appear in everything from jeans to three-piece suits and large parties are accommodated with ease.

The food is Israeli-Egyptian-Lebanese in inspiration. What really sparkles, and what regulars rely on, is the copious, excellent mezze, the varied appetizers that make up a satisfying meal for two at $15. Good warm pita bread, with a little dish of briny green and black olives along with pickled hot green chili peppers, whets your appetite. Another giveaway is harissa, the scorchingly hot chili pepper sauce-relish that is traditionally stirred into couscous. Here, brave souls dip into it with pita or stir a drop or two into some of the appetizers. In that selection is the eggplant purée, baba ghannouj, for which the eggplants are grilled over flame so they develop the characteristic smoky flavor. Beaten with oil and lemon, it is a delectable jade-green dip for the pita. That is the way other mezze are scooped up as well, including the chick-pea and sesame spread, hommus, and the parsley, mint, and scallion salad that is tabbouleh. I like more bulgur in that salad than they use here, but it is sprightly and tantalizing nonetheless. Tahini is a velvety dip of sesame seeds, somewhat like a gorgeous liquid halvah, and enough oil is drizzled over it to make it dippable. Felafel, the croquettes of mashed beans, onions, and subtle Middle Eastern spices such as cumin, is golden and greaseless, as are the croquettes of ground lamb (kibbee) filled with bulgur. Yogurt drained until curds form the cheese called labanee is pungent and creamy and is served with added yogurt and icy slices of cucumber. Grape leaves stuffed with herbed rice are also good, if slightly less so than the meat-filled variety served as a main course. Foul moudammas, the red beans that are the mainstay of the Egyptian diet, are stewed to softness, then dressed with oil and lemon to round out the mezze. This is a course much like Spanish tapas in spirit. You drink (ouzo or arack or beer), talk, dip, nibble, and drink again.

One specialty I like to add to the standard assortment is raw kibbee, much like a lamb tartare. One has to wait while the lamb is ground, mixed with bulgur, and served with slivers of raw onion. Gentle hints of cinnamon and allspice mellow this combination.

The only really good main courses here are the kafta kebob (marinated ground beef grilled on skewers), and the meat-stuffed vine leaves. Shish kebob of lamb or chicken are dry and relatively flavorless and stewed or braised meats are overcooked and greasy.

Baklava remains heavy going here. Unfortunately, the once moist and seductive sesame halvah is now gummy and pallid. Settle for hot and sweetly fragrant mint tea.

SCANDINAVIAN

AQUAVIT

13 West 54th Street, between Fifth and Sixth avenues
Telephone: 307-7311

Favorite meals:
Swedish West Coast shellfish salad
Snow grouse with cream and lingonberries
Brambleberry sorbet in almond basket
or
Smörgasbörd plate
Poached turbot with brown butter and horseradish
Chocolate cake with burned almond crust
Other favorite dishes: Gravlax, smoked Swedish salmon, wild mushroom salad, Arctic venison pâté, shellfish soup, salmon soufflé, juniper smoked salmon, poached salmon with hollandaise sauce, poached tenderloin in bouillon, loin of Arctic venison, Smalandsk cheesecake, blueberry clafoutis.
Setting: Spacious, handsome atrium dining room downstairs; upstairs is cramped and noisy.
Service: Polite, helpful, and professional, if somewhat cool and distant.
Dress code: Downstairs—jackets required for men, but no ties. Upstairs—no rules.
Facilities for private parties: None.
Hours: Lunch, Monday through Friday. Dinner, Monday through Saturday. Closed Sunday.
Reservations: Downstairs—recommended, especially for lunch. Upstairs—not accepted.
Prices: Downstairs—moderately expensive. Upstairs—moderate.
Credit cards: AE, MC, V.

Excellent Scandinavian food is back in town in a setting that is civilized and handsome. It's time for a skoal or two with a plain, aged, or flavored aquavit (all available here) as we toast the return of the much-missed, fresh, and airy foods of Denmark, Sweden, Norway, and Finland. About twenty-five years ago, New York had several superb Scandinavian restaurants, but whether because the interest in Scandinavian design waned, or because the public associated that cooking only with herring, pork, and plates overloaded at the smörgasbörd table, those restaurants disappeared.

Now, fortunately, Aquavit is with us, offering stylized versions of traditional Scandinavian dishes, and a handsomer representation would be hard to find. There are two dining rooms in this 54th Street town house just across from the Museum of Modern Art garden. The upper floor (a few steps below street level) features a blond wood bar, royal blue and white tiles, and silver-blue marble-topped tables. Here one can have the Danish open sandwiches, smörrebröd, or simple home-style dishes for light lunches or dinners. Downstairs is the more formal, beautiful, and far better dining room, spaciously laid out in a sort of atrium between two buildings. The soaring space with skylight, light gray marble walls, a gray tiled waterfall wall, stands of white birches, and a big fabric mobile that resembles Japanese kites is bright and cheery by day, but more atmospheric at dinner. Packed for business lunches, it is more relaxed at night.

Comfortable black leather chairs and elegant tableware add to the stylish effect. So does the friendly help, with the only distant coolness exhibited by the women who do the greeting upstairs.

The menu stresses fish in simple, perfect preparations that make the specimens at Le Bernardin seem hopelessly complex. Those who like fish simply adorned can do no better than the thick slab of turbot, moist yet not rare, bathed in melted brown butter and garnished with freshly grated horseradish. Salmon appears in three guises, two of which I can vouch for: the juniper smoked slice, hot-smoked over powdered wood on the premises, so that it has a dusky flavor as it nestles under a pleasantly saline sauce of trout roe, and the pink, perfect poached salmon with dilled hollandaise sauce. Both come with impeccable boiled potatoes, as do all fish dishes here. But there are meats too, including roseate snow grouse, soothed with a lingonberry cream sauce and a crisp potato cake, and the pink Arctic venison sauced with apple and juniper, all gentled with a celery root purée.

Most surprising and delightful among meats is the poached beef tenderloin, blush pink within and tender, in a pristine white, deep plate with tiny potatoes, kohlrabi, cabbage, and leeks.

There is no smörgasbörd table here, but there is a lovely assorted appetizer plate with pâtés, satiny gravlax, and woodsy Swedish smoked salmon, several kinds of herring (alas, a weak spot, so far), and frills of delicate sprays of dill, mâche, and oak leaf lettuce. This, like the West Coast salad, carries a small supplement on the menu. That salad, though not the authentic toss of lobster, shrimp, and mussels, is nevertheless delicious, with all of those elements separately arranged alongside greens, peas, and tips of asparagus. A warm wild mushroom salad with crunches of walnuts and greens, a creamy, tomato-blushed shrimp soup, and a rich dense soufflé of salmon in puff pastry sauced with tomato and dill are all better than the herrings and the crumbling, overly creamy liver pâté.

One garnish on many of the appetizers is called bleak roe, a depressing name for the tiny-grained, coral caviar the Swedes call löjröm (pronounced lói-rum). It also dots a few of the piquant, teeny giveaway appetizers that one can nibble while downing the first aquavit, chosen from the menu of the "water of life" variations. My preference is for the classic caraway, rather than other flavors, as it is a clean foil for the foods that go with it.

Desserts are few and generally well made, whether one has the winy brambleberry sherbet in a thin almond-flavored cookie tulip, the blueberry clafoutis that lacks the traditional custard of that French pastry but is rather an intense, chewy fruit tart, and both the crusty, cracklingly Smalandsk cheesecake and the nut-veneered chocolate cake. Ice cream with warm cloudberries is less exciting. Breads are much too marvelous—the chewy, sourish sunflower seed rye, the grainy pumpernickel, and the crackling hardtack that is Swedish crispbread. So are the petits fours, most especially the tiny pyramid-shaped Danish almond cakes, kransekage.

Were the upstairs lunches as good as the downstairs dinners, and if a few more great Scandinavian specialties were added, Aquavit would deserve four stars. As it is, open sandwiches up there are badly crafted of toppings not very well prepared.

Other luncheon dishes upstairs are better choices, among them the fillet of ruby red, salty, maatjes herring with boiled potato, herbs, and capers, the fried whole herring with chive cream sauce, and the Swedish meat balls in cream sauce with lingonberries. Pastries are chilled beyond flavor recognition.

With all of this goes a selection of glorious golden beers, my choice being Carlsberg, either on tap, or in bottles if I want the powerful Elephant brew.

SEAFOOD

Always among the most popular restaurants in New York, the institution known as the seafood house has undergone an enormous change. Until about thirty years ago, almost all seafood restaurants looked alike. The theme was Cape Cod nautical, with fishnets, cork floats, anchors, and ships' wheels as the main motifs. Tabletops were usually scrubbed oak, walls were pine, and the menu consisted of Manhattan and New England clam chowders, steamed clams, oysters and clams that could be had fried, stewed, or raw on the half shell, broiled or fried fish, boiled or broiled lobster, and a few fancy preparations such as curries, Creoles, gratins, and Newburgs of shellfish, deviled crabs, and a few salads. Hot biscuits, pilot crackers, coleslaw, and french fries were standards, as were pies for dessert. When well prepared, as the food often was, it was superb and a true fish lover's joy. Outstanding examples were The Lobster near Times Square, Lundy's in Brooklyn, the original Sea Fare in Greenwich Village, and both Sloppy Louie's and Sweets in the Fulton Fish Market.

Gradually, in the fifties and sixties, such restaurants began to disappear. Sloppy Louie's and Sweets still exist but, like the South Street Seaport around them, are sorry imitations of their former, genuine selves. Gloucester House (37 East 50th Street) follows the old formula and does serve some excellent broiled and fried fish, fluffy homemade biscuits, and, at times, first-rate french fries. But anything cooked, including soup, sauces, and other kinds of potatoes, is dismal. Considering the sky-high prices, that batting average is not high enough. Le Bernardin, the newly opened branch of the Paris restaurant, in the Equitable Building, remains much overrated in all respects.

New Yorkers have finally learned that excellent fish can be had at many places not specializing in that alone—French, Italian, Chinese, and Japanese restaurants being the most delectable examples. And fish is also important on the menus of "new American" restaurants, even though there is a tendency to undercook it, as much a mistake as the old crime of overcooking used to be. Cool raw fish, as in sushi and sashimi, is delicious. Warm raw-to-rare fish is disgusting. Properly cooked, fish will be moist and pearly, much like set custard. It should separate easily from the bone and not show any traces of blood.

A new style in seafood has been evolving in the past few years and is best realized at the favorites below. Among them, John Clancy's and the re-created Oyster Bar in Grand Central Station combine American and Continental classics with their own inventions.

THE CAPTAIN'S TABLE

860 Second Avenue, corner 46th Street
Telephone: 697-9538

Favorite meal:
Mussels marinière or seafood salad
Broiled whole fish (especially pompano) with Provençal herbs
Arugula, radicchio, and endive salad, shared by two
Fresh fruit
Other favorite dishes: Langoustines, oysters, artichoke vinaigrette, spinach salad, baked clams casino, oysters and clams on the half shell, New England clam chowder, all broiled fish and shellfish, steak au poivre.
Setting: Fanciful café-garden atmosphere, with flowery fabrics, colored lamp shades, and amusing bric-a-brac; some tables are cramped; moderately noisy when full.
Service: Generally prompt and polite but slows at peak hours; unknown customers may be treated summarily.
Dress code: None.
Facilities for private parties: None.
Hours: Lunch, Monday through Friday. Dinner, Monday through Saturday. Closed Sunday and major holidays.
Reservations: Necessary for lunch; recommended for dinner.
Prices: Moderately expensive.
Credit cards: AE, MC, V.

In its fanciful garden setting with colorful glass lampshades, bouquets, and floral-patterned tablecloths, The Captain's Table remains one of the better options for serious fish eaters. If it rates one star fewer than formerly, it is because of a tendency to overcook some of its former specialties, such as poached salmon and the red snapper baked in a foil "papillotte," now so mushy it falls apart in the handling. What remains impeccable is the dazzling selection of fish presented on a giant board for the customer's selection. There is something about examining the bright eyes and firm flesh of a fish that whets a fish lover's appetite and suggests which specimen looks best and how it might be prepared. Noble and humble fish share this plank: steaks of mako shark and swordfish, halibut and tilefish, blowfish and pompano, tuna, flounder and gray sole, salmon and white or red snapper, and, in season, shad roe. Flown-in imports include French rouget and Italian spigola. Whole broiled fish profit from a sprinkling of the aromatic herbs of Provence.

Frying is also crisply, greaselessly accomplished on flounder or sole, or at times for squid and an hors d'oeuvres giveaway, tiny whitebait. Sea urchins may be on hand as appetizers, as is a variety of oysters and clams. Coolly bright seafood cocktails are well prepared, as are sautéed wild mushrooms, and the mussels marinière in a heady white wine and garlic broth is perfection. So are the salads of calamari and shellfish in a sunny lemon and oil dressing, and the baked clams casino, smoky with curls of bacon. New England clam chowder can be fine if it has not cooked down too much and so become overly thick.

Steak, plain or au poivre, is provided for non–fish eaters. The au poivre is preferable, for, though a bit tough, it has the right peppery belt. French fries would be more appropriate with that steak than the baked potato. Well-cooked rice and firm, fresh vegetables accompany other dishes.

Baked desserts are disappointing and the once light crème caramel is now dark and chewy. Better to stick to cut fresh fruits.

Service is generally good, but there is the unfortunate habit of giving away the poor tables first, even if the room is empty. Things also get a bit slow at peak meal times. Menus, by the way, with their hand-painted flourishes, are especially beautiful.

Although there is a wide range of price options among white wines, the reds are, for the most part, expensive with few choices in the $18 to $25 range. There is now a lounge menu, offering appetizers and small dishes at the bar end of the restaurant, and a daily "spa" selection with nutrient counts available.

Claire, *see* Cuban, Caribbean, and Tropical

JOHN CLANCY'S

181 West 10th Street, corner Seventh Avenue South
Telephone: 242-7350

Favorite meals:
Lobster bisque
Sautéed shad roe with bacon
or
Barbecued jumbo Ecuadorian shrimp

Chocolate whipped cream roll
or
Mixed green and endive salad
Lobster Americaine
Lemon meringue tart
Other favorite dishes: Oysters and clams on the half shell, smoked trout with horseradish cream, gravlax with crème fraiche and caviar, New Zealand mussels in saffron white wine broth or in tomato broth, broiled clams with garlic butter, soft-shell crabs, sautéed shrimp with garlic butter or green garlic sauce, shrimp with jalapeño peppers, all mesquite-grilled fish except skewered swordfish and trout with rosemary butter, all desserts except trifle.
Setting: Trim, intimate low-ceilinged gray and white dining room with Art Deco accents; upstairs is similar if less effective, but quieter.
Service: At times very slow and a bit careless, but always polite and well-meaning. Slow upstairs.
Dress code: None.
Facilities for private parties: None, but will do take-out from daily menu.
Hours: Dinner until 11:30 P.M., Monday through Saturday; until 10 P.M. on Sunday. Closed Labor Day, Thanksgiving, and Christmas days.
Reservations: Usually necessary, especially before performances in nearby Off-Broadway theaters.
Prices: Expensive.
Credit cards: AE, CB, DC, MC, V.

Named for its founder, the extraordinary chef-author—cooking school teacher John Clancy, this intimate, stylish gray and white Greenwich Village boîte earned early praise for its subtle and inventive seafood dishes and for its seductive pastries and desserts. Always expensive, it too often had good and bad days, due to Mr. Clancy's busy travel schedule, and so the kitchen's performance became uneven. But now this low-ceilinged, Art Deco—accented duplex is owned by Clancy's former partner, Sam Rubin, who has put it on a steady keel, and a very good one at that. Flowers, delicate art posters, decorative china, and a polite, friendly staff help things along, and only the airless back room near the kitchen is to be avoided.

The luxurious seafood creations would make this restaurant welcome in any neighborhood, but it is doubly so here, so close to many Off-Broadway theaters in the Sheridan Square area. For that reason, it is wise to book a table well in advance.

Among the menu features that attract a staunch following despite fairly high prices are the appetizers, which, like the rest of the selections, range from simple classics (impeccable shrimp cocktail, clams and oysters on the half shell, smoked trout with horseradish cream) to such enticing inventions as New Zealand mussels in a gossamer tomato broth lightly scented with garlic, or Maine mussels in a fragrant saffron and white wine broth, or marinated tuna in a sesame-ginger sauce and Maryland crab meat doused with mayonnaise whipped with avocado. Gravlax is marinated to silky perfection with the fresh breath of dill about it, and garlic butter bathes clams broiled so carefully they remain tender and spurtingly hot. Lobster bisque always has the right shellfish crackle of a true coral-colored bisque.

One original main-course winner that still appears from time to time is shrimp sautéed with a fiery fillip of jalapeño peppers, and I rarely resist it when it is on the menu. Also sautéed carefully enough to retain moisture and flavor are shrimp sauced with either hefty garlic butter or the more verdant, herbed green garlic sauce. When in season, shad roe with bacon and soft-shell crabs are sautéed to delicate, moist succulence, with a variety of sauces and garnishes. The early use of Mexican and Oriental spicing has continued here and become refined, and Clancy's stands out as being one of the first restaurants to do serious grilling over mesquite. The mesquite grilling that in the early days might have been too pallid or too overpowering is now well accomplished and so adds a soft, pleasant burnishing to fish such as halibut, which may get a touch of red onion butter and tarragon or a mild saffron ginger sauce, or thick slabs of Norwegian salmon or jumbo Ecuadorian shrimp glossed with a tangy barbecue sauce.

The only mesquite offerings that seem not to profit from this cookery are the chunks of swordfish that dry out on skewers, and trout, because it is zapped with rosemary butter, that piney herb not really being suited to fish at all. Another house classic is lobster Americaine, a lush simmering of the crustacean, cut up and in the shell, in a sauce of tomato, wine, thyme, tarragon, cognac, and a hint of garlic. Fisherman's stew with or without a tail of Maine lobster, is closer to a sheer bouillabaisse, complete with a heady garlic and cayenne-tinted rouille mayonnaise.

Something that causes apprehension is the tendency toward overly complex seasonings that are now almost clichés in trendy fish cookery. At Clancy's, that means heavy green sauces (spinach and watercress) over mild-flavored shrimp, jam-sweet caramelized red onions and mustard-dill glaze for salmon, and the Italian bacon pancetta with salty Nice olives and roasted garlic obscuring the essence of monkfish. And as pleasant as it can be when used with restraint, ginger relied on a little too often.

One thing you can safely rely on without disappointment is the spectacular desserts, a legacy from John Clancy's expertise as a baker. His lemon meringue tarts with their sour-sweet citrus filling and their swirled domes of glazed meringues have never been better, nor has the airy, light chocolate roll filled with whipped cream. Flaky small pastries also hold berries of the season with drifts of whipped cream, and the thick, sensuous chocolate velvet cake surpasses the original at The Four Seasons. The trifle here looks magnificent in its crystal urn, and it is authentic, right down to the layering of raspberry purée, a feature that discourages me, because I dislike such intense sweetness. Those who feel otherwise may find this escalation of liqueur-soaked cake, whipped cream, custard sauce, and fruit, a dream come true. Wines tend to be as high-priced as the rest of the menu, with only limited choices at moderate levels.

OYSTER BAR & RESTAURANT

42nd Street, corner Vanderbilt Avenue;
Grand Central Station, lower level
Telephone: 490-6650

Favorite meals:
Oyster pan roast for a quick, satisfying lunch at the counter
or
A variety of clams or oysters on the half shell
Poached fillet of salmon with hollandaise sauce
Green salad
Old-fashioned apple tart
or
New England clam chowder
Halibut flakes on fresh spinach with lemon-mustard dressing
Rice pudding
Other favorite dishes: Smoked salmon, smoked trout, oyster stew, squid salad with avocado, crabcakes without sauce, fresh salmon salad, all broiled fish, fried oysters, broiled or steamed lobster, chocolate nougat dome, pear caramel torte, cheesecake.
Setting: Wonderful old landmark with huge cavernous tile and wood-paneled walls and counters for full meals in addition to back dining room and front bar-grill; noise seems appropriate here.
Service: Always excellent at the counters; generally good at tables but can be perfunctory in main dining room, especially at dinner.
Dress code: None.
Facilities for private parties: None.
Hours: Lunch and dinner, Monday through Friday. Closed Saturday, Sunday, and major holidays.
Reservations: Necessary for lunch except at counter; recommended for dinner, especially for bar-grill.
Prices: Moderately expensive.
Credit cards: AE, CB, DC, MC, V.

In a city where so many great architectural landmarks have disappeared, the Oyster Bar is a treasure. Opened about seventy years ago, it has always been famous for clams and oysters on the half shell—opened as ordered at a stand-up bar or sit-down counter (or at tables, of course)—and most especially for its oyster stew and pan roast. Those marvels of creamy, peppery salinity are still bubbled up in their original chafing dishes, which pivot over the flame to be poured into deep bowls and dusted with paprika. I usually add a shot or two of Tabasco as well. That, with plenty of oyster crackers, makes one of my favorite quick, solitary lunches. And as I often like to have early brunch-lunch and the Oyster Bar opens at 11:30, we seem to be made for each other. At times, the stew or pan roast can be disappointing if stray bits of cracked shell find their way into the soup. Otherwise, all is as expected.

So is the general action in this restored setting, with a crossroads hustle and bustle, a masculine air of hearty, turn-of-the-century–style eating, combined with new, fashionable dishes and a huge variety of fish, which varies on a daily basis. Japanese customers are always in evidence, considering the oysters and boiled lobsters irresistible bargains at their exchange rates.

The management tries hard for such unusual specimens as walleyed pike, channel bass, Virginia spots, wolffish, Lake Winnipeg goldeye, sand dabs, and so on. There are also many types of oysters on hand—Apalachicola, Belons, box, Wellfleet, Malpeques, Marennes, Chincoteague, and more. Like the varieties of clams, they are priced singly, as in Europe, so a sampler assortment can be ordered. A dozen oysters of mixed origins is the quick lunch I favor most as an alternative to pan roast. I prefer oysters and clams with only lemon juice and, for variety, a drop of Tabasco or two. Those who like a more sophisticated touch get it with the shallot- and tarragon-scented mignonette sauce.

Broiling and poaching are the most dependable cooking techniques here. The cold fish salads, such as the salmon and fresh tuna, are fine. The most exceptional is billed as flakes of halibut (more like snowy chunks) on spinach salad. Frying can be properly crisp or limp, the reason behind the difference being a mystery, and complex preparations show the same inconsistency. Soup is the prime example. It may be New England or Manhattan clam chowder at its best, or either can be overly thick. Recently the New England has outclassed the overly thick Manhattan, but that has not always been true. Broiled giant freshwater prawns, though delicious, were so difficult to extricate from shells that there was virtually nothing to eat. On the other hand, crabcakes have been good right from the start *if* you forgo the sauce. Potatoes, coleslaw, and salads are fine, and though the homemade biscuits are still strong on baking soda, they are good when hot.

Home-baked cakes and pies are by and large excellent, the flaw being a few that are too sweet—blueberry almond pie being a case in point. But the lofty cheesecake, apple pie in whole-wheat crust, and pear caramel torte will make you glad you had nonfattening fish so you can splurge at the end. Ditto the fluff of cool rice pudding adrift with whipped cream.

Considering the enormous menu and the gigantic seating capacity, the Oyster Bar does a remarkable job of turning out good food.

White wines make up about nine tenths of the list, and all are American. There are only six reds, again California, and generally mediocre and expensive. Similarly, the good whites, such as the Acacia chardonnay, are pricey. But there are plenty of inexpensive whites for those who have a taste for the West Coast products, which I do not.

The best service is at the oyster bar itself and at the low comfortable counter. It also tends to be fine in the bar-grill but can range from indifferent to downright rude in the dining room, where waiters grunt and food is thrown onto tables.

PESCA

23 East 22nd Street, between Broadway and Park Avenue South
Telephone: 533-2293

Favorite meal:
Mediterranean seafood chowder
Grilled salmon with coarse-grained mustard and dill
or
Soft-shell crabs
Fruit sherbet
Other favorite dishes: Clams and oysters on the half shell, tuna barbarian, a "rose" of cured striped bass and salmon, smoked Norwegian salmon, chilled mussel salad with sauce mustardine, grilled tuna Japanese style, cioppino, ganache of chocolate, ice cream profiteroles with hot chocolate sauce, crème caramel.
Setting: Romantically glowing, spacious café setting with dramatic lighting; moderately noisy. Tables for two tend to be cramped.
Service: Polite, accommodating, and efficient.
Dress code: None.
Facilities for private parties: None.
Hours: Lunch, Monday through Friday. Dinner, seven days. Open late (to 11 or 11:30 P.M.), Tuesday through Saturday. Closed major holidays. Live jazz, Tuesday through Friday.
Reservations: Recommended.
Prices: Moderately expensive.
Credit cards: AE, Transmedia.

Since it opened in 1979, Pesca has had intermittent changes in chefs and owners, and with those changes have come ups and downs in food. Fortunately it seems to have settled down nicely and, once again, offers rich, divertingly creative seafood in a soignée setting.

This was one of the first of the theatrical restaurants and a pioneer in the Park Avenue South area. The decor has held up well, with enameled walls of peach to mauve pink (stage lights with colored filters account for the impressionistic color variation) and shiny cream-colored stamped metal ceilings; the huge floral bouquets give the room an air of silken luxury. Light shining through from the faux courtyard beyond the dining-room windows heightens the effect, as do silk shades on wall sconces and the attractive prints, photographs, and paintings of fish and sea themes.

Flaws in the setting are the many uncomfortably placed tables, especially for parties of two, usually crammed against the wall in the noisy front bar area or at the entrances to kitchen or washrooms. Noise can be a problem even in the pretty back area, but at least conversation is possible there even on Tuesday through Friday nights, when a live jazz combo plays up front.

Although the menu no longer includes such Pesca originals as the Portuguese cataplana (sausage and clams steamed in the round, hinged casserole that gives the dish its name), or the Bermuda and Valencia fish chowders, the replacements are equally stylish and savory. Cioppino, the San Francisco–Italian fish soup-stew, is still here and rendered as a lusty tomato-based soup, bright with green peppers and onions, and heaped with lobster, scallops, mussels, clams, and shrimp heightened by herbs, saffron, and white wine. Exhibiting a slight tendency toward inconsistency, the kitchen sent out a spicy version of this dish to me. Later, when a friend arrived mid-meal and ordered the same dish, it was just a bit blander, though delicious. It would also be more appropriate to serve that hot soup in a china bowl rather than in one of glass.

Appetizers do indeed show consistent excellence, whether as simple as the perfect iced oysters or littleneck clams on the half shell or as intricate as the "rose" formed of dill-salt-sugar cured striped bass enfolding petals of salmon, also cured in that way and, therefore, known as gravlax. An edging of black peppercorns and a fresh dill sauce lend elegance to this delicate arrangement. Served in the style of steak tartare, raw tuna gets the same pungent spicing for a delectable first course. Other good choices are the chilled mussels in a salad sauced with mustard and mellowed with avocado, and the wonderful smoked Norwegian salmon.

Mediterranean seafood chowder, chock full of fish and shellfish in a creamy tomato-blushed soup, is a welcome replacement for the soups now gone.

If soft-shell crabs are in season, by all means try them, carefully gilded in the sauté pan, graced with herbs and bedded down on julienne slivers of vegetables. If not, such grilled offerings as tuna Japanese, brushed with a teriyaki-style soy–rice wine glaze, and the grilled salmon that gets a zesty accent from coarse-grained mustard counterpointed with mild dill are fine alternatives.

Not all is gastronomic bliss at Pesca. The most notable failures are the seafood pastas, which are mushy and sodden. Seafood cannelloni is a pasty case in point, the green pasta overcooked and almost melting into the heavy cheese sauce that obscures the flavor and texture of the shellfish filling. There is also a tendency to overcomplicate fish combinations such as ginger and hot orange juice on grouper or mahi-mahi masked with avocado and a heavy Creole tomato sauce.

Desserts are much improved, the best being the cool, refreshing homemade fruit sherbets, sublime cream puff profiteroles bursting with vanilla ice cream and napped with dark chocolate sauce, and the light yet authoritative chocolate ganache layer cake. Crème caramel is also a welcome cool finish after fish, and it has just the right burnishing of caramelized sugar syrup.

Service has lost its original preppy self-consciousness and is friendly and generally efficient. Daily specials are described, but are also thoughtfully presented on a table menu, with prices.

SPANISH

THE BALLROOM

253 West 28th Street, between Seventh and Eighth avenues
Telephone: 244-3005

Favorite meal:
An assortment of tapas, as described below
An assortment of desserts, as described below
Other favorite dishes: Boar stew with spaetzle, grilled duck with figs, grilled rack of lamb or venison, codfish aioli, cazuela of seafood.
Setting: Attractive modern café–dining room with beautiful bar hung with hams, sausages, cheeses, dried peppers, etc.; the renowned mural of the SoHo art set that hung in the West Broadway original is now here; noisy but convivial.
Service: Sometimes slow, but polite and accommodating.
Dress code: None.
Facilities for private parties: Can be arranged for Sunday and Monday, when restaurant is closed. Three rooms are available and can accommodate between 80 and 300. Tapas picnic boxes are available for take-out.
Hours: Lunch, Tuesday through Friday. Dinner, Tuesday through Saturday, until 1 A.M. Closed Sunday, Monday, and all major holidays, but open for Thanksgiving.
Reservations: Recommended for lunch; necessary for dinner.
Prices: Moderate to moderately expensive. Those tapas can add up.
Credit cards: AE, CB, DC, MC, V.

One of my favorite dining places since it opened in its original SoHo location in 1973, The Ballroom specializes in tapas, the progression of small dishes that in Spain are nibbled at bars as customers talk, drink, and get in the mood for dinner. Prepared by Felipe Rojas-Lombardi, the Peruvian chef who has worked with James Beard and in a number of catering enterprises, the tapas here are so rich, brightly fresh, and satisfying that they become dinner for most Americans into the grazing habit—eating small amounts of many dishes to make a meal. That may not be the Spanish way with tapas, but it is clearly becoming ours, even though there are main courses to be had at The Ballroom. And it is a custom that works especially well for lunch at The Ballroom, when tapas can be ordered singly, or taken from an eat-all-you-want buffet with dessert, cheeses, and a beverage for $18.50. It's a diverting bargain to remember for those who find this location, close to the Fashion Institute of Technology and the fur district, convenient.

Those tapas are virtually the only dishes that designate this restaurant as Spanish, but they are the overwhelming feature of its format. Always a cabaret-restaurant, The Ballroom now has a separate cabaret for acts that range from Blossom Dearie to Larry Adler, and here too tapas are served. The dining room is bright, modern, and casual, and if the noise and closely set chairs are not conducive to formal dining, they are much in the café spirit. The focal point of that room is the famed Marion Pinto mural of the SoHo art set, created for the original Ballroom and still as bright and stunning as ever. In fact, it casts its own spell over the room, making Larry Rivers & Company seem a living part of the scene.

The most colorful point of the room is the huge bar from a 1922 Bronx speakeasy (Bronx provincial would probably be the decorator's appellation), turned Spanish by the hangings of air-dried hams, winged slabs of dried salt codfish, ropes of dried peppers and garlic, and pale mahogany to dark, blood-red sausages, all of which suggest an edible mobile. The tapas assortment is laid out in sections on that bar, with a whole suckling pig often part of the choice, as are red beans with snails, fusilli in pesto, little white squid chubby with their filling of pork, nuts, and raisins, curried scallops, a light and yet chewy potato and onion omelet (tortilla española), fresh anchovies in grape leaves, mussels vinaigrette, escabeches of various sorts, grilled eggplant slices, and more.

It is a good idea to shop this array if you plan to sit at a table, because though waiters bring many choices for perusal, they do not bring all. Among cold tapas I especially like are, in addition to those mentioned above, pepper salad with eggplant, nuggets of suckling pig with cracklings, mussel and potato salad crunchy with flecks of vegetables, escabeche of chicken, ceviche of scallops tinted with turmeric, mushrooms à la grecque, pasta with coriander sauce, white beans vinaigrette, and Serrano-style ham.

Among hot tapas, only veal on skewers is lackluster. More savory choices include crunchy fried whitebait, squid in a garlicky pepper sauce, grilled shrimp with garlic and bulgur, and fried plantains. With the tapas, one can choose from a variety of sherries or good strong Spanish wines and nibble on chewy, hard-crusted bread.

Then comes the main-course menu, and things pale somewhat but not entirely. The choice is more Continental–new American.

Two improvements on the menu are Spanish fish specialties: tender, ivory chunks of poached fresh codfish that get a lift from an aioli mayonnaise that is good although lacking in a true garlic heft, and cazuela, a lusty version of bouillabaisse that is more than enough for two. Boar stew in a slightly sharp sauce was tender and fragrant with spicing. The spaetzle with it seemed dry at first, but the dark, rich gravy they absorbed worked like magic in improving them. Grilled duck with figs that were plumped in red wine could not have been better and a broiled rack of lamb though a little too rare was nonetheless delicious. Grilled venison, with fried sticks of crisp yucca, is also a fine choice.

There is a tantalizing display of desserts, and these too can be had tapas style, a concession to the American sweet tooth. My favorites in that assortment are the orange pound cake, the Linzer torte, with its tawny hazelnut crust, an ethereal custard with a burnt-sugar glaze, pears in red wine, and the chocolate Rigo Janci torte. Cheesecake is unpleasantly gummy.

If the spirit of tapas eating is virtually lost in America, at least the pleasures are not, and The Ballroom, with its friendly service, festive setting, and lively crowd, adds much to that pleasure.

One of the best take-out options in the city is available here—neatly boxed assortments of tapas, packed with bread, fruit, and a bottle of water. It is an enticing, original picnic idea that includes five different tapas. The box that serves two is $22.50.

The Ballroom will also do off-premise catering for parties of 50 to 100. Food can be delivered or picked up. Obviously, the price varies with the menu selected.

EL RINCÓN DE ESPAÑA

226 Thompson Street, between Bleecker and Third streets
Telephone: 260-4950

Favorite meal:
Grilled chorizo sausage, shared by two
Octopus à la Carlos
Vanilla custard (natilla)
Other favorite dishes: Grilled shrimp with garlic (gambas à la plancha), mussels in hot red sauce (mejillones à la Carlos), all soups, any shellfish (except king crab) with green, garlic, or egg sauce, codfish with potatoes and onions (bacalao à la Gallega), all paellas, flan.
Setting: Jam-packed, noisy, and predictably corny Spanish decor but with a lively, friendly informality. Guitar music, Wednesday through Sunday.
Service: Good natured and helpful but drags between courses on busy weekend nights.
Dress code: None.
Facilities for private parties: None.
Hours: Lunch and dinner, seven days. Dinner until midnight.
Reservations: Necessary, especially from Wednesday through Sunday.
Prices: Inexpensive.
Credit cards: AE, CB, DC, MC, V.

With such a paucity of really great Spanish food in New York, El Rincón has in recent years represented one of the better options. (Years ago—say thirty or forty—places like Jai-Alai and the old Granados in the Village and Fornos in the Theater District were nothing short of wonderful.) Although not as consistently expert as it used to be, the kitchen still turns out the most dependable version of sauced shellfish dishes, paellas, and so on in town. Having learned the hard way, I never eat meat dishes here, but that leaves a number of fragrant, hot, and richly flavored choices.

It is difficult to plan a meal at El Rincón because the main courses I like are more or less shellfish stews, and shellfish dishes are also the best appetizers. The only option is the oily, peppery grilled chorizo sausages, which I often have. Then too, I like the soups—the cool, crunchy gazpacho, the lentil with ham (if it is fresh), and caldo Gallego, a mix of kale, pork, and potato. But soups do not work well before those sauced shellfish, so I usually try one when I am having the gently salty, antique-tasting dried salt codfish bacalao, stewed with potatoes and onions in a paprika-burnished sauce that has a mild chili sting, all garnished with a hard-boiled egg.

Mariscados—the mix of shellfish that includes mussels, clams, shrimp, scallops, and sometimes lobster—can be had in big potfuls, graced with one of three delectable sauces: the parsley and garlic green sauce, the lightly garlicked, sunny egg sauce, and the frankly garlicked garlic sauce. There is also a tingling hot red sauce, superb with tender octopus simmered with herbs, spices, and, of course, garlic. For zarzuela de mariscada, shellfish are bedded down on rice and topped with egg sauce, a little lighter and easier to negotiate than paella. For that Spanish classic, big pots of moist rice flecked with peppers, olives, and onions are baked with seafood (paella marinera), with chicken and seafood (paella Valenciana), or with lobster (paella Valenciana con langosta), my favorites being the first and the third. As in all dishes, mussels here are remarkably sweet and free of that sewer taste those mollusks so often take on, shrimp never hint of iodine staleness, and lobster is tender though apparently precooked. Chicken is not always fresh, however, and is the weak point in the mix as is the occasional tendency to let the rice dry out. Not all the ingredients seem to have been cooked from scratch for each order of paella, but at least they are together long enough to trade flavors a little.

Because of the chancy chicken, I never have arroz con pollo. Tough, sinewy meats carelessly cooked are unpleasant. Flan is hefty and cooling and the vanilla custard, natilla with cinnamon and creme de cocoa, is restoring.

Guitar music Wednesday through Sunday adds to the already intense din, but because food is less good on slow, non-guitar nights, I brave the noise.

TIDBITS

Harlequin, 569 Hudson Street, corner West 11th Street (255-4950), though announcing Spanish food as its specialty, features more all-Continental nouvelle dishes badly prepared. Two very good dishes, however, are truly Spanish and worth trying, even if it means putting up with the detached, indifferent, but polite service. The winning appetizer is the brandada de bacalao, a purée of salt codfish whipped with potatoes, olive oil, and garlic that requires only a dusting of freshly ground black pepper to be thoroughly satisfying. Paella is the best (and only really good) main course, lightly and freshly cooked, gentled with a hint of saffron, and with moist rice topped by a briny assortment of shellfish, chicken, and sausages, at $36 for two. Desserts are skippable, most especially the inexplicably miserable flan that is a deep, dark orange color with the texture of wet cake. The pale gray setting, with fake Picasso-like harlequins, has not worn well, but it is pleasant enough and the paella is worth the trip downtown, considering local alternatives.

STEAK

MOE'S

112 Duane Street, between Broadway and Church Street
Telephone: 406-1043

Favorite meal:
Endive, arugula, and radicchio salad
Rumanian tenderloin or porterhouse steak
Cottage fries
Halvah (What else?)
Other favorite dishes: String bean and onion salad, baked clams, all broiled meats, mashed or baked potatoes.
Setting: Typical SoHo soaring café/dining room with big, lively bar. Can be depressing when sparsely filled.
Service: Relaxed and attentive, if unpolished.
Dress code: None.
Facilities for private parties: None, but can accommodate large parties in separate sections.
Hours: Lunch, Monday through Friday. Dinner, Monday through Saturday. Closed Sunday and major holidays.
Reservations: Generally recommended.
Prices: Moderately expensive.
Credit cards: AE.

The big beef in TriBeCa is at Moe's. And that beef, along with other grilled meats, is not only dished up in huge portions, but is just about the most succulent and flavorful in town. I didn't think they made restaurants like this anymore, now that beef has become a four-letter word and the cholesterol watchers have infiltrated the ranks of the gourmet establishment.

Opened in 1986 by Manny Feldman, a retired Seventh Avenue manufacturer who missed the action, this is a noisy, lusty macho scene, catering to what may be the very last of the big spenders. His smaller and more intimately convivial first home one block west became so jammed that he moved to these premises, which some will remember as Le Saint Jean des Prés. The once lipstick-red walls have been muted to burgundy with somewhat cheerless results, and the sprawl of tables is not so felicitous as the former arrangement, especially when the place is half empty. Fortunately, that does not happen too often. Usually, there is a crowd at the long bar being glad-handed and kibitzed by Manny, who circulates like a proud father at his son's bar mitzvah, wanting to be sure everyone is happy and getting enough to eat. Similarly, waiters are friendly and prompt, if not professionally polished, a trade-off that can be a welcome relief from the Stanislavsky school of waiters.

Moe's menu is an only-in-New York ethnic hybrid—a little bit of the Palm with its steaks and Italian food here, and a little more of Sammy's Famous Roumanian Restaurant there. Once seated you are served, courtesy of the house, small, hot, and crunchy potato pancakes along with applesauce, best bypassed if you are having drinks. A sprinkling of salt does more for those pancakes than the cold, sweet fruit dip. Next comes a bowl of first-rate, firm and pungent kosher pickles, green tomatoes, and vinegar-marinated red peppers, nested on sauerkraut that is inexplicably limp and sweet.

As you look at the menu, keep the meat and potatoes firmly in mind. Nothing else comes up to them and they are the reasons for the trek downtown. Among appetizers, only clams on the half shell or baked with bits of bacon have been consistently top notch. Shrimp cocktail can be mushy, and a slippery sherry-sweetened sauce mars the hot shrimps' Moe, strangely placed apostrophe and all. A spicy red sauce on hot mussels was delicious but several of the mollusks were overpoweringly rank, a flaw that could be avoided if farmed mussels were bought. And so, start in a refreshing and healthful way, with an excellent string bean and red onion salad or another of bristly bright arugula, endive, and radicchio.

Skippables on this menu include all bland and overcooked poached or broiled fish, and the Italian chicken and veal dishes.

If you have a hankering for pasta after potato pancakes and before meat and potatoes, you may be in trouble in more ways than one. Most here taste about as Italian as subgum. The only passable choices are two based on simple tomato sauces—the rigatoni filetto di pomodoro and the capellini with tomato and basil.

But ah, those grilled meats and the array of nicely marbled, richly savory beefsteaks! The plump, juicy belt of skirt steak known as Rumanian tenderloin is on the menu along with bone-in porterhouse for two; either a mouth-watering combination of tenderness with just enough texture to add interest. Sirloins and filet mignons are as good as they get and nowhere are a thick loin veal chop or double lamb chops handled with such impeccable skill, the meat properly, securely seared, yet rose-pink within, if so ordered. Broiling calves' liver requires real skill as it tends to dry out before the inside is cooked, but it too reaches sheer perfection here, as does its crisp and meaty slices of bacon.

All that meat with no potatoes is a depressing thought, so opt for either the crisp-skinned, fluffy baked potato, the made-from-scratch mashed potatoes topped with meltingly soft sautéed onions, or the cottage fries, which are more like Sammy's silver dollars in spirit than like the Palm's thinner chips. Never mind vegetables. That salad should take care of vitamins, and with a lot more style.

There are genuine desserts here such as chocolate mousse and grotesque bread pudding. Shun them in favor of the giveaway, a dish of gently sweet, oily halvah that is surprisingly good nibbled along with coffee. That dish also contains chocolate-covered marshmallow twists and Mallomars, but neither is my cup of tea and so I pass.

In addition to all of its advantages, which include ample parking space, Moe's costs about one-third less than most of the first class uptown steak houses. Beer is preferable to wine with this food and in the milieu, and drinks are generously poured.

PALM

837 Second Avenue, between 44th and 45th streets
Telephone: 687-2953

Favorite meals:
Shared by two hungry eaters
Chopped tomato and onion salad
Shared lobster followed by shared sirloin steak, with half orders of cottage fries and onion rings
One portion of cheesecake and two forks
or
Clams Posillipo or linguine with white clam sauce
Lamb chops with hash brown potatoes
Cheesecake, shared by two
Other favorite dishes: Minestrone when available, steak tartare, roast beef, veal chop, steak à la Stone, corned beef and cabbage, roast beef or corned beef hash when available for lunch.
Setting: Wildly noisy and convivial, colorful old New York atmosphere, with celebrity cartoons on the wall and sawdust on the floor.
Service: Superprofessional and adept, although the house style of brusqueness can put off the timid. If you do not want steak, chops, or lobster, insist that the waiter tell you about other dishes, as no menu is offered.
Dress code: None.
Facilities for private parties: None.
Hours: Lunch, Monday through Friday. Dinner, Monday through Saturday. Closed Sunday and major holidays.
Reservations: Necessary for lunch; not accepted for dinner.
Prices: Expensive. Ask prices of choices waiter describes.
Credit cards: AE, CB, DC, MC, V.

Few restaurants in New York continue to be as controversial as this sixty-two-year-old steak house begun by the Bozzi and Ganzi families, who named it after their native Parma. It took a city licensing clerk to write down Palm, thereby giving the restaurant its unlikely tropical name. Half the people I know detest the Palm for its noise, the huge quantities of food served and eaten, and an overall style they regard as vulgar. Imagine! The other half adore it as I do, finding the noise convivial, the plain setting a signal that all is genuine, and the frankly macho esprit, well, sort of sexy.

Not that the Palm is what it was twelve years ago, which is why it gets three stars instead of four. Somehow, the cleaning of the cartoons on the wall signaled a subtle change in the consistency of the cooking, although that is probably more traceable to the management's spreading itself too thin with Palm clones across the street (Palm Too, which I advise you to forget) as well as across the country. Then too, with new beef-grading regulations, a lot of what used to be top choice is now passing for prime, so at times the extra edge of beefy flavor is lacking. And if this steak house takes itself seriously, it should offer steak on the bone and, the best cut of all, a porterhouse. Such cavils aside, I think the Palm still does what it does better than any other restaurant in town, and it is my choice for sirloin steak, for the sensational chubby and pink double-rib lamb chops with their burnishing of charred fat, and for the gigantic broiled lobsters ($55 for $4^{1}/_{2}$ pounds) that are miraculously sweet and tender (only the claw meat sticks to the shell at times, from being overcooked).

Right from the start, the Palm provides a feast. The firmest, crispest kosher-style pickles and pickled green tomatoes are on the table with icy red radishes. All are fine with the rough-textured Italian bread. Waiters hurriedly call off "steaks-chops-lobsters" in hopes of pushing an order through quickly, but it is worth pressing on to learn what variety there is. That way you get a chance to start with the clams Posillipo with or without shrimp in a thick, garlicky tomato sauce, or with the linguine with white clam sauce. You might prefer the thick minestrone or a tomato and onion salad, which is much better chopped than sliced. Grilled veal chop, always pink and moist, is juicy and delicious as is the roast prime rib of beef, the broiled chicken, and the steak tartare. At lunch on certain days there is mildly saline, tender corned beef with cabbage. Hash brown potatoes are done in a firm pancake style, and the famed cottage fries are tender but crisp and, with the greaseless, crackling onion rings, good foils for the rich meats.

Other cooked dishes, including overly sweet roast beef hash, are not as good as they used to be, but steak à la Stone—sliced beef on toast given the cool, satin contrast of roasted peppers and sautéed onions—is again satisfying. Skip vegetables. The only dessert worth saving room for is the S & S cheesecake, a matchless blend of the creamy and the solid. There is a very basic Italian wine list here, but somehow beer seems more appropriate.

SWISS

CHALET SUISSE

6 East 48th Street, between Fifth and Madison avenues
Telephone: 355-0855

Favorite meals:
Cheese and onion pie
Sautéed calves' liver with bacon
Coupe au chocolat
or
Ramequin
Bratwurst with onion sauce
Surprise Valaisanne
or
For a one-course pre-theater meal, Fondue Neuchâteloise
Other favorite dishes: Herring, air-cured beef (Bündnerfleisch), air-cured ham (Bündnerschinken), cervelat salad, medallions of veal with morels, kidneys and liver, rack of lamb, Zuger Kirschtorte, chocolate fondue.
Setting: Travel-poster Swiss chalet; you can almost hear the yodel; comfortable and cheerful.
Service: There are still people who care and here they are; waitresses are polite, concerned, efficient, and helpful.
Dress code: Jacket required for men.
Facilities for private parties: None.
Hours: Lunch and dinner, Monday through Friday. Closed Saturday, Sunday, major holidays, and for the month of August.
Reservations: Necessary.
Prices: Moderate to moderately expensive.
Credit cards: AE, DC, MC, V.

In some ways, the Chalet Suisse is my Brigadoon, an enchanted bygone dreamland where service is everything it should be—concerned, polite, helpful. Waitresses really want guests to like the food and, except at the busiest times, always check back to see if anything is needed. Whenever I go back for the rich, substantial homespun Swiss food, I expect it to have all disappeared. True, the chalet setting, with cowbells and the folk costumes on the waitresses, is cornily travel poster in inspiration, but if that's what it takes to have the committed staff, the glowingly spotless table settings, and the comfortable food, I'll pass on a more stylish come-on.

For obvious reasons, fall and winter are my favorite seasons for the Chalet Suisse. Everything about the place and its food seems suited to crisp weather, Christmas, and snowfall, and it provides a glowing cheerfulness to gray midwinter days. Simple products are always perfect. The air-cured beef and ham from the Grison Alps (Bündnerfleisch and Bündnerschinken, respectively) have the right saline meatiness, the appropriate sheen and chewiness, much like good prosciutto. With sweet butter and the yeasty bread, either makes a fine first course. So does the herring, its saltiness gentled by the sour cream and onion topping. Sliced wurst (cervelat) in a pungent vinaigrette dressing is a refreshing appetizer, as are the mushrooms Ascona, really à la grecque with tomato and onion.

Hot appetizers include two famous specialties of the Swiss kitchen, both based on cheese, not too surprisingly. Onion and cheese tart, a sort of quiche, is served bubbling hot, and the ramequin, a frothy cross between a soufflé and pudding, requires a twenty-minute wait—one I have never regretted. Snails and ravioli glazed with cheese are also good, if not quite up to other choices. Soups vary, from flavorful to stodgy.

Main courses range from humble offerings, such as bratwurst in a golden onion sauce on sauerkraut or with braised spinach, to an elegant rack of lamb crunchy with a bread-crumb veneer. Calves' liver is remarkably fresh and is as delicious sautéed with bacon and onions as it is combined with veal kidneys. Tender, moist veal medallions with cream and morels is a more savory choice than one of Switzerland's favorite dishes. Geschnetzeltes Kalbfleisch—slivered veal in cream sauce, a special taste and perhaps soothing when one has had a bad day. In the past, daily specials such as roast pork and grilled chicken have been fine, as has poached salmon with dill sauce.

Spätzli, the flecks of pasta dumplings, and rösti, the crisp-crusted Swiss potato pancake, are the right foils for most of the dishes. Vegetables, like soups, are likely to be institutionally bland. Get your vitamins someplace else and save room here for dessert. Of the two Swiss fondues—Neuchâteloise, made with cheese, and Bourguignonne, consisting of beef cooked at the table in hot oil—I much prefer the former and consider it a satisfying yet uncomplicated pre-theater meal.

Chocolate is, of course, another Swiss triumph, so the excellent desserts made with it are worth trying. Fondue (melted chocolate into which fresh fruit is dipped) and the coupe au chocolat (a hot bittersweet chocolate fudge sundae of sorts) are cases in point.

Layers of whipped cream, meringue, and strawberries form Surprise Valaisanne, while kirsch is the operative flavor sharpening the butter cream that is layered between meringue and genoise cake in the Zuger Kirschtorte. The apple tart, served icy cold, is soggy and commercial; not even a fluff of fresh whipped cream saves it.

Beer or Dôle de Sion, one of the better Swiss red wines, is the right accompaniment to the food. With cheese fondue, a white wine is preferable. There is a complete dinner that includes appetizer, soup, main course, dessert, and coffee for $37.50, still an exceptional bargain. Lunch is more crowded than dinner, at which time Chalet Suisse is a real find.

TIDBITS

Auberge Suisse, in the Market of the Citicorp building, 153 East 53rd Street (421-1420), is a smart little clubby setting for an elegant fondue Vaudoise made with all-Gruyère cheese, wine, and kirsch and served in a colorfully glazed earthenware pot. Also here is raclette, made not with the very smelly cheese that gives the dish its name, but with the milder Bel Sano. Served simmering hot in a gratin dish, this melted cheese treat may be had with boiled potatoes as an appetizer or with the crisp, grated potato pancake, roesti, as a main course. I much prefer the boiled potato even with the main course. Both versions come with the mandatory pickled onions and tiny green cornichons, for a cold, crisp, sharp contrast to the warm, supple cheese.

Smoked trout and the juicy veal and pork bratwürst sausage, grilled and topped with brown onions, are the other two winners here. Too bad the same cannot be said for the personalities of the pushy, perfunctory staff.

THAI

SIAM GRILL

585 Ninth Avenue, between 42nd and 43rd streets
Telephone: 307-1363

Favorite meals:
Shared by two to four
Kingfish patties (tod mun)
Chinese sausage with chili and onion
Grilled chicken gai yang
Fried flounder with chili sauce or garlic and pepper
Fried crisp rice noodles (mee krob)
Fresh fruit, if any, or ice cream
or
Shared by four
Beef satays
Shrimp soup with lime juice (tom yum koong) and/or chicken soup with coconut cream (tom ka kai)
Frogs' legs with basil and chili (gob pad kaiprau)
Minced pork with lime juice and peanuts (nam sod)
Chicken or beef with Thai hot curry (gai or neau padped)
Rice stick noodles (pad Thai)
Fresh fruit, if any, or ice cream
Other favorite dishes: Marinated baby ribs; frogs' legs with garlic and black pepper; steamed flounder with vegetables, shrimp, squid, or beef salad with onion and chilies; ba me noodles with chicken curry.
Setting: Small, informal, but attractive with Thai decorative touches; tables are close and small.
Service: Polite, accommodating, but slow at peak hours because of kitchen limitations.
Dress code: None.
Facilities for private parties: None.
Hours: Lunch and dinner, Monday through Friday. Dinner, Saturday and Sunday. Closed major holidays.
Reservations: Not accepted; go early if planning a visit to theaters on West 42nd and 43rd streets.
Prices: Inexpensive.
Credit cards: AE, CB, DC, MC, V.

What first seemed to me merely a convenience in an otherwise gastronomically barren area has grown to be a favorite even without that consideration. Small, trim, and attractively paneled and mirrored, with a cheerful and obliging staff, Siam Grill turns out some of the better versions of standard Thai dishes, and does so at amazingly low prices. It has a fairly good lunch following, and early dinner is crowded with customers going to off-Broadway theaters on 42nd and 43rd streets, in the Manhattan Plaza area.

Grilling is especially well done here, both for the tender, juicy beef satays and the barbecued chicken gai yang, which has a zesty glaze of garlic, curry spices, and lemon and gets added spark from a pungent sauce. Spareribs are not usually meaty enough; marinated baby ribs, when available, are far better. Minced kingfish patties (tod mun) are tender and accented by vinegared cucumber slices, and the soups described above are delicate and bracing; the dry strawlike strands of lemon grass can be annoying in these Thai soups as they are meant to be avoided, not eaten. Crab soup is the only disappointment—a watery, characterless brew. Mee krob, the Thai fried rice noodles, is not too sweet and remains crisp throughout the eating.

Fried flounder, with a thick, hot, sweet-and-sour chili sauce, is perhaps the most exceptional dish and one I rarely resist. For a lighter sauce, the same fish, moistly, carefully cooked, can be had with a veneer of brown garlic and black pepper, the same combination that distinguishes frogs' legs and shrimp. Minced pork brightened with lime juice and peanuts is delicious rolled in lettuce leaves and eaten out of hand. Salads of onion and green chilies with sausage, shrimp, beef, or squid are equally good as shared appetizers or as a light lunch for one. Curries of all meats and fish, mild-to-hot, are nicely done, if not quite up to other dishes.

A slight unevenness mars the kitchen's batting average, as does a reluctance to flavor food with enough chili, even when a fervent plea is made. Noodle dishes, described above, are good, but fried rice is sometimes greasy and cold. Beer is the best accompaniment to this aromatic fare.

SIAM INN

916 Eighth Avenue, between 54th and 55th streets
Telephone: 489-5237

Favorite meals:
Shared by two
Sautéed squid with chili and onion
Beef curry with coconut milk, bamboo shoots, and chili
Sautéed chicken with basil leaves and chili

Mee krob
Coconut ice cream
or
Shared by four
Kingfish patties (tod man pla)
Beef or squid with cucumber, onion, and chili
Shrimp soup or chicken soup with coconut milk
Bangkok duck
Whole fried fish with chili and garlic sauce (pla lad prig)
Pad Thai or white rice
Mango or coconut ice cream
Other favorite dishes: Seafood combination (shellfish, squid, and fish in garlicky tomato sauce, steamed in foil packet); frogs' legs any style; deep-fried whole fish with ground pork, mushrooms, and ginger (pla jearn); all shrimp dishes; chicken or beef with basil and chili or with garlic and pepper; mussels steamed in white wine and garlic.
Setting: Pleasant café–dining room with long, attractive bar; back of dining room is a bit roomier than the narrow front.
Service: Excellent.
Dress code: None.
Facilities for private parties: None.
Hours: Lunch, Monday through Friday. Dinner, seven days.
Reservations: Recommended, especially before theater.
Prices: Inexpensive to moderate.
Credit cards: AE, CB, DC.

Every now and then I hear of a new Thai restaurant that is supposed to be sensational, and, of course, I invariably go and eat for myself. So far none has matched this one for consistent excellence at dinner. Lunch, unfortunately, is far less even. Perhaps the biggest improvement since the last edition of this book is the kitchen's courage in spicing dishes as hot as the menu indicates them to be. Two asterisks, now, stand for pretty damn hot and, as for three, be sure you mean incendiary when you order. As attractive as it is functional, the Siam Inn is decorated with basil-green tablecloths topped with glass, dark wood paneling, and fresh flowers. Tables in back have a bit more space around them than those in front but are still somewhat small for four people and all the dishes they might order.

What the efficient and polite staff serves forth is a palate-tingling assortment of beautifully cooked dishes. Among those might be plump, sweet mussels, steamed in white wine and garlic, much like the French marinière version, or tender squid fried with chili, onions, and lemon grass. I like to share either as a first course. Both are good forerunners to beef curry with coconut milk, bamboo shoots, and chili—marked with three asterisks and actually hot if you insist. Fork-size pieces of chicken sautéed with chili and Thai basil, which is stronger and more mentholated than our own, adds a soothing, satisfying note, as does the mee krob—sticky sweet and pungent fried thin rice noodles. Only pork is dry and bland.

Sharing food among four (or even six), as when eating Chinese food, is the most fun here. It allows for other excellent dishes, such as the satays or a crisp cool salad of thin slices of beef or tenderized squid sprinkled with green chilies, sliced onion, and slightly lemony fish sauce. Egg rolls and spring rolls are skippable, but, when available, Thai steamed dumplings make good hors d'oeuvres with drinks. Soups, both the shrimp and lemon (tom yom koong) and the chicken with coconut milk (tom ka kai), are bracing introductions to heartier dishes. Bangkok duck, braised in a chili and tamarind juice curry, has mild overtones of anise, and the meat is lean, greaseless, and meltingly tender. By contrast, the big crisp fried fish with a thick sauce of chili and garlic (pla lad prig) is piercingly hot. In another version the fish is sauced with ginger and mushrooms (pla jearn). Frogs' legs are a Thai specialty, and at the Siam Inn they are equally delicious seasoned with coconut milk and basil or with garlic sauce. One very ambitious dish that requires a very ambitious eater is the combination of crab meat, shrimp, squid, and sometimes scallops steamed with fish in an almost Provençale tomato-garlic sauce, zapped with chili and arriving at the table as bubbling hot as an active volcano. Modest appetites might better choose poached whole fish.

As in other Thai restaurants, avoid dishes that include pineapple and stick to ice creams for desserts, the mango being a velvety alternative to the coconut.

The problem at lunch may be the short shrift the kitchen gives the less expensive dishes featured at that time of day.

TOONS

417 Bleecker Street, corner Bank Street
Telephone: 924-6420 or 243-9211

Favorite meal:
Shared by two
Sausage salad
Frogs' legs with basil and chili pepper sauce
Whole deep-fried fish with hot chili and garlic sauce (pla muk pad tua)
Soft sautéed rice noodles with shrimp (pad Thai)
Pumpkin custard or orange crème caramel
Other favorite dishes: Sautéed squid with chili paste and herbs (pla muk); steamed red snapper with ginger and scallions (pla bae sa); "special honor to the king" (boneless fried chicken breasts with red curry sauce); eggplant in soybean, garlic, and chili sauce (makuur pad); marinated and grilled chicken (kai yung); fried rice noodles (mee krob).
Setting: Theatrical café setting with huge windows, flowers, and candlelight; tables are cramped, and there is no provision for checking coats.
Service: Helpful, well meaning, and prompt.

Dress code: None.
Facilities for private parties: Back room accommodates up to 40.
Hours: Dinner, seven days.
Reservations: Recommended, especially for parties larger than 2 and for peak dinner hours.
Prices: Moderate.
Credit cards: AE, MC, V.

With its dramatic spotlighting, sprays of purple orchids, plants, and decorative artifacts, Toons is as pretty as a movie set. Big windows give it a café atmosphere, spoiled only at a few tables as oncoming automobile headlights flash into the eyes of diners. It's too bad that the tables are touchingly close and that there are no provisions for checking, or even hanging coats; as it is, winter outer clothing must be stuffed onto vacant chairs, adding to the crowded feeling at the height of busy dinner hours.

Earlier, or on slower nights, Toons is a delightful option for Thai food in Greenwich Village. Since it is close to my home, I go fairly often and have learned that about one third of the menu is dependable. Even so, what is good is very good, hence its inclusion here.

What is not good is the appetizer assortment; fried choices are greasy, including a shrimp fritter that many regulars seem to favor. A sprightly sausage salad (more salad than sausage) is a refreshing alternative when it is on the menu, as is the frogs' legs with basil and chili pepper, meant as a main course but fine shared by two as a starter.

Fish is generally well prepared at Toons, most especially the big, moistly meaty, crisp-coated fried sea bass or snapper that is enriched by a hefty, chili-sparked sauce. Lighter, but no less appealing, is the steamed red snapper with ginger and scallions, a dish that owes much to the Chinese kitchen. "Special honor to the king," boneless chicken fried and topped with a red curry sauce accented by cool, vinegar-marinated cucumbers, is far better than "special honor to the queen," a mishmash fish combination overcomplicated with bean curd and pineapple. (Could there be overtones of sexism in the kitchen?)

Chicken kai yung, marinated and grilled, is as juicy and tender as the menu promises. Sautéed squid, either with chili paste or with string beans, is satiny and delicate, and eggplant with soybeans and the heady array of traditional Thai herbs is soothing. Mee krob, the crisp, fine fried rice noodles, and pad Thai, softer fried noodles, are better than the greasy, often cold fried rice.

Desserts are unusually good for a Thai restaurant; a version of the coconut custard sankhaya is steamed in acorn squash (pumpkin custard), and the crème caramel has a sunny orange accent. Beer is the right, cool beverage for such strongly flavored food.

TIBETAN

TIBETAN KITCHEN

444 Third Avenue, between 30th and 31st streets
Telephone: 679-6286

Favorite meals:
Shared by two
Steamed beef dumplings (momo)
Spicy mixed cabbage (tang tsel)
Tibetan chicken curry (chashah shamdeh)
Tibetan lamb curry (shamdeh)
Rice with yogurt and raisins (deysee)
or
Shared by four
Mixed-vegetable dumplings (tsel momo)
Fried beef dumplings (fried momo)
Spicy mixed cabbage (tang tsel)
Sautéed sliced steak with hot Asian bread (shapta)
Sautéed noodles with vegetables (tsel gyathuk ngopa)
Mixed fresh fruits with yogurt
Other favorite dishes: Peas with beef and egg, peas sautéed with shredded beef and egg, spicy hot potato dish. Beer and white wine go best with this food. No liquor license; take your own.
Setting: Simple, crowded storefront dining room with a few Tibetan artifacts; noisy and cramped, especially when there is a line waiting at the door.
Service: Concerned, naive, and polite; slow at peak hours because of kitchen limitations.
Dress code: None.
Facilities for private parties: Claustrophobic downstairs room accommodates up to 25.
Hours: Lunch, Monday through Friday. Dinner, Monday through Saturday. Closed Sunday and holidays.
Reservations: Necessary for more than four people; recommended even for two (though there may be a wait anyway) on Friday and Saturday nights.
Prices: Inexpensive.
Credit cards: None.

It is not only the pleasant and unusually diverting food that continues to make this inexpensive little restaurant one of my favorites. Add to that the endearing staff, which is polite, gracious, and genuinely concerned. As an added convenience, the small menu describes dishes in detail so no one need fly blind, gastronomically.

Professionalism is not the word to use here; this is more like a cottage-industry effort. The long, narrow storefront setting has a few decorative Tibetan motifs, and at peak hours—Friday and Saturday nights—it is cramped and noisy.

But at other times it is less hectic and, therefore, more enjoyable. Tibetan food combines elements of the Chinese kitchen (stir-fried dishes and meat or vegetable dumplings, or momo, which are steamed or fried) with Indian-style foods such as curries and filled flat breads such as the chapati-like shapta and shaphali that accompany sliced beef. A hot chili paste, sephan, lends fire to other seasonings, such as garlic, onions, coriander, and soy sauce, in dips and sauces.

Among stir-fried dishes are the Chinese cabbage with chicken (patsel), a variety of noodles combined with vegetables and beef, and curries (shamdeh) of lamb or chicken.

A hot and spicy cabbage salad with carrots (tang tsel) provides coolness and crunch with either appetizers or main courses such as the gentle, chewy combination of peas sautéed with shredded beef and egg threads. Soups and vegetarian dishes tend to be uninteresting in flavor, but there is a spicy potato salad (shogog khatsa) with hot bread that is especially good, as is spicy cauliflower with bean curd (Himalayan khatsa).

Deysee, a dessert described as being served at all religious ceremonies in Tibet, is indeed soul food and a lovely surprise, much like rice pudding. The firm white rice is served hot, studded with raisins and topped with cool yogurt. Mixed fresh fruits, also with yogurt, is the acceptable second choice. Thara, a yogurt shake, should make you feel as though you could conquer the world. Bocha, tea that is buttered and salted, may make you feel as though you'd like to retire from it. Tibetan black tea is a far more viable alternative, as they say.

VIETNAMESE

SAIGON RESTAURANT ★

60 Mulberry Street, near Bayard Street
Telephone: 227-8825

Favorite meals:
Shared by four
Barbecued shrimp on sugarcane (chao tom)
Barbecued pork ball (nem nuong)
Chicken salad (ga xe phay)
Crab cooked in beer (cua lave)
Chicken with lemon grass (ga xao xa)
Red bean ice cream (dau do nuoc dua)
or
For a quick one-dish lunch when alone, raw and cooked beef noodle soup (pho tai chin)
Other favorite dishes: Spring roll (cha gio), steamed pork roll (banh cuon), pork and shrimp salad (goi tom sua), Vietnamese salami (cha lua gio heo), shrimp or lobster steamed in beer or fried in salt and pepper, beef in vinegar (thit bo nhung giam), pork chops with lemon grass (thit suon), steamed pork with crab and egg (cha chung), curried eel (luon xao xa), shrimp in satay sauce (tom satay), chicken curry rice (com ga cari), steamed chicken rice (com ga tay cam), all rice noodle soups and rice vermicelli dishes.
Setting: Clean, bright downstairs, luncheonette.
Service: Charming and helpful, if occasionally forgetful.
Dress code: None.
Facilities for private parties: None.
Hours: Lunch and dinner, seven days.
Reservations: Necessary for more than five.
Prices: Inexpensive.
Credit cards: AE, MC, V.

If I have always enjoyed jury duty, it is not only because I have been on interesting cases and feel jurors are treated with consideration and respect in New York. It is also because I can have many lunches at Saigon, a cheerful, good, and inexpensive Vietnamese restaurant in Chinatown. It is a short walk from the various courts. I simply go through the Criminal Courts Building, then cross the little park behind it, and there is the downstairs restaurant, a neat, shining sort of luncheonette with a young, polite, and accommodating staff. Perhaps a little more careless than it used to be, the kitchen still usually turns out diverting fare.

The food of Vietnam is beyond doubt the most beguiling in Southeast Asia. Having first tried it in 1960, both in Saigon and then in Cambodia, where there were several Vietnamese restaurants, I hoped for years that it would become available in New York. The flavor contrasts of lemon grass, garlic, coriander, chili, ginger, and peanuts, combined with the textural counterpoints of the soft and silken and the crackling crisp, make it an unusually diverting cuisine. There are elements of both the Chinese and the Thai kitchens, with many Malaysian accents, such as satays and the use of peanuts as a soothing base for the fiery chili oil.

Although New York has several restaurants featuring this food, Saigon remains the best. If I am alone for lunch, I have one of the marvelous soups adrift with rice or noodles, vegetables and beef, chicken and shrimp. The raw and cooked beef noodle soup is a particular favorite, with a steaming hot broth that slowly, gradually cooks carpaccio-thin slices of raw beef so that they're eaten half-raw-to-rare and flavor the broth. Soft egg noodles are satisfying, as are the bean sprouts meant to be added to the soup as the eating progresses. The effect is sustaining and yet not deadening and, at $2.95, probably the biggest bargain in town. Despite the hot pineapple in them, which I dislike, the sweet and sour soups, most especially the shrimp, are also good, assuming you can avoid the pineapple as you go along.

Appetizers are intriguing, not only the meaty beef satays with their peanut-chili dip but also barbecued pork balls, the ground shrimp grilled on sugarcane skewers, and the pungent chicken salad. Fried spring rolls tend to be greasy, but both the steamed and shredded pork roll and the shrimp and pork roll are expertly prepared. The most spectacular main course is the crab or lobster steamed in beer—a kind of eggy, puffy near-soufflé. Extracting the meat from the shell is a bit difficult, but the effort is worthwhile as the warm yeasty beer mellows the shellfish. Shrimp can also be had that way and are easier to handle, if less breathtaking to taste. Saigon special beef (thit bo vi) is fried in the dining room in ginger- and lemon grass–flavored oil, as is thit bo nhung giam, thinly sliced beef cooked at the table in vinegar-flavored beef broth. Both now have become bland and uninteresting. Chicken stir-fried with lemon grass is pleasant if a bit mild in flavor; it provides a soothing foil to other dishes. Hot chili in many forms is a staple of the Vietnamese kitchen, and it does well by the casseroles of eel or frog in a curry sauce, the barbecued fish, and the chicken curry rice.

Pork and seafood are combined with delectable results throughout—in appetizers such as the spiced pork and shrimp crackers and the rock shrimp with pork and in main courses such as the steamed pork with crab and egg.

Desserts tend to be stickily sweet, the red bean ice cream being a notable exception. French filtré coffee is disappointingly weak; better to opt for tea. There is full bar service, and beer lends itself best to the food.

TIDBITS

Bo Ky Restaurant, 80 Bayard Street, between Mott and Baxter streets (406-2292), offers bracing, savory main course soups with a variety of noodles, shrimp, meats, and vegetables, in the best hot pot tradition, all at incredibly low prices ranging from $2.50 to $4. Flat wheat noodles with slivers of beef is especially bracing, as is the lusty curried chicken rice noodle that has a fiery belt. The setting is strictly luncheonette, and be prepared to share tables at crowded times. There are Chinese overtones to the soups here, many of which are described as "teo chew," meaning that they are native to the Quangdong province of China. Open from 8 A.M. to 9 P.M., seven days.

THE VIEW, THE SETTING, AND THE SCENE

Only occasionally is food the secondary reason for my going to a restaurant, but there are a few instances where some other aspect draws me. It might be a view I want to show out-of-town friends or to take another look at for myself, or an interior I find beautiful and uplifting, or a scene that is amusing or exciting, or a particular time of day or season that appeals to me.

Some of these restaurants have better food than others, but none are consistently good enough to attract me for that alone. That, in short, is the test that determined which restaurants go into this category, and I have developed a strategy for eating, choosing those dishes that have proved the most likely to succeed. **The ratings represent an averaging of food and setting, in this case with emphasis on the latter.**

AMERICA

9–13 East 18th Street, between Fifth Avenue and Broadway
Telephone: 505-2110

Favorite meals:
Shared by four
New Orleans Cajun popcorn
Buffalo chicken wings
Albuquerque blue corn tostadas with sour cream, guacamole, salmon caviar, and scallions
Traditional pizza with cheese, tomato, and basil
or
New Mexican black bean cakes with sour cream, chilies, and salsa, shared by two

Grilled whole chicken with garlic and herbs
Brownie with vanilla ice cream
Other favorite dishes: None.
Setting: More a town square than a room, with airy murals and deafening noise level when crowded.
Service: Friendly and good-natured, but at times forgetful.
Dress code: None.
Facilities for private parties: One large room can accommodate as many as 30.
Hours: Lunch and dinner, seven days, until midnight.
Reservations: Recommended, especially at peak meal hours.
Prices: The range is enormous, from inexpensive to moderately expensive.
Credit cards: AE, MC, V.

When it opened about three years ago, America was a wild parody of a restaurant. In some ways it still is, but the changing neighborhood around it, with its advertising and publishing firms, has made the management here take itself a bit more seriously. That is especially true at lunch, when a well-dressed, young, and creative clientele drops in to graze or really dig into the 200-plus-item menu. Food and service are still a bit on the wild side, but America has become a cheerful and useful facility.

It is (of course) in the trendiest new lower Fifth Avenue neighborhood, and (also of course) its sign is invisible until you are on the top step leading to the doorway. There, embedded in concrete, is the restaurant name in brass. And brass is what it took to put this together, to dare to try a 10,000-square-foot space and to offer a cookbook index of a menu that reflects every hot food trend, from the Southwest and Louisiana to New England, Buffalo, and Rochester, by way of France, Italy, and Japan. There are down-home culinary memorabilia such as meat loaf with onion gravy (awful), baby food such as a fluffernutter sandwich (marshmallow whip with peanut butter, and disgusting), sushi, alligator sausages (dry), nuova pastas, and green eggs and ham, for Dr. Seuss fans in the audience. Most of the kitchen's efforts are dismal, and the service is a perfect match. But the young staff is so good-natured and unpretentious that though they approach with trays, asking not "Who gets what?" but "Does this table get this food?" I am inclined to forgive them.

There is a three-deep bar scene at night and a constant promenade of people looking for friends to join, so they can mix-match shared choices from the menu. It might be a salad, a pizza or pasta, and some Cajun popcorn, the fried, breaded crawfish tails, or lobster-filled ravioli in a tomato-cream sauce.

But the chairs are comfortable, the action is diverting, and the pastel, wide-horizon abstract murals are fresh and bright, and so I rely solely on the dishes recommended above for favorite meals. Friends from out-of-town or out-of-country get as much of a kick out of this as I do. After all, there are lots of places to get good food, but only one America. Also, prices can be low, with sandwiches and burgers (fair) at $2.95 and $5.95, or as high as $18.95 for hefty meat main courses or lamb chops (just edible). Oversize bowls and coffee cups and larger-than-life portions indicate food is merely a prop in this theatrical production, but there is no minimum, and kids have a wonderful time. America is great for large groups and small children. An assortment of appetizers, as indicated, should keep you from starving.

America is brought to us by the same wonderful restaurant group that gave us The Saloon and Ernie's, among others, but those places are no laughing matters. America is at least a pleasant chuckle.

CAFÉ DES ARTISTES

1 West 67th Street, between Central Park West and Columbus Avenue
Telephone: 877-3500

Favorite meals:
Brunch or lunch
Asparagus vinaigrette
Grilled swordfish
Key lime pie
or
Salmon, four ways
Boiled beef with vegetables in broth (pot-au-feu)
Strawberry sherbet
Other favorite dishes: Assorted pâtés and sausages (charcuterie), asparagus with hollandaise sauce, Chef Andrés pâté, duck liver terrine, clams on the half shell with Mexican relish, seafood gazpacho, sweetbread headcheese, cauliflower salad, eggs Benedict with smoked salmon, chicken salad Waldorf, mocha dacquoise, orange savarin, chocolate Ilona cake, sour cream apple walnut pie, Grand Dessert.
Setting: One of New York's most beautiful; a romantic Continental café with flowery murals and a wonderful glow of daylight coming through plant-trimmed windows; tables are close and noise level can be a bit high.
Service: Friendly, helpful, and efficient.
Dress code: Jackets required for men after 5 P.M.
Facilities for private parties: None.
Hours: Lunch, Monday through Friday. Dinner, Monday through Sunday. Open late. Brunch, Saturday and Sunday.
Reservations: Necessary.
Prices: Moderate to moderately expensive.
Credit cards: AE, CB, DC, MC, V.

As romantic and sentimental as a Viennese waltz, Café des Artistes is a beautiful Continental café that I prefer for brunch or lunch. The effect of daylight (with luck, sunshine) pouring through the small windowpanes reflecting greens, pinks, and reds of plants seems a continuation of the lush sylvan murals painted by Howard Chandler Christy for the café's opening in 1917.

Through the years the kitchen's performance has been uneven, but the same sort of dishes that have always been good for brunch and lunch still are. And since that is the time of day I prefer, it raises no problems.

The buffet of appetizers and desserts in the center of the front room is a tip-off to the kitchen's strong points. There is always a nice, coarse saucisson to be had warm in a crust (en croûte) and assorted pâtés and terrines that may be ordered singly or in combination. Chef André's pâté, a meaty and subtly fat loaf, has the pleasant crunch of big, crisp, dark walnut meats, while a more sophisticated and elegant terrine of duck livers has a mousselike texture and rich flavor. To this has been added a cool, chewy headcheese with a gentle inset of sweetbreads, all sparkled with a piquant cucumber and vinaigrette dressing. Too bad better, coarser breads are not served with these; the pumpernickel and rye on the table look far better than they taste. There is, however, nice hot Dijon-style mustard.

Much is made of asparagus in season, when asparagus-based dishes are listed on a separate card as in Germany. Asparagus is as good served cold in vinaigrette dressing as it is served hot with hollandaise sauce. As unlikely as seafood gazpacho may sound, it can be delicious with its thickening of fish and its garnishes of minced cucumber, peppers, and onions enlivening the tomato blend.

If in the mood for an egg dish, I have the poached eggs Benedict Café des Artistes, with smoked salmon substituted for ham. But next time I'll remember to remind the waiter about toasting both sides of the English muffin and bringing the eggs steaming hot. The lovely tarragon-flecked hollandaise and the nicely cooked eggs and asparagus deserve that extra attention.

Certainly it is a choice I prefer to the darkly wet roast beef hash, a veritable football-size oval turned mushy by its gravy. Lovers of Waldorf salad should revel in the stylish, bright presentation here, with the fresh mayonnaise-and celery-tossed chicken heaped in a dome that is roofed with toasted walnuts and shingled around the sides with snow peas and matchsticks of nice, tart Granny Smith apples.

Pastas generally seem too rich and complex, witness such combinations as fettuccine with salmon, mushrooms, and asparagus. A far better choice is the house pot-au-feu, that fragrant boiled beef, tender in its golden broth and garnished with leeks, carrots, potatoes, coarse salt, and gently sharp horseradish sauce. A cut of the marrow bone is presented along with a proper marrow spoon so the soft fatty substance can be extracted gracefully, to be spread on the rounds of croutons.

That dish, by the way, is also on the dinner menu and makes Café des Artistes a convenient option for a before– or after–Lincoln Center meal. Cold raw clams topped with a spicy Mexican pepper and onion relish and cold poached salmon are dishes I have enjoyed in the past, and there are some attractive cold plates (buffet platters) I mean to try on future visits. I also mean to repeat the excellent grilled swordfish steak, one of the dewiest I have ever had.

Bourride, the creamy, garlicky fish soup-stew of Provence, is a standby here, but, though very well flavored, it contains only a small proportion of fish to broth and salmon is much out of character in the mix. Steak au poivre is acceptable, but not so the baby chicken stuffed with mushily overcooked fettuccine.

If the dazzlement of desserts makes choosing impossible, then share with a friend the Grand Dessert, a killer of a finish unless it is divided and unless it follows a light main course. Then on future visits you will know if you want to restrict yourself to the cool, creamy, and airy Key lime pie, the moist orange-accented savarin pound cake, the thick apple pie made with sour cream and walnuts, or the creamy and seductive layered chocolate Ilona cake. Mocha dacquoise with rosettes of butter cream hiding between layers of crisp meringue is also delicious and preferable to the cloying marzipan torte or a thinner, cocoa-dusted chocolate torte with a name I don't remember. Pastries are not quite all, as there have always been refreshing fruit sherbets, my current favorite being the strawberry.

The bar shakes up a perfect bloody Mary, cold but without ice if ordered that way, and with lemon juice instead of lime, all my preferences and beautifully executed.

THE FOUR SEASONS

99 East 52nd Street, between Park and Lexington avenues
Telephone: 754-9494

Favorite meals:
In Bar Room grill at lunch
Mushroom ravioli in broth (Spa cuisine)
Broiled shad roe with bacon
or
Grilled quail
Fruit sherbet

In Pool dining room at dinner
Terrine of pike and salmon
Crisp farmhouse duck au poivre
Grand Marnier soufflé
Other favorite dishes: Pasta with game sauce, crisped shrimp with mustard fruits, seviche of scallops or red snapper, fettuccine primavera, oysters or clams on the half shell, Scotch smoked salmon, gravlax with dill sauce, game pâtés, calves' liver with onions or avocado, breast of pheasant with Gorgonzola polenta, double lamb chops, chocolate velvet cake.
Setting: Perhaps the world's most beautiful and classic modern restaurant, with a tailored, clublike Bar Room grill, which I like for the lunchtime scene, and the large, flowery Pool Room, which I like for the setting. Unfortunately, some tacky touches are compromising the overall effect.
Service: Excellent if you are known; offhand, if you are not.
Dress code: Jacket and tie required for men.
Facilities for private parties: Three private rooms accommodate between 10 and 200. Entire restaurant can be booked for Sunday.
Hours: Bar Room grill—Lunch and dinner until 11:30 P.M., Monday through Saturday. Pool Room—Lunch, Monday through Friday; dinner until 11:30 P.M., Monday through Saturday. Closed Sunday and major holidays.
Reservations: Recommended, especially for Bar at lunch.
Prices: Expensive. Spa menu and pre- and post-theater dinners are moderately expensive.
Credit cards: AE, DC, MC, V.

When The Four Seasons opened in the summer of 1959, its interior by Philip Johnson and William Pahlmann became an instant design landmark, perhaps the first modern restaurant to be formal and substantial. Until that time it was assumed that any restaurant offering serious food at very serious prices had to be traditional. But following the lines established by Mies van der Rohe, the architect of the Seagram Building, which houses The Four Seasons, the interior designers came up with a result as distinguished as the exterior. The proof of its excellence is in the classic quality it has taken on. The Bar Room grill, with its dark "leather" and wood and the glittering brass rod sculptures by Richard Lippold that hang over bar and balcony dining area, is crisp and handsome. The Pool Room, with its white marble reflecting pool and hanging plants, presents a less tailored, more glamorous aspect, and in both rooms swags of metal chains curtain windows.

Unfortunately, intermittent refurbishings and tacky economies now compromise the overall elegance of this setting. Dreary, black-patterned carpet, glitzy, metallic-threaded plastic partitions between the bar itself and the grill dining room, two overlapping tablecloths doing the work of one that is properly large, ever-cheaper paper for menus, and dented hollowware take a heavy toll. It is that deterioration of design quality that makes The Four Seasons a little less of a pleasure than it used to be. This is all especially disappointing in a building designed by Mies, whose observation that "God is in the details" should guide the operators of this restaurant.

Nevertheless, I still enjoy an occasional meal at The Four Seasons, most especially at lunch, when daylight filters through the chain curtains, making them translucent. At night when the chains become opaque, they are less magical, and their upward movement (an illusion caused by ripples of rising air currents) makes me feel as though I am going under.

What actually can go under at almost any time of day is my bank account, for this is New York's most exorbitantly expensive restaurant, which is why I have relegated it to this category. For as good as dishes can be here, there has never been enough culinary consistency to justify the price. There are a few special dinners (pre- and post-theater and a diet Spa menu) that are $41.50 prix fixe, but that means eating lean and dull, or too early or too late.

Yet lunch in the Bar Room grill is a special kind of delight, the grill being a meeting place for movers and shakers in the publishing world, and I see many people I know and like and so have a good time. The lunch menu in that room is trim and easygoing with simple dishes that get diverting flourishes and that are slightly less costly than those in the Pool Room. But sitting on comfortable banquettes or chairs and watching the action is something I enjoy now and then, especially if someone else is paying the check. When I am feeling more festive, or having lunch with someone from out of town or the suburbs (usually a woman) who prefers a little saucing of glamour, I go to the Pool Room, where roomy tables and chairs rim the watery center and everyone gets bowls of tiny, flaky croissants.

Even though I am recognized here (though rarely expected in advance), I get food that may be good, indifferent, and even, at times, bad. Bad would be the rating for a few very salty dishes I have had, such as crabcakes or swordfish obscured by a heavy olive paste. And I have had meat paillards both dry and succulent and scampi grilled perfectly or dried out. What has never failed for lunch in the grill is pasta, whether the wide pappardelle with game sauce or porcini, or the vegetable-tossed fettuccine primavera, or the risotto with a dark sauce of squid ink, as dense and rich as caviar. Ravioli are always delicate and often afloat in spicy, herb-strewn broth, whether they are filled with seafood or wild mushrooms, as they sometimes appear on the Spa menu, which has gained staunch followers. Seviche, whether of scallops or red snapper, has a nice limey edge that is sparked with red peppers, and both game birds and charcoal-grilled fish dishes have been fine. This menu is cleverly devised to be entertaining but not intrusive. No dish requires tableside service to distract the big-dealers in their manipulations, nor is any complicated to eat.

The Pool Room menu is far more ambitious and includes one of the house's original dishes that I love—crisp shrimp breaded and fried and garnished with the sweet-sour preserved mustard fruits of Cremona. Clams or oysters on the half shell with grated fresh horseradish and a wine-vinegar mignonette dip are sparkling and clear. Smoked Scottish salmon has the right drypoint finish, and marinated salmon, gravlax, is silky and airy with dill. Chef Seppi Renggli is Swiss and so has a special talent for game, in pâtés or with main-course birds and meats. I especially like grilled pheasant or pigeon breast with Gorgonzola-zapped polenta or wild rice.

Most recently, two excellent main courses were the tender, cushiony double lamb chops, grilled to rose-rare perfection, and the roast duck, its crisp skin pavéd with crunches of black peppercorns that heightened the subtleties of the moist, pink meat. Rack of lamb and the ultimate beef rib steak, côte de boeuf, are dinner main courses I always mean to try again, but other options interfere; so do their ferocious price tags—$37 per person for the rack of lamb and $40 for the steak, strictly à la carte and served only for two.

Fruit tarts and cakes are not what they were when baked by master pastry chef Albert Kumin, but the dense, chocolaty velvet cake has held up well as have fruit sherbets (the grapefruit is beautiful) and poached fruit compotes.

There are still adorably enticing coffee cup soufflés, equally good flavored with Grand Marnier or chocolate. Also still on hand from the old days are tiny, flaky croissants and wheaty rolls in the Pool Room, and, at dinner, delightful assortments of olives, black radishes, and a few hot savories such as little potato crêpes with crème fraîche and good caviar and the chewy, satisfying liver satays.

Service varies here, being impeccable for regulars and often indifferent to unknowns, who may be guided to the worst tables, including the out-of-it upstairs dining rooms, even if the Pool Room is not full.

The present operators, Paul Kovi and Tom Margittai, have maintained much of the original policy as to wines, offering an enormous and thoughtful selection, always at prices that are relatively reasonable, if not quite the bargains they once were.

RUSSIAN TEA ROOM

150 West 57th Street, between Sixth and Seventh avenues
Telephone: 265-0947

Favorite meals:
Assorted zakuska appetizer
Cheese pancakes (sirniki)

Russian tea with cherry preserves
or
Blini with red caviar and sour cream
Pepper vodka
Other favorite dishes: Eggplant Orientale, seviche of scallops, Swedish matjes herring, chicken Kiev, calves' liver, Caucasian shashlik, blintzes (blinchiki).
Setting: Avoid the upstairs room. Downstairs is *the* scene in a festive, lavish stage set of eternal Christmas; noisy and cramped.
Service: The most authentically Russian feature here, it is usually brusque and slapdash.
Dress code: No shorts, running suits, or blue jeans permitted.
Facilities for private parties: Two upstairs rooms accommodate from 20 to 200.
Hours: Lunch, Monday through Friday. Dinner until 11:30 P.M., seven days. Brunch, Saturday and Sunday.
Reservations: Recommended, especially for lunch and before and after theater.
Prices: Moderately expensive to expensive.
Credit cards: AE, CB, DC, MC, V.

Take away the year-round Christmas ornaments, the festive red, green, and gold color scheme, the colorful paintings, and the glittering brass samovars—as well as the lively show-biz and publishing set during lunch and late evening—and you are left with a place I would never walk into. It is those attractions that make this a jumping, very New York scene and one that is fun to watch during lunch or after theater. The meal to avoid is dinner, first because the room is usually half empty, and then because those who are there are uninteresting to observe. Most important of all, the dinner menu eliminates most of the dishes I like best and offers only a mandatory table d'hôte of food that is indifferently prepared.

Perhaps as an antidote to the worst food of the day comes the best service. The dinner staff seems friendlier and more willing to please. At other times, unknowns are treated with an indifference or even rudeness that can be matched only in the Soviet Union itself. To that extent, the Russian Tea Room is indeed authentic. I have been served stale bread and have had a waiter ask if he could have my uneaten salt stick roll for another table because, he said, they were in short supply.

Yet at its most festively crowded hours in the main dining room, this is fun to be part of, especially as there are several delicious things to eat on the lunch and late-night à la carte menus. Among such is the Russian appetizer assortment zakuska, based on rich and oily tidbits intended to bolster the system against the effects of vodka. That means several good herrings, with the thick, silky, and saline Swedish raw matjes being the best, followed by spicy pickled herring with sour cream. One or the other will be in the assortment, as will a slice of boiled potato topped with sour cream and red salmon caviar, a slice of smoked salmon pinwheeled around capers, a gentle eggplant purée Orientale, savory after being simmered with onions and tomato, and, at times, an unauthentic but pleasing seviche of tiny scallops in a sparkly herb marinade. The only off note is the hideous chopped liver, puréed to near liquid and seemingly creamed to pale insignificance. Roszolnick, traditionally a sour-cream thickened soup based on chicken giblets with vegetables and pickled cucumber, is delivered here as a tasteless, thin porridge, such as one expects on a hospital tray. Cold beet borscht contains too much sour cream and is annoyingly sweet. With soups come hot (well, warm) pirojok, flaky, puff-pastry turnovers containing a pleasantly mild meat filling.

All of these appetizers can be had in large single portions or in the smaller dibs and dabs that make up the combination. Caviar, of course, is another option, but though the qualities are acceptable when served with the blini buckwheat crêpes and sour cream, they do not stand up to solo performances. Those blini, by the way, though somewhat soggy from being kept hot at the table in a covered casserole, come through nicely once slathered with melted butter, caviar, and cream. They are available on all menus and are a satisfying indulgence before or after theater, or for weekend brunches. The red salmon caviar is my favorite with these, because given their prices other more expensive caviars are not worthwhile.

Hot cabbage borscht, once a reliable and bracing starter, may now be truly hot or disappointingly tepid. It may or may not come with sour cream and at times may reek of stale cabbage, having been reheated once too often.

Sirniki, the small round and puffy cheese pancakes, are delicious, especially as redesigned, apparently by the new consulting chef, Jacques Pepin. More soufflélike than formerly, they seem to have an extra bite, as though, perhaps, a bit of ripened cream cheese had been added for piquancy. Topped with sour cream, they too are suited to all non-dinner meals, as are the crisply fried cheese-filled blinchiki, better known in these parts as blintzes.

The lunch menu features some popular salads that unfortunately are disappointing, most especially the chicken salad, in which it is hard to find the chicken for the mayonnaise.

Only a few heftier dishes hold up, among them the huge, well-fried chicken cutlet Kiev, the tender breast meat rolled around a knob of butter that melts and spurts properly when the meat is cut into, and the onion-flavored Caucasian shashlik of tender lamb chunks grilled medium rare as ordered. The filet of lamb with a nugget of kidney that is known as Karsky shashlik is also good, but meagerly portioned for the staggering $45.50 price tag it carries on the complete dinner. (The table d'hôte dinner here, by the way, has too many surcharges for appetizers and desserts.) The only other wise choice is the fresh calves' liver, nicely broiled and crested with a lean slice of bacon. Not worth ordering are the other creations such as mushy nalistniki (crêpes filled with ground meat and topped with a creamy mushroom sauce), versions of Pojarski cutlets (ground chicken or veal croquettes also sodden with sauce), and duck that is often overcooked and stringy.

If desserts have changed at all it is for the worse, with some of the sorriest French pastry, kissel (a red fruit pudding) that tastes of pure starch, overly sweetened kasha à la Gourieff (a sort of sweet semolina pudding), and baklava that, twice at least, contained rancid nuts.

But the cherry preserves are just fine when stirred into good hot tea served à la Russe, in a glass, if not, alas, with water drawn from one of the beautiful old samovars on display.

There is a long list of vodkas here, two of the most diverting being the Pretsovka, or pepper-flavored, and the palate-warming 90-proof Russian Okhotnichya, or "hunter," vodka. To be avoided are the sickening vodka cocktails that combine ingredients such as Triple Sec, lemon, and pineapple, or dry vermouth and apricot liqueur. Also to be avoided is the totally out-of-it upstairs dining room that gives special meaning to the term Siberia.

TAVERN ON THE GREEN

Central Park at West 67th Street
Telephone: 873-3200

Favorite meal:
Brunch or lunch
Smoked duck breast salad
Crab meat omelet with chives
Baked Brazil
Other favorite dishes: Smoked salmon with dill corn blinis, salmon-wrapped sea bass, clams or oysters on the half shell, seafood salad, hamburger, cold veal with lentils, pepper-cured roast beef with potato salad, rack of lamb, roast veal, banana split, chocolate truffle cake, coconut ice cream with pineapple.
Setting: The Crystal Room with Baccarat chandeliers and flowery accents is the place to be, especially for brunch or lunch, as is the outdoor garden in summer.
Service: Ranges from polite and helpful to mindless and inefficient, but not rude.
Dress code: None.
Facilities for private parties: Three adjoining rooms accommodate between 20 and 1,000.
Hours: Lunch, Monday through Friday. Dinner, until 1 A.M., seven days. Brunch, Saturday and Sunday. Pre-theater dinner, 5:30 to 6:45 P.M., Monday through Friday.
Reservations: Recommended, especially in good weather and for pre-theater menu.
Prices: Moderate to moderately expensive.
Credit cards: AE, CB, DC, MC, V.

This is the sort of setting everyone wants to enjoy midst the concrete and dust of New York—a sylvan, flowery fairyland of a restaurant right in Central Park. That it has never been the place for good food or professional service makes visits there near-challenges, the point being to develop a menu strategy that enables one to take out-of-towners, children, or anyone else who has a romantic, bucolic bent. I go only during the day, for weekend brunch or mid-week lunch, because the Crystal Room is then at its most magical, with the trees of the park and the sparkling, jewel-toned Baccarat chandeliers and carousel pastel frosting around the room.

There have been some construction changes here, eliminating the pleasant bar that wrapped around a tree trunk and requiring that all pass through a cheap hall of mirrors. Therefore, the Crystal Room and, in summer, the outdoor garden terrace are the only places I would consider sitting. Even then there are uncomfortable features—the very slow service outdoors and the faded flowers often in the indoor planters. (Why brown-edged mums should be the choice for mid-summer is hard to understand.)

Still, it can have appeal. The trick is to find things to eat that are esthetically safe, no easy task ever since Warner LeRoy took over in 1976. Perhaps now that he has given up the ghost at Maxwell's Plum (at its worst under its last celebrated chef), he can devote some attention to this kitchen. As it is, stick to the simplest dishes based on good products—the icy cold, sea-fresh clams or oysters on the half shell and the fine-grained, moist, and saline smoked Scottish salmon that comes with tiny corn blinis and a dill sauce. Marinated slices of raw bass wrapped around the same smoked salmon make another fine appetizer, fleshed out with tiny, red-skinned new potatoes boiled to the right firm but tender texture—a good foil for the rich fish. At a recent brunch there was also a substantial, palate-intriguing salad of sliced smoked duck breast tossed with mincings of apple, walnuts, and corn kernels with the slim French green beans haricots verts, on field greens dressed with a sparkly vinaigrette. In fact, if one had the salmon with blinis followed by the duck breast salad, it would be a fine brunch or lunch.

Less successful starters are the wet and bland pâtés and terrines, the pallid soups, and the pastas that tend to be watery and in need of salt, as though they had gone through a cycle in a dishwasher.

Crab meat, shrimp, and scallops, all cool and fresh, are combined in a seafood salad with avocado, tomato, and lacy greens for a restorative main course. Omelets, though a bit on the heavy side, are nevertheless satisfying with fillings of snowy lump crab meat and chives, or lustier accents of Gruyère or Cheddar cheese. Salade Niçoise is strangely presented, the dry, gray tuna, string beans, and other vegetables arranged separately on a flat plate so it is difficult to toss them with dressing. Cold poached salmon can be stiffly contorted, as though it had been cooked too rapidly, then held in the refrigerator too long.

More dependable cold dishes include sliced veal with marinated lentils, and pepper-encrusted roast beef slices nestling beside a salad of new potatoes. Only two hot main courses have been acceptable at dinner—the rack of lamb with light touches of garlic and thyme, and roast veal with wild mushrooms. Mushy duck in a cloying peach sauce is eminently skippable and fish is usually half-raw or overcooked.

There are very good batons of sour dough bread, *if* the waiter can find them. At times, the house runs out, even quite early in the dinner hour, and all one has then is faux pumpernickel, almost as soft and sweet as devil's food cake. If not the best hamburger in town, the specimen here is fresh and usually broiled as ordered, and should satisfy children who will eat nothing else.

Desserts are lavish enough to appeal to children and the childish alike, and are designed for the big birthday-crowd-with-balloons set that frequents this place. Dark, rich chocolate truffle cake with a smooth, fudgelike glaze, hot butterscotch or fudge sundaes, and light, fresh-tasting coconut ice cream that gets a nice astringent edge from fresh pineapple are among better choices. So is Baked Brazil, a sort of individual baked Alaska, with a golden brown meringue igloo holding coconut and vanilla ice cream, all bathed in a bittersweet chocolate sauce. Crème brûlée rarely has the properly glassy sugar-glaze, and fruit tarts are soggy.

As at Maxwell's Plum, there is a lot of changing of chefs here, so one never knows which of the specialties will be available even a few weeks after this writing.

WINDOWS ON THE WORLD ★

1 World Trade Center, 107th floor of the North Tower
Telephone: 938-1111

Favorite meal:
Clams and oysters on the half shell
or
Asparagus vinaigrette
Rack of lamb, James Beard
Hot apple tart with Calvados sherbet
Other aesthetically safe choices: Clam and mussel bisque, beef consommé with pasta, roast tenderloin of beef with morel or Périgourdine sauce on the side, roast chicken, hazelnut dacquoise, lemon tart.
Setting: Glowing, theatrical dining room with the world's most spectacular view; two can

rarely get a window table so try going with four, but some views can be glimpsed from other points in the room.
Service: Friendly, well-meaning, but sometimes slow.
Dress code: Jacket and tie required for men.
Facilities for private parties: Sixteen handsome private rooms and four ballrooms can accommodate between 6 and 1,000.
Hours: For main restaurant only: Lunch, Monday through Friday, is a private club, charging a $7.50 surcharge to each nonmember. Dinner, Monday through Saturday. Grand buffet brunch, Saturday and Sunday.
Reservations: Necessary, but available on short notice if weather is bad; unknowns may have a hard time getting 7 to 8:30 reservations for dinner.
Prices: Moderate to moderately expensive. Prix fixe dinner is $29.95 to $33.95. Grand buffet is $21.
Credit cards: AE, CB, DC, MC, V.

Take away the magnificent view of New York and the city lights, and what you're left with is a lousy restaurant. But as only God takes away the view now and then with curtains of fog, rain, or snow, that generally leaves a breathtaking experience. It's one I like to introduce to young people from out of town and to foreign visitors who have not seen it before. It's also one I like to experience and so I am always tempted to go back, especially if I'm not too hungry.

The kitchen here has never managed to turn out consistently good food, and only a few choices are reliable. Among such is the rack of lamb James Beard, though its presentation has been altered a bit since the late food writer and consultant created it. Now the small but flavorful rack (really more suited to one than two as demanded on the menu) is garnished with sautéed slivers of leeks, herbed tomatoes, and new potatoes. The former sauté of Provençale-style tomatoes was preferable. Nevertheless, on my last visit the lamb was done exactly as ordered. Roast tenderloin of beef, if rare, is a fine second choice but ask to have the sauce of the evening served on the side, in case it is dull and thin, as it so often is. Roast chicken is a third possibility, but not so the dry, tough, grilled pheasant. Despite its thyme marinade, it is bland and watery and not helped by a stodgy succotash labeled "autumn" although served on May 31. Perhaps it had been around since October.

Before you get to the main course, you'd be best off with the clear, icy array of clams and oysters on the half shell with grated horseradish, or the firm, bright asparagus in a nice oily, sweet pepper–flecked vinaigrette dressing. Both the clam and mussel bisque, with its creamy, saline edge, and the strong beef consommé are fine, although the latter was garnished with carrot pasta when the menu promised green spinach pasta.

Many of the original spectacular desserts are left off the menu from time to time, but the hazelnut dacquoise, with its alternate layers of meringue and mocha cream, and the sharp, fresh lemon tart are reliable. Poached pear or figs in red wine are nicely complemented by walnut ice cream, and a crunchy hot apple tart is accented by cool, sharp Calvados sherbet.

There is an eat-all-you-want grand buffet on Saturday and Sunday that enables guests to enjoy the daytime view of the city. Because it is a big buffet, there are usually some more-than-merely passable choices. It seems simpler to have a drink at the bar or brunch in the Hors D'Oeuvrerie, but then you see only the Statue of Liberty or New Jersey, which is the lesser view. The restaurant affords the real dazzler, looking over Manhattan north to the Empire State Building and south to Brooklyn and Queens, all linked by necklaces of lights on bridges, rivaling the sparkle of a Van Cleef and Arpels window.

There have been some unfortunate changes here, probably in the interest of cutting costs. Tan uniforms on waitresses suggest a hotel coffee shop and the cheap-looking graphics and paper for the menus are a far cry from the original stylishness. The staff, however, is friendly and attentive. On a felicitous note, the rose-gold lushness of the dining room, designed in ocean-liner tiers by Warren Platner, has held up remarkably well and is as sparkling as ever.

The original policy of offering interesting wines at modest prices still prevails. A 1985 Acacia Pinot Noir, one of California's best reds, is a good buy at $24, and a light, fragrant 1983 Château de Sales is reasonable at $22.

INDEX

Bold numbers indicate primary review; other numbers indicate secondary references.

Abyssinia, 85
Adam's Rib, 23
Albero D'Oro, 177
America, **254**
Anatolia, 215
Aquavit, **218**
Arcadia, **5**
Arturo's Pizzeria and Restaurant, 181
Auberge Suisse, 243
Auntie Yuan, 56, 62

The Ballroom, **231**
Beijing Duck House Restaurant, **57**, 67, 68
Le Bel Age (Beverly Hills), 32
Le Bernardin, xiv, 219, 221
Bernstein-on-Essex Street, 207
Le Biarritz, **88**
Bice, 23, **146**
Bleecker Luncheonette, 47
The Blue Nile, **85**
Bo Ky Restaurant, 253
Bouley, **89**
Brasserie Lipp (Paris), 109, 120
Brazilian Pavilion, **40**
Brive, **92**
Bukhara, **134**

Cabana Carioca, 40, **42**
Café de Bruxelles, **35**, 108
Le Café de la Gare, **94**
Café des Artistes, **256**
Café Luxembourg, **9**, 23, 25, 87
Café Marimba, 63, 213
Il Cantinori, 128
The Captain's Table, **222**
Carnegie Delicatessen & Restaurant, **201**
Carolina, **11**, 158
Cent' Anni, **149**, 151
Chalet Suisse, **241**
Chanterelle, **96**
Charles' Green Tree Hungarian Restaurant, **130**
Chez Brigitte, 47
Chez Garin (Paris), 123
Chikubu, **185**
China Grill, 56
Chinatown Seafood, 56, **59**
Chin Chin, 56, **61**
Christine's Polish Restaurant, 48
Le Cirque, **98**
Claire, **80**
The Coach House, **13**
Corner Bistro, 53, 54
La Côte Basque, **101**

269

La Coupole, 9
Le Cygne, **105**

Darbar, **136**
Da Umberto, **151**
David K's, **63**
David K's Café, 79
Dawat, **138**
Dodin-Bouffant, 92
Due, 161, 182

Elephant & Castle, 45
Erminia, **153,** 177
Ernie's, 256

Felidia, **155**
Le Festival, 103
Flamand, **37**
Fornos, 234
The Four Seasons, 225, **258**
Fu's, 56

Garden, 208
La Gauloise, 35, **107**
Gloucester House, 221
La Goulue, 120
Granados, 234
Gray's Papaya, 54
La Grenouille, **110**
Guinea Grill (London), 14

H.S.F. (Hee Sung Feung), 78
Hamburger Harry's, 54
Hammer's, 208
Harlequin, 235
Hatsuhana, **187**
Helen Lane's Tearoom, 14
Hsin Yu, 79
Huberts, **15,** 23
Hwa Yuan Szechuan Inn, 65

Inagiku, **188**

Jai-Alai, 234
John Clancy's, 222, **223**
John's Pizzeria, 181

Katz's Delicatessen, 55
Kiev Luncheonette, 48
Kitcho, **189**

Lan Hong Kok Seafood House, 77, 78
Larmen Dosanko, 197
Lattanzi, 153, **157,** 177
La Lavandou, 103
The Lobster, 221
Lone Star Café, 53, 54
Lundy's, 221
Lusardi's, **160,** 175
Lutèce, **113**

Manganaro's Hero Boy, 181
Manhattan Chili Co., 53
Manhattan Island, 11, **19**
Maurice, **118**
Maxwell's Plum, 265, 266
Memphis, **21**
Metro, **23**
Mocca Hungarian Restaurant, **132**
Moe's, **236**
Montrachet, 90

Nanni, **163**
Il Nido, **165**
Il Nido Café, 45, 168

Odeon, 10, 23, **25,** 87
Omen, **191**
Oriental Town Seafood Restaurant, 78
Orso, 181
Oyster Bar & Restaurant, 222, **226**

Paley Park, 55
Palm, 173, 237, **238**
Palm Too, 239
Pamir, **3**
Pasta & Cheese Café, 46
Patisserie J. Lanciani, 48
Le Pavilion, 102
Peking Duck West, 58, **67**
Le Périgord Park, 16
Periyali, **127,** 215
Pesca, **228**
Petrossian, **50**

Pig Heaven, 56
The Pink Tea Cup, 46
Positano, **169**

Quatorze, **120**

R. Gross Dairy Restaurant, 208
Raga, **141**
Rao's, **171**
Rappaport's, 208
Ratner's Dairy Restaurant, 208
Le Régence, 99
El Rincón de España, **233**
Russian Tea Room, **261**

Sabor, **82**
Safari Grill, 63
Saigon Restaurant, **251**
Le Saint Jean des Prés, 236
The Saloon, 256
Sammy's Famous Roumanian Restaurant, 172, **204**, 237, 238
Sam's, **27**
Santa Fe Bar and Grill (Berkeley), 28
Sant' Ambroeus, 49
Sapporo, 199
Sarabeth's Kitchen, 46
Savant, 30
Say Eng Look, **69**
Sea Fare, 221
2nd Avenue Kosher Delicatessen and Restaurant, 208
Serendipity, 46, 55
Seryna, **193**
Shinwa, **194**
Shun Lee Palace, **70**

Shun Lee West, 71, **73**
Siam Grill, **244**
Siam Inn, **245**
Sido Abu Salim, **215**
Sistina, 161, **174**
Siu Lam Kung, 59, **75**
Sloppy Louie's, 221
Sushisei, **196**
Sweets, 221

Takesushi, **198**
Tanjore, **143**
Taste of the Apple, 54
Tavern on the Green, **264**
Terrace, **122**
Terrace-five, 47
Texarkana, 29
Tibetan Kitchen, **249**
Time & Again, **31**
Tony Roma's, 137
Toons, **247**
Trastevere Ristorante, 155, 158, 159, 160, **177**
La Tulipe, **124**
The "21" Club, xv, 6, 99

Viand Coffee Shop, 48
Vico, **179**

Windows on the World, **266**
Woo Lae Oak of Seoul, **209**, 212

Yellow Rose Café, **33**
Young Bin Kwan, **211**

Zarela, **213**

MIMI SHERATON'S TASTE

The candid newsletter guide to restaurants, hotels, and more, in New York and beyond . . .

As an addendum to this book, Mimi Sheraton publishes an insider's newsletter, available by subscription only. Issued ten times a year, with enlarged, combined issues for July–August and December–January, it will keep you informed on the changing scene, particularly of restaurants that opened after this book went to press. Reviews include restaurants in all parts of the city and in all price ranges. Unlike this book, which covers only favorite restaurants, Mimi Sheraton's newsletter includes reviews both positive and negative, as well as the following:

CHECKING IN—Mimi Sheraton checks into New York hotels and reports on room, bath, room service, and all amenities. This is a guide for out-of-town visitors and New Yorkers who are asked for hotel recommendations.

MORSELS—You'll find saucy tidbits such as where to have a great hamburger or pizza after midnight, the lustiest pot-au-feu or pasta, the quietest spot for a business breakfast, the best private banquet rooms . . . and more.

BEYOND NEW YORK—Restaurants, hotels, and points of interest elsewhere in the United States and the world are reported on here.

To receive this candid, personal newsletter, subscribe to "Mimi Sheraton's Taste" today.

One year (10 issues) $48   Two years (20 issues) $79
           Add $12 per year for foreign airmail.

Please make your check payable to Mimi Sheraton's Taste and remit to:

         Mimi Sheraton's Taste
         P.O. Box 1396, Old Chelsea Station
         New York, NY 10011

Please write to the above address for special rates for corporate gift subscriptions.

You have nothing to lose by subscribing. If "Mimi Sheraton's Taste" does not please yours within the first three months, you receive a full refund.